FINTECH

In this comprehensive, accessible work, Ross P. Buckley, Douglas W. Arner, and Dirk A. Zetzsche offer an ideal reference for anyone seeking to understand the technological transformation of finance and the role of regulation: the world of FinTech. They consider financial technologies including artificial intelligence, blockchain, BigData, cloud computing, cryptocurrencies, central bank digital currencies, and distributed ledger technologies and provide a unique perspective on FinTech as an interactive system involving finance, technology, law, and regulation. Starting with an evolutionary perspective, the authors then consider the major technologies transforming finance, arguing for approaches to balance the risks and challenges of innovation. They address the central role of infrastructure in digital financial transformation, highlighting lessons from China, India, and the EU, as well as the impact of pandemics and other sustainability crises, while considering the risks generated by FinTech. They conclude by offering forward-looking regulatory strategies to address the challenges our world faces today.

Ross P. Buckley is one of the world's most cited and read FinTech scholars. Professor Buckley leads a major, six-year Laureate research project at the University of New South Wales (UNSW), Sydney, into the regulation of FinTech. He advises governments and regulators around the world and has twice been a Fulbright scholar, at Yale and Duke.

Douglas W. Arner is one of the leading policy researchers on the interaction of finance, technology, regulation, and development. Professor Arner is the Kerry Holdings Professor in Law, RGC Senior Fellow in Digital Finance and Sustainable Development, Senior Fellow of the Asia Global Institute, and Associate Director of the HKU-Standard Chartered FinTech Academy at the University of Hong Kong. He works with international organisations, governments, regulators, and leading private sector firms around the world.

Dirk A. Zetzsche holds the ADA Chair in Financial Law (inclusive finance) and leads the House of Sustainable Governance & Markets at the University of Luxembourg. Professor Zetzsche is one of the most well-known authors on FinTech regulation, a frequent consultant to regulators and parliaments, and a regular guest at all the leading universities and academic conferences across the globe.

FinTech

FINANCE, TECHNOLOGY AND REGULATION

ROSS P. BUCKLEY

University of New South Wales, Sydney

DOUGLAS W. ARNER

University of Hong Kong

DIRK A. ZETZSCHE

University of Luxembourg

Shaftesbury Road, Cambridge CB2 8EA, United Kingdom

One Liberty Plaza, 20th Floor, New York, NY 10006, USA

477 Williamstown Road, Port Melbourne, VIC 3207, Australia

314–321, 3rd Floor, Plot 3, Splendor Forum, Jasola District Centre,
New Delhi – 110025, India

103 Penang Road, #05–06/07, Visioncrest Commercial, Singapore 238467

Cambridge University Press is part of Cambridge University Press & Assessment,
a department of the University of Cambridge.

We share the University's mission to contribute to society through the pursuit of
education, learning and research at the highest international levels of excellence.

www.cambridge.org
Information on this title: www.cambridge.org/9781316514405

DOI: 10.1017/9781009086943

First published 2024

A catalogue record for this publication is available from the British Library

Library of Congress Cataloging-in-Publication Data
NAMES: Buckley, Ross P., author. | Arner, Douglas W., author. | Zetzsche, Dirk A., author.
TITLE: FinTech : finance, technology and regulation / Ross P. Buckley, University of New South
Wales, Sydney; Douglas W. Arner, University of Hong Kong; Dirk A. Zetzsche, University of
Luxembourg.
DESCRIPTION: Cambridge, United Kingdom ; New York, NY : Cambridge University Press, 2024. |
Includes bibliographical references and index.
IDENTIFIERS: LCCN 2023017041 | ISBN 9781316514405 (hardback) | ISBN 9781009078214
(paperback) | ISBN 9781009086943 (ebook)
SUBJECTS: LCSH: Financial services industry – Law and legislation. | Financial institutions – Effect
of technological innovations on. | Financial services industry – Technological innovations – Law
and legislation.
CLASSIFICATION: LCC K1066 .B83 2024 | DDC 346/.082–dc23/eng/20230802
LC record available at https://lccn.loc.gov/2023017041

ISBN 978-1-316-51440-5 Hardback
ISBN 978-1-009-07821-4 Paperback

Contents

Figures

Acknowledgements

We thank sincerely our co-authors on the research who have shaped our thinking in this field profoundly and provided the groundwork for this book, including Filippo Annunziata, Linn Anker-Sørensen, Janos Barberis, William Birdthistle, Kuzi Charamba, Anton Didenko, Scott Farrell, Linus Föhr, Jon Frost, Natalia Jevglevskaja, Luca Enriques, Emilija Pashoska, Maria Louisa Passador, Brian Tang, Lucien Van Romburg, Robin Veidt, Rolf Weber, Andreas Wehrli, and Jannik Woxholth.

This earlier foundational research has been expressed in the following publications:

1. Douglas W Arner, Jànos Barberis, and Ross P Buckley, 'The Evolution of FinTech: A New Post-Crisis Paradigm?' (2016) 47(4) *Georgetown Journal of International Law* 1271–320.

2. Ross P Buckley and Sarah Webster, 'FinTech in Developing Countries: Charting New Customer Journeys' (2016) 44 *Journal of Financial Transformation* 151–9.

3. Douglas W Arner, Jànos Barberis, and Ross P Buckley, 'FinTech, RegTech and the Reconceptualization of Financial Regulation' (2017) 37(3) *Northwestern Journal of International Law and Business* 371–414.

4. Dirk A Zetzsche, Ross P Buckley, Janos Barberis and Douglas W Arner, 'Regulating a Revolution: From Regulatory Sandboxes to Smart Regulation' (2017) 23(1) *Fordham Journal of Corporate and Financial Law* 31–104.

5. Dirk A Zetzsche, Ross P Buckley, Douglas W Arner and Janos Barberis, 'From FinTech to TechFin: The Regulatory Challenges of Data-Driven Finance' (2018) 14(2) *New York University Journal of Law and Business* 393–446.

6. Dirk A Zetzsche, Ross P Buckley, and Douglas W Arner, 'The Distributed Liability of Distributed Ledgers: Legal Risks of Blockchain' (2018) (4) *University of Illinois Law Review* 1361–406.

7. Douglas W Arner, Dirk A Zetzsche, Ross P Buckley and Janos Barberis, 'The Identity Challenge in Finance: From Analogue Identity to Digitized Identification to Digital KYC Utilities' (2019) 20 *European Business Organisation Law Review* 55–80.

8. Anton N Didenko and Ross P Buckley, 'The Evolution of Currency: Cash to Cryptos to Sovereign Digital Currencies' (2019) 42(4) *Fordham International Law Journal* 1041–94.

9. Dirk A Zetzsche, Ross P Buckley, Douglas W Arner and Linus Föhr, 'The ICO Gold Rush: It's a Scam, It's a Bubble, It's a Super Challenge for Regulators' (2019) 60(2) *Harvard International Law Journal* 267–316.

10. Dirk A Zetzsche, Douglas W Arner, Ross P Buckley and Rolf H Weber, 'The Future of Data-Driven Finance and RegTech: Lessons from EU Big Bang II' (2020) 25(2) *Stanford Journal of Law, Business and Finance* 245–88.

11. Luca Enriques and Dirk A Zetzsche, 'Corporate Technologies and the Tech Nirvana Fallacy' (2020) 72(1) *Hastings Law Journal* 55.

12. Douglas W Arner, Ross P Buckley, Dirk A Zetzsche and Robin Veidt, 'The Road to RegTech: The (Astonishing) Example of the European Union' (2020) 21(1) *Journal of Banking Regulation* 26–36.

13. Douglas W Arner, Ross P Buckley, Dirk A Zetzsche and Robin Veidt, 'Sustainability, FinTech and Financial Inclusion' (2020) 21(1) *European Business Organisation Law Review* 7–35.

14. Ross P Buckley, Douglas Arner, Robin Veidt, Dirk A Zetzsche, 'Building FinTech Ecosystems: Regulatory Sandboxes, Innovation Hubs and Beyond' (2020) 61 *Washington University Journal of Law and Policy* 55–98.

15. Dirk A Zetzsche, Ross P Buckley, Rolf H Weber, Dirk Zetzsche, 'The Evolution and Future of Data-Driven Finance in the EU' (2020) 57(2) *Common Market Law Review* 331–60.

16. Ross P Buckley, Douglas W Arner, Dirk A Zetzsche, 'TechRisk' [2020] *Singapore Journal of Legal Studies* 35–62.

17. Ross P Buckley, Douglas W Arner, Dirk A Zetzsche and Eriks Selga, 'Building Australia's FinTech Ecosystem: Innovation Hubs for a Competitive Advantage' (2020) 31(2) *Journal of Banking and Finance Law and Practice* 133–40.

18. Dirk A Zetzsche, Douglas W Arner, and Ross P Buckley, 'Decentralized Finance' (2020) 6(2) *Journal of Financial Regulation* 172–203.

19. Dirk A Zetzsche, William A Birdthistle, Douglas W Arner and Ross P Buckley, 'Digital Finance Platforms: Toward a New Regulatory Paradigm' (2020) 23(1) *University of Pennsylvania Journal of Business Law* 273–339.

20. Linn Anker-Sørensen and Dirk A Zetzsche, 'From Centralized to Decentralized Finance: The Issue of "Fake-DeFi"' (Working Paper, University of Luxembourg, 2021).

21. Dirk A Zetzsche, Linn Anker-Sørensen, Maria Lucia Passador and Andrea Wehrli, 'DLT-Based Enhancement of Cross-Border Payment Efficiency: A Legal and Regulatory Perspective' (2021) 15(1) *Law and Financial Markets Review* 70–115.

22. Ross P Buckley, Dirk A Zetzsche, Douglas W Arner and Brian W Tang, 'Regulating Artificial Intelligence in Finance: Putting the Human in the Loop' (2021) 43(1) *Sydney Law Review* 43.

23. Ross P Buckley et al, 'Sovereign Digital Currencies: Reshaping the Design of Money and Payments Systems' (2021) 15(1) *Journal of Payments Systems and Strategies* 7–22.

24. Dirk A Zetzsche, Ross P Buckley, and Douglas W Arner, 'Regulating Libra' (2021) 41(1) *Oxford Journal of Legal Studies* 80–113.

25. Dirk A Zetzsche, Filippo Annunziata, Douglas W Arner and Ross P Buckley, 'The Markets in Crypto-assets Regulation (MICA) and the EU Digital Finance Strategy' (2021) 16(2) *Capital Markets Law Journal* 203–25.

26. Dirk A Zetzsche and Jannik Woxholth, 'The DLT Sandbox under the Pilot-Regulation' (2022) 17(2) *Capital Markets Law Journal* 212–36.

27. Douglas W Arner, Ross P Buckley, Andrew M Dahdal and Dirk A Zetzsche, 'COVID-19, Digital Finance and Existential Sustainability Crises: Opportunities and Challenges for Law and Regulation in the 2020s' (2021) 33(2) *National Law School of India Review* 384–416.

28. Ross Buckley et al, 'Regional Solutions to Global Payments Challenges: Towards a Single Rulebook' (2022) 38 *Banking and Finance Law Review* 81–115.

29. Dirk A Zetzsche, Ross P Buckley, Douglas W Arner and Maria L Passador, 'From "Best Friends" to "Best Execution": Rethinking Cross-border Payments' (2022) (8) *Journal of Business Law* 682–709.

30. Douglas Arner et al, 'Governing FinTech 4.0: BigTech, Platform Finance, and Sustainable Development' (2022) 27(1) *Fordham Journal of Corporate and Financial Law* 1–72.

31. Anton N Didenko and Ross P Buckley, 'Central Bank Digital Currencies as a Potential Response to Some Particularly Pacific Problems' (2022) 30(1) *Asia Pacific Law Review* 44–69.

32. Ross P Buckley, Natalia Jevglevskaja and Scott Farrell, 'Australia's Data-Sharing Regime: Six Lessons for Europe' (2022) 33(1) *King's Law Journal* 61–91.

33. Natalia Jevglevskaja and Ross P Buckley, 'The Consumer Data Right: How to Realise This World-Leading Reform' (2022) 45(4) *University of New South Wales Law Journal* 1589–622.

34. Douglas W Arner, RP Buckley, and DA Zetzsche, 'FinTech and the Four Horsemen of the Apocalypse' (2022) 39(1) *Banking and Finance Law Review* 5–31.

35. Ross P Buckley and Mia Treczinski, 'Central Bank Digital Currencies and the Global Financial System: The Dollar Dethroned?' (2023) 18(2) *Capital Markets Law Journal* 137–71.

We would also like to express our gratitude to the many postdoctoral research fellows and research assistants who have contributed to this book, especially in the final intensive stage of manuscript polishing and preparation. In particular, in alphabetical order, we thank: Sijuade Animashaun, Katharine Cheng, Georgia Fink-Brigg, Tom Hodgson, Jarrod Li, Areti Kovolou Nikolakopoulou, Luisa Künzel, Carmen Preda, Triston Qian, Georgie Robertson, Stamatia Stylianopoulou, and Marian Unterstell.

We would like to thank the Australian Research Council (in particular the ARC Lauraute Fellowship Programme), the Hong Kong Research Grants Council (in particular the RGC Research Impact Fund for support of Parts I and II and the RGC Senior Research Fellowship Scheme for support of Parts III and IV) as well as the sponsors of the ADA Chair in Financial Law (inclusive finance).

Abbreviations and Technical Terms

ABCD	AI, Blockchain, Cloud, and Data or AI, Big Data, Cloud, and DLT
AFI	Alliance for Financial Inclusion
AFM	Authority for the Financial Markets (the Netherlands)
AI	Artificial Intelligence
AIFMD	Alternative Investment Fund Managers Directive; Directive 2011/61/EU of the European Parliament and of the Council of 8 June 2011
AIS	Account Information Services
AISP	Account Information Service Provider
Aladdin	Asset, Liability and Debt and Derivative Investment Network (Blackrock's platform)
AML	Anti-money Laundering
AMLD V	Fifth Anti-money Laundering Directive – Directive (EU) 2018/843 of the European Parliament and of the Council of 30 May 2018 amending Directive (EU) 2015/849 on the prevention of the use of the financial system for the purposes of money laundering or terrorist financing, and amending Directives 2009/138/EC and 2013/36/EU, OJ L 156/44-74
APAC	Asia-Pacific
API	Application Programming Interface
APS	Accrediting Principal Swap
ASIC	Australian Securities and Investments Commission
ATM	Automated Teller Machine
BACS	Bankers' Automated Clearing Services
BaFin	Bundesanstalt für Finanzdienstleistungsaufsicht (Germany)
Basel Committee	Basel Committee on Banking Supervision
Basel I	Basel Capital Accord

Basel II	Basel II: International Convergence of Capital Measurement and Capital Standards: A Revised Framework
Basel III	Basel III: A Global Regulatory Framework for More Resilient Banks and Banking Systems
BATs	Baidu, Alibaba, Tencent
BCBS	Basel Committee on Banking Supervision
BCCI	Bank of Credit and Commerce International
BIS	Bank for International Settlements
CBDC	Central Bank Digital Currency
CBM	Central Bank Money
CDD	Customer Due Diligence
CDO	Collateralised Debt Obligation
CFPB	Consumer Financial Protection Bureau (US)
CFT	Combatting the Financing of Terrorism
CFTC	Commodity Futures Trading Commission
CGAP	Consultative Group to Assist the Poor
CHAPS	Clearing House Automated Payment System
CHIPS	Clearing House Interbank Payments System
CIO	Chief Investment Officer
CLOUD Act	Clarifying Lawful Overseas Use of Data Act (United States)
CLS	Continuous Linked Settlement
COVID-19	Coronavirus Disease 2019
CPSS	Committee on Payment and Settlement Systems
CRD	Capital Requirements Directive: Directive 2013/36/EU on access to the activity of credit institutions and the prudential supervision of credit institutions and investment firms (CRD IV), amending Directive 2002/87/EC and repealing Directives 2006/48/EC and 2006/49/EC OJ L 176/338
CRD IV	Fourth Capital Requirements Directive – see CRD
CRR	Regulation (EU) No. 575/2013 on prudential requirements for credit institutions and investment firms and amending Regulation (EU) No 648/2012 OJ L 176/1
CRS	Common Reporting Standards
CSD	Central Securities Depository
CSSF	Commission de Surveillance du Secteur Financier (Luxembourg)
CTF	Counter Terrorist Financing
DAO	Decentralised Autonomous Organisation

Data Protection Directive	Directive 95/46/EC of the European Parliament and of the Council of 24 October 1995 on the protection of individuals with regard to the processing of personal data and on the free movement of such data, OJ L 281/31-50
DeFi	Decentralised Finance
DEX	Decentralised Exchange
DFP	Digital Finance Platform
DFS	Digital Financial Services
DLT	Distributed Ledger Technology
DNA	Deoxyribonucleic Acid
DORA	*Digital Operational Resilience Act* – Regulation of the European Parliament and of the Council on digital operational resilience for the financial sector and amending Regulations (EC) No 1060/2009, (EU) No 648/2012, (EU) No 600/2014 and (EU) No 909/2014
DP	Discussion Paper
DSL	Data Security Law of the People's Republic of China (Adopted at the 29th Meeting of the Standing Committee of the Thirteenth National People's Congress on 10 June 2021)
e-Banking	Electronic Banking
EC	European Commission
ECB	European Central Bank
ECtHR	European Court of Human Rights
ECHR	European Convention on Human Rights; The Convention for the Protection of Human Rights and Fundamental Freedoms of the Council of Europe
eCNY	Electronic Chinese Yuan
e-Commerce	Electronic Commerce
ECR	European Court Report
EEA	European Economic Area
EEC	European Economic Community
eID	Electronic Identification
eIDAS	Electronic Identification, Authentication, and trust Services
eIDASR	Regulation (EU) No 910/2014 of the European Parliament and of the Council of 23 July 2014 on electronic identification and trust services for electronic transactions in the internal market and repealing Directive 1999/93/EC, OJ L 257, 28.8.2014
e-Krona	Electronic Krona

eKYC System	Electronic Know-your-customer System
e-Liquidity	Electronic Liquidity
EMIR	European Market Infrastructure Regulation – Regulation (EU) No 648/2012 of the European Parliament and of the Council of 4 July 2012 on OTC derivatives, central counterparties and trade repositories Text with EEA relevance, OJ 201/1-59.
e-Money	Electronic Money
e-Payment	Electronic Payment
e-Personhood	Electronic Personhood
EPN	Electronic Payments Network
ESA	European Supervisory Authority
ESG	Environmental, Social and Governance
e-Signature	Electronic Signature
ESMA	European Securities and Markets Authority
ESRB	European Systemic Risk Board
ETH	Ether
eTrust Services	Electronic Trust Services
EU	European Union
EUR	Euro
e-Yuan	Electronic Yuan
FATF	Financial Action Task Force
FCA	Financial Conduct Authority (UK)
FEAT	Fairness, Ethics, Accountability, and Transparency Principles
FinHub	The Strategic Hub for Innovation and Financial Technology
FINMA	Financial Market Supervisory Authority (Switzerland)
FINRA	Financial Industry Regulatory Authority
FinTech	Financial Technology
FMI	Financial Market Infrastructure
FMU	Financial Market Utility
FR	Final Report
FSAP	Financial Services Action Plan
FSB	Financial Stability Board
FSOC	Financial Stability Oversight Council
FTC	US Federal Trade Commission
G20	The Group of Twenty
G2P	Government-to-Person
G7	The Group of Seven Industrialised Countries
GBP	Pound Sterling
GDP	Gross Domestic Product

GDPR	General Data Protection Regulation – Regulation (EU) 2016/679 of the European Parliament and of the Council of 27 April 2016 on the protection of natural persons with regard to the processing of personal data and on the free movement of such data, and repealing Directive 95/46/EC, O.J. L119/1 of 4 May 2016
GFC	Global Financial Crisis
GFIN	Global Financial Innovation Network
GPFI	Global Partnership for Financial Inclusion
GSC	Global Stablecoin
HKMA	Hong Kong Monetary Authority
HSBC	The Hongkong and Shanghai Banking Corporation Limited
ICO	Initial Coin Offering
ID	Identification Document
IMF	International Monetary Fund
IMS	Innovation Market Solutions
InsurTech	Insurance Technology
IOSCO	International Organization of Securities Commissions
IoT	Internet of Things
IPO	Initial Public Offering
IRS	Internal Revenue Service (USA)
ISD	Investment Services Directive
IT	Information Technology
JC	Joint Committee
JOBS	Jump Start our Businesses Act (US)
KYC	Know Your Customer
LEI	Legal Entity Identifier
LHoFT	Luxembourg House of Financial Technology
LIBOR	London Interbank Offered Rate
LU	Luxembourg
MAGMA	Meta, Apple, Google, Microsoft, and Amazon
MAS	Monetary Authority of Singapore
MiFID	Markets in Financial Instruments Directive; Directive 2004/39/EC of the European Parliament and of the Council of 21 April 2004 on markets in financial instruments amending Council Directives 85/611/EEC and 93/6/EEC and Directive 2000/12/EC of the European Parliament and of the Council and repealing Council Directive 93/22/EEC OJ L 145/1
MiFID II	Markets in Financial Instruments Directive (recast); Directive 2014/65/EU of the European Parliament and

	of the Council of 15 May 2014 on markets in financial instruments and amending Directive 2002/92/EC and Directive 2011/61/EU (recast) OJ L 173/349
MiFID II (Commission) Directive	Commission Delegated Directive (EU) 2017/593 of 7 April 2016 supplementing Directive 2014/65/EU of the European Parliament and of the Council with regard to safeguarding of financial instruments and funds belonging to clients, product governance obligations and the rules applicable to the provision or reception of fees, commissions or any monetary or non-monetary benefits
MiFID Organisation Regulation	Commission Delegated Regulation (EU) 2017/565 of 25 April 2016 supplementing Directive 2014/65/EU of the European Parliament and of the Council as regards organisational requirements and operating conditions for investment firms and defined terms for the purposes of that Directive
MiFID Reporting Regulation	Commission Implementing Regulation (EU) 2017/2382 of 14 December 2017 laying down implementing technical standards with regard to standard forms, templates and procedures for the transmission of information in accordance with Directive 2014/65/EU of the European Parliament and of the Council, OJ L 340/6-31
MiFIR	Markets in Financial Instruments Regulation – Regulation (EU) No 600/2014 of the European Parliament and of the Council of 15 May 2014 on markets in financial instruments and amending Regulation (EU) No 648/2012, OJ L173/84-148
MoU	Memorandum of Understanding
MSMEs	Micro, Small, and Medium Enterprises
NASDAQ	National Association of Securities Dealers Automated Quotations
NGO	Non-Governmental Organisation
NMS	National Market System
NPCI	National Payments Corporation of Indi
NYSE	New York Stock Exchange
OCC	Office of the Comptroller of the Currency
OECD	Organisation for Economic Cooperation and Development
P2P	Peer-to-Peer
PBoC	People's Bank of China

PE	Private Equity
PilotR	Regulation (EU) 2022/858 of the European Parliament and of the Council of 30 May 2022 on a pilot regime for market infrastructures based on distributed ledger technology, and amending Regulations (EU) No 600/2014 and (EU) No 909/2014 and Directive 2014/65/EU, OJ L151/1-33
PIPL	Personal Information Protection Law of the People's Republic of China (Adopted at the 30th Meeting of the Standing Committee of the Thirteenth National People's Congress on 20 August 2021)
PIS	Payment Initiation Services
PISP	Payment Initiation Service Provider
PlatFin	Platform FinTech
PPP	Public–Private Partnership
PR Passport	Passport provided under the EU Prospectus Regulation
PS	Policy Statement
PSA	Public Securities Association Standard Prepayment Model
PSD1	First Payment Services Directive; Directive 2007/64/EC of the European Parliament and of the Council of 13 November 2007 on Payment Services in the Internal Market Amending Directives 97/7/EC, 2002/65/EC, 2005/60/EC and 2006/48/EC and Repealing Directive 97/5/EC, 2007 O.J. (L 319) 1
PSD2	Second Payment Services Directive; Directive (EU) 2015/2366 of the European Parliament and of the Council of 25 November 2015 on payment services in the internal market, amending Directives 2002/65/EC, 2009/110/EC and 2013/36/EU and Regulation (EU) No 1093/2010, and repealing Directive 2007/64/EC, OJ L 337/35
PSP	Payment Service Provider
R&D	Research and Development
RBI	Reserve Bank of India
RegTech	Regulatory Technology
RMB	Renminbi
RTGS	Real-Time Gross Settlement
S&P	Standard & Poor's
SAR	Special Administrative Region
SDG	Sustainable Development Goal

SEC	Securities and Exchange Commission
SEPA	Single Euro Payments Area, referring to Regulation (EU) No 260/2012 of the European Parliament and of the Council of 14 March 2012 establishing technical and business requirements for credit transfers and direct debits in euro and amending Regulation (EC) No 924/2009
SF	Sustainable Finance
SIFI	Systematically Important Financial Institution
SMEs	Small and Medium Enterprises
SRI	Socially Responsible Investment
SRO	Self-Regulatory Organisation
SSS	Securities Settlement System
STO	Securities Token Offering
SupTech	Supervisory Technology
SWIFT	Society for Worldwide Interbank Financial Telecommunication
TBTF (or TB2F)	Too Big To Fail
TCTF (or TC2F)	Too Connected To Fail
TDIF	Trusted Digital Identity Framework
TechRisk	Technology Risk
TFEU	Treaty on the Functioning of the European Union, OJ C 326/47
TTI	Top Tier Intermediary
UIDAI	Unique Identification Authority of India
UK	United Kingdom
UN	United Nations
UN SDG	United Nations Sustainable Development Goal
UPI	United Payments Interface
US	United States
US$ or USD	United States Dollar
VaR	Value at Risk
VISA	Visa International Service Association
WTO	World Trade Organization

1

Introduction

Finance and technology have been central to human societies and economies since the advent of settled human civilisations almost 10,000 years ago, and for almost as long, efforts have been made to govern and regulate both.

While innovation has always affected finance, over the past 50 years, finance and technology have evolved incredibly rapidly due to digitalisation. Digitalisation combines processes of digitisation and datafication. Digitisation is the process of moving data from physical (analogue) to electronic (digital) form, while datafication is the process of deriving data from activities and analysing them, typically via a range of information technologies, including artificial intelligence (AI). The resulting opportunities and risks are challenging the evolution of financial policy, governance, law, and regulation domestically and internationally.

This book considers this ongoing evolution. In particular, we enquire into how law and regulation can best balance the opportunities and risks of finance and technology, and how finance and technology respond to advancing and expanding financial regulation.

When in 2008 the financial world changed and the Global Financial Crisis (GFC) plunged the world into the worst recession since the Great Depression, millions of people lost their homes, jobs, and life savings. Some of the unemployed were financial services professionals. Young talented finance people with good tech skills were looking for new opportunities, conventional credit sources were contracting due to the Crisis and post-Crisis regulatory reforms, internet penetration was extensive in many markets, and the first widely successful smartphone, the Apple iPhone, was launched in mid-2007. The scene was set for dramatic change in finance. The result was a truly dramatic growth in the application of technology to finance – known as FinTech.

Accordingly, when most people think of FinTech today they think of it starting around 2008. However, we argue that FinTech is not new, because finance and technology have always danced well together – technology has long assisted in information provision which is (and always has been) crucial for financial decision-making. Today, money is intangible. It moves in response to information that comes to us on computers and is directed via electronic systems. At the same time, technological innovation helps to overcome distances, both physical and temporal. This is important in a world where financial markets are the most globalised segment of the economy, and one of the largest investors in information technology (IT) systems has long been the financial services industry, in its competitive race for new information and speed.

We show that since the 1960s, finance has gone through a profound process of digital transformation, involving digitisation and datafication and the creation of massive amounts of digital infrastructure. Finance today is the most digitised, datafied, and, due to both its destructive and constructive potential, regulated sector in developed societies.

FinTech, as we lay out in this book, is best understood as including four major elements: first, global wholesale markets where digitisation means speed, crucial for capitalising on information advantages; second, an explosion of financial technology (FinTech) start-ups particularly since 2008 in the aftermath of the GFC seeking regulatory lenience that was available to the small but not the large; third, the unprecedented digital financial transformation in retail finance in an increasing number of countries, most dramatically China and India; and fourth, the increasing role of large technology companies (BigTechs) moving into financial services and digital financial platforms.

The changes since 2008 have been unprecedented, particularly in terms of the speed of technological evolution and emergence of new entrants, including start-ups and BigTechs. These changes have brought greater financial inclusion and efficiency and new risks. Regulators seek to maximise the former and ensure that financial intermediaries well accommodate the latter.

This long-term process of digitisation and datafication of finance has been increasingly combined over the past 15 years with a group of technologies commonly termed 'ABCD': Artificial Intelligence (A), Big Data (B), Cloud Computing (C), and Distributed Ledger Technology (D). The latter typically uses blockchains and makes possible the smart contracts that underpin cryptocurrencies and central bank digital currencies. These technologies have together, on the one hand, prompted the need for digital identification and, on the other hand, triggered the extraordinary growth we have seen in use of technology for regulatory and supervisory purposes: Regulatory Technologies (RegTech) and Supervisory Technologies (SupTech).

We include all of these aspects of the revolution through which we are all living in the rubric, FinTech. Its ambit is broad and extends from innovations with disruptive effects on existing intermediaries, such as crowdfunding and crowdlending among many others, through to the entry into financial services of the BigTechs and the existential threats they pose to traditional banks.

While this process of digitisation and datafication and emergence of new technologies extends across both developed and developing markets, the latter often display faster digital financial transformation because of the absence of legacy systems and the demand driven by large-scale financial exclusion.

During the 2020s, factors beyond digitisation and datafication have driven this revolution. The COVID-19 pandemic and its attendant lockdowns around the world drove ever better presenceless payments and security measures. If the pandemic had struck a mere decade earlier, the then technology would have allowed far fewer of us to work, shop, and communicate well from home. FinTech likewise has been central in times of conflict and in our current sustainability crisis. Only a digital financial system has the capacity and versatility to deal with the plethora of objectives that regulators now impose on financial systems.

We consider the history, evolution, and scaffolding of 'FinTech' in Part I of this book.

We commence in Chapter 2 by analysing the evolution of FinTech since 1865 in four periods. The first period involved electrification and lasted for a century until the mid-to-late 1960s. It was dominated by analogue processes and traditional banks. The second period lasted 40 years and was marked by digitisation, including across securities markets (NASDAQ), payments (ATMs and SWIFT), computerisation (financial calculators and PCs), and mass communication (Internet and mobile). From around 2007 onwards, a new period commenced which was driven by the application of a range of new transformative technologies to finance, the impact of the 2008 crisis on finance, and the massive concomitant increase in regulation. These three driving forces underpinned the emergence of huge numbers of tech-driven financial services start-ups commonly called 'FinTechs'. This period lasted just over 10 years and included a rapid rise in the algorithmic analysis of data that has transformed finance. The fourth and most recent period commenced in 2020 driven by the COVID pandemic and is characterised by the rise of new scale and impact in technology, for instance with the emergence of large digital platforms, central bank digital currencies and AI.

These ever-shortening time periods are no coincidence, for it is the nature of technological change to build upon itself and thus be ever accelerating. The current period may only last five years. It has been a wild ride so far, and only likely to get faster and wilder.

In Chapter 3, we argue for smarter regulatory approaches and measures. Since the 2008 GFC, financial regulation has increased dramatically in scope and scale. Post-crisis regulation, plus rapid technological change, has spurred the development of FinTech and RegTech firms and data-driven financial service providers. Financial regulators increasingly seek to balance the traditional objectives of financial stability and consumer protection with promoting growth, innovation, and sustainability. This chapter analyses possible new regulatory approaches, ranging from doing nothing (which spans being permissive to highly restrictive, depending on context), cautious permissiveness (on a case-by-case basis, or through special charters), structured experimentalism (e.g., sandboxes or piloting), and development of specific new regulatory frameworks. We argue for a new balanced, risk-based, proportionate approach that incorporates these rebalanced objectives, which we term 'smart regulation'.

Chapter 4 considers the evolution of the use of technology for regulatory and supervisory purposes: RegTech for short. RegTech is the use of technology, particularly IT, in monitoring, compliance and regulatory reporting by industry, and in supervision and enforcement by regulators. The latter use by regulators is sometimes termed 'SupTech', which then narrows the ambit of the term RegTech to the use by industry. Either way, for industry, regulators, and policymakers, the pace of transformation in digital financial products and systems requires ever greater use of RegTech. In this substantial sense, FinTech demands RegTech. While the principal regulatory objectives of financial stability, consumer protection, market integrity, and support for growth and development remain, their attainment increasingly requires the deployment of sophisticated technology by both reporting entities and regulators. The increasing use of RegTech in turn enables a paradigm shift involving a reconceptualisation of financial regulation which we analyse.

Chapter 5 considers the impact of COVID and how the digital financial infrastructure that emerged in the wake of the 2008 Crisis assisted to address the financial, economic, and health challenges presented by the COVID-19 pandemic. While the 2008 Crisis was a financial crisis that impacted the real economy, COVID-19 was a health and geopolitical crisis that impacted the real economy. Remarkably, during the pandemic, the financial system proved to be highly resilient and, in fact, turned from problem child to crisis response facilitator.

Chapter 6 analyses the drivers of the recent digital financial transformation as the quest for (i) efficiency, (ii) financial inclusion, and (iii) sustainability. These three factors are necessarily intertwined: financial inclusion underpins long-term-oriented economies, and sustainability is required longer term for efficiency, and vice versa. More efficient and innovative financial systems support responses to crises such as the COVID pandemic and enable financial inclusion and sustainable development across the full range of the United Nations Sustainable Development Goals (SDGs).

Having set the scene historically with a conceptual framework within which to understand the FinTech Revolution, we then proceed to consider the breadth of FinTech. We analyse its various elements, which taken together comprise nothing less than a revolution in finance.

In Part II, we consider the major new technologies that characterise the FinTech age. Chapter 7 addresses the use of AI and machine learning in finance. The chapter develops a framework for understanding and addressing the increasing role of AI in finance. It focuses on human responsibility as central to any solution to the AI 'black box' problem – which is the risk of undesirable results arising from people's difficulties in understanding the internal working of an AI or from an AI's independent operation outside human supervision or involvement.

The next two chapters (Chapters 8 and 9) in Part II address distributed ledger technology (DLT) and blockchain, and the evolution of decentralised finance (DeFi) and embedded regulation.

In Chapter 8, we consider how DLTs and blockchain are contributing to the creation of a new foundational infrastructure for financial services, including crypto-assets and smart contracts. We classify the new business models, analyse the opportunities, and highlight the regulatory challenges.

In Chapter 9, we analyse the meaning, legal implications, and policy consequences of DeFi. Decentralisation has the potential to undermine traditional forms of accountability and erode the effectiveness of traditional financial regulation and enforcement. At the same time, where parts of financial services are decentralised, there will be a reconcentration in a different (but possibly less regulated, less visible, and less transparent) part of the financial services chain. DeFi regulation could and should focus on this reconcentrated portion to ensure effective oversight and risk control. Paradoxically, DeFi may well require regulation in order to achieve its core objective of decentralisation. Furthermore, DeFi facilitates 'embedded regulation', by allowing regulatory measures to be built into the decentralised infrastructure, potentially decentralising both finance and its regulation in the ultimate expression of RegTech.

Chapter 10 considers the role of data and data regulation. Against the background of the big data age, this chapter explores the relationship between data and financial regulation in four major jurisdictions: the EU, the United States, China, and India. We argue that data regulation provides a crucial foundation upon which FinTech infrastructure is designed, built, and operated. Data regulation thus profoundly shapes the emergence of FinTech ecosystems. For FinTech, data regulation is a new form of financial regulation.

Chapter 11 presents a framework for a balanced proportional approach to supporting innovation, focusing on the role of innovation hubs and regulatory sandboxes. This chapter argues that innovation hubs provide most of the benefits that the policy discussion associates with regulatory sandboxes, while avoiding most of the downsides of formal regulatory sandboxes. Consequently, we argue, regulators should focus their resources on developing effective innovation hubs, including, in appropriate cases, a sandbox as part of the hub.

In Part III, we move from the questions around new technologies to the strategies for building better financial systems, focusing on the role of digital financial infrastructure, so as to allow societies to capitalise on the true potential of FinTech.

Chapter 12 explores the infrastructure for digital financial transformation and suggests it be built on four primary pillars. The first pillar comprises digital identity, simplified account opening, and e-KYC systems. The second is open interoperable electronic payment systems. The third involves the electronic provision of government services and payments. The fourth is the design and development of digital financial markets and systems, which supports broader access to finance and investment.

Chapter 13 focuses on the role of digital identity as a core enabling infrastructure and explores the various requirements for identification in the financial sector and the evolving nature of identity. We argue that technology enables the solution of the identity challenge through the development of digital identity infrastructure and related identity utilities. The establishment of such utilities for digital or electronic identification requires addressing design questions, such as registration methods, data availability, and cross-jurisdictional recognition, and offers massive efficiencies to financial services.

Chapter 14 explores the digital transformation of payments and the emergence of cryptocurrencies, stablecoins, and central bank digital currencies ('CBDCs'). In the future, we expect domestic money and payment systems to involve public central banks cooperating with (old and possibly new) private entities, including commercial banks, to launch digital currencies which will underpin profoundly better monetary and payment systems at both domestic and international levels.

Chapter 15 highlights the experience of the European Union in bringing these elements together to support digital financial transformation. Europe's path to digitisation and datafication in finance has rested upon four apparently unrelated pillars: (1) extensive reporting requirements imposed after the GFC to control systemic risk and change financial sector behaviour; (2) strict data protection rules; (3) the facilitation of open banking to enhance competition in banking and particularly payments; and (4) a legislative framework for digital identification imposed to further the European Single Market. We suggest that together these seemingly unrelated pillars have driven a transition to data-driven finance. The EU experiences provide insights for other countries in developing regulatory approaches to the intersection of data, finance, and technology.

Part IV then focuses on the risks of FinTech, which we term 'TechRisk'. It explores the risks to competition that arise because both finance and technology industries tend towards winner-takes-all outcomes and the other risks that increasing dependence upon technology brings.

Chapter 16 highlights the emergence of a range of new platforms that are transforming finance far more than have the FinTech start-ups which characterised the 2010s. These massive data companies moving into financial services we refer to as 'TechFins'. China has led this change, with Alibaba establishing the online financial conglomerate Ant Group. The chapter also considers the emergence of digital finance platforms and the entry of BigTech firms (the tech behemoths Microsoft, Apple, Google, Meta, and Amazon) into finance. These changes are a natural outcome of the economies of scope and scale that characterise finance combined with the network effects of data and technology. These major trends are at the heart of the current era of FinTech and bring the major risks we explore in Chapters 17, 18, and 19.

Chapter 17 provides a framework to understand the emerging risks in digital finance, and in particular, we focus upon systemic, cybersecurity risks and privacy risks.

Chapter 18 considers the emergence of new systemically important financial institutions (SIFIs) and financial market infrastructures, and the risks that this brings and how best to regulate these SIFIs, many of which will not trigger the traditional thresholds of financial regulation.

Chapter 19 analyses platformisation, one of the trends transforming finance, with examples including the rise of Ant Financial in China's financial landscape and of Blackrock's Aladdin in the US mutual funds industry. This chapter considers how to regulate these emerging massive digital finance platforms in the light of their impact on financial regulation objectives, competition, and innovation.

Our analysis then concludes in Chapter 20, in which we argue that contemporary digital finance, which emerged from the crisis of 2008, has become a crisis impact mitigation tool able to assist in dealing with the plethora of challenges and crises mankind is facing, be they wars, a pandemic, or the climate-related sustainability crisis. Better financial systems may not only promote efficiency and stability but also support resilience in future crises whatever their source.

We argue that the digitisation of finance has been central to the positive contributions of today's financial systems. To ensure our financial systems continue as a force for good, financial regulation must simultaneously pursue the objectives of efficiency, resilience, inclusion, innovation, and sustainable development. This is particularly challenging because the rise of the TechFins and of digital financial platforms means two of the major players in contemporary finance will often be systemically significant without activating the traditional triggers for financial regulation – and thus will lie outside the purview of financial regulation. This is the core challenge facing financial regulation globally today. Digital finance, well regulated, will be essential to respond well to the increasing range of crises likely in coming decades. To realise this potential, FinTech and digital finance require a fundamental readjustment of approaches to the regulation of finance and technology. How this may be brought about is the subject of this book.

PART I

Digital Transformation of Finance and Regulation

2

Evolution of FinTech

SUMMARY

This chapter analyses the evolution of finance and technology. In the modern era, we mark this in four major periods. The first focused on electrification and lasted for a century until the mid to late 1960s. It was dominated by analogue processes and traditional banks. The second period was marked by digitisation, including across securities markets (NASDAQ), payments (ATMs, Swift), mass computerisation (financial calculators, PCs), and communications (Internet, mobile), and lasted 40 years. From around 2007 onwards, a new trend emerged as a result of the application of a range of new financial technologies, combined with the impact of the 2008 Global Financial Crisis on finance and regula- tion. These three driving forces – the 2008 Crisis, the application of new and transformative technologies to finance, and a massive increase in regulation globally in response to 2008 and a range of financial scandals – underpinned the emergence of FinTech, short for 'financial technology'. This third period lasted just over 10 years and saw the rise of data and its algorithmic analysis in a process called datafication which has transformed finance. The most recent era, driven by the COVID-19 pandemic, commenced in 2020 and is characterised by the emergence of scale in technology, in the form of large digital platforms, CBDCs and AI.

I. INTRODUCTION

'Financial technology' or 'FinTech' refers to the use of technology in finance. The term dates back to the early 1990s and the Financial Services Technology Consortium, a Citigroup-led project to facilitate technological cooperation.[1] In 2014, the number of Google searches for the term began to increase exponentially and

---

[1]   See Marc Hochstein, 'Fintech (the Word, That Is) Evolves', *American Banker* (Web Page, 5 October 2015) <www.americanbanker.com/bankthink/fintech-the-word-that-is-evolves-1077098-1.html>.

the sector began to attract the focus of regulators.[2] FinTech can be seen narrowly (as in the context of new entrants and business models focusing on new technologies) or broadly (as in the use of technology across financial services of all forms). By 2020, narrow FinTech – in the form of new entrants and start-ups – was a massive, fast-growing sector that accounted for some US\$ 121.5 billion in investment.[3] At the same time, from a broader standpoint, every aspect of finance has been transformed since the late 1960s through digitisation and datafication.

While FinTech is typically seen as a uniquely recent phenomenon, finance has been based upon transmission and manipulation of information for centuries. For instance, the introduction of the telegraph in 1838[4] and the laying of the first successful transatlantic cable in 1866[5] by the Atlantic Telegraph Company provided the fundamental infrastructure for the first major period of financial globalisation in the late nineteenth century.

For nearly 30 years, traditional financial services have driven the information technology (IT) industry. The financial services industry is often the largest purchaser of IT,[6] with total accumulated spending exceeding US\$ 4.40 trillion from 2005 to 2021.[7] Today, for most consumers, the automated teller machine (ATM) is often the only point at which finance shifts from being a purely digital experience to one involving a physical commodity, that is, cash. With the rapid advancement of e-payments,[8] even this singular experience is decreasing rapidly.

Since FinTech is not a new story, its opportunities, risks, and legal implications should not be novel.[9] Industry activities and regulators' concerns arise now not so much from the technology itself but from *who* is applying the technology to finance and the *speed* of change.

---

[2] A Google trend search reveals that the interest over time for the word 'fintech' increased exponentially in 2014. 'Fintech: Interest over Time', *Google Trends* (Web Page) <www.google.com/trends/explore#q=fintech> (parameters set at 'Worldwide'; '2004-present'; 'All categories'; 'Web Search').

[3] 'Australian fintech Investment Hits US\$890 m in First Half of 2021' *KPMG* (Web Page, 11 August 2021) <https://home.kpmg/au/en/home/media/press-releases/2021/08/australian-fintech-investment-hits-us890m-first-half-2021-11-august-2021.html>.

[4] See Giancarlo Barbiroli, *The Dynamics of Technology: A Methodological Framework for Techno-Economic Analyses* (Springer, 1997) 58.

[5] See Jill Hills, *The Struggle for Control of Global Communication: The Formative Century* (University of Illinois Press, 2002) 35.

[6] See Khalid Kark, *Reinventing Tech Finance: The Evolution from IT Budgets to Technology Investments* (CIO Insider Report, Deloitte Insights, January 2020) 2 <www2.deloitte.com/content/dam/insights/us/articles/6300_CIO-insider-tech-finance/DI_CIO-Insider_Tech-Finance-Budgets.pdf>.

[7] Kimberly Mlitz, 'Information Technology (IT) Worldwide Spending from 2005 to 2023' *Statista* (Web Page, July 2021) <www.statista.com/statistics/203935/overall-it-spending-worldwide>.

[8] See McKinsey & Company, *The Great Divergence: McKinsey Global Banking Annual Review 2021* (Report, December 2021) 15 <www.mckinsey.com/industries/financial-services/our-insights/global-banking-annual-review>.

[9] See, generally, Roy Goode, *Electronic Banking: The Legal Implications* (Institute of Bankers, 1985) for discussions about the legal consequences of the increased use of electronic payments and authentication in banking.

In this chapter, we first track developments across the four main eras of modern FinTech evolution. In the FinTech 1.0 era of around 1866 to 1967, the financial services industry, while heavily interlinked with technology, remained largely analogue. In the late 1960s, the advent of the ATM and handheld financial calculators marked the beginning of FinTech 2.0. The development of digital technology for communications and processing of transactions was to increasingly transform traditional finance over the next 40 years, beginning with the advent of NASDAQ and SWIFT in the early 1970s. FinTech 3.0, beginning in 2007–2008, with the iPhone, mPesa and Bitcoin, was characterised by new start-ups and big technology companies (BigTechs) delivering financial products and services directly to businesses and the public. These included new payment systems, peer-to-peer (P2P) lending, financial platforms, and robo-advice. These developments, posing an existential threat to incumbent banks, are forcing banks to transform how they deliver financial services to their customers.[10] In 2020, the COVID-19 pandemic marked the beginning of FinTech 4.0. This was heralded by an incredible growth in financial platforms; the rise in value and number of cryptocurrencies; the development of stablecoins; and the piloting of central bank digital currencies (CBDCs), as well as convergence in major FinTech trends across developed and developing financial services markets. We now consider each period in more detail.

II. FINTECH 1.0 (1866–1967): FROM ANALOGUE TO DIGITAL

A. Early 'FinTech'

From their earliest stages of development, finance and technology have been interlinked and mutually reinforcing. Finance originated in the state administrative systems that supported the transition from hunter-gatherer groups to settled agricultural and commercial states. For example, in Mesopotamia, written records facilitated management of administrative and economic systems, including financial transactions.[11] Similarly, the development of money and finance are clearly intertwined. According to Mervyn King, former governor of the Bank of England (2003–13):

> The history of money is.... The story of how we evolved as social animals, trading with each other. It starts with the use as money of commodities—grain and cattle in Egypt and Mesopotamia as early as 9000 BC.... The cost and inconvenience of using such commodities led to the emergence of precious metals as the dominant form of money. Metals were first used in transactions in ancient Mesopotamia and Egypt, metal coins originated in China and the Middle East and were in use no

---

[10] See David Gyori, 'FinTech Is the Future Itself' in Susanne Chishti and Janos Barberis (eds), *The FINTECH Book: The Financial Technology Handbook for Investors, Entrepreneurs and Visionaries* (Wiley, 1st ed, 2016) 265.

[11] Matthew Rowlinson, *Real Money and Romanticism* (Cambridge University Press, 2010) 7.

later than the fourth century BC. The earliest banknotes appeared in China in the seventh century AD.[12]

Money is a technology that evidences transferable value and is a defining character-istic of a modern economy.[13] Early calculation technologies like the abacus greatly facilitated financial transactions. Finance evolved from an early stage to support trade (e.g., financing and insuring ships and infrastructure such as bridges, railroads, and canals), and the production of goods for that trade. Double-entry bookkeep-ing – another technology fundamental to a modern economy – emerged in the late Middle Ages and the Renaissance.

Many historians today believe that Europe's financial revolution in the late 1600s involving joint stock companies, insurance, and banking was essential to the Industrial Revolution.[14] Access to capital supported the development of technolo-gies that underpinned industrial development. The mutual relationship between finance and technology is thus longstanding; the two are in fact co-developmental.

B. *The First Age of Financial Globalisation*

In the nineteenth century, finance and technology combined to produce the first period of financial globalisation. Technology such as the telegraph, railroads, canals, and steamships underpinned financial interconnections across borders, allowing rapid transmission of financial information, transactions, and payments around the world. The financial sector provided the resources to invest in these technolo-gies and the technologies provided the means to invest throughout the world.[15] J M Keynes, writing in 1919, provided a clear picture of the interlinkage between finance and technology in this first age of financial globalisation:

> The inhabitant of London could order by telephone, sipping his morning tea in bed, the various products of the whole earth, in such quantity as he might see fit, and reasonably expect their early delivery upon his door-step; he could at the same moment and by the same means adventure his wealth in the natural resources and new enterprises of any quarter of the world, and share, without exertion or even trouble.[16]

---

[12] Mervyn A King, *The End of Alchemy: Money, Banking and the Future of the Global Economy* (Little, Brown, 2016) 55–7.

[13] Indeed, one can make the argument that paper is a technology that allows us to store value. The same size bank note can 'store' $10 or $100 and be worth this much for as long as there is a state or central bank guaranteeing to pay the bearer of the note. The amount written on the bank note itself has theo-retically no limit.

[14] Charles More, *Understanding the Industrial Revolution* (Routledge, 2000) 36.

[15] See, generally, Ralf Roth and Günter Dinhobl (eds), *Across the Borders: Financing the World's Railways in the Nineteenth and Twentieth Centuries* (Routledge, 2016); Werner Baer, 'The Promoting and Financing of the Suez Canal' (1956) 30(4) *The Business History Review* 361.

[16] John Maynard Keynes, *The Economic Consequences of the Peace* (Harcourt, Brace, and Howe, 1919) 10–12.

C. *The Early Post-war Period*

After World War I, financial globalisation was constrained for decades, but communications and IT used in war advanced rapidly, as firms such as International Business Machines (IBM) turned code-breaking tools into early computers. Credit cards were first introduced in the 1950s, such as Diners Club in 1950 and American Express in 1958.[17]

The next decade introduced the true game changers. Texas Instruments produced the first handheld financial calculators in 1967. What is now MasterCard was built in the United States in 1966 and would in time underpin a global consumer payments revolution. A global telex network was already in place, and the successor to the telex, the fax machine, was introduced by Xerox in 1964.[18] In 1967, Barclays deployed the world's first ATM in England, leading Paul Volcker, former chairman of the US Federal Reserve, to famously comment in 2009:

> The most important financial innovation that I have seen the past 20 years is the automatic teller machine, that really helps people and prevents visits to the bank and it is a real convenience.[19]

In our characterisation, these developments were a necessary precondition for the emergence of FinTech 2.0.

III. FINTECH 2.0 (1967–2008): DEVELOPMENT OF TRADITIONAL DIGITAL FINANCIAL SERVICES

From 1967 through 1987, financial services transitioned from an analogue to a digital industry.

A. *The Modern Foundations: Digitalisation and Globalisation of Finance*

In the late 1960s and 1970s, electronic payment systems – the basis of today's internet and mobile payment systems – advanced rapidly for domestic and cross-border transactions. The Inter-Computer Bureau was established in the United Kingdom in 1968, forming the basis of today's Bankers' Automated Clearing Services (BACS),[20] and the Clearing House Interbank Payments System (CHIPS) was established in

---

[17] Jerry W Markham, *From Christopher Columbus to the Robber Barons: A Financial History of the United States 1492–1900* (Routledge, 2002) 306.

[18] 'The History of Fax (From 1843 to Present Day)', *Fax Authority* (Web Page, 9 August 2021) <https://faxauthority.com/fax-history>.

[19] See Reuters, 'The Only Thing Useful Banks Have Invented in 20 Years Is the ATM', News (online, 13 December 2009) <http://nypost.com/2009/12/13/the-only-thing-useful-banks-have-invented-in-20-year-is-the-atm/>.

[20] Brian Welch (ed), *Electronic Banking and Treasury Security* (Woodhead Publishing, 2nd ed, 1999).

the United States in 1970.[21] Fedwire, originally established in 1918, became an electronic (instead of telegraphic) system in the 1960s.[22] Reflecting the need to connect domestic payment systems across borders, the Society of Worldwide Interbank Financial Telecommunications (SWIFT) was established in 1973, followed soon after by the collapse of Herstatt Bank in 1974, which clearly highlighted the risks of increasing international financial linkages.[23] This crisis triggered the first major regulatory focus on FinTech issues, with the establishment of the Basel Committee on Banking Supervision of the Bank for International Settlements (BIS) in 1974 as well as a series of international soft law agreements on developing robust payment systems and related regulation.[24]

The BIS Committee on Payment and Settlement Systems (CPSS) was established in 1990, building on an earlier group established in 1980.[25] The combination of finance, technology, and appropriate regulatory attention is the basis of today's US$ 7.5 trillion-per-day global foreign exchange market, the largest, most globalised, and most digitised component of the global economy.[26]

Michael Bloomberg started Innovation Market Solutions (IMS) in 1981 after leaving Salomon Brothers, where he had designed in-house computer systems. Bloomberg, with its iconic Bloomberg Terminal, is therefore one of the first and most successful of FinTech start-ups; many traditional financial institutions that adopted advanced technologies early on could be so classified. Throughout this period, FinTech was dominated by incumbents that increasingly used technology to provide financial products and services to consumers. Financial institutions increasingly used new IT developments in their internal operations, gradually replacing most paper-based mechanisms.

In securities, the establishment of NASDAQ[27] in the United States in 1971, the end of fixed securities commissions, and the eventual development of the National Market System marked the transition from physical trading of securities dating from the late 1600s to today's fully electronic securities trading.[28] In 1987, the stock market crashed on 'Black Monday', clearly showing the interlinkage of global markets through technology. Indeed, Hollywood's take on this era in Oliver Stone's

---

[21] 'About CHIPS', *The Clearing House* (Web Page) <www.theclearinghouse.org/payment-systems/chips>.

[22] *Assessment of Compliance with the Core Principles for Systemically Important Payment Systems* (Report, The Fedwire Funds Service, July 2014) 7–8 <www.federalreserve.gov/paymentsystems/files/fedfunds_coreprinciples.pdf>.

[23] 'SWIFT History', *SWIFT* (Web Page) <www.swift.com/about-us/history>.

[24] 'History of the Basel Committee', *Bank for International Settlements* (Web Page) <www.bis.org/bcbs/history.htm>.

[25] This was renamed the Committee on Payments and Market Infrastructures (CPMI) in 2016.

[26] See Bank for International Settlements, *Triennial Central Bank Survey: Foreign Exchange Turnover in April 2022* (Report, 27 October 2022).

[27] Acronym for National Association of Securities Dealers Automated Quotations.

[28] See NASDAQ, 'NASDAQ Celebrates 50 Years of Innovation' (Press Release, 8 February 2021) <https://ir.nasdaq.com/news-releases/news-release-details/nasdaq-celebrates-50-years-innovation>.

1987 film *Wall Street* produced an iconic popular image: an investment banker wielding a clunky early mobile telephone, an IT innovation first introduced in the United States in 1983. While over 30 years later, there is still no clear consensus on what caused the crash, focus has fallen on financial institutions' use of 'program trading' through systems that bought and sold securities automatically based on preset price levels.[29]

This reaction led to the introduction by exchanges and regulators of a variety of mechanisms, particularly in electronic markets, to control the speed of price changes ('circuit breakers'). It also led securities regulators around the world to begin working on mechanisms to support cooperation in cross-border securities markets.[30] In addition, the *Single European Act* of 1986 established the framework for what would become the single financial market in the European Union. This Act, in addition to the Big Bang financial liberalisation process in the United Kingdom in 1986, the 1992 Maastricht Treaty, and the increasing introduction of 'European Passports' for financial services from the late 1980s onwards, underpinned the eventual full interconnection of European Union financial markets by the early twenty-first century.[31]

By the late 1980s, financial services were becoming mostly digital, relying on electronic transactions between financial institutions, market participants, and customers around the world. By 1998, financial services had become, for all practical purposes, a *digital industry*. This period also showed the initial limits and risks in complex computerised risk management systems with the collapse of Long-Term Capital Management (LTCM) in the wake of the Asian and Russian financial crises of 1997–98.[32]

The emergence of the widespread use of the Internet set the stage for the next level of development. In the consumer banking sector, online banking was first introduced in the United States in 1980 (although it was abandoned in 1983) and in the United Kingdom in 1983 by the Nottingham Building Society.[33] Then again in 1995, Wells Fargo began providing online banking to US consumers. By 2001, eight US banks had at least one million customers online, with other major jurisdictions to follow.[34] By 2005, the first direct banks without physical branches had emerged and gained wide public acceptance (e.g., ING Direct, HSBC Direct).

[29] See Richard Bookstaber, *A Demon of Our Own Design: Markets, Hedge Funds, and the Perils of Financial Innovation* (Wiley, 2008) 7–32.

[30] See Marc I Steinberg, *International Securities Law: A Contemporary and Comparative Analysis* (Kluwer Law International, 1st ed, 1999).

[31] See George A Walker, *International Banking Regulation: Law Policy and Practice* (Kluwer Law International, 1st ed, 2001).

[32] See, generally, Philippe Jorion, 'Risk Management Lessons from Long-Term Capital Management' (2000) 6(3) *European Financial Management* 277.

[33] Harry Choron and Sandra Choron, *Money: Everything You Never Knew about Your Favorite Thing to Find, Save, Spend and Covet* (Chronicle Books, 2011) 22.

[34] See, generally, Mary J Cronin (ed), *Banking and Finance on the Internet* (Wiley, 1997).

By the beginning of the twenty-first century, banks' internal processes, interactions with outsiders, and an ever-increasing number of interactions with retail customers became digitised. This growth in digitisation led to corresponding growth in IT spending by the financial services industry.

B. *Regulatory Approaches to FinTech 2.0*

As technology changed, so too did regulatory structure and strategies. By the late 1990s, computerised trading systems and records had become the regulators' principal source of information about market manipulation in securities markets. The internationalisation of finance supported by new technologies underpinned major developments in cross-border regulatory cooperation, particularly through the Basel Committee and IOSCO (International Organisation of Securities Commissions). In the United States and Europe, major efforts were focused on regulating new risks emerging in e-payments and exchanges.[35] Naturally, there was limited benefit in regulating *all* new innovations applicable to the financial sector. Pre-emptive regulation would increase the workload of regulatory agencies and stifle innovation without providing substantial benefits.[36] Hence, regulators focused during FinTech 2.0 on innovations of major scope and scale.

Regulators during FinTech 2.0 focused primarily on the new risks of e-banking (which was understood to simply constitute a digital version of the traditional brick and mortar banking model). By providing direct and virtually unlimited access to their accounts, technology removed the need for depositors to be physically present at a branch to withdraw funds. The development of e-banking could thus facilitate electronic bank runs (a risk that will be increased by an order of magnitude if and when CBDCs become common).[37]

> In addition, regulators identified new credit risks. Competitive pressure, given that borrowers have access to a greater pool of lenders with the removal of geographical limits, may put systemic financial stability at risk. Further, the potential stability-inducing constraints arising from being known personally by a loan officer are lost as loan origination is automated.

The benefits of online banking have, to date, outweighed the risks. Better organised and analysed data have underpinned improved assessments of borrower credit risk. However, FinTech start-ups introduce new risks relative to online banks. While

---

[35] See David Carse, Deputy Chief Executive, Hong Kong Monetary Authority, 'Regulatory Framework of E-banking' (Keynote Speech, Symposium on Applied R&D: Enhancing Global Competitiveness in the Next Millennium, 8 October 1999) <www.bis.org/review/r991012c.pdf>. See Section VI for more details on this point.

[36] Ravi Menon, Managing Director, Monetary Authority of Singapore, 'Fintech: Harnessing Its Power, Managing Its Risks' (Panel Remarks, Singapore Forum, 2 April 2016) <www.mas.gov.sg/news/speeches/2016/fintech-harnessing-its-power-managing-its-risks>.

[37] David Carse (n 35).

risks during FinTech 2.0 stem from technological innovations being used only by licensed financial institutions, the advent of entirely new entrants marked the turning point between FinTech 2.0 and FinTech 3.0.

IV. FINTECH 3.0 (2008–2019): DEMOCRATISING DIGITAL FINANCIAL SERVICES?

A. *The World of Finance at a Turning Point*

In the aftermath of the 2008 Global Financial Crisis (GFC) a shift in mindset occurred among retail customers in many places as to *who* had the resources and legitimacy to provide financial services. In parallel, there was unprecedentedly rapid technological development and change. An alignment of factors post-2008 supported the emergence of innovative market players and novel applications of technology to financial services. Among these factors were public perception, regulatory scrutiny, political demand, and economic conditions. All in all, 2008 clearly represents the beginning of FinTech 3.0.

B. *FinTech and the GFC: Evolution or Revolution?*

The 2008 financial crisis trashed perceptions of banks and bankers[38] as some 8.7 million American workers lost their jobs.[39] Many finance professionals also lost their jobs or high salaries and found new roles in FinTech start-ups.[40] These professionals were complemented by a younger generation of highly educated graduates who were facing a difficult job market and were often educationally well equipped to understand finance and markets. In turn, the brand image of banks and their perceived stability was severely shaken. A 2018 Bain & Company survey of 151,894 consumers in 29 countries showed that 54 per cent of respondents trust at least one technology company more than banks in general.[41] For example, respondents who reposed higher trust in Amazon are open to trying banking services offered by the company. Beyond such well-established corporations, an increasing number of non-listed companies and start-ups entered the stage at this time to compete for customers' money and financial data.

---

[38] See, generally, Sumit Agarwal et al, 'Predatory Lending and the Subprime Crisis' (2004) 113 *Journal of Financial Economics* 29.

[39] See John Kell, 'U.S. Recovers All Jobs Lost in Financial Crisis', *Fortune* (Web Page, 6 June 2014) <http://fortune.com/2014/06/06/us-jobs-may>.

[40] See Mark Esposito & Terence Tse, 'The Lost Generation: What Is True about the Myth…', *The London School of Economics and Political Science* (Web Page, 7 April 2014) <http://blogs.lse.ac.uk/eurocrisispress/2014/04/07/the-lost-generation-what-is-true-about-the-myth>.

[41] See Katrina Cuthell, 'Many Consumers Trust Technology Companies More than Banks', *Bain & Company* (Web Page, 9 January 2019) <www.bain.com/insights/many-consumers-trust-technology-companies-more-than-banks-snap-chart>.

China clearly illustrated this phenomenon with over 6,000 essentially unregulated P2P lending platforms before a major government crackdown caused almost all to close.[42] Likewise, the reputational factors that suggest only banks can offer banking services were weak for the 1.7 billion unbanked individuals on our planet.[43] As has been well put, 'banking is necessary, banks are not'.[44] Post-2008, financial regulation increased banks' compliance obligations and altered their commercial incentives. In particular, universal banks were subject to costly ring-fencing obligations and increased regulatory capital that changed their incentive or capacity to originate low-value loans. Furthermore, the (mis)use of certain financial innovations, such as collateralised debt obligations, contributed to the crisis by detaching the credit risk of the underlying loan from the loan originator.[45] Finally, the necessity to ensure orderly failure of banks drove the implementation of financial institution resolution regimes across jurisdictions, with banks required to prepare Recovery and Resolution Plans and conduct stress tests to evaluate their viability. In short, since 2008, the business models and structures of banks have been utterly reshaped.

C. From Post-Crisis Regulation to FinTech 3.0

The regulatory responses to the GFC were necessary in the light of the social and economic impact of the crisis and to reduce the prospects of the next financial crisis having similar causes.[46] Yet, unintentionally, these post-crisis reforms encouraged new technological players and limited the capacity of banks to compete. For example, Basel III led to higher capital requirements for banks. This enhanced market stability but also diverted capital away from small and medium enterprises (SMEs) and individuals. Many individuals then turned to P2P lending platforms or other innovations to meet their credit needs.

During FinTech 2.0, the expectation was that e-banking solutions would be provided by supervised financial institutions. However, in FinTech 3.0, financial services provision no longer rested solely with regulated financial institutions.

---

[42] Regulators in China announced new rules around the P2P industry, mainly around credit-worthiness checks and regulatory capital requirements in 2019. See 'China Gives P2P Lenders Two Years to Exit Industry', *Reuters* (online, 28 November 2019) <www.reuters.com/article/us-china-p2p-iduskbn1y2039>.

[43] See Asli Demirgüç-Kunt et al, *The Global Findex Database 2017: Measuring Financial Inclusion and the Fintech Revolution* (World Bank Group, 2018) 4.

[44] As stated by Richard Kovacevich, see Bethany Mclean, 'Is This Guy the Best Banker in America?', *Fortune* (Web Page, 6 July 1998) <http://archive.fortune.com/magazines/fortune/fortune_archive/1998/07/06/244842/index.htm>. This quote is often wrongly ascribed to Bill Gates, but he seems to have said, '[b]anks are dinosaurs, we can bypass them.' See 'Culture Club', *Newsweek* (online, 10 July 1994) <www.newsweek.com/culture-club-189982>.

[45] Miguel Segoviano et al, 'Securitization: Lessons Learned and the Road Ahead' (Working Paper WP/13/255, International Monetary Fund, 2013) 14–21.

[46] On what may cause the next crisis, and the inadequacy of regulatory reforms to date to avert it, see generally Ross P Buckley, 'Reconceptualizing the Regulation of Global Finance' (2016) 36(2) *Oxford Journal of Legal Studies* 242.

The public demand for greater access to credit in the United States was answered in part by the *Jump Start Our Business Startups (JOBS) Act* in 2012. The *JOBS Act* tackled unemployment and credit supply. On employment, the *JOBS Act* aimed to promote the creation of start-ups by providing alternative ways to fund their businesses.[47] On credit, the *JOBS Act* assisted start-ups to bypass the credit contraction caused by banks' increased costs and reduced capacity to lend by making it possible for start-ups to access capital on P2P platforms, thereby bolstering the growth of FinTechs.

In summary, the financial services industry from 2008 to 2019 was affected by a combination of factors, financial, political, and public, that supported a new generation of market participants in establishing the new era we have called FinTech 3.0. But, consistent with the ever-accelerating rate of change in our modern world, this era was destined to only last a decade.

V. FINTECH 3.5: A NEW SYNTHESIS IN ASIAN AND AFRICAN EMERGING MARKETS

As FinTech 3.0 was progressing in developed nations, quite different forces were at work in developing nations. In the West, the main drivers were the pursuit of profits and the opportunities created by post-2008 regulation. In Africa and Asia, the main drivers were the pursuit of economic development and government policies focused on improving financial inclusion, especially in Africa. We characterise the era in these two regions as FinTech 3.5 because the time frame is the same as for FinTech 3.0 in developed nations, but the phenomena are quite distinct.

A. *Africa: A FinTech Greenfield*

FinTech in Africa emerged most notably in Kenya in 2007 with the launch by Vodafone of M-Pesa. Its tremendous growth surprised everyone involved, and came about because of need, generally underdeveloped banking services, and the very rapid spread of mobile telephones.

The reach of banks in Africa is circumscribed, generally much more so than in Asia. At most, 55.1 per cent of African individuals have a bank account as of 2021 as compared to 67.9 per cent in South Asia.[48] As a result, telecommunications companies, rather than banks, took the lead. While mobile money was pioneered in the Philippines, it rose to prominence in East Africa.[49]

---

[47] *Jump Start Our Business Startups Act*, Public Law 112–106, 126 Stat. 306 (2012).

[48] 'Databank: Global Financial Inclusion', *The World Bank* (Web Page, 2022) <https://databank .worldbank.org/reports.aspx?Source=global-financial-inclusion>. Parameters set as 'Sub-Saharan Africa (all income levels)'/'South Asia', 'Account (% age 15+)', '2021'.

[49] In the Philippines, SMART Money was launched in 2001 and GCASH in 2004. See Global System for Mobile Communications Association, *Mobile Money in the Philippines: The Market, the Models and*

Africa's FinTech journey began with mobile money facilitating the core functions of payments and savings, and subsequently the higher-order services of credit and micro-insurance. The typical African provider of Digital Financial Services (DFS) is a telecommunications company that encourages customers to purchase e-money, usually in the same way and place as buying airtime (i.e., by paying cash to a retail agent). The agent is typically a small shopkeeper who sells e-money, airtime, cigarettes, snacks, and the like.[50] This profile is rather similar to mobile money developments in some Asian nations, such as Cambodia and Laos, but dramatically different from the profile of DFS in China or India.

M-Pesa's great success caused excessive optimism elsewhere. Companies in other countries offering mobile money services have often needed screen savers on their corporate computers warning, 'Beware – you are not in Kenya.' Providers have had to learn over and over that replicating what had worked in Kenya did not necessarily work elsewhere. Many designers of DFS products from an IT background were charged with rolling out DFS products across a range of quite disparate countries, and in doing so typically ignored local needs.

B. *FinTech Opportunities and Limitations in the Asia-Pacific*

While DFS in Africa was instrumental for financial inclusion, it is in Asia, particularly in China and India, where the more sophisticated, and potentially transformative, developments have been occurring. The growth of Asia-Pacific (APAC) FinTech is attributable to various factors ranging from clunky banks with relatively limited branch networks through to some of the highest mobile and smartphone penetration rates in the world. On the regulatory side, most Asian regulators sought to promote FinTech with the Monetary Authority of Singapore soon serving as pacemaker and expert regulator for the region.

Following the government market reform process initiated in the late 1970s, China went from a mono-banking model[51] to a largely commercialised financial system, with some 20 large and over 4,000 small domestic banks.[52] To put this in perspective, the retail banking licence issued to Metro Bank in 2010 was the first new licence issued in the UK in over 150 years.[53]

Regulation (Report) <www.gsma.com/mobilefordevelopment/wp-content/uploads/2012/06/Philippines-Case-Study-v-X21-21.pdf>.

[50] Evan Gibson, Federico Lupo-Pasini, and Ross P Buckley, 'Regulating Digital Financial Services Agents in Developing Countries to Promote Financial Inclusion' [2015] (1) *Singapore Journal of Legal Studies* 26.

[51] See Bin Wu, Shujie Yao, and Jian Chen (eds), *China's Development and Harmonization: Towards a Balance with Nature, Society and the International Community* (Routledge, 1st ed, 2013) 171.

[52] See 'Number of Banking Institutions in China from 2009 to 2021', *Statista* (Web Page, 2 May 2022) <www.statista.com/statistics/259910/number-of-banks-in-china>.

[53] See Jill Treanor, 'UK Challenger Banks Aim to Loosen Grip of Big Four', *The Guardian* (Business Blog, 2 June 2015) <www.theguardian.com/business/2015/jun/01/uk-challenger-banks-aim-to-loosen-grip-of-big-four>.

FinTech 3.5 in developing countries was not driven by essentially post-crisis forces as in the West but by need and entrepreneurial forces coupled with highly supportive and focused government policies. It was supported by: (1) young digitally savvy populations equipped with mobile devices; (2) inefficient financial services and capital markets creating opportunities; (3) a shortage of physical banking infrastructure; (4) less stringent data protection and competition rules than in the West; (5) a patchwork of financial regulation creating many opportunities for those who knew how to manoeuvre through the regulatory landscape; and (6) governments welcoming market reform and innovation to drive financial inclusion and economic growth. To these factors should be added, in India and China, very large numbers of engineering and computer science professionals.

To further development, Asian countries used new tools of regulation, in particular tiered licensing systems. Digital banking licences were first established in China in 2015 and have since become widespread throughout the region.[54] These developments matter because they reflect a FinTech dynamic in the APAC that is based on regulatory policy that favours the development of specific sub-sectors to promote national policy objectives.

C. *China: Transitioning Its Financial Market for the Twenty-First Century*

In China specifically, technology has enlarged customer perceptions of who can properly deliver a financial service. Furthermore, the speed of FinTech evolution and development in China has been nothing short of astounding. China's AliPay serves more over 1 billion people and processes over 175 million transactions[55] each day by means that resemble those of a traditional bank – payments can be made using deposits held in a Yu'E Bao account which pays interest and is redeemable on demand – without being a bank. Primarily due to the BATs (Baidu, Alibaba, and Tencent), the percentage of people (age 15+) with a bank account in China grew from 63.8 per cent in 2011 to 88.7 per cent in 2021.[56] Furthermore, 67.2 per cent of the population (age 15+) used a mobile phone or Internet to make payments and purchases, or to send or receive money using a financial institution account in 2021. In the first quarter of 2020, the number of online banking users reached 421 million.[57] Likewise, roughly 500 million Chinese have been credit-scored by

---

[54] Raphael Bick et al, Joining the Next Generation of Digital Banks in Asia (Report, McKinsey & Company, January 2021) 2.

[55] Craig Smith, 'Alipay Statistics and Facts (2022)' DMR (Web Page, 19 October 2022) <https://expandedramblings.com/index.php/alipay-statistics>.

[56] 'Databank: Global Financial Inclusion' (n 48). Parameters set as 'China', 'Account (% age 15+)', '2011'–'2021'.

[57] Daniel Slotta, 'Leading Mobile Banking Applications of Chinese Commercial Banks in 1st Quarter 2020, Based on Average Daily Users', *Statista* (Web Page, 21 March 2021) <www.statista.com/statistics/1171331/china-leading-mobile-banking-apps-based-on-average-daily-users/#:~:text=In%20the%20first%20quarter%20of,to%20enhance%20their%20online%20services>.

an alternative credit bureau, Sesame Credit Management, part of Alibaba, using alternative data points.

The benefits of digital finance are many. Ant Financial has supported the creation of millions of jobs and provided credit to many SMEs. The Chinese FinTech industry leads innovation in finance globally. AliPay introduced facial recognition payments in March 2015, four months before MasterCard. Similarly, lending to SMEs using alternative credit-scoring data from an e-commerce platform was introduced by Alibaba in 2010, one year before this happened in the United States and Japan.

With digital finance companies furthering the public good, regulatory policies need to strike a difficult but important balance in the current competitive dynamic between banks and digital finance companies. Unlike in the West, tech companies in China are a real threat to the market share of banks. Regulators and legislators must support this digital financial transition and develop the necessary understanding and scope of operations to oversee the use of technology within the financial industry. The regulatory burden on banks and FinTech 3.0 companies that offer similar products should be comparable. Yet start-ups do need a regulatory framework that allows them to develop their business before becoming subject to expensive compliance costs. We will examine in Chapters 18 and 19 how regulators might best shape such a system that is open to innovation and competition, while risks are properly identified, monitored, and managed.

VI. FINTECH 4.0: TODAY AND TOMORROW

In our view the next step change occurred in 2020.

This latest era is characterised by the pandemic-induced digitisation (see Chapter 5), the rise of cryptocurrencies and early development of CBDCs (see Chapter 14), and the extraordinary growth of all-encompassing financial platforms (see Chapters 18 and 19). On the regulatory side, FinTech 4.0 is characterised by the marked popularity of regulatory sandboxes and innovation hubs. Regulators seek to promote competition in financial services in their jurisdictions by making them more FinTech-friendly, while trying to balance rapidly emerging risks of concentration and dominance.[58]

The announcement by Facebook in 2019 of its plans to launch its Libra stablecoin elicited a sharp regulatory backlash and demonstrated that financial regulators are not like the more malleable telecommunications regulators with which it was familiar, particularly when ignored in a proposal's development as they had

---

[58] Ross P Buckley et al, 'Building Fintech Ecosystems: Regulatory Sandboxes, Innovation Hubs and Beyond' (2020) 61 *Washington University Journal of Law and Policy* 55; Dirk A Zetzsche et al, 'Regulating a Revolution: From Regulatory Sandboxes to Smart Regulation' (2017) 23(1) *Fordham Journal of Corporate and Financial Law* 31.

been in this case. In the evolution of FinTech, Facebook's Libra/Diem is crucial as it triggered the development of CBDCs. In China, the Chinese CBDC project now called the eCNY brings together both money and payments. The eCNY demonstrates that CBDCs may have a huge role in the future, with many developed nations well advanced in their research and development efforts, as is analysed in Chapter 14.

Another feature of FinTech 4.0 was developed in response to the economies of scale and scope inherent in software, data, and liquidity. This was the rise of financial platforms, such as the all-encompassing Ant Financial, the wings of which the Chinese government decided to clip by obstructing its initial public offering, and Aladdin, the platform operated in the United States by Blackrock and indispensable at both the front and back ends of the US mutual fund industry. The rise of these platforms, which we discuss further in Part IV, poses massive challenges to regulators as without crossing any of the traditional thresholds for financial regulation, these platforms can become systemically significant, and their collapse could bring down a financial system.

One fascinating aspect of the current FinTech 4.0 period is that the bifurcation between developed and developing markets is ending. FinTech 4.0 spans geographically the regions covered by both FinTech 3.0 and 3.5. Developing country governments are exploring CBDCs as potential responses to the dual challenges of domestic financial exclusion and expensive international remittances and other payments. Developing country regulators have established, or are looking to establish, innovation hubs and regulatory sandboxes. At the national level, the world's most sophisticated FinTech innovations are being developed in China and the most sophisticated digital identity platform in India. Most of the FinTech developments today in developed nations are being mirrored in developing nations as entrepreneurs from Nigeria to Uganda, and Cambodia to the Philippines, drive these developments ever onward.

Another fascinating progression over time has been in who provides FinTech services. Between FinTech 2.0 and FinTech 3.0, the type of entity using technology to deliver a financial product or service changed, such that FinTech was no longer the preserve of traditional financial institutions. This change was reinforced in FinTech 3.5 in emerging markets, in which technology and especially telecommunications companies were increasingly more important in delivering financial services than the often inefficient and underdeveloped traditional banks. This evolution has continued into FinTech 4.0 in which it is the BigTechs that are moving into the provision of financial services, such as payments, and in other fields, offering to customers financial services sourced from incumbent financial institutions. However, as many incumbents have understood the scale economies that flow from adding data to their control of their clients' liquidity, many traditional financial institutions have copied a FinTech model and are seeking to establish financial ecosystems in the same vein as FinTechs and BigTechs.

VII. CONCLUSION

This chapter has illustrated the evolution of FinTech through four major eras, culminating in today's FinTech 4.0.

In developed markets, the shift to FinTech 3.0 emerged out of the 2008 Crisis and was driven by public expectations and demands, the movement of technology companies into finance, and political demands for a more diversified banking system. In contrast, in developing countries, particularly in Africa and Asia, the corollary to FinTech 3.0 has been FinTech 3.5, which has been driven by the needs of development and government policy combined with the rapid introduction and reach of new technology, particularly mobile phones.

The recent shift to FinTech 4.0 was driven by the explosion in the number, and value, of cryptocurrencies, the development of stablecoins and CBDCs, and the rise of platforms in financial services, which mirror their rise in e-commerce and other sectors. We are currently in the early stages of FinTech 4.0, but one apparent certainty going forward is that the ever-accelerating rate of technological change and development will contribute to ever faster growth and change in FinTech, RegTech, SupTech, and related fields. FinTech today has moved from the outer suburbs of global finance to Main Street and Wall Street, which is why it is the focus of this book.

3

Smart Regulation

SUMMARY

Since the 2008 Global Financial Crisis, financial regulation has increased dramatically in scope and scale. Post-crisis regulation, plus rapid technological change, have spurred the development of FinTech and RegTech firms and data-driven financial service providers. Financial regulators increasingly seek to balance the traditional objectives of financial stability, market integrity, and consumer protection with promoting growth, innovation, and sustainability. This chapter analyses possible new regulatory approaches, ranging from doing nothing (which spans across being permissive to highly restrictive, depending on context), cautious permissiveness (on a case-by-case basis, or through special charters), structured experimentalism (e.g., sandboxes or piloting), and development of specific new regulatory frameworks. We argue for a new balanced, risk-based, and proportionate approach that incorporates these rebalanced objectives, and which we term 'smart regulation'.

I. INTRODUCTION

As we argued in Chapter 2, reforms in the aftermath of the Global Financial Crisis (GFC) of 2008 signalled a swing in the regulatory pendulum from a laissez-faire to an comprehensive regulatory approach. This policy swing coincided with rapid technological innovation; the meeting of legal and technological change prompted FinTech and RegTech. Start-ups (FinTechs), established technological and e-commerce companies (which we call TechFins, see Chapter 16), and incumbent financial firms entered into competition with one another for clients to recuperate their immense investments in technology.

FinTech promises innovation and economic growth, yet poses major challenges to the post-Crisis regulatory paradigm. Financial regulators, of late, are attempting to balance the traditional regulatory objectives of financial stability and consumer protection with promoting growth, innovation, and sustainability. Across the world's regulators, we see four approaches, ranging from doing nothing (which could be restrictive or permissive, depending on context), cautious permissiveness (where existing rules are relaxed in specific contexts), restricted experimentation (e.g., sandboxes or piloting), and development of specific new regulatory frameworks and tools, such as innovation hubs.

Section II of this chapter introduces these four approaches through the lens of a comparative study. Section III considers the traditional regulatory approaches of regulating or not regulating. Section IV considers case-by-case approaches. Section V then suggests possible elements of a new approach that transcends these boxed ways of thinking – a comprehensive review of existing regulatory approaches in the light of today's rebalanced objectives that we term 'smart regulation'.

II. THE GFC'S IMPACT ON REGULATORY PERSPECTIVES

A. *Pre-Crisis: Permissive vs Restrictive, Rules vs Principles*

Competition drives innovation. Regulators can create anti-competitive rules and restrict entry to banking and other financial services activities – the 'financial repression' practised by most economies until the 1980s – or they can take 'light touch' approaches.[1]

Prior to the 2008 Crisis, regulatory approaches to financial innovation were typically framed as 'restrictive' or 'permissive'.[2] This analysis often framed common law systems as permissive and civil law systems as restrictive.[3] While such framing has limitations,[4] it provided the starting point for most analyses of the interaction of regulation and innovation.

Further, financially repressive systems in many developing and centrally planned economies restricted innovation and growth, limiting development. Research suggested that while crises might be more common in more permissive systems, increases in growth and development over the medium to long term outweighed this cost.

This analytical approach, coupled with the Efficient Markets Hypothesis, was the guiding policy paradigm before the Crisis and focused on combining financial liberalisation with appropriate systems of prudential regulation to prevent and address

---

[1] Michael Snyder et al, *Big Bang 20 Years On: New Challenges Facing the Financial Services Sector* (City of London Center for Policy Studies, 2006). See Foreword by Nigel Lawson at iv. See also 'All Regulation Is Bad' in the same book at 24, as published on the eve of the GFC by Andrew Hilton, the director of City of London's Center of Policy Studies.

[2] See Dan Awrey, 'Regulating Financial Innovation: A More Principles-Based Proposal?' (2011) 5(2) *Brooklyn Journal of Corporate, Financial and Commercial Law* 273; Roger Brownsword and Karen Yeung (eds), *Regulating Technologies: Legal Futures, Regulatory Frames And Technological Fixes* (Hart Publishing, 2008).

[3] For a seminal treatment, see Rafael La Porta, Florencio Lopez-de-Silanes, and Andrei Shleifer, 'The Economic Consequences of Legal Origins' (2008) 46(2) *Journal of Economic Literature* 285.

[4] See, for example, Katharina Pistor, 'A Legal Theory of Finance' (2013) 41(2) *Journal of Comparative Economics* 315.

crises. This favoured financial innovation with (i) financial stability and consumer protection to be achieved through risk-based prudential regulation, (ii) disclosure to provide market discipline, and (iii) enforcement to protect consumers. Wholesale institutional participants were largely left to protect themselves through processes of private ordering.[5]

Finding balance between regulation and permissiveness towards innovation was often framed as tension between rules and principles.[6] This analytical framework contrasted systems with highly specific rules designed to address all possible questions (e.g., the United States) and systems based on guiding principles to be applied to a variety of situations (e.g., the United Kingdom).

Since the 2008 Crisis, this dominant paradigm has been reconsidered. From 2008 to about 2016, international regulatory considerations were dominated by the need to install new regulatory frameworks which would have prevented or ameliorated the Crisis and hopefully avert the next.[7]

During this period, regulatory discussions shifted from the pre-Crisis frameworks of restrictive versus permissive and rules versus principles to comprehensive macro and micro prudential frameworks combined with broader consumer protection efforts. Regulation has moved beyond market failures and the Efficient Markets Hypothesis. In the language of the G20, all aspects of the financial sector should be subject to appropriate levels of regulation, with efforts directed at both too-big-to-fail institutions that were central to the 2008 Crisis and many other activities which were previously unregulated or under-regulated and often referred to as 'shadow banking'.[8]

In this post-Crisis regulatory environment, FinTech posed a significant challenge. The choice remained: to regulate or not?

B. *Post-Crisis Blues*

After the Crisis, regulators were tasked with answering that question – to regulate or not – under very different circumstances than before 2008. On the one hand, regulators were aware of positive pro-innovation effects, including enhanced market efficiency by reducing transaction and financial mediation costs, financial exclusion, and agency and compliance costs, while also improving the quality of consumer decision-making.

On the other hand, the 2008 Crisis reminded regulators that financial innovation brings massive risks. Securitisation and derivatives, due to their ability to shift

---

[5] For discussion of private ordering, see Dan Awrey, 'The Limits of Private Ordering within Modern Financial Markets' (2014) 34(1) *Review of Banking and Financial Law* 183.

[6] See Robert Baldwin and Julia Black, 'Really Responsive Regulation' (2008) 71(1) *Modern Law Review* 59.

[7] See Ross P Buckley and Douglas W Arner, *From Crisis To Crisis: The Global Financial System Regulatory Failure* (Kluwer Law, 2011).

[8] See Douglas W Arner, 'Adaptation and Resilience in Global Financial Regulation' (2011) 89(5) *North Carolina Law Review* 1579, 1585–6.

risk, are indispensable to sophisticated financial management. Yet certain forms of securitisation (e.g., collateralised debt obligations) and credit derivatives (e.g., credit default swaps)[9] were significant contributors to the Crisis, as was deregulation generally.[10] While the risks of innovation were well known before 2008, pre-Crisis research suggested that the benefits outweighed the costs of periodic crises.[11] Since 2008 this view has been severely questioned. As Paul Volcker said, he 'found very little evidence that vast amounts of innovation in financial markets in recent years has had a visible effect on the productivity of the economy'.[12]

Among traditional financial regulatory mandates, two were key as the Crisis unfolded: consumer protection, particularly of retail clients, investors, and depositors;[13] and financial stability, particularly in the macroprudential context. While the *microprudential* dimension of regulation focuses on individual institutions, the *macroprudential* perspective considers the impact of counterparty interrelationships and/or systemically important financial institutions (SIFIs).[14] Since the Crisis, a major process of re-regulation occurred to address pre-Crisis weaknesses in regulation around macroprudential linkages.

FinTech emerged against this backdrop of post-Crisis regulatory change. FinTech start-ups, and information technology and e-commerce firms (here discussed as TechFins in Chapter 16), entered into competition with incumbent institutions. Regulators encouraged this *disruptive* innovation since it enhanced the service level through entirely new methods and technologies and also furthered diversification in local banking markets. This pro-innovative reasoning was supplemented by policy pressure to restart economic growth.[15] At the same time, new regulatory objectives have been recognised on an international level, such as fostering financial inclusion[16] and furthering sustainability. All of these trends together

---

[9] See Warren E Buffett, *Berkshire Hathaway Inc 2002 Annual Report* (Report, 2002) 15, describing credit default swaps as 'financial weapons of mass destruction'. René M Stulz, 'Financial Derivatives: Lessons from the Subprime Crisis' (2009) 11(1) *The Milken Institute Review* 58, 59.

[10] See Lynn A Stout, 'Derivatives and the Legal Origin of the 2008 Credit Crisis' (2011) 1(1) *Harvard Business Law Review* 1, 37; also see Buckley and Arner, *From Crisis To Crisis* (n 7).

[11] See Douglas W Arner, *Financial Stability, Economic Growth, and The Role of The Law* (Cambridge University Press, 1st ed, 2007).

[12] Reuters, 'The Only Thing Useful Banks Have Invented in 20 Years Is the ATM', *New York Post* (online, 13 December 2009) <http://nypost.com/2009/12/13/the-only-thing-useful-banks-have-invented-in-20-years-is-the-atm>.

[13] Sumit Agarwal et al, 'Predatory Lending and the Subprime Crisis' (2014) 113(1) *Journal of Financial Economics* 29.

[14] Iman Anabtawi and Steven L Schwarcz, 'Regulating Systemic Risk: Towards an Analytical Framework' (2011) 86(4) *Notre Dame Law Review* 1349; Steven L Schwarcz, 'Systemic Risk' (2008) 97(1) *Georgetown Law Journal* 193, 204.

[15] *Jumpstart Our Business Startups Act*, Pub L No 112–106, 126 Stat 306 (2012) (codified in scattered sections of 15 USC).

[16] Reflected in Goal 8 of the United Nations Sustainable Development Goals: '8 Promote Sustained, Inclusive and Sustainable Economic Growth, Full and Productive Employment and Decent Work for All', *United Nations* (Web Page) <https://sdgs.un.org/goals/goal8>.

pressured regulators to balance support for innovation with their core mandates of financial stability and consumer protection.

III. INNOVATIVE APPROACHES TO FINTECH INNOVATION

The rapid technological change underlying the FinTech boom challenged regulators trained primarily in banking, accounting, and financial regulation, but usually not engineering or computer technologies. Similarly, new entrants in financial markets with, from a financial and regulatory perspective, inexperienced executives looked for regulatory approval. Regulators across the globe responded to this challenge differently.

Four main approaches have emerged. We discuss each.

1. Regulators do nothing: either by intent or inertia. Doing nothing can involve simply not regulating FinTech, and the result can be either permissive or laissez-faire depending upon whether banking regulation applies to the sector. China, especially before 2015, is often highlighted as the leading example of a permissive approach that delivered a positive, yet unexpected outcome.[17]
2. Regulators can apply flexibility on a case-by-case basis under a cautiously permissive approach. Many regulators encountering innovation, and with mandates encompassing growth and/or financial development along with financial stability and consumer protection, have granted no-action letters, restricted licences, special charters, or partial exemptions for firms testing new technologies. This allows regulators to acquire data and experience with innovation.
3. Regulators can provide a structured context for experimentation, by instituting a regulatory sandbox or (as in China and elsewhere) structured piloting exercises.
4. A formal approach which reforms existing regulations or develops new regulations could be adopted to provide a more balanced framework for new entrants and activities. Indeed, many countries, among them some of the largest integrated markets,[18] have reviewed existing rules from the perspective of proportionality.

In the rest of the chapter and in fact throughout the book, we argue for a balanced proportional risk-based approach to innovation and traditional regulatory objectives. This approach includes elements of structural experimentation but also integrates other regulatory approaches that encourage innovation while managing its risks by

---

[17] See Jing Wang, '"The Party Must Strengthen Its Leadership in Finance!": Digital Technologies and Financial Governance in China's Fintech Development' (2021) 247 *The China Quarterly* 773, 775 (2021).

[18] For instance, the EU submitted many smaller investment firms with simple businesses to less strict rules, while certain DLT-based trading, clearing, and settlement platforms were subjected to a time-limited pilot regime. See Dirk A Zetzsche and Jannik Woxholth, 'The DLT Sandbox under the Pilot-Regulation' (2022) 17(2) *Capital Markets Law Journal* 212.

taking proportionate regulatory steps. We term this balanced approach 'smart regulation'. We first discuss the four approaches separately before drawing conclusions on the recommended regulatory strategy.

A. *The Zen Approach: Regulating a Revolution by Doing Nothing*

Beyond the financial context, debates around the best ways to regulate innovation typically focus on whether to regulate in advance or allow innovation to develop and then, if necessary, regulate afterwards.[19]

Doing nothing can take various forms. It may involve requiring FinTechs to comply with existing financial regulations, often with highly restrictive results. This may protect against risk but at the cost of stifling innovation. If regulation is a barrier to entry, increased regulation will reduce the competitive threat posed by currently non-regulated technology firms to regulated financial institutions. Abolishing legislation can help to even the playing field between these two groups. However, most financial markets, especially post-Crisis, are highly regulated. In this environment reducing regulation can be difficult, slow, and fraught.

But doing nothing may also further FinTech in the absence of a sophisticated regulatory system. China is often applauded for first adopting a laissez-faire approach and then developing a comprehensive regulatory system for the new environment. Their pre-2015 approach allowed testing by FinTechs without immediate regulatory repercussions. However, China abandoned this approach after the wake of financial turmoil in 2015. This was then taken even further after the rapid emergence of a small number of dominant financial platforms, culminating in decision to cancel the global initial public offering of Ant Financial in 2020. As only one example, after Alibaba Group issued new pooled products, regulators awoke one morning to discover Yu'e Bao had grown to be the world's fourth largest (USD $90 billion) money market fund in only nine months.[20] China subsequently pursued a comprehensive new regulatory approach.[21]

The relative inefficiencies of China's financial system, combined with the government's prioritisation of growth and innovation, largely explain the allowing of development without regulatory intervention.[22] However, the Chinese experience

---

[19] See Ross P Buckley, Douglas W Arner, and Michael Panton, 'Financial Innovation in East Asia' (2014) 37(2) *Seattle University Law Review* 307.

[20] Angela Huyue Zhang, 'Agility over Stability: China's Great Reversal in Regulating the Platform Economy' (2022) 63(2) *Harvard International Law Journal*.

[21] Weihuan Zhou, Douglas W Arner, and Ross P Buckley, 'Regulating FinTech in China: From Permissive to Balanced' in David Lee and Robert H Deng (eds), *Handbook of Block Chain, Digital Finance, and Inclusion (Volume 2): ChinaTech, Mobile Security, and Distributed Ledger* (Elsevier, 2018) 45.

[22] See Christian Haddad and Lars Hornuf, 'The Emergence of the Global Fintech Market: Economic and Technological Determinants' (2019) 53(1) *Small Bus Economics* 81, arguing that the soundness of the financial system has a negative effect on FinTech start-up dynamics, that is, financial systems with many deficits provide a vibrant environment for start-ups.

both before and since 2015 also proves that innovation can bring risks, resulting in a more cautious, and for some sectors even restrictive, regulatory approach once their evolution reaches a certain size.[23]

It is unsurprising that innovation is less restricted in less regulated regions.[24] Even without prescriptive rules, regulation can weaken innovation as new, solution-driven, potentially innovative firms are more expensive to establish in strictly regulated environments than in accommodative ones.

Most financial rules have their origin in crises or scandals. The principle underlying a rule may be sound, but its crisis-driven extreme variant may not be. For instance, the core of the Volcker Rule[25] in the United States is that a bank's own speculative trading should not put at risk the safety of clients' deposits. Similar approaches have been taken elsewhere to insulate state-backed deposits from trading risks.[26] The underlying rationale is probably sound. Trading using state-guaranteed deposits increases moral hazard due to the bail-out guarantee. Similarly, inadequate sales practices in financial services put consumers' funds at risk and render efficient decision-making even more difficult than when proper information is disclosed. Accordingly, the solicitation of clients is regulated. Removing these laws would unlock innovation – but much of it may well not benefit society.

The proponents of free markets often characterise regulation as an unnecessary cost to business. Yet, beyond the traditional benefits of protecting consumers and preventing financial crises, good regulation in fact benefits efficiency, facilitates standardisation and reduces transaction costs.

Standardisation delivers economies of scale benefits and thus appeals in large markets (e.g., the European Union) but less so in smaller markets (e.g., Singapore). Harmonisation is coordinated by regulators worldwide who interact through bodies such as the Financial Stability Board (FSB), the Basel Committee on Banking Supervision (BCBS), the International Organization of Securities Commissions (IOSCO), and the International Association of Insurance Supervisors (IAIS). Any move away from harmonised regulatory approaches will undermine the equivalence of different jurisdictions' legal systems, possibly hindering global access and certainly raising compliance costs for providers operating across markets. Equivalence

---

[23] Weihuan Zhou, Douglas W Arner, and Ross P Buckley, 'Regulation of Digital Financial Services in China: Last Mover Advantage?' (2015) 8(1) *Tsinghua China Law Review* 25, 27.

[24] Global System for Mobile Communications Association, *Access to Mobile Services and Proof of Identity 2021: Revisiting SIM Registration and Know Your Customer (KYC) Contexts during COVID-19* (Report, April 2021) <www.gsma.com/mobilefordevelopment/wp-content/uploads/2021/04/Digital-Identity-Access-to-Mobile-Services-and-Proof-of-Identity-2021_SPREADs.pdf>.

[25] See John C Coates IV, 'The Volcker Rule as Structural Law: Implications for Cost-Benefit Analysis and Administrative Law' (2015) 10(4) *Capital Markets Law Journal* 447.

[26] See generally Financial Stability Board, *Structural Banking Reforms: Cross-Border Consistencies and Global Financial Stability Implications* (Report to G20 Leaders for the November 2014 Summit, 27 October 2014) <www.fsb.org/wp-content/uploads/r_141027.pdf>.

enables foreign firms to avoid costly target markets' rules when offering financial services, a practice often referred to as substituted compliance.[27]

An example of regulation reducing transaction costs is mandatory disclosure. As the issuer or originator of a financial product has access to information about it at the lowest cost, any solution other than requiring disclosure by the issuer or originator will require multiple market participants to gather the information, or negotiate for it, separately. These sizable transaction costs are removed by mandatory disclosure.[28] Thus, even with the Efficient Markets Hypothesis, disclosure requirements remain important.

For these reasons, plus the business certainty afforded by regulation, the complete disengagement of regulators in financial markets is highly unlikely and highly undesirable.

B. *Specific Regulatory Frameworks*

At the other extreme is the traditional approach of developing specific regulations for new products and/or institutions.

An increasing number of jurisdictions have implemented new legislative and/or regulatory frameworks to address specific forms of FinTech innovation. According to the FSB:

> [T]here is a risk of potential regulatory gaps as FinTechs' and BigTechs' financial service product offerings expand rapidly. In this light, a number of jurisdictions have already taken actions on the scope of regulation…. Countries such as Nigeria, Ghana and Kenya are introducing new legislation to regulate FinTech products and services.[29]

To date, most such measures have focused on new payments providers and alternative financing techniques, such as equity crowdfunding and peer-to-peer (P2P) lending.[30] In particular, the *JOBS Act*[31] with its Securities and Exchange Commission

---

[27] The United States Commodity Futures Trading Commission (CFTC) relies on substituted compliance to determine the eligibility of swap counterparties. See *Dodd-Frank Wall Street Reform and Consumer Protection Act*, Pub L No 111–203, §§ 701–74, 124 Stat 1376, 1641–1802 (2010); *Cross-Border Application of Certain Swaps Provisions of the Commodity Exchange Act*, 77 Fed Reg 41213 (2012) (codified at 17 CFR ch 1). See also Howell E Jackson, 'Substituted Compliance: The Emergence, Challenges, and Evolution of a New Regulatory Paradigm' (2015) 1(2) *Journal of Financial Regulation* 169.

[28] On mandatory disclosure, see Christian Leuz and Peter D Wysocki, 'The Economics of Disclosure and Financial Reporting Regulation: Evidence and Suggestions for Future Research' (2016) 54(2) *Journal of Accounting Research* 525, 555–60.

[29] Financial Stability Board, *FinTech and Market Structure in the COVID-19 Pandemic: Implications for Financial Stability* 14–15 (Report, 21 March 2022) <www.fsb.org/wp-content/uploads/P210322.pdf>.

[30] Johannes Ehrentraud et al, 'Policy Responses to Fintech: A Cross-Country Overview' (FSI Insights on Policy Implementation No 23, January 2020) 17 <www.bis.org/fsi/publ/insights23.pdf>.

[31] *Jumpstart Our Business Startups Act*, Pub L No 112–106, 126 Stat 306 (2012). Title III, also known as the Crowdfund Act, created a way for companies to use crowdfunding to issue securities. At §§ 301–05, 126 Stat at 315–23.

(SEC) regulation of crowdfunding[32] was introduced to liberalise the existing framework. The BIS has since reported that around two-thirds of jurisdictions surveyed have FinTech-specific regulations for equity and/or loan crowdfunding.[33]

The other major area where new frameworks are being developed is payment and settlement with the BIS reporting that most jurisdictions surveyed have FinTech-specific regulations for digital payment services.[34] The most significant legislative response to these new technologies has been the Payment Service Directive (PSD2) implemented by the European Union.[35]

PSD2 aims to remove the monopoly of credit institutions and banks on their customer's account information and payment services.[36] PSD2 enables bank customers to use third-party providers to manage their finances. Banks are required to give these third-party providers access to their customers' accounts through open Application Program Interfaces (APIs).[37] In turn, third-party providers can offer financial services using bank data and infrastructure as either an Account Information Service Provider (**AISP**) using the account information of bank customers or as a Payment Initiation Service Provider (**PISP**) by initiating a payment or P2P transfer on the customer's behalf.[38] These third-party providers can include telecommunication companies, social media, shopping platforms, or value-added service providers, offering, for instance, facilitated transfers, an aggregate overview of a user's account information from several banks, or financial analysis and advice, while the customers' money remains safely stored in the current bank account. Going beyond merely adding new elements to an existing framework, PSD2 aims at a fundamental change of the payments value chain, business profitability, and customer expectations.[39] The extent to which this will be achieved over time remains to be seen.

Reforms are seeking to facilitate FinTech in many jurisdictions. For instance, India has implemented regulations barring any one third-party app from processing more than 30 per cent of transactions, which aims to benefit smaller players who rely on app or transaction-based models.[40] Another example is Peru, which

---

[32] See *Crowdfunding*, 80 FR 71387 (2015) (codified at 17 CFR 200, 227, 232).

[33] Ehrentraud et al (n 31).

[34] Ibid.

[35] The core of the new payments framework is the Payment Services – *Directive (EU) 2015/2366 of The European Parliament and of the Council of 25 November 2015 on Payment Services in the Internal Market* [2015] OJ L 337/35, 53–4 ('PSD 2').

[36] Ibid.

[37] Ibid.

[38] Ibid.

[39] Pinar Ozcan and Markos Zachariadis, 'Open Banking as a Catalyst for Industry Transformation: Lessons Learned From Implementing PSD2 in Europe' (SWIFT Institute Working Paper, September 2021) <https://ssrn.com/abstract=3984857>.

[40] Saurabh Thukral and Saloni Sachdeva, 'Protecting UPI, a Jewel among Indian Fintech Innovations', *NITI Aayog* (Web Page, 2022) <www.niti.gov.in/protecting-upi-jewel-among-indian-fintech-innovations>.

recently amended its laws to allow online-only financial entities.[41] Japan has also revised its laws to allow companies to sell a range of financial products – banking, securities, and insurance – under a single financial services brokerage licence, which will make it easier for consumers to access such products via a mobile app.[42]

Finally, the United Kingdom altered the mandate of the FCA to require considerations of innovation and economic competitiveness in regulatory decisions.[43] In other jurisdictions, such as Luxembourg, furthering innovation is treated as one aspect of maintaining financial system stability, which is exercised through the establishment of an innovation hub for innovative payment services. At the same time and under the same EU financial regulations, the German regulator BaFin requires an explicit mandate to further innovation as a precondition for waiving licensing conditions; but notwithstanding this, BaFin has undertaken steps to further payments innovation, for instance by organising an annual FinTech conference, the 'BaFinTech'. Similar issues arise between federal and state regulators in the United States.

Beyond these traditional approaches lie a range of alternatives to addressing innovation, the first being the cautiously permissive case-by-case approach.

C. *The Case-by-Case Approach: Forbearance,*
Restricted Licences, and Special Charters

In between the traditional choices of doing nothing and developing new regulatory frameworks, regulators can carve out activities (i.e., defined by product, scope, or scale) where participants can benefit on a case-by-case basis from regulatory forbearance (e.g., 'no-action' letters in the United States) or from restricted licences or special charters.[44] In return, the no-action letter or restricted licence may come with conditions seeking to uphold the principles underlying the regulation.

---

[41] 'Peru Encourages the Entry of New Participants in the Local Financial System', *Garrigues News* (online, 22 March 2022) <www.garrigues.com/en_GB/new/peru-encourages-entry-new-participants-local-financial-system#:~:text=Peru%20encourages%20the%20entry%20of%20new%20participants%20in%20the%20local%20financial%20system,Peru%20Banking%20%20%26%20Finance&text=The%20recent%20amendment%20to%20the,new%20entities%20in%20the%20sector>.

[42] See Wataru Suzuki, 'Japan's Digital Banks Emerge as Regulatory Easing Gains Momentum', *Nikkei Asia* (online, 21 October 2021) <https://asia.nikkei.com/Business/Finance/Japan-s-digital-banks-emerge-as-regulatory-easing-gains-momentum>.

[43] See Elena Carletti and Agnieszka Smolenska, '10 Years on from the Financial Crisis: Co-operation between Competition Agencies and Regulators in the Financial Sector' (OECD Paper No DAF/COMP/WP2(2017)8, 4 December 2017) 27 <www.oecd.org/officialdocuments/publicdisplaydocumentpdf/?cote=DAF/COMP/WP2%282017%298&docLanguage=En>.

[44] See Office of the Comptroller of the Currency, 'OCC Issues Draft Licensing Manual Supplement for Evaluating Charter Applications from Financial Technology Companies, Will Accept Comments through April 14' (News Release, 15 March 2017) <www.occ.gov/news-issuances/news-releases/2017/nr-occ-2017-31.html>.

The Dutch regulators DNB/AFM have given the following example of where some dispensation from mandatory law governing client onboarding is in order:

> An innovative type of asset management enables customers to gradually build their wealth through incremental accounts, with the investment company conducting a step-by-step inventory of customers' financial position, knowledge, experience, objectives and risk appetite as time goes on. If supervisors find the investment company to be acting in the spirit of the law, i.e. to be scrupulously observing its duty of care, they may judge that it is unreasonable to demand the same thorough initial intake process as is customary in asset management where initial outlays are substantially steeper and a full profile is drawn up at a first meeting.[45]

1. Regulators' Discretion

The extent regulators can make use of forbearance through no-action letters or restricted licensing depends on their legislative context. While some discretion is available in most jurisdictions, the relation between the generic and specific provisions, as established in the country's legal framework (particularly administrative case law), determines the extent to which regulators may require legislative action before granting exemptions. For instance, in 2016 the German regulator BaFin re-read the German banking act in a way to enable video chat identification of bank clients but could not re-read the German investment fund act, applying to fund management companies and depositories, in the same way. Comparatively, the Luxembourg CSSF read basically the same European Union rules in a way that enabled fund managers and investment firms to allow video authentication. Innovation is moving rapidly in this field and has led, for instance, Irish regulators to allow the client identity verification using the biometric features embedded in all EU passports by way of mobile applications. Needless to say, app-based biometric ID is much better suited for retail applications aiming at millions of potential clients who seek to open bank or crypto-asset accounts.

While some legislation allows no-action letters and/or restricted licensing,[46] at times special charters are issued, without explicit legislation, to provide regulatory dispensation on a case-by-case basis.[47] Major regulators, with hundreds of

---

[45] See The Netherlands Authority for the Financial Markets and De Nederlandsche Bank, *More Room for Innovation in the Financial Sector: Market Access, Authorisations and Supervision* (Report, December 2016) 4 <www.afm.nl/~/profmedia/files/onderwerpen/innovation-hub/publicaties/2016/room-for-innovation-in-financial-sector.ashx>.

[46] For Europe, see the dispensation from capital requirements granted to certain banks and investment firms meeting the conditions of the Capital Requirements Regulation: *Regulation (EU) No 575/2013 of The European Parliament and of the Council of 26 June 2013 on Prudential Requirements for Credit Institutions and Investment Firms* [2013] OJ L 176/1; also see the license for 'small' managers of alternative investment funds pursuant to *Directive 2011/61/EU of the European Parliament and of the Council of 8 June 2011 on Alternative Investment Fund Managers* [2011] OJ L 174/1.

[47] See, for example, Office of the Comptroller of the Currency, *Exploring Special Purpose National Bank Charters for Fintech Companies* (Report, December 2016) 3–4 <www.occ.gov/topics/responsible-innovation/comments/special-purpose-national-bank-charters-for-fintech.pdf>.

institutions under supervision, have extensive experience that positions them to identify conduct that represents minor risks, or may even be good market practice, and they can accordingly then reduce the regulatory burden through no-action letters, conditional dispensations (restricted licensing), or an official special charter policy. Yet, the fate of special charters is dependent on the regulatory framework in which these charters are released. In 2019, a legal challenge by New York's banking regulator against the validity of a FinTech special charter issued by the OCC on the grounds that the OCC lacks a mandate to further innovation succeeded, though it was later overturned on procedural grounds.[48]

2. Upsides

Communication between regulators and FinTechs through innovation hubs facilitates partial exemptions and educates regulators. Hubs connect regulators with a fast-changing innovative marketplace and enable the adjustment of approaches on a case-by-case basis accordingly.

One upside of case-by-case assessment is risk control. Exemptions end the flow of information from licensed entities. Hubs empower regulators with oversight of evolving business models and practices and facilitate ongoing risk assessments and control.

Financial centres increasingly find themselves competing for innovative start-ups. A partial exemption approach demands a level of regulatory expertise that not all regulators possess. Moreover, restricted licences may come with cross-border recognition, that is the licence may grant market access. A licence granted by a regulator of the European Union and European Economic Area Member States includes the right to offer services cross-border in all European Union and European Economic Area states, markets currently comprising 450 million consumers. Case-by-case flexibility and dispensations provide a comparative advantage for major regulators.

3. Risks

However, this approach comes with limitations. While small or highly specialised FinTech ecosystems are well suited to this bespoke model, the strain on regulators increases as the number and variety of actors requesting exemptions grows. Additionally, ensuring equal treatment is difficult. Case-by-case assessment comes with risks of errors, which can distort competition and produce suboptimal outcomes. Alternatively, the permitted conduct may harm customers or the financial system at large, damaging the regulators' reputation and generating liability.

If judges hold the no-action letter, restricted licence, special charter, or other forbearance approach to violate mandatory law, the regulators' conduct may be found

---

[48] *Lacewell v Office of the Comptroller of the Currency*, No. 19–4271 (2nd Cir, 2021).

to be negligent if not supported by explicit legislation. This prospect likely often leads to suboptimal levels of dispensation practice.

Moreover, the benchmarks for a regulator's dispensation practice may be questioned: should consumer protection and systemic risk prevention dominate, or should the focus be on competitiveness and innovation? For instance, should the regulator of a state that produces financial products focus on job creation, while a regulator of a state that only distributes such products shield local market participants from foreign competition?

Forbearance-based case-by-case experimentation has downsides for regulators, FinTechs and society. Regulators risk liability for their decisions. For FinTechs, the process of obtaining such forbearance is often costly. Given that determination is on a case-by-case basis, each application will require in-depth development and will not be a standardised off-the-shelf solution. Some FinTechs will find themselves falling within existing laws or regulations and may need to develop detailed arguments justifying special treatment. The associated costs raise the minimum capital necessary to start an innovative firm. For society, the principal costs may arise either from a suboptimal level of dispensation or from excessive dispensation leading to unacceptable risks and consumer losses.

On balance, cautious experimentation on a case-by-case basis through forbearance via no-action letters, restricted licences, special charters, and the like doubtless provides a useful tool for regulators to perform market discovery (i.e., acquire knowledge of start-ups and understanding of business models, and identify regulatory perimeters of modern technologies). However, this approach is not suitable for market-wide use given its case-by-case nature. Further, it fails to provide long-term legal certainty for business development and is not conducive to regional or international standardisation.

D. *Structured Experimentalism: Innovation Hubs and Regulatory Sandboxes*

An increasing range of jurisdictions are therefore experimenting with more structured approaches, such as innovation hubs and regulatory sandboxes.

Structured experimentalism requires regulators to embrace mutual learning: tools allowing for extensive interaction between regulators and market participants are increasingly seen as necessary for the cautious experimentation with, and regulation of, financial and technological innovation. Technological innovation has thus prompted regulatory innovation. From 2014 onwards (with the Luxembourg Commission de Surveillance du Secteur Financier (CSSF), the United Kingdom's Financial Conduct Authority (FCA), and the Australian Securities and Investments Commission (ASIC) as first movers), communication has been increasingly facilitated through the development of innovation departments in regulatory agencies. Institutional access points for innovative firms dubbed Innovation Hubs have now been established in many jurisdictions. We will discuss Innovation Hubs in more detail in Chapter 12 ('Facilitation').

A major trend in structured experimentalism has been the great popularity of regulatory sandboxes and a range of piloting and test-and-learn approaches that we consider in Chapter 11. In finance, a regulatory sandbox refers to a regulatory 'safe space' for experimentation with new technologies. At the highest level, the sandbox enables businesses to test products with less risk of regulatory enforcement. In return, regulators require applicants to incorporate appropriate safeguards. Eligibility is standardised and publicised, requiring participants to articulate their added value in a pre-defined format.[49] This is cost-effective for participants and resource-effective for regulators, allowing for easier comparison among potential entrants. At least 73 sandboxes across 57 countries have been implemented.[50]

However, while providing transparency in entry criteria and processes, sandboxes remain human driven and analogue in monitoring. Sandboxes, as currently conceived, are not scalable – the total 166 participants in the UK FCA sandboxes are insignificant relative to the over 56,000 licensed market participants in the United Kingdom.[51] Sandboxes must be made smarter and equipped to self-monitor activity. We will discuss Regulatory Sandboxes more in detail in Chapter 12 ('Facilitation').

IV. TOWARDS SMART REGULATION: BUILDING A REGULATORY STACK

The increasing commoditisation of core technologies in finance is opening a Pandora's box of new FinTech and RegTech solutions. We argue that innovation requires smart regulation, and two elements form the basis of such a framework.

A. *Focus on (Risk) Fundamentals*

First, the new automated and proportionate 'smart' regime should be built upon the fundamentals of financial regulation. Regulators must focus on their broader mandates as defined by applicable legislation (i.e., consumer protection, financial stability, competition, and prudential regulation) as opposed to attempting to apply overly prescriptive rules-based approaches which will inevitably trail the velocity of innovation and overly stretch regulatory resources.

Being 'technologically neutral' should not be used as an argument that excuses regulators from the need to understand the impact of new technologies on processes

---

[49] See Zetzsche et al, 'Regulating a Revolution: From Regulatory Sandboxes to Smart Regulation' (n 19).

[50] Finance, Competitiveness and Innovation Global Practice of World Bank, 'Global Experiences from Regulatory Sandboxes' (FinTech Note No. 8, 2020) 55–6.

[51] 'Regulatory Sandbox Accepted Firms', *Financial Conduct Authority* (Web Page, 16 August 2022), <www.fca.org.uk/firms/innovation/regulatory-sandbox/accepted-firms>.

(e.g., biometric identification for payments) or business models (e.g., alternative data credit scoring). Instead, 'technological neutrality' should mean that regulators do not seek to 'regulate' technological innovations, but instead focus on the financial processes that technology enables and that ought to be subject to regulation.

B. *Focus on Lower Entry Barriers*

Second, we believe that the key is not the regulation of innovative processes but instead the regulation of competition in financial markets. Defining the boundaries of competition and innovation is a challenge for regulators, which we address in detail in Part IV. Structured experimentalism may be an example of how innovative financial regulation can balance traditional objectives with competition. Of course, a closer look reveals that both are two sides of the same coin: innovation enables competition, and competition drives innovation in that one competitor seeks to distinguish itself from the others. So competition on the merits (i.e., where all participants follow the same rules and bear the same costs) is, generally speaking, a good thing for financial markets. In the context of FinTech, however, it is difficult to determine whether a new entrant is a competitor or collaborator.

On balance, at least for jurisdictions that wish to compete by signalling regulatory flexibility to the market, the express inclusion of innovation in their mandate could be most useful. In addition, the fact that competition spurs the arrival of new participants is facilitating regulatory capacity to experiment with new supervisory and reporting models. The bargaining power of start-ups with regulators is disproportionately low compared to that of large incumbent licensed enterprises.

In practice, this provides regulators with the opportunity to engage in a sequenced reform process. This allows experimentation at the margin (as supported by the low numbers of firms in sandboxes) while the bulk of the industry is gradually brought to new standards via the digitisation of regulatory requirements themselves, in short: RegTech.

V. FOUR STAGES OF SMART REGULATION

From the basis in Section IV, a reasonable regulatory approach could comprise four sequenced stages:

1. A testing and piloting environment
2. A regulatory sandbox, which widens the scope of testing and piloting
3. A restricted licensing/special charter scheme, under which innovative firms can further develop their client base and financial and operational resources
4. When size and income permits, the move to operating under a full licence.

Regulatory complexity and the fixed costs of regulation increase with each stage, as does the FinTech's operational space in terms of clients, resources, and scope.

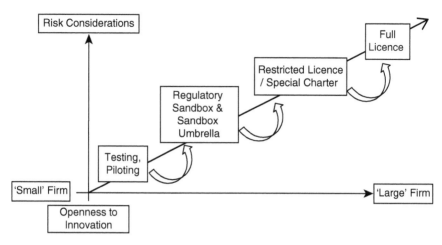

FIGURE 3.1 The progressive approach of smart regulation

This should lead to a desirable lowering of the entry barriers to financial markets. Figure 3.1 shows the resulting four stages of Smart Regulation.

With every stage, the Smart Regulator assesses risk considerations bearing in mind the firm's ability to cover costs and the need to maintain a similar regulatory burden for licensed entities.

Many of the regulatory details depend on the technology employed, which is the focus of Part II.

4

RegTech and the Reconceptualisation
of Financial Regulation

SUMMARY

RegTech is the use of technology, particularly information technology, in monitoring, compliance and regulatory reporting by industry, and in supervision and enforcement by regulators. For industry, regulators, and policymakers, the pace of transformation in digital financial products and systems requires ever greater use of RegTech. In this sense, FinTech demands RegTech. Whilst the principal regulatory objectives of financial stability, market integrity, consumer protection, and promoting development remain, their attainment increasingly requires the deployment of sophisticated technology by both reporting entities and regulators. The increasing use of RegTech prompts a paradigm shift necessitating the reconceptualisation of financial regulation.

I. INTRODUCTION

RegTech is a contraction of the terms *regulatory* and *technology*, and comprises the use of technology, particularly information technology (IT), in regulatory implementation, compliance, reporting, monitoring, and enforcement. The rapid evolution and development of FinTech described in Chapter 2 demands a similar evolution and development of RegTech.[1] RegTech has been described as 'technological solutions to regulatory processes'[2] with a focus on risk identification and regulatory compliance. With RegTech, financial institutions and their regulators can monitor and analyse real-time financial information from across the global financial system to improve efficiency and safety.[3] For instance, artificial intelligence can be used to improve risk management.

---

[1] See Susannah Hammond and Mike Cowan, *Fintech, Regtech, and the Role of Compliance 2021* (Report, Thomson Reuters Regulatory Intelligence, 2021) 4.

[2] Institute of International Finance, *Regtech: Exploring Solutions for Regulatory Challenges* (Report, October 2015) 2 <www.iif.com/portals/0/Files/content/Innovation/10_01_2015_regtech_exploring_solutions.pdf>.

[3] See Andrew G Haldane, Chief Economist of Bank of England, 'Managing Global Finance as a System' (Speech at the Maxwell Fry Annual Global Finance Lecture, Birmingham University, 29

The 2008 Global Financial Crisis (GFC) was a turning point in the development of both FinTech (cf Chapter 2) and RegTech, but the factors underlying, and the beneficiaries of, the growth in FinTech and RegTech are quite different. FinTech growth has been led by start-ups to challenge incumbents. RegTech growth was mostly a response to the huge costs of complying with new reporting requirements imposed after the 2008 Crisis.[4] The massive increases in the volume and types of data required for mandatory reporting to regulatory authorities presented a major opportunity for the automation of compliance and monitoring processes of financial firms. The fines imposed on financial institutions of over US$560 billion in the period from 2009 to 2020[5] sent the clear message that noncompliance was no viable option for the industry.

For *regulators*, RegTech enables a more proportionate risk-based approach where analysis of data enables more granular and effective supervision of markets and market participants.[6] This is a natural response to the increasingly digital nature of global finance,[7] with the bonus that it should reduce the risks of the regulatory capture seen in the run-up to the 2008 Crisis. If regulators can directly access financial data from supervised firms, this will allow them to form their own evidence-based opinions as opposed to relying on the firm's self-reporting. Similarly, as the amount of data available to regulators increases, the impact of their policy decisions on financial markets may be better simulated to predict the consequences of regulatory action, instead of relying on market participants' potentially self-serving opinions. Applying technology to regulation also facilitates the monitoring of financial market participants who are becoming increasingly diverse with the emergence of new FinTech start-ups.[8]

In this chapter, we consider the rise of RegTech and its role in shaping financial systems. Section II considers the evolution of RegTech. Section III deals with the

---

October 2014) <www.bankofengland.co.uk/speech/2014/managing-global-finance-as-a-system>. The idea of using technologies to carry out real-time monitoring of financial institutions and markets is now widespread but was very progressive when proposed by Andrew Haldane in 2014.

[4] See Douglas W Arner, Jànos Barberis, and Ross P Buckley, 'FinTech, RegTech, and the Reconceptualization of Financial Regulation' (2017) 37(3) *Northwestern Journal of International Law and Business* 371, 374.

[5] See Boston Consulting Group and Freshfields Bruckhaus Deringer, *Cross-Border Investigations: A New Era of Regulatory Enforcement* (Report, 15 March 2021) 2 <www.freshfields.com/en-gb/our-thinking/knowledge/insight/2021/03/cross-border-investigations-a-new-era-of-regulatory-enforcement-4418>.

[6] See Imran Gulamhuseinwala, Subas Roy, and Abigail Viljoen Imran, *Innovating with RegTech: Turning Regulatory Compliance into a Competitive Advantage* (Report, EY, 2016) 10, observing that the development of RegTech will eventually lead financial supervision to a 'Compliance by Design' framework which enables automated monitoring of compliance standards by the regulators.

[7] See Douglas W Arner and Jànos Barberis, 'FinTech in China: From the Shadows?' (2015) 3(3) *Journal of Financial Perspectives* 78.

[8] Global Partnership for Financial Inclusion, *G20 High-Level Principles for Digital Financial Inclusion* (Report, 2016) 12, highlighting key action plans that 'encourage the use of digital technologies, as appropriate, to improve their processes and capacity for supervision.'

use of technology by financial institutions to meet regulatory requirements. Section IV discusses the technology used by regulators. Section V analyses the relationship of FinTech and RegTech, and concludes.

II. REGTECH: A FRAMEWORK OF ANALYSIS

A. *Post-Crisis Regulation*

The 2008 Crisis and post-crisis regulation transformed how financial institutions operate, combining to reduce their risk-taking and spectrum of operations.[9] That regulation increased the compliance burden on financial institutions and the extent of regulatory penalties. Sectors like anti-money laundering stand out, with fines imposed on financial institutions exceeding US$5.4 billion in 2021.[10]

Fines and penalties have gone from being rare for financial institutions to an ordinary cost of doing business. Bank of America was fined by US agencies alone 251 times between 2000 and 2021, on average more than 10 times a year, amounting to approximately $82.9 billion in fines and exceeding an average of $3.9 billion a year.[11] Naturally enough, financial institutions are taking major steps to reduce these cost burdens, most of which centre on the deployment of RegTech.

B. *FinTech*

Along with this groundbreaking change has come the rapid evolution of FinTech, as discussed in Chapter 2. Each of the three major evolutionary trends related to FinTech supported the rise of RegTech.

The digital transformation in developed markets, starting in the late 1960s (see Chapter 2), continues to this day. It has provided for the progressive large-scale data-fication of payments, lending, and securities markets.

The long partnership in the 1980s and 1990s between major central banks and financial institutions aimed at the facilitation of, and reduction of risk in, cross-border payments (particularly systemic risks).[12] The establishment of early RegTech institutions like SWIFT (Society for Worldwide Interbank Financial Telecommunications)[13] and

---

9   For a brief overview of the post-crisis global mandated reforms and the profound changes in global finance over the past 40 years, see Ross P Buckley, 'Reconceptualizing the Regulation of Global Finance' (2016) 36(2) *Oxford Journal of Legal Study* 242.

10 See Fenergo, *Enforcement Actions in a COVID Climate: A Global Research Report on Financial Institution Fines and Enforcement Actions* (Report, 2021) 7.

11 See Bence András Rózsa, 'Investment Fines', *Broker Chooser* (Web Page, July 2021) <https://brokerchooser.com/education/news/investment-fines>.

12 See George G Kaufman and Kenneth E Scott, 'What Is Systemic Risk, and Do Bank Regulators Retard or Contribute to It?' (2003) 7(3) *The Independent Review* 371, 378.

13 SWIFT was founded in the 1970s. See, for example, Susan V Scott and Markos Zachariadis, 'Origins and Development of SWIFT, 1973–2009' (2012) 54(3) *Business History* 462.

VISA in the 1970s,[14] real-time gross settlement (RTGS) systems,[15] and the launch of CLS (Continuous Linked Settlement) in 2002[16] not only contributed to today's US$7.5 trillion-a-day global foreign exchange markets[17] but resulted in a global infrastructure as well, underpinned by alternative payment systems such as PayPal and AliPay.[18]

Another example of RegTech can be seen in the governance of today's virtual electronic markets characterised by high frequency and algorithmic trading: the world of the 'flash boys'.[19] Following NASDAQ's establishment in 1971 (the first fully electronic securities market), the 1987 stock market crash (caused by programme trading), the dot-com bubble in 2001, and the flash crash of 2010, lead major market participants and regulators collaborate to improve market efficiency and risk management.[20] The outcome of their efforts can be seen in the National Market System (NMS) in the United States and the Investment Services Directive (ISD), Markets in Financial Instruments Directive (MiFID), and European Market Infrastructure Regulation (EMIR) in the EU. In turn, most securities trading today involves computers trading with computers – humans are minority participants.[21]

Finally, increasing digitalisation of financial services and rise of mobile money in developing countries (see Chapter 2) further accelerated RegTech.

C. *RegTech*

RegTech is not a subset of FinTech. While FinTech is inherently financial in focus, RegTech applies in a growing range of contexts across regulated industries, from monitoring COVID data to trucking companies for speeding infractions to pesticide

---

[14] VISA was launched as BankAmericard in 1958 and renamed as VISA in 1976. 'Unlocking Opportunities for Everyone', *VISA* (Web Page) <https://usa.visa.com/about-visa/our_business/history-of-visa.html>.

[15] See Peter Allsopp, Bruce Summers, and John Veale, *The Evolution of Real-Time Gross Settlement: Access, Liquidity and Credit, and Pricing* (Financial Infrastructure Series Report, February 2009). For a more recent example in developing countries like Zambia, see the Zambia Interbank Payment and Settlement System (ZIPSS): 'ZIPSS', *Bank of Zambia* (Web Page) <www.boz.zm/zipss.htm>.

[16] See Jürg Mägerle and David Maurer, *The Continuous Linked Settlement Foreign Exchange Settlement System* (Report, Swiss National Bank, November 2009) 2 <www.snb.ch/en/mmr/reference/continuous_linked_settlement/source/continuous_linked_settlement.en.pdf>.

[17] See 'Triennial Survey of Central Banks of Foreign Exchange and Over-the-Counter (OTC) Derivatives Markets in 2022', *Bank for International Settlements* (Web Page, October 2022) <www.bis.org/statistics/rpfx22.htm>.

[18] Morten Bech and Jenny Hancock, 'Innovations in Payments' in Bank for International Settlements, *Quarterly Review* (Report, March 2020) 21, 33 <www.bis.org/publ/qtrpdf/r_qt2003f.htm>.

[19] See Michael Lewis, *Flash Boys: A Wall Street Revolt* (W W Norton, 1st ed, 2015).

[20] For a brief but comprehensive summary of the role of regulators and regulations in the development of electronic markets and high frequency trading, see Anuj Agarwal, *High Frequency Trading: Evolution and the Future* (Report, Capgemini, 2012) 19–20.

[21] Trading is now dominated by high-frequency and computerised trading. See Khairul Zharif Zaharudin, Martin R Young, and Wei-Huei Hsu, 'High-Frequency Trading: Definition, Implications, and Controversies' (2022) 36(1) *Journal of Economic Surveys* 75. See also Esteban Medina, 'Should High Frequency Trading Be Regulated?', *Harvard College Economics Review* (Web Page, July 2021) <www.economicsreview.org/post/should-high-frequency-trading-be-regulated>.

levels from farm run-off in water in which oysters are being grown to energy companies safety and climate compliance.

Within financial services, new entrants providing niche and supplementary services have emerged, often as FinTech start-ups, but also from other technology fields. For example, social media data might now be utilised for portfolio analysis and risk insurance pricing. As one of the most regulated and datafied industries, technology offers massive cost savings to established financial institutions and potentially similar opportunities to emerging FinTech start-ups, IT firms, and advisory firms. From a regulator's perspective, RegTech enables more continuous monitoring and should improve efficiency by sharply decreasing the time it takes to investigate a firm following a compliance breach.[22]

RegTech further can be used to underpin a paradigm shift in regulation. In particular, RegTech can provide near real-time insights into the functioning of national and global markets. These insights can be gathered from continuous monitoring, leveraging advancements in deep learning and artificial intelligence (AI). This allows regulators to identify problems in advance rather than being limited to ex-post enforcement action. Relative to the tools that regulators have today, this will be profoundly transformative for finance and its regulation.

It is therefore critical to distinguish RegTech from FinTech. The emergence of RegTech is attributable to: (1) post-crisis regulation mandating massive data disclosures;[23] (2) developments in data science that enable the structuring of unstructured data;[24] (3) economic incentives to minimise rising compliance costs; and (4) regulators' efforts to enhance the efficiency of supervisory tools to foster competition and promote financial stability and market integrity.[25]

The emergence of FinTech is attributable to: (1) GFC-induced financial market deficiencies and post-GFC regulation; (2) public distrust in financial services, particularly in the United States and EU; (3) political pressure for small and medium enterprises to be given alternative sources of finance; (4) unemployed financial professionals seeking to apply their talents; and (5) the commoditisation of technology, through the Internet and smart phones.

---

[22] Ioannis Anagnostopoulos, 'FinTech and RegTech: Impact on Regulators and Banks' (2018) 100 *Journal of Economics and Business* 7, 19.

[23] See Institute of International Finance, *RegTech in Financial Services: Technology Solutions for Compliance and Reporting* (Report, March 2016) 5–8.

[24] The IIF identified several new technologies that could improve data management and analysis, which include new cryptographic technology, data mining algorithms, machine learning, blockchain, robotics, and visual analytics. Ibid 12–14.

[25] For example, Principle 9 of the Basel Committee on Banking Supervision (BCBS)'s 'Core Principles for Effective Banking Supervision' requires financial supervisors to use an appropriate range of techniques and tools to effectively implement the supervisory approach and deploy supervisory resources. This includes a criterion that '[t]he supervisor uses a variety of tools to regularly review and assess the safety and soundness of banks and the banking system': Basel Committee on Banking Supervision, *Core Principles for Effective Banking Supervision* (Report, Bank for International Settlements, September 2012) 30–1.

From a post-2008 perspective, FinTech has grown organically as a bottom-up movement led by start-ups and IT firms. In contrast, RegTech grew largely in response to top-down institutional demand.

III. FINANCIAL INSTITUTIONS: COMPLIANCE AND REGTECH

A. *Globalisation of Finance*

Global financial regulation is historically an iterative process of liberalisation, crisis, and reactive regulatory response. As markets advanced internationally from the late 1960s and globally from the 1980s, domestic regulation could no longer adequately address the challenges of cross-border, international, and global financial markets and institutions. In response, a network of cooperative arrangements between national and global regulators addressed the new risks of global finance, with the Bank for International Settlements (BIS), the Basel Committee on Banking Supervision (Basel Committee), the Financial Action Task Force on Money Laundering (FATF), the Financial Stability Forum, and the Group of Seven (G7) Industrialised Countries as central institutions.[26] These organisations staffed by national regulators convened following each major crisis (Herstatt in the 1970s, the Developing Country Debt Crisis of the 1980s, the Mexican and Asian Financial Crises, the failures of BCCI and Barings of the 1990s) to agree on regulatory responses to prevent future crises. Major examples include the 1988 Basel Capital Accord (Basel I),[27] its replacement (Basel II),[28] and the FATF's 40 Recommendations.[29]

The period from the late 1960s to the 2008 GFC was one of continual expansion in scope and scale, culminating in large global financial conglomerates.[30] This was achieved through organic growth and, more significantly, through an extraordinary series of mergers and acquisitions in which, for instance, between 1990 and 2009, 12 banks were to merge into Bank of America and 10 into JPMorgan Chase such that in this period 37 banks became the 'Big Four'.[31]

---

[26] Lawrence G Baxter, 'Understanding the Global in Global Finance and Regulation' in Ross P Buckley, Emilios Avgouleas, and Douglas W Arner (eds), *Reconceptualising Global Finance and Its Regulation* (Cambridge University Press, 2016) 28–48.

[27] See Basel Committee on Banking Supervision, *International Convergence of Capital Measurement and Capital Standards* (Report, Bank for International Settlements, 1998) <www.bis.org/publ/bcbsc111 .htm> ('Basel I').

[28] See Basel Committee on Banking Supervision, *International Convergence of Capital Measurement and Capital Standards: A Revised Framework* (Report, Bank for International Settlements, 2006) <www.bis.org/publ/bcbs128.htm> ('Basel II').

[29] See Financial Action Task Force, *FATF 40 Recommendations* (Report, October 2003) <www.fatf-gafi.org/ publications/fatfrecommendations/documents/the40recommendationspublishedoctober2004.html>.

[30] See Ross P Buckley, 'The Changing Nature of Banking and Why It Matters' in Ross P Buckley, Emilios Avgouleas, and Douglas W Arner (eds), *Reconceptualising Global Finance and Its Regulation* (Cambridge University Press, 2016) 9–27.

[31] Jeremy C Kress, 'Modernizing Bank Merger Review' (2020) 37(2) *Yale Journal on Regulation* 435, 454–6.

As these financial institutions expanded, they faced additional operational and regulatory challenges requiring increased risk, legal and compliance oversight. Throughout the 1990s and 2000s, financial engineering and Value at Risk (VaR) systems were routinely used in major financial institutions.[32] The financial industry – particularly stakeholders in large global financial institutions – grew overconfident in their ability to manage risk through quantitative finance and IT.[33] In fact, as the GFC demonstrated, quantitative, IT-based finance proved to be one of the great failures that led to the crisis.

Regulators similarly placed excessive faith in this quantitative framework to manage risk, as is clearly demonstrated by the Basel II Capital Accord's heavy reliance on quantitative risk management systems.[34] As a result, financial regulation was essentially left to self-enforcement by the regulated entities. These aspects of risk management could be characterised as the first iteration of RegTech. This pre-crisis partnership between financial institutions and their regulators created a false sense of security and confidence, which was eventually shattered by the GFC.

B. *The 2008 GFC*

Financial institutions have progressively transformed into major users of RegTech solutions, motivated primarily by their risk management and compliance needs. While the financial services industry has always demanded automated reporting and compliance tools, massively increased regulatory costs since 2008 have further incentivised the digitisation and automation of processes required to meet new regulatory obligations.

This regulatory environment is marked by a *complex, fragmented,* and *ever-evolving* global financial regulatory regime which calls for greater granularity, precision and frequency in data reporting, aggregation, and analysis. RegTech has emerged in response to reduce the vast compliance and supervision costs of regulators and the regulated.

Examples include the capital and liquidity regulations under Basel III, stress testing and risk assessments particularly in the most developed nations, and the reporting requirements imposed on OTC derivatives transactions agreed between the Group of 20 (G20) and Financial Stability Board (FSB).[35] In 2020 alone, financial institutions spent in excess of US$213 billion on compliance.[36] It is no wonder industry turned to RegTech for cost-effective solutions.

---

[32] Margaret Woods, Kevin Dowd, and Christopher Humphrey, 'The Value of Risk Reporting: A Critical Analysis of Value-at-Risk Disclosures in the Banking Sector' (2008) 8(1) *International Journal of Financial Services Management* 45, 54–5.

[33] David Blake, 'The Great Game Will Never End: Why the Global Financial Crisis Is Bound to Be Repeated' (2022) 15(6) *Journal of Risk and Financial Management* 245, 29.

[34] Katalin Mérő, 'The Ascent and Descent of Banks' Risk-Based Capital Regulation' (2021) 22(4) *Journal of Banking Regulation* 308.

[35] For discussion in the context of the United States, see Financial Stability Oversight Council, *Study of the Effects of Size and Complexity of Financial Institutions on Capital Market Efficiency and Economic Growth* (Report, March 2016).

[36] LexisNexis Risk Solutions, *True Cost of Financial Crime Compliance Study* (Global Report, June 2021) 8.

This complexity is intensified by deepening regulatory fragmentation, resulting from differences in the detail of rules in domestic markets that seek to implement international frameworks. In this context, RegTech has served to optimise compliance management. Further, the rapidly evolving post-crisis regulatory landscape introduced uncertainty into future regulatory requirements, placing a premium on financial institutions being able to enhance their *adaptability* in regulatory compliance. Iterative modelling and testing by RegTech has served to assist in this exceedingly dynamic environment. Finally, regulators are increasingly motivated to explore RegTech solutions to ensure financial institutions comply with regulations in a responsive manner (cf Part IV).

Leading RegTech examples include anti-money laundering (AML), know-your-client (KYC), prudential regulatory reporting, and stress-testing compliance requirements.

1. AML and KYC

Established in 1989 and hosted by the OECD, the FATF devises international soft law standards on money laundering and terrorist financing. Most jurisdictions have, in turn, adopted these standards,[37] especially as the UN is active in issuing sanction lists of prohibited or restricted countries, firms, and individuals that fail to meet these standards. Unlike FATF recommendations, UN sanction lists have a formal international legal basis.

FATF rules and UN sanctions have dramatically influenced the operations of financial institutions globally, with large financial institutions typically having major divisions tasked with implementing the AML rules of the various jurisdictions in which they operate. In addition to financial institutions, infrastructure such as SWIFT and CLS are important implementers of AML procedures and sanctions.[38]

Domestic law will generally reflect international standards in various ways, but details may vary. From a compliance standpoint, several issues arise.[39]

First, every client or potential client of a financial institution must be reviewed under the core AML requirement of knowing one's customer. This is an intensive process requiring documentation of information including identity, income, and funding sources. For large financial institutions with thousands of customers in multiple countries, this process is demanding and generally monitored through the firm's internal IT, risk management, and compliance systems.

---

[37] FATF, *International Standards on Combating Money Laundering and the Financing of Terrorism & Proliferation: The FATF Recommendations* (Report, March 2022) <www.fatf-gafi.org/media/fatf/documents/recommendations/pdfs/FATF%20Recommendations%202012.pdf>.

[38] See Arner et al (n 4), 371, 391. See also 'Financial Crime Compliance: Setting the Standard in Financial Crime Compliance', SWIFT (Web Page) <www.swift.com/our-solutions/compliance-and-shared-services/financial-crime-compliance>.

[39] See Institute of International Finance (n 24), 10.

Second, because of differences between the requirements of individual jurisdictions, firms operating across multiple markets must implement systems (usually IT-based) that address not only the general global requirements but also the specific requirements of individual markets, and in some cases of individual regulatory authorities within those markets.

Third, the United States is particularly active in enforcing its rules on both US financial institutions and foreign financial institutions operating within the United States. Many major financial institutions including HSBC, Standard Chartered, Barclays, Deutsche, and BNP Paribas have been subjected to US regulatory action and enormous fines. Through deferred prosecution agreements, US regulators typically require financial entities to implement AML and sanctions compliance systems that meet US standards throughout their entire global operations.

Fourth, the AML investigation and reporting processes of suspicious transactions within large financial institutions is onerous and requires significant human and IT resources. These processes include both subjective elements (e.g., unusual account behaviour) and objective elements (e.g., reporting any cash transaction over a certain size, often $10,000).[40]

2. Prudential Regulatory Reporting and Stress Testing

Prior to the 2008 Crisis, prudential regulation was typically embedded in capital and trading reporting requirements. Trade reports focused on exchange traded activities, designed to address market conduct issues (particularly market manipulation and insider trading). Capital requirements centred on the prudential safety and soundness of the individual financial institution.

Capital requirements have been a major focus of cross-border regulatory cooperation since the development of the Basel I Capital Accord in the 1980s. The Accord responded to insufficient levels of capital in internationally active financial institutions after the 1980s Developing Country Debt Crisis. While initially fairly simple, its complexity and resulting compliance costs steadily increased throughout the 1990s after a series of amendments.[41]

In the aftermath of the 1997 Asian Financial Crisis, Basel II was developed to bring together regulatory, economic, and accounting capital into a single market-friendly framework. This reflected the consensus view of the reliability of quantitative

---

[40] FATF, *Anti-Money Laundering and Terrorist Financing Measures and Financial Inclusion: With a Supplement on Customer Due Diligence* (FATF Guidance, November 2017) 5–6, 40–1 <www.fatf-gafi.org/media/fatf/Updated-2017-FATF-2013-Guidance.pdf>; 'Reporting Transactions of $10,000 and over: Threshold Transaction Reports (TTRs)', AUSTRAC (Web Page) <www.austrac.gov.au/business/how-comply-guidance-and-resources/reporting/cash-transactions-over-10000-ttr>.

[41] See Andrew G Haldane and Vasileios Madouros, 'The Dog and The Frisbee' (Speech at the Federal Reserve Bank of Kansas City's 366th economic policy symposium, 31 August 2012) 1, 6–8 <www.bis.org/review/r120905a.pdf>, a source worth reading for its entertainment value and illumination about heuristics.

financial risk management systems (despite some evidence to the contrary provided by the rescue of LTCM in 1999). Basel II extended the internal models-based approach, initiated by the 1995 Basel I Market Risk Amendment, to all aspects of capital regulation.[42] Effectively, financial regulators outsourced the setting of capital requirements to the financial institutions.

Following 2008, attention has shifted to developing Basel III, aiming to dramatically increase capital (particularly equity capital), reduce leverage, enhance liquidity, and implement crisis management systems for individual institutions, including by limiting reliance on the firms' internal risk modelling systems. This framework is massive in its internationally agreed soft law form. It will be even more substantial upon implementation in the legal and regulatory systems of individual jurisdictions.

As with AML, prudential regulation requires global institutions to understand, monitor, and report all aspects of their activities to regulators in their operative jurisdictions. These requirements continue to multiply, with thousands of data points requiring reporting to multiple regulators in different jurisdictions now the norm for internationally active banks. Financial institutions must now produce all necessary data in the frequency and form set by individual regulators. While the overall approaches may be harmonised, the details frequently are not.[43] Institutions have focused on developing their compliance teams and IT systems to implement these requirements, with these requirements continually evolving as stages of the G20/FSB reforms are agreed and implemented in individual jurisdictions.

Unlike the pre-2008 environment, regulators no longer rely on the internal risk management systems of individual financial institutions but instead establish complex rules. The rules set capital, leverage, and liquidity at levels sufficient to protect financial stability and are continuously monitored through periodic reviews and 'stress tests.'[44] Overall, these changes have greatly increased the demand for RegTech solutions in the financial industry.

C. *RegTech: A FinTech Opportunity*

In addition to regulatory factors, RegTech is also being driven by FinTech developments. An increasing range of IT firms, advisory firms, and start-ups are meeting regulatory requirements by deploying data gathering and analytical solutions.

---

[42] See Basel Committee on Banking Supervision, *An Internal Model-Based Approach to Market Risk Capital Requirements* (Report, Bank for International Settlements, April 1995).

[43] This is probably why some private sector standards promoters, such as ISO and the IIF, call for data standardisation and definition harmonisation. See Institute of International Finance (n 24) 19–21.

[44] See, for example, regulatory capital rules issued by Office of the Comptroller of the Currency, Board of Governors of the Federal Reserve System and Federal Deposit Insurance Corporation: *Changes to Applicability Thresholds for Regulatory Capital and Liquidity Requirements*, 84 Fed Reg 59230 (1 November 2019).

In the field of AML/KYC, solutions focus on automating and simplifying processes in addition to identifying and reporting suspicious transactions. Other aspects of financial institution RegTech involve building strategic platforms that aggregate data to comply with capital and stress-testing requirements. Data analysis models can evaluate how thousands of variables impact financial institutions. Further, algorithmic margin requirements can ensure compliance with trading book risk management rules by managing the market risk of traders' portfolios and transactions. In general, at the more advanced levels, RegTech can enable near to real-time data analysis and customised reporting.

As these examples demonstrate, RegTech today is not only about cost reduction but also about enhancing effectiveness of the rules implemented.

D. *Looking Forward: Shared Services Utility and Global Compliance*

In 2014, Goldman Sachs introduced a new campus in Bangalore (Bengaluru), India. Bangalore is now Goldman's second largest office (with approximately 7,000 staff, compared to 22,828 in the United States), and are expecting to hire an additional 2,000 staff on a second campus in Hyderabad by 2023.[45] Other major financial institutions, including JPMorgan, Citibank, Morgan Stanley, Barclays, Deutsche Bank, HSBC, and Standard Chartered, among others, have large proportions of their staff in centralised support operations in India, especially in Bangalore, Mumbai, New Delhi, and Chennai. These offices have grown from traditional back offices and call centres into major integrated global risk management and regulatory compliance operations. For instance, all operations of a global financial services firm around customer onboarding, account opening, and KYC can now be centralised in India (or elsewhere).

Likewise, extensive prudential reporting requirements have prompted financial institutions to centralise operations that collate global data. Ironically, these operations look like pre-2008 trading floors, with rows of desks, telephones, and screens facilitating continuous monitoring and communication across the institution. As these companies are generally separately incorporated subsidiaries, they are not considered to conduct licensed 'banking' activities requiring targeted regulation. The subsidiaries remain constrained only by their group entity's domestic outsourcing rules.[46]

These new compliance strategies have been the first elements of a post-crisis RegTech 2.0. This increased use of RegTech has required regulators to adapt and

---

[45] Goldman Sachs employs 43,900 staff, 52 per cent based in the United States and 30 per cent in Asia. See Goldman Sachs, *The Goldman Sachs Group Annual Report 2021* (Report, 2021) 8. Shilpa Phadnis, 'Goldman Sachs Services Has Over 1k Open Positions', *The Times of India* (online, 11 October 2021) <https://timesofindia.indiatimes.com/city/bengaluru/goldman-sachs-services-has-over-1k-open-positions/articleshow/86947875.cms>.

[46] For a summary of the regulatory issues concerned with shared services, see Deloitte, *Shared Services Handbook: Hit the Road* (Report, 2011).

adopt their own regulatory technologies in response, which comprise the second element of RegTech today and are the subject of Section IV.

IV. REGULATORS: COPING WITH COMPLIANCE

Regulators are generally accepted to be under-resourced in hiring human capital, and especially under-resourced in acquiring and implementing technology. However, regulators have seen notable successes using Supervisory Technologies (SupTech) in the context of technology and regulation.[47]

Technology has actively monitored and enforced market integrity since the 1980s, with the US Securities and Exchange Commission (SEC) being the global leader.[48] Regulators and industry participants have long worked to address issues with cross-border electronic payment, securities trading, and settlement systems by building robust technology and regulatory solutions. However, the use of AI and deep learning systems to address the regulatory information explosion may hold further potential in advancing SupTech.

A. *RegTech and SupTech: A Regulator's Tools for the Twenty-First Century*

Regulators are increasingly aware of the gap between the masses of data reported to them and their own data analysis capacity. A failure by regulators to develop their analytics capabilities in response to growing datasets undercuts the policy objectives of these reporting requirements.

B. *Big Data: Matching Reporting with Analytical Tools*

One example of an area where regulators are considering advanced technological solutions is the suspicious transactions reports produced by financial services firms. Exploring these solutions raises an important opportunity for collaboration between regulators and academia (particularly for quantitative finance and economics academics with highly developed capabilities in analysing datasets and a constant hunger for new datasets to analyse).

Over the past 20 years, regulators have successfully used technology to monitor and analyse the reporting of transactions in public securities markets. Today,

---

[47] Chris Brummer, 'Disruptive Technology and Securities Regulation' (2015) 84(3) *Fordham Law Review* 977.

[48] See Technical Committee of the International Organisation of Securities Commissions, *Regulatory Issues Raised by the Impact of Technological Changes on Market Integrity and Efficiency* (Final Report FR09/11, October 2011) for an overview of the major movements the SEC has led in regulation; The Board of the International Organisation of Securities Commissions, *The Use of Artificial Intelligence and Machine Learning by Market Intermediaries and Asset Managers* (Consultation Report CR02/2020, June 2020).

regulators rely heavily on trade reports from securities exchanges to detect wrongdo-ing. Analysis of such data underpins regulatory investigation and enforcement, for instance, insider trading ahead of major corporate announcements. As securities exchanges maintain data on all trades, it is simple to review trading activity prior to major corporate events and detect unusual trading activity.

Since the GFC, these systems have demonstrated a limited ability to monitor off-exchange activities. Regulatory changes in the United States and EU have increased the observability of OTC transactions by mandating reporting of all of the listed financial instrument transactions (including securities and derivatives), regardless of whether these transactions are cleared via formal exchanges or over the counter. Obviously, SupTech monitoring systems must retain the ability to draw from these expanded datasets for analysis.

While the advancement of regulators in RegTech is the second element of an emerging RegTech 2.0, we argue that further progress is necessary. Beyond cyber-security (discussed at length in Part IV), macroprudential policy holds perhaps the greatest potential for RegTech.

C. *Macroprudential Policy*

Macroprudential policy focuses on the stability of the entire financial system, based on a holistic analysis focused on interconnections and evolution over time.[49] It was the focus of global regulatory efforts in the aftermath of the GFC, as the suscepti-bility of the entire financial system to collapse from interlinkages among financial institutions was revealed by that crisis. This new focus prompted an increasing num-ber of jurisdictions to implement new institutional frameworks supporting macro-prudential policy, including the Financial Stability Oversight Council (FSOC) in the United States and the European Systemic Risk Board (ESRB) in the EU. Along with the IMF, FSB, and BIS, these frameworks seek to develop and implement macroprudential policies that prevent financial crises and support financial stability. Macroprudential policy thus seeks to leverage the massive amounts of reported data to identify patterns and reduce the severity of the financial cycle.

Though this process is challenging, progress is apparent in identifying potential leading indicators for future financial instability.[50] To date, these processes involve

---

[49] See International Monetary Fund, Financial Stability Board, and Bank for International Settlements, *Elements of Effective Macroprudential Policies: Lessons from International Experience* (Report, 31 August 2016).

[50] Ibid. See Committee on the Global Financial System, 'Experiences with the Ex Ante Appraisal of Macro-Prudential Instruments' (CGFS Papers No 56, Bank for International Settlements, July 2016); Blaise Gadanecz and Kaushik Jayaram, 'Macroprudential Policy Frameworks, Instruments and Indicators: A Review' (Working Paper for Irving Fisher Committee workshop on 'Combining Micro and Macro Statistical Data for Financial Stability Analysis: Experiences, Opportunities and Challenges', Bank for International Settlements, December 2015).

utilising quantitative analysis to search for interconnections and implications in large volumes of data. Reporting by financial institutions and infrastructure providers of these massive datasets may feed into these analytical processes. Major central banks such as the Federal Reserve, the European Central Bank, and the Bank of England are already employing data 'heat maps' to visualise the masses of reported data (such as stress tests) they receive to highlight potential issues. These efforts highlight the likely future direction of RegTech in macroprudential policy. Moreover, these analyses are causing regulators to identify needs for yet more data.[51] This trend is particularly pronounced in sustainable finance where reporting often includes data on how firms impact external sustainability factors (see Chapter 6).

Ultimately, reporting requirements for financial institutions continue to expand, further driving the necessity for RegTech processes and centralised support services that collect and produce the required data at the required frequency and in the required format. Significantly, the FSB and IMF have identified a strong need to harmonise reporting templates for systemically important financial institutions, thereby decreasing the complexity of data collection and analysis.

V. RECONCEPTUALISING FINANCIAL REGULATION

Moving forward, RegTech must move beyond the efficiency gains it has provided to date and seek to leverage its potential as a transformative tool to revolutionise financial regulation. Indeed, the speed of FinTech innovation, combined with the dramatic progress witnessed in some developing countries, means that not only should RegTech be used to make financial regulation more effective and affordable, but also that RegTech be used to reconceptualise and redesign financial regulation in line with the transformation of financial market infrastructure. As such, RegTech will move beyond supervision to help steer the whole financial system, and quite possibly the economy at large.

As FinTech gradually moves from digitisation of money to embrace the monetisation of data, the regulatory framework for finance will need to cover new fields such as data sovereignty and algorithm supervision. At this stage, the sustainable development of FinTech will need to be built around a new framework, namely RegTech. Doing so requires a sequenced approach.

First a holistic approach is needed, focusing on building twenty-first century infrastructure to support market functions. This is most clear in the context of SWIFT, with efforts now centred on improving the structure of global payments infrastructure. Second is the challenge of developing appropriate regulatory responses to FinTech innovation. While RegTech 2.0 has largely concerned streamlining and

---

[51] See Financial Stability Board and International Monetary Fund, *The Financial Crisis and Information Gaps: G20 Data Gaps Initiative (DGI-2), Progress Achieved, Lessons Learned, and The Way Forward* (Report, 9 June 2022).

automating regulatory compliance and reporting, RegTech 3.0 is more forward looking. Progress in RegTech 3.0 has changed both market participants and infrastructure, with data as the common denominator and universal facilitator.

The emergence of FinTech companies, combined with the wider use of regulatory sandboxes, offers a unique opportunity to pilot this novel kind of proportionate, efficient, and data-driven regulatory architecture before market-wide implementation. FinTech requires RegTech. The challenge for regulators globally is 'to boldly go where no man has gone before' in conceptualising and implementing the possibilities of RegTech.

5

COVID-19, Digital Finance, and Existential Sustainability Crises

SUMMARY

This chapter examines how the digital financial infrastructure that emerged in the wake of the 2008 Global Financial Crisis assisted to address the financial, economic, and health challenges presented by the COVID-19 pandemic. While the 2008 Crisis was a financial crisis that impacted the real economy, COVID-19 was a health and geopolitical crisis that impacted the real economy. In fact, during COVID-19 the financial system turned from problem child to crisis manager, providing effective tools to support the crisis response. Notwithstanding the former, digital finance has also created new forms of risk (which we will address as TechRisk in Part IV of this book).

I. INTRODUCTION

The origins and impacts of the 2008 Global Financial Crisis (GFC) and the COVID-19 crisis of 2020 are very different and thus demanded different responses and approaches: 2008 was a financial crisis that spilt over into the real economy.[1] COVID-19 as a pandemic was a health and geopolitical crisis – in fact an existential sustainability crisis – that spilt over into the real economy.[2]

The COVID-19 pandemic shook nations around the world. It tested their healthcare infrastructure, battered their economies, and left whole populations in fear and periodic lockdowns. While first and foremost a human health and sustainability crisis, its economic and social consequences will extend for years. In the words of the United Nations:

> The COVID-19 pandemic is far more than a health crisis: it is affecting societies and economies at their core. While the impact of the pandemic will vary from

---

[1] Ross P Buckley and Douglas W Arner, *From Crisis to Crisis: The Global Financial System and Regulatory Failure* (Kluwer Law, 2011).

[2] Douglas W Arner, Ross P Buckley, and Dirk Zetzsche, 'FinTech and the Four Horsemen of the Apocalypse: Building Financial Ecosystems for Resilience, Innovation and Sustainable Development' (2022) 39(1) *Banking and Finance Law Review* 5.

country to country, it will most likely increase poverty and inequalities at a global scale, making achievement of SDGs even more urgent.[3]

The UN suggests that COVID-19 set back human development around the world by several years.[4] In sharp contrast, in 2009, following the 2008 Crisis, the global economy contracted by only 1.7 per cent.[5] The pandemic's impact has been devastating across the whole planet, leaving no region unaffected. Its immediate impact on most developed countries was massive, and its longer-term impact on the developing world, in particular less-developed countries and Indigenous communities, may yet prove to be even greater, given weaker healthcare systems and infrastructure, and the dependency on global trade of many of these countries.[6] Disparate impact in terms of race, poverty, and inequality is being seen strongly in developed economies, with the wealthiest being able to dodge the crisis impact best and the poor suffering the most. The trend noticeable through the pandemic has been reinforced with the war in Ukraine commenced in 2022; its impact on fossil energy and nutrition prices was massive and has hit many societies that bled out in the preceding pandemic years. With these and other climate-related sustainability crises emerging with increasing frequency and force around the world, the 2020s are presenting a very difficult decade indeed for billions of people.

We examine in this chapter how the financial infrastructure – in particular digital financial infrastructure – has been tested and is being leveraged to both overcome the immediate challenges of the COVID-19 pandemic and manage some of the longer-term economic impacts. We explore some of the lessons from the recent use of digital financial platforms. Our examples underscore the versatility and agility of financial technology and demonstrate how the digital financial infrastructure can be robust, resilient, and most importantly, responsive in the face of fluid and unpredictable events. We argue that crisis-resilient digital financial systems are mankind's best recipe to address future crises, including the sorts of existential sustainability crises which are likely to become increasingly common in coming decades. At the same time, from late 2020 through 2022, digitisation of finance combined with massive amounts of central bank liquidity appears to be contributing to new asset price bubbles in the tech and e-commerce sectors around the world, increasing the

---

3   'COVID-19: Socio-Economic Impact', United Nations Development Programme (Web Page, 2022) <www.undp.org/coronavirus/socio-economic-impact-covid-19>.

4   United Nations Development Programme, *Human Development Report 2021/2022: Uncertain Times, Unsettled Lives, Shaping our Future in a Transforming World* (Human Development Report, 8 September 2022) <https://hdr.undp.org/content/human-development-report-2021-22> 32–3.

5   Elisabeth WaelbroeckRocha and Nariman Behravesh, 'COVID-19 Recession to be Deeper than That of 2008–2009', *S&P Global Market Intelligence* (Web Page, 30 March 2020) <www.spglobal.com/marketintelligence/en/mi/research-analysis/covid19-recession-to-be-deeper-than-that-of-20082009.html>.

6   Dirk A Zetzsche and Roberta Consiglio, 'Ten Million or One Hundred Million Casualties? COVID-19 Crisis and Europe's Sustainability Agenda' in Beate Sjåfjell, Georgina Tsagas, and Charlotte Villiers (eds), *Sustainable Value Creation in the EU: Towards Pathways to a Sustainable Future through Crises* (Cambridge University Press, 2022) 26–57.

potential for new financial stability risks: second-order effects arising from the initial financial responses to the crisis in 2020. These effects can be seen both in the rise of inflationary pressures and central bank responses across 2022–2023, combined with a series of crises in the context of digital assets (the Crypto Winter of 2022–2023) and the failure of a number of technology-related banks including Silicon Valley Bank in 2023, as well as the failure of Credit Suisse as a result of longstanding management issues and finally a range of developing country financial crises resulting from higher interest rates combined with commodity and food prices in the wake of Russia's invasion of Ukraine in early 2022. This chapter focuses on the role of digital finance in non-financial crises, particularly sustainability crises such as the 2020–2022 global pandemic.

II. THE FOUR-LEVEL INTERRELATIONSHIP BETWEEN FINANCE AND THE REAL ECONOMY

From a financial sector standpoint, the starting point in any crisis – be it a financial, an economic, or a sustainability crisis – is to understand the situation and context, and, from there, to deploy appropriate strategies to prevent or mitigate the financial crisis while minimising damage to the real economy and laying the foundations for a return to financial stability and sustainable development. In the wake of any crisis, legal and regulatory reforms will be necessary to address the issues and lessons which arose, and to enhance systems prior to the next test, whatever that might be.

The 2008 Crisis originated with a financial crisis. This in turn impacted the real economy as financial resources became unavailable to support economic activity. Conceptually, the 'real economy' is distinct from the financial economy in that it refers to the physical production of goods and delivery of services. The 'financial economy', in contrast, refers to financial transactions entered into to create wealth. This damage to the real economy, therefore, in turn worsened financial sector issues (through both liquidity and solvency channels) causing a dangerous spiral (including spillovers to various governments around the world).[7]

In 2020, the triggering events were different. The initial situation was primarily a health and existential sustainability crisis, with the COVID-19 pandemic starting at the end of 2019. This was followed by a geopolitical crisis. The pandemic became a domestically politicised issue in much of the world, and then had strong international consequences as it widened existing fissures in global trade, economic interactions, and geopolitics. In addition to the existing trade tensions between the United States, China, the European Union (EU), the United Kingdom, and Canada, among others, the trade relationship between Australia and China, for example, deteriorated

---

[7] Ross P Buckley, Emilios Avgouleas, and Douglas W Arner, 'Three Major Financial Crises: What Have We Learned?' in Douglas W Arner et al (eds), *Systemic Risk in the Financial Sector: Ten Years after the Great Crash* (Centre for International Governance Innovation Press, 2019) 47.

greatly following the Australian government calling for an independent inquiry into the origins of the pandemic. Relations between China and India also deteriorated, resulting in an increasingly competitive and tense environment.

While the most significant impact of the COVID-19 pandemic was on humans, the immediate consequences of quarantine measures and lockdowns reverberated through supply chains (i.e., reduced operation of factories and logistic networks) and through demand channels (i.e., reduced demand and prohibitions on certain services such as travel and hospitality) globally and locally.

As the early economic and human toll increased, so did the strain on the financial sector. Most economic actors initially sought to maximise their access to cash – albeit mostly in digital form as opposed to physical cash or gold – with a rush for liquidity around March 2020. Largely as a result of the post-2008 financial regulatory reforms coupled with technological developments described in Chapter 2, the financial sector was able to withstand these initial challenges and facilitate liquidity and financial support throughout economies across the world. The levels of central bank liquidity support proved to be an essential public good and withstood the global panicked rush for liquidity remarkably well, and far better than in 2008. Having said that, the high liquidity support promoted price rises in asset markets, some of which, such as housing, may well have enduring deleterious social consequences.

So while the impact of this crisis has not fallen mainly on the financial sector, the robustness and effectiveness of the financial sector has proven central in the overall battle against COVID-19. Nonetheless, for the financial sector to operate efficiently it requires trust between actors and certainty in economic outlook, and the latter element may be severely challenged given the current global economic strains.

Targeted intervention to address such outcomes highlight the central role that digital financial channels can play in alleviating prevailing ills. From this perspective, we identify four levels of intervention around the role of digital finance.

The *first level*, from the standpoint of the financial sector, is the infrastructure of the financial system, particularly payment systems and securities markets (for both companies and governments). One of the greatest concerns is failure in this core infrastructure, which is almost entirely digital. This digital plumbing lies at the core of all financial systems, domestic and international.

To the extent this digital financial infrastructure functions as intended, it underpins the financial sector in performing its key functions of payments facilitation, liquidity management, and financial resource allocation, which are necessary to support economic activity and sustainable development (see Chapter 6). Since 2008, governments have placed considerable attention on these key areas, and overall, this infrastructure has coped well with the massive challenges posed by the COVID-19 crisis.[8]

---

[8] International Monetary Fund, *A Year Like No Other: IMF Annual Report 2020* (Report, 2020) 20 <www.imf.org/external/pubs/ft/ar/2020/eng/downloads/imf-annual-report-2020.pdf>.

Ensuring resilience of this core infrastructure is essential, as the consequences of failure in times of crisis can be devastating. As we further lay out in Part IV, cybersecurity has emerged as a major source of operational, financial, systemic, and national security risk. Before the pandemic, cyber-risk was already being seen by some as being larger than credit and financial risk, particularly as most firms struggled to deal with it. This risk has only increased given the rise in working from home increases opportunities for potential breaches by malicious actors and the risks of technical failures. We categorise and discuss these risks as TechRisks in Part IV.

The *second level*, from the standpoint of liquidity, focuses on identifying where solvency problems in both the real economy (individuals, firms, governments) and the financial sector (bank runs, etc.) may emerge and deploying financial resources where possible to avoid the emergence of solvency problems as a result of lack of liquidity.

At the heart of any financial sector are wholesale electronic systems which must be carefully monitored for stress by domestic liquidity providers (generally the central bank). In times of crisis, expansive credit lines from major central banks and assistance from international organisations can be essential. This is particularly true if consumers respond to rumours on the crisis' impact on financial institutions and seek to withdraw cash, prompting a banking crisis on top of a health and economic crisis. A similar phenomenon is mirrored in the government sector where mass and rapid unemployment may result in 'welfare runs'. Government welfare services can become quickly inundated by support seekers overstretching the capacity of the public service and immediately skewing fiscal projections.

Yet liquidity supply alone will not ensure demand in the real economy if consumers choose to save rather than spend or if the choice of goods remains limited. Where choice of goods is limited, excess liquidity may well translate into higher prices for the few goods available.

The *third level*, from the standpoint of solvency of financial institutions, focuses on having closer to real-time reporting in order to coordinate timely responses and identify emerging solvency issues as early as possible. Batch reporting of financial data, for both listed and private companies, is retrospective and fails to capture dynamic financial changes. This pertains, for instance, to all annual, quarterly, or monthly reports required by financial regulators. These numbers, once received by decision-makers, are outdated and may well be inadequate to steer an economy through a crisis.

RegTech and SupTech systems provide important tools in this context.[9] For example, historically, on-site supervision played a central role in financial supervision. During COVID-19 however this became impossible, requiring non-face-to-face interactions between financial institutions and their regulators (SupTech).

---

[9] See Financial Stability Board, 'Regulatory and Supervisory Issues Relating to Outsourcing and Third-Party Relationships' (Discussion Paper, 9 November 2020) 8 <www.fsb.org/2020/11/regulatory-and-supervisory-issues-relating-to-outsourcing-and-third-party-relationships-discussion-paper>.

While digital regulatory reporting was already developing rapidly – particularly in the United States and EU[10] – COVID-19 has increased attention for the digital agenda globally.[11] In addition, technology is playing an important role in health monitoring and compliance – another form of RegTech/SupTech which we discussed in Chapter 4, albeit outside finance. For instance, in countries such as Qatar, electronic ID repositories underpinned all COVID-19 testing and national vaccination strategies.[12] Given the very rapid change in economic conditions, systems for collecting and analysing data and their impact through RegTech and SupTech can offer more granular and real-time information about health, finance and otherwise.[13] The same infrastructure, in place for longer periods, could facilitate regulators requiring systemically significant institutions to report core data that policymakers can use for economic projections and crisis modelling. Regrettably, while RegTech and SupTech systems could provide vital tools in this respect, they cannot be put in place quickly in the middle of a crisis due to the disruption typically associated with upgrading legacy systems. However, going forward, this is a major opportunity for legal and regulatory reform.

The *fourth level*, from the standpoint of the financial health of individuals, businesses, and governments, focuses on leveraging existing FinTech solutions. These are primarily digital payments, digital commerce (with respect to delivery services for necessities), and digital funding (with respect to rapidly growing sectors such as online education). The increased reliance on grocery and food delivery services in the COVID-19 pandemic has proven to be a blessing and a curse. On the one hand, these services enable physical distancing and self-isolation. On the other hand, if delivery systems are poorly designed or implemented or if delivery staff are undertrained or overworked, these systems can (and have) put workers at risk with tragic consequences. Online learning, tutoring, education, and marketing have all evolved with incredible rapidity virtually everywhere during the pandemic. Most of these changes will outlive the pandemic and continue to evolve and grow, requiring further financial resources for technological infrastructure.

[10] Douglas W Arner, Jànos Barberis, and Ross P Buckley, 'FinTech, RegTech and the Reconceptualization of Financial Regulation' (2017) 37(3) *Northwestern Journal of International Law and Business* 371; Douglas W Arner et al, 'The Future of Data-Driven Finance and RegTech: Lessons from EU Big Bang II' (2020) 25(2) *Stanford Journal of Law, Business and Finance* 245.

[11] See Financial Stability Board, *The Use of Supervisory and Regulatory Technology by Authorities and Regulated Institutions: Market Developments and Financial Stability Implications* (Report, 9 October 2020) <www.fsb.org/wp-content/uploads/P091020.pdf>.

[12] Douglas W Arner, Emilios Avgouleas, and Evan C Gibson, 'Financial Stability, Resolution of Systemic Banking Crises and COVID-19: Toward an Appropriate Role for Public Support and Bailouts' (Research Paper No. 2020/044, University of Hong Kong Faculty of Law, 2020).

[13] Jànos Barberis, Douglas W Arner, and Ross P Buckley, *The RegTech Book* (Wiley, 2019); Douglas W Arner, Jànos Barberis, and Ross P Buckley, 'FinTech, RegTech and the Reconceptualization of Financial Regulation' (2017) 37(3) *Northwestern Journal of International Law and Business* 371, 375; Luca Enriques, 'Financial Supervisors and RegTech: Four Roles and Four Challenges' (2017) *Revue Trimestrielle de Droit Financier* 53.

Financial stability is central in all of this. The financial system has to be regulated and supported to function properly in order to achieve its core functions of supporting economic and other activities; and financial crises need to be avoided, if possible, or ameliorated when they do occur.[14] Fortunately, the impact of the pandemic on the financial sector has not amplified the COVID-19 health crisis. Indeed, digital finance and commerce have emerged as pillars supporting financial stability and underpinning the economic and social responses to the crisis.

III. REDUCING ECONOMIC IMPACT: DIGITAL FINANCIAL ASSISTANCE

Digital finance offers potentially important tools in directing resources quickly and efficiently to the stakeholders that need them the most. In particular, we focus on strategies and solutions to mitigate economic and human impact.

In an existential sustainability crisis such as the COVID-19 pandemic, the initial economic, social, human, and financial impact results from short-term factors. As a crisis extends for longer, these can turn into structural factors, which then require different strategies, as seems to be happening in a number of areas as the COVID-19 pandemic evolves from a short-term shock to a longer-term challenge. As we discussed more in detail in Chapter 4, digital financial and regulatory tools are capable of achieving traditional crisis management objectives with greater potency and accuracy than has ever been possible. This may be one unprecedented advantage for some governments in the current crisis. The data-driven nature of digital finance provides policymakers with the ability to structure and scale stimulus with precision.[15] The potential benefits are obvious. The core questions, however, are whether the information is available, readable, and in front of decision-makers and if the technical capability is sufficiently mature to meet the challenge. Consolidating, curating, and monitoring collected information in near to real time has been a pillar of crisis response in some countries or areas at some times (and the need to have effective systems in place permanently to do this is probably one of the major policy lessons of this pandemic).

In times of upheaval, people need the means to secure the essentials of food, shelter, and clothing. As long as basic market conditions hold, and riots and looting have not taken hold, commercial exchange and public assistance will remain the only legitimate ways to secure such essentials. In recent years, financial technology has spearheaded the financial inclusion agenda by enabling more people than ever before to access financial services through their mobile devices in China, India, and large parts of Africa. In terms of publicly directed assistance and crisis fallout alleviation, the dynamics of the traditional public–private divide are also being witnessed

[14]   Douglas W Arner, *Financial Stability, Economic Growth and the Role of Law* (Cambridge University Press, 1st ed, 2007).

[15]   Jessica Kent, 'Big Data Analytics Show COVID-19 Spread, Outcomes by Region', *Health IT Analytics* (Web Page, 21 September 2020) <https://healthitanalytics.com/news/big-data-analytics-show-covid-19-spread-outcomes-by-region>.

upon a new axis. That new dimension, which we discuss in more detail in Chapters 16 and 17, is incumbent banks or financial institutions (BigFin) versus giant technology firms (BigTech) in the financial services market.

In addition to providing mechanisms for monitoring financial and economic conditions, digital finance enables the direct targeting of financial resources rapidly to those in the greatest need. The combination of digital identity frameworks and widespread availability of financial and mobile money accounts along with interoperable electronic payment systems provides great potential for delivering resources directly across an entire society.[16] In countries with such systems, they can provide the foundations for the design of appropriate programmes and the delivery of financial resources using algorithms prioritising different factors such as age, health, social commitments, professional qualifications, and others. To date, at least, it appears that the politics surrounding these types of social programmes and assessments are less polarised than would normally be the case, and more conciliatory.

Governments, NGOs, and international organisations have to work with payment, financial, and telecommunications providers to use whatever resources are available to enable rapid targeted delivery. Cheques mailed over a period of months are clearly far less effective. For example, the US government mailed cheques and prepaid debit cards to approximately 35 million Americans for the first round of the US COVID-19 support payments, as the government did not have their direct deposit information on file, causing significant delays.[17] Even in the second and third rounds of these payments, many Americans' cheques were delayed by months.[18]

For SMEs, short-term response tools included the capacity to unlock future income through invoice factoring solutions. However, this requires digitisation of invoices, which might not be commonplace in developing markets.[19] Another tech approach heavily reliant on current and accurate information included strategic government cash injections into businesses to avoid mass unemployment, loss of infrastructure, and deterioration of workforce skills, thus preserving readiness for a rapid restart post crisis. For instance, some states through tax authorities triggered reverse transactions based on the latest VAT, corporate tax, or income/salary tax

---

[16] Douglas W Arner, Ross P Buckley, and Dirk A Zetzsche, *FinTech for Financial Inclusion: A Framework for Digital Financial Transformation* (Special Report, Alliance for Financial Inclusion, September 2018); Douglas W Arner et al, 'The Identity Challenge in Finance: From Analogue Identity to Digitized Identification to Digital KYC Utilities' (2019) 20 *European Business Organisation Law Review* 55.

[17] Tanza Loudenback, '9 Reasons Your Full Stimulus Payment Might Be Delayed, and What to Do about It', *Insider* (Web Page, 4 June 2020) <www.businessinsider.com/personal-finance/stimulus-check-delayed-what-to-do-answers-2020-4>.

[18] Tara Siegel Bernard, 'Stimulus Checks Delayed, but I.R.S. Says They're Coming', *The New York Times* (online, 26 March 2021) <www.nytimes.com/live/2021/03/26/business/stock-market-today>.

[19] Financial Stability Board, *BigTech Firms in Finance in Emerging Market and Developing Economies: Market Developments and Potential: Financial Stability Implications* (Report, 12 October 2020) 7–8 <www.fsb.org/2020/10/bigtech-firms-in-finance-in-emerging-market-and-developing-economies>.

records. Certain types of businesses may also be suitable for crowdfunding (see Section IV). Governments that have at various times limited the use of crowdfunding platforms in their jurisdictions may revisit this stance, or at times support suitable campaigns by officially declaring their conditional regulatory blessing.

A. *Digital Identity*

Digitally identifying people by connecting to official repositories of identity data will continue to grow in importance. This can enable governments to implement remedial policies particularly by direct fiscal assistance. The GFC of 2008 saw substantial resources in some jurisdictions wasted through the misallocation of stimulus payments to deceased or non-existent citizens. Digital identity verification and authentication should ensure only intended recipients receive stimulus payments. The threat of fraud and identity theft can be greatly minimised through strengthened digital identity infrastructure.[20] It is important to note, however, that authentication and verification of an identity via a digital channel should be the focus, and not the creation of separate 'digital identities' or avatars. The need, during the pandemic, for non-face-to-face on-boarding and other activities has dramatically highlighted the importance and role of sovereign digital identity systems, particularly for constraining money laundering and terrorist financing.

B. *Behaviour Management*

Social distancing and quarantine policies in many parts of the world saw a massive increase in e-commerce. The use of digital platforms to shop, pay, and organise delivery of all types of goods grew exponentially across 2020, and the resultant behavioural and purchasing pattern changes seem set to endure, and continue to grow, long beyond the pandemic.

The wisdom of crowds was perhaps most apparent in the context of mass consumer behaviour. The purchasing behaviour of the consuming public provided real-time information and highlighted public consternation and full-blown panics. Using digital financing tools to aggregate purchase information (of medical supplies, for example, or toilet paper) can help identify emerging panics in time to facilitate possible government interventions, by way of either product supply or reassurance.

C. *Information Sharing*

Trusted data and information are the lifeblood of the digital economy. From advertising to public health to detection of criminal activities, the ability to access and use data and information is critical. As in war, in this crisis, accurate and factual data

---

[20] Arner, Buckley, and Zetzsche (n 16); Douglas W Arner et al (n 16).

and information have meant the difference between life and death. Establishing a well-funded, national coordinating body – such as a Health Stability Board – as a crisis management tool could ensure timely information exchange – especially between the public and private sectors. Emergency government powers may be used to overcome data privacy and protection obstacles and intensify information exchange on health *and* financial/economic matters. Legal frameworks that mediate principles of data sharing and broader digital governance policies, such as Open Banking in many jurisdictions, and the far broader Consumer Data Right regime in Australia,[21] will be imperative in such an approach.

D. *Collective Decision-Making*

Corporate decisions often depend on collective decision-making by boards and general meetings of shareholders. This can, among other things, relate to dividends, share buy-backs, or recapitalisation. Keeping the economy afloat in the pandemic required alternatives to in-person meetings. For this reason, many Parliaments around the globe provided for digital, instead of in-person, meetings in corporate governance rules. In particular, most advanced economies, by way of crisis legislation, allowed for some type of remote voting and/or virtual shareholder meetings.[22]

E. *Tokenisation*

Tokens, online banking, and mobile money schemes could also be used to channel funds faster to consumers to provide financial support and to promote economic activity.

IV. DIGITAL FINANCIAL TRANSFORMATION

Starting in the 1960s and building on foundations of electrification in the late nineteenth century, finance has undergone a process of digital transformation, involving digitisation and datafication. Today, finance is not only the most globalised segment of the world's economy but also perhaps the most digitised, datafied, and regulated. This process can be seen across four major axes: (1) global wholesale markets, (2) an explosion of financial technology (FinTech) start-ups particularly since 2008, (3) the unprecedented digital financial transformation in some countries particularly China and India, and (4) the increasing role of large technology companies (BigTechs) and digital financial platforms in financial services. This process of digital financial transformation brings with it massive changes. These changes have

---

[21] Ross P Buckley and Natalia Jevglevskaja, 'Australia's Consumer Data Right: A World Leading Innovation' (UNSW Law Research Paper No. 22–2, February 2022).

[22] Dirk A Zetzsche et al, 'Enhancing Virtual Governance: Comparative Lessons from COVID-19 Company Laws' (2022) 22(1) *Journal of Corporate Law Studies* 115–50.

positive aspects such as greater financial inclusion and negative aspects such as new risks. As we have laid out in detail in Chapter 2, the changes since the 2008 GFC have been unprecedented, particularly in terms of the speed of technological evolution and of new entrants, including BigTechs and start-ups.

This long-term process of digitisation and datafication of finance has been increasingly combined with related technologies including big data[23] and AI,[24] distributed ledgers and blockchain,[25] cryptocurrencies,[26] smart contracts,[27] RegTech and SupTech,[28] and digital identity,[29] in a new era of FinTech. The result of these new technologies, which will be discussed in detail in Part II, is novel services with disruptive effects on existing intermediaries, such as crowdfunding and crowdlending, among many others.[30] This process of digitisation and datafication with new technologies can be seen across developed and developing markets, with the latter often displaying even faster digital financial transformation. In this environment, COVID-19 has driven digitalisation further and faster, particularly in finance.

Technology and finance have together been central in enabling resilient responses to the pandemic, especially its attendant lockdowns around the world. Lockdowns and social distancing rapidly accelerated digitalisation worldwide. If the pandemic had struck a mere decade earlier, the technology of that era would have provided

[23] Solon Barocas and Andrew D Selbst, 'Big Data's Disparate Impact' (2016) 104(3) *California Law Review* 671; Dirk A Zetzsche et al, 'From FinTech to TechFin: The Regulatory Challenges of Data-Driven Finance' (2018) 14(2) *New York University Journal of Law and Business* 393; Dirk A Zetzsche et al, 'The Evolution and Future of Data-Driven Finance in the EU' (2020) 57(2) *Common Market Law Review* 331.

[24] Ross P Buckley et al, 'Regulating Artificial Intelligence in Finance: Putting the Human in the Loop' (2021) 43(1) *Sydney Law Review* 43.

[25] See Christian Catalini and Joshua S Gans, 'Some Simple Economics of the Blockchain' (Working Paper No 22952, National Bureau of Economic Research, December 2016); Dirk A Zetzsche, Ross P Buckley, and Douglas W Arner, 'The Distributed Liability of Distributed Ledgers: Legal Risks of Blockchain' [2018] 2018(4) *University of Illinois Law Review* 1361; Usha R Rodrigues, 'Law and the Blockchain' (2019) 104(2) *Iowa Law Review* 679.

[26] Philipp Hacker and Chris Thomale, 'Crypto-Securities Regulation: ICOs, Token Sales and Cryptocurrencies under EU Financial Law' (2018) 15(4) *European Company and Financial Law Review* 645; Dirk A Zetzsche et al, 'The ICO Gold Rush: It's a Scam, It's a Bubble, It's a Super Challenge for Regulators' (2019) 60(2) *Harvard International Law Journal* 267.

[27] Jeremy M Sklaroff, 'Smart Contracts and the Cost of Inflexibility' (2017) 166(1) *University of Pennsylvania Law Review* 263; Kevin Werbach and Nicholas Cornell, 'Contracts Ex Machina' (2017) 67(2) *Duke Law Journal* 313; Max Raskin, 'The Law and Legality of Smart Contracts' (2017) 1(2) *Georgetown Law Technology Review* 305.

[28] Douglas W Arner, Jànos Barberis, and Ross P Buckley, 'FinTech, RegTech and the Reconceptualization of Financial Regulation' (2017) 37(3) *Northwestern Journal of International Law and Business* 371; Kristen Silverberg et al, *RegTech in Financial Services: Solutions for Compliance and Reporting* (Report, Institute of International Finance Report, March 2016).

[29] Douglas W Arner et al, 'The Identity Challenge in Finance: From Analogue Identity to Digitized Identification to Digital KYC Utilities' (2019) 20 *European Business Organisation Law Review* 55.

[30] John Armour and Luca Enriques, 'The Promise and Perils of Crowdfunding: Between Corporate Finance and Consumer Contracts' (2018) 81(1) *Modern Law Review* 51; Dirk Zetzsche and Christina Preiner, 'Cross-Border Crowdfunding: Towards a Single Crowdlending and Crowdinvesting Market for Europe' (2018) 19(2) *European Business Organisation Law Review* 217.

far fewer of us an ability to work from home. Likewise, shopping and the like would have entailed far more face-to-face interactions between people.

Since 2020, there are four major areas where the digitalisation of finance is moving forward rapidly as a result of the 'digitisation of everything': electronic payments, use of technology for regulatory and supervisory purposes, digital identity and market integrity, and BigTech and digital finance platforms.

A. *Electronic Money and Payments*

The most obvious and immediate impact of COVID-19 on finance was in the dramatic expansion in electronic payments.[31] This was necessary due to lockdowns and an increase in e-commerce participation.[32] This continued the trend of consumers preferring digital payments over cash and of many governments preferring electronic funds as the means by which to provide financial support. These trends have been supported by a range of national projects to make digital wallets widely available and to launch fast payment systems.

The era of COVID-19 has also been marked by dramatic increases in interest and engagement with digital money. This can be seen directly in the increase in prices and use of cryptocurrencies and other digital assets and tokens. It can also be seen in the dramatic increase in the number of jurisdictions working on, experimenting with and, in the case of the Bahamas and Nigeria, launching central bank digital currencies (CBDCs).

Technologies – both centralised and decentralised – are revolutionising payments and money. Reflecting these trends, the Group of 20 has launched a payments roadmap,[33] incentivised by the announcement of the Facebook Libra/Diem project in 2019[34] and the evolution of cryptocurrencies, reflecting the potential to use technology to build better money and payment systems. All of these major technological developments will be considered in more detail in Part II.

B. *RegTech and SupTech*

The second pandemic-driven evolution in digital finance has come in RegTech and SupTech. Starting from the status ex ante as described in Chapter 3, faced with the need to work from home, financial institutions, and their staff – from trading to

---

[31] Committee on Payments and Market Infrastructures, *Covid-19 Accelerated the Digitalisation of Payments* (Report, Bank for International Settlements, 12 September 2021) 1–2 <www.bis.org/statistics/payment_stats/commentary2112.pdf>.

[32] Viviana Alfonso et al, *E-commerce in the Pandemic and Beyond* (Bank for International Settlements Bulletin No. 36, 12 January 2021) 1–2 <www.bis.org/publ/bisbull36.pdf>.

[33] Financial Stability Board, *G20 Roadmap for Enhancing Cross-border Payments: First Consolidated Progress Report* (Report, 13 October 2021) <www.fsb.org/wp-content/uploads/P131021-1.pdf>.

[34] Dirk A Zetzsche, Ross P Buckley and Douglas W Arner, 'Regulating Libra' (2021) 41(1) *Oxford Journal of Legal Studies* 80.

legal, and from compliance to management – have had to rapidly implement digitised communications and working systems. Globally, this process has accelerated
the digitalisation of finance, particularly that of the incumbents and large financial
institutions which had been lagging. This has driven a stampede to cloud-based
infrastructure to support the full range of processes and activities.

COVID-19 has also transformed the attitudes and approaches of regulators, supervisors, and central banks around the world to the use of technology in their own
operations.[35] Where pre-COVID-19 meetings were invariably face to face, now they
are mostly virtual. Supervisory functions, including those that would have been on
site, have had to move online. Interactions with industry compliance staff have also
moved online. Consequently, central banks, regulators, and supervisors are looking
not only at how their technological infrastructure can be improved but also at digitising and datafying their own operations and systems. Beyond finance, other regulated
industries are also increasingly using technology for compliance, monitoring, implementation, and enforcement, with health, travel, and energy all growing very rapidly.

C. *Market Integrity and Digital Identity*

A third major area where COVID-19 has transformed approaches is in market
integrity, particularly relating to money laundering (AML) and terrorist financing
(CFT).[36] Prior to COVID-19, while a range of jurisdictions were implementing
sovereign digital identification systems for individuals (with India's Aadhaar a particularly high profile and effective example that we have discussed in Chapter 3),
the Financial Action Taskforce (FATF) was slow to recognise that digital identification could not only be as good as traditional paper-based systems but *better*.[37] This
reflects an increasing understanding among law enforcement and policy communities of the potential to build better systems for market integrity based on digital identification (for both individuals and entities) combined with systems for tracking and
tracing transactions. The EU is emerging as a leader in this context, but the trend is
clear among major jurisdictions around the world.

In addition to individual digital identity, there are also an increasing range of
efforts to develop digital identities for firms and businesses, which has the potential
to have a huge impact, particularly on SMEs.

---

[35] See, for example, Kenton Beerman, Jermy Prenio, and Raihan Zamil, 'Suptech Tools for Prudential
Supervision and Their Use during the Pandemic' (Financial Stability Institute Insights on policy
implementation No. 37, Bank for International Settlements, December 2021) <www.bis.org/fsi/publ/
insights37.pdf>.

[36] See Juan Carlos Crisanto and Jermy Prenio, 'Financial Crime in Times of Covid-19: AML and Cyber
Resilience Measures' (Financial Stability Institute Briefs No. 7, Bank for International Settlements,
May 2020) <www.bis.org/fsi/fsibriefs7.pdf>.

[37] Financial Action Task Force, *COVID-19-Related Money Laundering and Terrorist Financing: Risk
and Policy Responses* (Report, May 2020) 14, 18 <www.fatf-gafi.org/media/fatf/documents/COVID-19-
AML-CFT.pdf>.

D. *BigTech and Digital Finance Platforms*

Long-term trends of digitisation and datafication, combined with COVID-driven digitalisation, the network effects which characterise data, and the economies of scope and scale which characterise finance, have led to a global trend towards the emergence of large digital platforms. This is evident in payments (e.g., PayPal, Visa, MasterCard, Alipay, WeChatPay), in asset management (e.g., BlackRock, Vanguard), in market-making (e.g., Citadel, Virtu), and in lending (e.g., Ant, Amazon). Facebook's announcement of its Libra project in 2019 and the decision to halt the Ant IPO in 2020 clearly mark the beginning of a new period of digital finance – FinTech 4.0 – characterised by dominant platforms and ecosystems, emerging from BigTechs, incumbents, FinTechs, and TechFins.[38] Going forward, the challenge will be formulating a strategy to balance the benefits of these platforms with their risks.

V. CONCLUSION

As a result of the post-2008 regulatory reforms combined with the technological transformation of finance over the past decade, digital financial infrastructure around the world has proven robust to the incredible strains placed upon it by the COVID-19 pandemic. In this rapidly evolving and unprecedented context, digital financial innovations are being relied upon at both micro and macro levels to address everything from basic logistical means of transacting to the strategically important financial fundamentals – and everything in between. These fundamentals include liquidity, systemic stability, and the ability of the economy to weather unforeseen economic or geopolitical shocks. The primary measure taken to combat the spread of COVID-19 – 'social distancing' – advanced digitisation and embedded e-commerce and FinTech into modern life. Beyond behavioural adaptation, widespread exposure to the cost savings, convenience and hygiene associated with digital finance are consolidating FinTech usage more broadly, with potentially important and enduring benefits for financial inclusion and sustainable development.[39] This can be seen particularly in the context of electronic payments.

The digital financial infrastructure has performed resiliently and responsively in the context of COVID-19. This is hugely significant and should not be undervalued. It highlights the value of regulations geared towards financial stability, and more generally, the critical role of digital finance within the contemporary financial

---

[38] Douglas Arner et al, 'Governing FinTech 4.0: BigTech, Platform Finance and Sustainable Development' (2022) 27(1) *Fordham Journal of Corporate and Financial Law* 1.

[39] Dirk A Zetzsche, Ross P Buckley, and Douglas W Arner, 'FinTech for Financial Inclusion: Driving Sustainable Growth' in Julia Walker, Alma Pekmezovic, and Gordon Walker (eds), *Sustainable Development Goals: Harnessing Business to Achieve the SDG's through Finance, Technology and Law Reform* (Wiley, 2019) 179; Douglas W Arner et al, 'Sustainability, FinTech and Financial Inclusion' (2020) 21(1) *European Business Organisation Law Review* 7.

system. Digital finance has also played and is continuing to play an important role in supporting health and economic responses to this existential sustainability crisis. For sure, nothing is without costs. In the case of COVID-19, the combination of central bank liquidity and digital finance is resulting in strong inflation, volatility, and asset price bubbles, each of which in turn brings new financial stability risks.[40]

Digitisation is proving to be a potential double-edged sword: digitisation of finance and everything else brings new opportunities for financial, economic, and social interactions and business, with great potential to support financial stability and sustainable development. At the same time, digitisation brings tremendous new risks and challenges: TechRisks, in particular, relating to cybersecurity, data concentration, and privacy. These risks are the subject of major policy debates around the world and present significant legal and regulatory challenges. What role will data and technology play in our financial systems, economies, and societies? In addition, how can governments, through law and regulation, balance the tremendous positive potential with the associated and emerging risks? These are the key emerging policy fault lines.

COVID-19 will not be the last pandemic nor the last existential sustainability crisis. If anything, as the pace of change accelerates, it is likely the world will face an increasing range of existential sustainability crises going forward, ranging from pandemics to climate change and geopolitics. The 2008 GFC offered an opportunity to build a more stable and resilient financial system. The experiences since 2020 with COVID-19 suggest these efforts were broadly successful. (Although the current stresses on the international financial system, arising in large measure from the long periods of quantitative easing, are different in kind and possibly scale.) The COVID-19 crisis offers an opportunity to build even more resilient and effective digital financial infrastructure that will prove robust in future existential sustainability crises and underpin vital new tools and systems to respond to such crises when they occur. At the same time, this digitisation brings with it important fundamental questions for societies around legal and regulatory approaches to digital finance so as to balance its positives with its potential for tremendous risk.

The reliability and consistency of this digital lifeline, should it continue to work well, is transforming FinTech – especially electronic payments – from an entrepreneurial novelty to an indispensable element of modern life, to the one crisis management tool humankind and regulators alike rely upon, to mitigate the impact of the ongoing crisis of various kinds: famine, warfare, pestilence, and droughts.

---

[40] See Financial Stability Board, *COVID-19 Pandemic: Financial Stability Implications and Policy Measures Taken* (Report to the G20, 15 April 2020) 1 <www.fsb.org/2020/04/covid-19-pandemic-financial-stability-implications-and-policy-measures-taken/>; Financial Stability Board, *Financial Policies in the Wake of COVID-19: Supporting Equitable Recovery and Addressing Effects from Scarring in the Financial Sector* (Final Report, 14 November 2022) <www.fsb.org/2022/11/financial-policies-in-the-wake-of-covid-19-supporting-equitable-recovery-and-addressing-effects-from-scarring-in-the-financial-sector-final-report/>.

6

Drivers of Change

Efficiency, Financial Inclusion, and Sustainability

SUMMARY

This chapter analyses the drivers of the digital financial transformation analysed in the previous chapters. We argue that the digital transformation of finance has been driven by the quests for (i) efficiency, (ii) financial inclusion, and (iii) sustainability. These three factors are necessarily intertwined: financial inclusion underpins long-term-oriented economies, and sustainable yet inefficient and unprofitable services are doomed to fail. Efficiency in turn supports inclusion and sustainable development.

I. INTRODUCTION

As detailed in previous chapters, over the past decade, regulators have had to respond to the digital transformation of finance, today referred to as FinTech. At the same time, sustainable development is a very high priority shared global objective, which increasingly centres upon the United Nations Sustainable Development Goals (UN SDGs) combined with UN climate change commitments. The UN SDGs provide a framework of detailed objectives and criteria for pursuing sustainable development. Central banks and financial regulators across the world are considering how to enhance sustainable development in the context of their wider mandates for financial and economic development, monetary and financial stability, financial integrity, and consumer protection.

Sustainable finance and FinTech are now major research interests and policy foci of most regulators, as demonstrated by a range of regulatory initiatives promoted by, inter alia, the United Nations (UN), the European Union (EU) and its Member States, the United Kingdom (UK), and a range of other Parliaments around the world.[1]

---

[1] See Cristina Chueca Vergara and Luis Ferruz Agudo, 'Fintech and Sustainability: Do They Affect Each Other?' (2021) 13(13) *Sustainability* 7012:1–19; David Mhlanga, 'The Role of Financial Inclusion and FinTech in Addressing Climate-Related Challenges in the Industry 4.0: Lessons for Sustainable Development Goals' (2022) *Frontiers in Climate* 4:949178.

Financial inclusion is likewise a focus of current global policy attention, driven by the G20,[2] World Bank,[3] and major development organisations.[4]

Yet few have linked sustainable finance, FinTech, and financial inclusion. We argue in this chapter that the three are linked as together they drive the development of stable, efficient financial digital systems. Further, we show that efficiency, financial inclusion, and sustainability are necessarily intertwined: each depends on the other. Financial inclusion is the precondition for a long-term-oriented economy, while efficiency is needed for businesses to be profitable so that they may deliver sustainability and environmental goals.

This cross-disciplinary perspective is crucial: while most research has focused on these three fields as separate, unrelated silos of knowledge,[5] this chapter follows the practical approach taken by development bodies. Their interdisciplinary tendency is demonstrated by widely acknowledged reports of the G20, UN,[6] and the Alliance for Financial Inclusion.[7]

We start in Sections II and III by analysing how efficiency and financial inclusion considerations, respectively, kickstarted the digital transformation of finance and then proceed in Section IV to show how sustainability has provided further impetus in recent years. We then analyse in Section V the interrelationship between the three factors, concluding that all three together explain the different elements of FinTech and RegTech seen today, before concluding in Section VI.

[2] See Global Partnership for Financial Inclusion, G20 2020 *Financial Inclusion Action Plan* (Report, 20 October 2020) <www.gpfi.org/publications/g20-2020-financial-inclusion-action-plan>.

[3] See the World Bank's financial inclusion policy work at <www.worldbank.org/en/topic/financialinclusion>.

[4] Including the International Monetary Fund, the Organisation for Economic Co-operation and Development, and others, non-governmental organisations such as Alliance for Financial Inclusion, The Toronto Centre, and Microfinance Centre, as well as the state-sponsored development banks (European Investment Bank, Asian Development Bank, Inter-American Development Bank, Federal Deposit Insurance Corporation, etc.).

[5] To our knowledge, there are three exceptions: Douglas W Arner et al, 'Sustainability, FinTech and Financial Inclusion' (2020) 21(1) *European Business Organization Law Review* 7; Iris HY Chiu and Edward F Greene, 'The Marriage of Technology, Markets and Sustainable (and) Social Finance' (2019) 20(1) *European Business Organisation Law Review* 139; Dirk A Zetzsche, Ross P Buckley, and Douglas W Arner, 'FinTech for Financial Inclusion: Driving Sustainable Growth' in Julia Walker, Alma Pekmezovic, and Gordon Walker (eds), *Sustainable Development Goals: Harnessing Business to Achieve the SDGs through Finance, Technology, and Law Reform* (Wiley 2019) 177.

[6] Global Partnership for Financial Inclusion (n 2); Global Partnership for Financial Inclusion, G20 *Financial Inclusion Action Plan Progress Report 2017–2020* (Report, October 2020); Douglas Arner et al, 'A Principles-Based Approach to the Governance of BigFintechs' (Technical Paper 3.3, UNDP, UNCDF Dialogue on Global Digital Finance Governance, October 2021) <www.undp.org/sites/g/files/zskgke326/files/2021-10/UNDP-UNCDF-TP-3-3-A-Principles-based-Approach-to-the-Governance-of-BigFintechs-EN.pdf>.

[7] AFI, 'Inclusive Green Finance' (Web Page, 2022) <www.afi-global.org/thematic-areas/inclusive-green-finance/>.

II. THE ECONOMICS OF FINTECH: DRIVING EFFICIENCY

At the heart of FinTech and RegTech lie the efficiencies and performance enhancements arising from technology. These are generated by three economic features of FinTech and technology generally: (i) conventional economies of scale, (ii) data-driven economies of scale, and (iii) network effects. These factors together explain why we often see FinTech firms develop *digital finance platforms* to offer their services.[8]

Information technology enables a financial institution to decrease the costs of output per service to a level where the income generated from each additional customer or client accrues almost entirely to its profits. While this may well prompt the need for a regulatory response to the resulting market concentration and monopoly power, to a real extent these factors drive the digital transformation of finance: if the winner takes almost all the profits, there is a strong incentive, as we have seen over and over again, to invest enormous resources to win.

1. Conventional Economies of Scale

Economies of scale refer to the reduction in per-unit production costs arising from the increased production of units.[9] FinTech business models exhibit these conventional economies of scale because the costs of providing the service to a high number of users are often fixed. Once the applications have been coded, the interfaces established, and the servers set up or leased, connecting each additional client incurs very low marginal costs. Where additional users mean additional marginal costs for energy and data warehousing, these additional costs per user are often offset by the additional data these users create. These data allow the platform provider to choose, more or less freely, which services will be charged for and which services will be provided ostensibly for free. This platform economy is often called the gig economy or sharing economy.

A useful example is the asset management industry – particularly with passive investment – where large entities can invest in software programming and development themselves, while small asset managers are usually price takers who must pay software licensing and data warehousing fees that are high, relative to their business size. The more important the technology is for the industry, and the more software tools that are required, the higher these costs are in proportion to other expenses,

---

[8] Daniel Haberly et al, 'Asset Management as a Digital Platform Industry: A Global Network Perspective' (2019) 106 *Geoforum* 167, 169.

[9] These scale economies are particularly present in software markets where the costs of the original application ('first copy') are enormous, while the costs of the second and subsequent copies are minimal and become close to zero. While licensing models and modern anti-piracy devices restrict software users from making use of these characteristics, the software producer and licensor are not bound by these restrictions and are able, in principle, if pressed by competitors to reduce the price.

and the greater the incentive to subscribe to an existing platform that relieves the small managers of this burden. Given technology is rapidly becoming ever more important, smaller asset managers have no choice but to contract with a platform or be inhibited in their growth by IT limitations and costs.

2. Data-Driven Economies of Scale

The second type of economies of scale result from the data collected and used for the application. In simple terms: '[m]ore information lets firms develop better services, which attracts more users, which in turn generate more data.'[10] Where risk management depends on data, such management should improve when the digital finance provider can collect more and better structured data.

For example, Blackrock, one of the largest service providers to investment funds worldwide, has developed a risk data aggregating and risk management system named Aladdin, which stands for 'Asset, Liability and Debt and Derivative Investment Network' and which we discuss further below. Aladdin monitors more than 2,000 risk factors each day, from interest rates to currencies, and performs 5,000 portfolio stress tests and 180 million option-adjusted calculations each week[11] – far more than any other risk analytics form in the world. Accordingly, no other risk analytics firm can match Aladdin's predictive capabilities.

3. Network Effects

Digital finance exhibits strong network effects. Network effects occur where an additional user of a service adds value to the product for other users – the more users, the greater the benefit.[12] For instance, a telephone is of little use if the phone network has few subscribers. The more people who can be called, the more valuable the phone. Network effects are particularly prominent in financial services for several reasons.

First, the value of a software-based 'network' grows in proportion to the numbers of copies installed in financial services firms, as the look and feel of software becomes embedded in human processes. Users know where to click, which shortcuts to use, and how to upload data or link to the Internet. The more particular software is used among specialist financial services firms, the more employees expect this software and its features in their work environment.

[10] The Economist, *A New School in Chicago: How Regulators Can Prevent Excessive Concentration Online* (Special Report, 28 June 2018) <www.economist.com/special-report/2018/06/28/how-regulators-can-prevent-excessive-concentration-online>.

[11] BlackRock, 'Risk Managers', *Aladdin* (Web Page, 2022) <www.blackrock.com/aladdin/benefits/risk-managers>.

[12] See Amrit Tiwana, *Platform Ecosystems: Aligning Architecture, Governance, and Strategy* (Morgan Kaufmann, 2014) 33–48 (analysing the benefits to users of greater total users).

Second, each additional user adds data to the existing pool. Take again the example of risk management and BlackRock's Aladdin: where risk management can draw on more data from more firms, the predictive power of the platform's algorithms improves. As Aladdin's risk management data reflect the exposure of the portfolios managed by the world's largest asset managers (although in an anonymised way and with information barriers preventing the transfer of inside information), the data provided and generated by their clients form the basis of Aladdin's 'collective intelligence'. This turns into a business rationale in itself: the data generated by its users provide the very reason other clients seek to license Aladdin's services; at the same time, since these data could be used for front-running the strategies of these managers, rules addressing data confidentiality, use, and protection are key.

In this way, Aladdin overcomes the main deficiency of firm-specific data pools which suffer from data shortages in relation to low frequency risk events. Among these, internal fraud, business disruption, and IT failures are potentially of 'high severity'; that is, these operational risks can threaten the existence of a financial institution. Aladdin's predictive power is not impaired by such data shortages as it can use the data of all of its asset manager clients rather than just the data generated by BlackRock itself. In this case, *all* network participants benefit from pooling risk data.

BlackRock is very clear in stressing the upsides of these network effects of Aladdin:

> More than just technology, Aladdin powers your firm's Collective Intelligence by providing tools to help your organization communicate effectively, address problems more quickly, and make decisions at every step of the investment process. And Aladdin's Collective Intelligence gets better with every new user, and every new asset that joins the platform.[13]

A. *Platforms*

The economic features described above are transforming the financial services industry into a platform industry. In plain language, platforms are 'a place or opportunity for communicating ideas and information.'[14] In the digital finance context, the term 'platform' refers to a systems architecture where multiple applications are linked to and through one technical infrastructure so that users can use one major integrating software system in order to run all applications written for that system. Platformisation produces financial ecosystems with multiple services provided to clients via the platform. The platform serves as the indispensable technical core that links all services and clients, and often also provides some services itself.

Functioning as a 'spider in the web', a digital finance platform gathers data concerning users and their activities, which is then used to further develop platform

---

[13] BlackRock, 'Powering Collective Intelligence', *Aladdin* (Web Page, 2022) <www.BlackRock.com/aladdin/benefits/organizations>.

[14] *Merriam-Webster* (online at 2 November 2022) 'Platform'.

applications and services to users, resulting in the gradual expansion of the platform in scale and scope. In turn, the overhead costs of the services provided gradually decline, compared to the economic value provided. The characteristic of platforms is 'some mixture of both technology-enabled efficiency enhancement, and technology-enabled organizational arbitrage', enabled by the control the platform providers gain over markets while enhancing their efficiency.[15]

Risk management systems drawing on deep data pools, for instance, are expected to gain ever-greater predictive powers; and platform providers can generate additional returns by leveraging this data power into related, yet new, types of business (in the absence of legal restrictions). For instance, if risk data suggest a certain asset combination assists in hedging a given type of risk, this insight can underpin the issuance of a derivative or fund product that offers that combination of assets.

Owing to the evolution of the MAGMAs and BATs, features of technology platforms have become a major focus of contemporary legal scholarship.[16] As has become obvious since the COVID-19 pandemic, e-commerce platforms provide unique benefits – centralised offerings of products and decentralised delivery of them. They also need e-payments, thus promoting digital finance. At the same time, the platform economy is seen as a catalyst for social issues that touch all aspects of society, ranging across privacy, product liability, public housing, discrimination, labour and employment law, and tax law. Platforms are also at the heart of the discussions about 'fake news' and electoral manipulation as well as manipulation of consumer prices, search results, and scoring power.

B. *Examples of Platforms*

It is instructive to consider examples of FinTech developments, from both private and public sectors, which demonstrate the benefits to be gained from combining conventional and data-driven scale economies and network effects.

1. BlackRock's Aladdin

At its core, Aladdin is a technology tool that allows asset managers to 'communicate effectively, address problems quickly, and make informed decisions at every step of the investment process.'[17] BlackRock began developing Aladdin for its own portfolio

---

[15] Daniel Haberly et al (n 8) 167, 168 (discussing cost reductions and efficiency enhancements resulting from disruptive platforms in markets not traditionally centred around information and communications technology).

[16] See Tianxiang He, 'Online Content Platforms, Copyright Decision-Making Algorithms and Fundamental Rights Protection in China' (2022) 14(1) *Law, Innovation and Technology* 71; Michael Guihot and Hannah McNaught, 'Platform Power, Technology, and Law: Consumer Powerlessness in Informational Capitalism' (2021) 13(2) *Law, Innovation and Technology* 510.

[17] Dirk A Zetzsche et al, 'Digital Finance Platforms: Towards a New Regulatory Paradigm' (2020) 23(1) *University of Pennsylvania Journal of Business Law* 273, 288.

and risk management, investment processes, and trade execution in 1993. From there, Aladdin moved into automatic position-keeping, record-keeping, and control of risk exposure. Aladdin's capabilities became known outside the asset management community during the 2008 GFC, when governments globally struggled to evaluate the risk exposure underlying the portfolios of global investment banks. By excluding the investment banks themselves, due to their obvious conflicts, and by using the reach of Aladdin's data and analytical tools, BlackRock was able to devise and value the multi-billion-dollar refinancing transactions necessary to prevent the collapse of the US financial system. The platform has since expanded into risk analysis and other parts of the investment process, and evolved into an end-to-end investment platform that 'combines sophisticated risk analytics with comprehensive portfolio management, trading and operations tools on a single platform to power informed decision-making, effective risk management, efficient trading and operational scale.'[18]

Aladdin is a hosted service: the technical infrastructure, system administration, and interfacing with data providers and industry utilities are operated by BlackRock's IT and technical staff, who focus on creating data and analyses for clients. The scale of Aladdin is impressive. More than $21.6 trillion in assets, around 10 per cent of the world's stocks and bonds, depend on Aladdin's services – a figure equal to four times the value of all cash in the world, the annual GDP of the United States, or the total US stock market capitalisation. Approximately 55,000 investment professionals globally rely on Aladdin and Aladdin Wealth. Aladdin hosts the portfolios of at least 240 institutions worldwide, including some of the largest asset owners (e.g., California State Teachers' Retirement System (CalSTRS) and competitors including Schroders and Vanguard).[19] The technology services revenue of BlackRock from Aladdin systems increased by 12 per cent in 2021 to US$1.3 billion.[20]

2. Ant Group

Although Aladdin is a giant, numerically, Ant Group, the provider of the world's largest financial ecosystem, is even more impressive. Ant Group is the financial arm of the Chinese BigTech, Alibaba. Developed originally as a support function for e-commerce in the form of Alipay, Ant (Ant Financial prior to July 2020 when renamed Ant) today comprises a payment system, a custody function for its clients, robo-advisory and asset management services, and credit, investment, and insurance products of its own and other firms. A particularly interesting service within the Ant

[18] Ibid.
[19] Ibid 279, 287–90; Rebecca Ungarino, 'Here Are 9 Fascinating Facts to Know about Blackrock, the World's Largest Asset Manager', *Insider* (Web Page, 11 March 2022) <www.businessinsider.com/what-to-know-about-blackrock-larry-fink-biden-cabinet-facts-2020-12>.
[20] BlackRock, *Investing with Purpose: BlackRock 2021 Annual Report* (Report, 2021) 11.

ecosystem is the money market mutual fund Yu'e Bao, which within three years of launching had grown to be the world's largest mutual fund.[21] While now no longer the largest, it remains one of the largest in the world.

Ant also became one of the largest providers of both consumer and SME lending in China. Ant's objective was to provide a comprehensive ecosystem that allows customers to buy whatever they want through e-commerce platforms and physical and virtual merchants throughout the world via Alipay. Ant funds itself through fees, sales of data, and borrowing in China's Interbank Bond Market. It then lends to individuals to help them buy products through Alibaba and other vendors while also providing credit to businesses to enable them to expand their operations, income, and profits. Ant in turn securitises those loans and is one of the largest issuers of asset-backed securities in China. More than 700 million Chinese active users can, in turn, use the funds in Ant's Alipay system for other payments or investments, earning attractive returns through money market funds, an increasing range of ETFs, and other investment products including insurance.

The Ant ecosystem covers all aspects of finance. Ant calls it 'Digital Life'. Hundreds of millions of individuals and firms participate in its financial ecosystem, interacting with third-company providers and funding commercial borrowers both directly and through the capital markets.

Ant is anything but a financial ant – it is one of the highest valued financial companies globally. In 2018, Ant raised $14 billion in venture capital financing, or 35 per cent of all venture capital funding worldwide that year, more than all US FinTech companies combined. At its height in October 2020, immediately prior to its planned IPO in Hong Kong and Shanghai, it had a valuation of US$280 billion. Had that IPO taken place, it would have been one of the world's largest financial companies.[22]

Alipay, its payments service, is estimated to have around 900 million users in China and 1.3 billion users globally.[23] It has over one-half of the Chinese payments market and executes more than $16 trillion in transactions, equivalent to four times China's nominal GDP. The number of merchants that accept payments by Alipay is around 80 million.[24] In August 2022, there were around 19 million visits to Alipay .com from around the world.[25] The reach of Ant extends beyond payments. All of

---

[21] Quan Yue and Denise Jia, 'China Curbs Money Market Funds, among Them Ant's Yu'e Bao', *NikkeiAsia* (online, 17 January 2022) <https://asia.nikkei.com/Spotlight/Caixin/China-curbs-money-market-funds-among-them-Ant-s-Yu-e-Bao>.

[22] If the IPO had proceeded as expected, Ant would have had about the market capitalisation of PayPal, about two-thirds that of JP Morgan, one-third that of Facebook, and one-fifth that of Google, though Ant and Alibaba combined would not be close in size to these US companies.

[23] Michael Singer, 'Alipay Statistics 2022: Market Share, Facts and Marketing Trends', *EnterpriseAppsToday* (Web Page, 10 November 2022) <www.enterpriseappstoday.com/stats/alipay-statistics.html#:~:text=To%20 date%2C%20Alipay%20has%20around,platform%20for%20the%20year%202022>.

[24] Ibid.

[25] Ibid.

China's 116 mutual fund managers are on the platform reaching an additional 180 million users. The potential scope of economic and financial disruption caused by a failure or hacking of Ant's platform is immense and these concerns – among many others – led to a decision to subject it to increased regulation by mainland Chinese and Hong Kong regulators, causing the IPO in November 2020 to be suspended indefinitely.

3. Aadhaar as Public Sector Example

Efficiencies are not only generated by private players seeking to dominate a market. The public sector can also seek to increase the efficiency of the financial system, making use of the same economic features. Take the example of India's Aadhaar system, analysed in detail in Chapter 10:[26] Aadhaar has proven extremely useful in terms of financial inclusion and efficiency, facilitating access to financial accounts and digitisation of government payments and services. This, when combined with other elements of the India Stack strategy, has enabled far faster and more secure public spending. Aadhar's standardised data interfaces have proven instrumental in increasing efficiency and lowering costs in the private sector. Drawing on Aadhaar, new suppliers created entirely new services, time for opening a bank account fell from weeks to minutes, and bank fees in India plummeted to a level reflecting digital rather than manual processes. All of this would have been impossible in the absence of data-driven and conventional economies of scale and the network effects created by the standards for customer and transactional identification, which lie at the heart of the Aadhaar system.

III. FINANCIAL INCLUSION

Along with efficiency, financial inclusion was one of the early drivers of the FinTech revolution in the Global South, especially in East Africa and parts of East Asia.

A. *Financial Inclusion: A Policy Agenda*

Financial inclusion involves delivering financial services at an affordable cost to all parts of society. It enables people to manage their financial obligations efficiently and think longer term. Financial inclusion thereby reduces poverty and supports wider economic growth.[27]

---

[26] Srijoni Sen, 'A Decade of Aadhaar: Lessons in Implementing a Foundational ID System' (Issue Brief No 292, Observer Research Foundation, May 2019); John Thornhill, 'India's All-Encompassing ID System Holds Warnings for the Rest of World', *Financial Times* (online, 11 November 2021) <www.ft.com/content/337f6d6e-7301-4ef4-a26d-a4e62f602947>.

[27] 'Financial Inclusion', *World Bank* (Web Page, 29 Mar 2022) <www.worldbank.org/en/topic/financialinclusion/overview>.

B. *Technology as Enabler*

Technology has proven critical for financial inclusion. As of 2021, just under 1.9 billion adults lacked access to a financial or mobile money account, some 24 per cent of the world's population.[28] Significantly, though, between 2011 and 2021, account ownership increased by 50 per cent, mostly in developing countries.[29] Much of this progress came from the impact of technology on finance. For example, mobile money has played a major role in increasing financial inclusion in Kenya and East Africa.[30] China has rapidly developed into perhaps the world's most digitised financial system.[31] India has dramatically increased financial access by building the infrastructure for a new digital economy, leading to hundreds of millions of people gaining accounts.[32]

Technology facilitates financial inclusion in three ways. First, technology helps overcome the last mile-issue in remote areas. Where bank branches are distant, the Internet enables digital substitutes. Second, technology allows for better tailoring of financial services to users. For instance, people with lower financial literacy can receive tailor-made services and information, mitigating their inability to make complex financial decisions, or auto-translation software may overcome language barriers in markets with high language diversity. Third, technology may be used to counter abuses, either by embedding financial inclusion requirements into technology ('compliance-by-design') or by detecting exclusive approaches. For example, algorithms employed by the financial institution itself or its regulator can detect whether the institution's credit scoring algorithm excludes certain customer groups in terms of race, age, or gender.

All of this explains the emphasis various regulatory bodies have put on FinTech for Financial Inclusion (FT4FI) initiatives. The 2008 financial crisis prompted sweeping regulatory responses coordinated by the G20 aimed at building a resilient global financial system. This led to the establishment of the Financial Inclusion Experts Group,[33]

---

[28] Asli Demirguc-Kunt et al, *The Global Findex Database 2021: Financial Inclusion, Digital Payments, and Resilience in the Age of COVID-19* (Report, 2022) 11 <www.worldbank.org/en/publication/globalfindex/Report>.

[29] See ibid.

[30] Seth Onyango, 'Africa Accounts for 70% of the World's $1 Trillion Mobile Money Market', *Quartz Africq* (online, 4 May 2022) <https://qz.com/africa/2161960/gsma-70-percent-of-the-worlds-1-trillion-mobile-money-market-is-in-africa/>; GSMA, *State of the Industry Report on Mobile Money 2022* (Report, 2022) 18, 90.

[31] Dagny Dukach, 'Understanding the Rise of Tech in China' (September–October 2022) *Harvard Business Review* <https://hbr.org/2022/09/understanding-the-rise-of-tech-in-china>.

[32] Douglas W Arner et al, 'The Identity Challenge in Finance' (2019) 20(1) *European Business Organization Law Review* 55, 64ff. See also Shruti Jain, 'The G20 Digital Economy Agenda for India' (Occasional Paper, Observer Research Foundation, 13 September 2022).

[33] G20 Financial Inclusion Experts Group, *Innovative Financial Inclusion: Principles and Report on Innovative Financial Inclusion from the Access through Innovation Sub-group of the G20 Financial Inclusion Experts Group* (Report, 25 May 2010) <www.gpfi.org/sites/gpfi/files/documents/Principles%20and%20Report%20on%20Innovative%20Financial%20Inclusion_0.pdf>.

Global Partnership for Financial Inclusion (GPFI), and the endorsement of the first Financial Inclusion Action Plan (FIAP) by G20 leaders in 2010, later revised in 2017 and 2020.[34]

GPFI recognised digital financial solutions as critical to facilitating global financial inclusion in 2016[35] and introduced the G20 High Level Principles for Digital Financial Inclusion (HLPs).[36] Alongside the Recommendations for Responsible Finance[37] and the ID4D,[38] the HLPs encourage and guide governments to embrace digital approaches to financial inclusion. In 2020, the FIAP was updated to reflect the pivotal role of digitisation.[39]

The Alliance for Financial Inclusion (AFI) was established in 2008 by the central banks of developing countries. In 2012, its members signed the historic Maya Declaration on Financial Inclusion, by which developing countries committed to financial inclusion targets and national policy changes.[40] Other agreements have followed.

The UN established the Task Force on Digital Financing in November 2018 to develop strategies that promote financial technology to advance the SDGs. It is committed to 'put[ting] people at the centre', supporting our view that FinTech is an important, possibly the most important, single accelerator for attaining the SDGs.[41]

---

[34] For the latest version, see Global Partnership for Financial Inclusion (n 2); Ross P Buckley, 'The G20'S Performance in Global Financial Regulation' (2014) 37(1) *University of New South Wales Law Journal* 63.

[35] Global Partnership for Financial Inclusion, 'G20 Financial Inclusion Indicators Update' (Research Report, 2016) <www.gpfi.org/sites/gpfi/files/documents/G20%20Financial%20Inclusion%20Indicators%20%282016%20Update%29.pdf>.

[36] Global Partnership for Financial Inclusion, 'G20 High-Level Principles for Digital Financial Inclusion' (Principles, 16 September 2016) <www.gpfi.org/sites/gpfi/files/G20%20High%20Level%20Principles%20for%20Digital%20Financial%20Inclusion.pdf>; Global Partnership for Financial Inclusion, *Digital Financial Inclusion: Emerging Policy Approaches* (Report, 23 May 2017); Global Partnership for Financial Inclusion, 'G20 High-Level Policy Guidelines on Digital Financial Inclusion for Youth, Women and SMEs' (Guidelines, 19 July 2020) <www.gpfi.org/sites/gpfi/files/G20%20High%20Level%20Principles%20for%20Digital%20Financial%20Inclusion.pdf>.

[37] See Centre for Financial Inclusion, 'Detailed Guidance on the Client Protection Principles' (Guidance, 1 June 2019) <www.centerforfinancialinclusion.org/detailed-guidance-on-the-client-protection-principles>; Responsible Finance Forum, *The Responsible Finance Forum (RFF) Begins a New Chapter* (Summary Report, August 2022).

[38] See 'Identification for Development', *World Bank* (Web Page) <https://id4d.worldbank.org/>.

[39] Global Partnership for Financial Inclusion (n 2).

[40] 'Maya Declaration', *AFI* (Web Page) <www.afi-global.org/global-voice/maya-declaration/>; 'Maya Declaration Continues to Evolve', *AFI* (Web Page, 6 November 2017) <www.afi-global.org/news/2017/11/maya-declaration-continues-evolve-financial-inclusion-commitments-66-countries>; AFI, *2021 Maya Declaration Progress Report: A Decade-Long Journey* (Report, 7 March 2022).

[41] 'Task Force on Digital Financing of Sustainable Development Goals', *United Nations Secretary General* (Web Page, 29 November 2018) <www.un.org/sg/en/content/sg/personnel-appointments/2018-11-29/task-force-digital-financing-sustainable-development>; Digital Financing Task Force, *People's Money: Harnessing Digitization to Finance a Sustainable Future* (Report, August 2020) <https://unsdg.un.org/resources/peoples-money-harnessing-digitalization-finance-sustainable-future>.

The COVID-19 pandemic discussed in Chapter 5 has disrupted many parts of the global supply chain. It also created difficulties for advancing the financial inclusion agenda where crucial elements of financial onboarding rely on manual work, particularly around client identification for AML/KYC purposes. Nonetheless, despite the challenges, the pandemic has on balance markedly accelerated financial inclusion, as it forced regulators to accept digital substitutes for in-person contact (see Chapter 5).

C. *Financial Inclusion: A Global South Topic?*

Formal financial exclusion is less widespread in countries in the Global North, but this does not mean that their populations know how to use their bank access well: as of 2014, only 33 per cent of all adults globally (and only 38 per cent of account-owning adults) were found to be financially literate (among them 57 per cent in major advanced economies and 30 per cent in major emerging economies).[42] Financial literacy means the ability to manage one's finances independently, without a financial advisor. Assuming that approximately one-third of the world's population are children, and subtracting the 1.7 billion formally excluded from the financial illiterate, there are *approximately 1.7 billion adults* globally who cannot put their financial services access to good use.

FinTech, if rightly designed and applied (e.g., through robo advisors), could come to these account holders' assistance. However, according to Eurostat, 39 per cent of EU individuals over age 65 did not use the Internet even once in the three-month period surveyed.[43] Despite many EU initiatives and initiatives of EU member states,[44] an analysis of how legislation, with the help of technology, could respond to financial illiteracy is sorely needed.[45] The UK Financial Conduct Authority estimates that 28 per cent of UK adults aged from 75 to 84 years are digitally excluded.[46] At a time where bank branches are being closed – and more bank branches tend to close in poorer quarters than in rich – technological exclusion translates into financial exclusion.

---

[42] See Leora Klapper, Annamaria Lusardi, and Peter Van Oudheusden, 'Financial Literacy around the World' (Research Report, 2015) 16 <https://gflec.org/wp-content/uploads/2015/11/Finlit_paper_16_F2_singles.pdf>.

[43] Eurostat, 'Individuals: Internet Use', *Data Browser* (Web Page, 30 March 2022) <https://ec.europa.eu/eurostat/databrowser/view/ISOC_CI_IFP_IU__custom_915519/default/table?lang=en&bookmarkId=1a84d7ea-0d93-40ff-a7c0-b3b3cfcd62e3>.

[44] See the overview on the European Commission's online platform for adult learning: 'Financial Literacy', *Finance* (Web Page) <https://finance.ec.europa.eu/consumer-finance-and-payments/financial-literacy_en>.

[45] See the recent proposal by Safeguarding Ireland: 'Identifying Risks, Sharing Responsibilities: The Case for a Comprehensive Approach to Safeguarding Vulnerable Adults' (Discussion Paper, May 2022) <www.safeguardingireland.org/wp-content/uploads/2022/05/6439-Safeguarding-Risks-Resp-Report-FA4_lowres.pdf>.

[46] Financial Conduct Authority, *Financial Lives 2020 Survey; The Impact of Coronavirus* (Report, 11 February 2021) 197.

Multiple regulators seek to draw lessons from (and implement) the UN's digital literacy framework,[47] with Kenya's Three-Step System of (1) gaining familiarity with, (2) using, and (3) creating and programming software, being an oft-followed example.[48] But despite all these efforts, digital and financial illiteracy will be with us for the foreseeable future and financial law has to accept widespread illiteracy as a regulatory precondition. In the light of this, customer-oriented effective FinTech is needed for the Financial Inclusion that is crucial on the journey towards a long-term, sustainable, and prosperous world.

IV. SUSTAINABILITY

The third and most recent driver of data-driven finance is sustainability.

A. *Regulatory Approaches to Sustainability*

Today, there are three major approaches to sustainability.

The first approach views climate change and the other UN SDGs from the standpoint of the traditional financial services' focus on risk and related disclosure and particularly centres around environmental, social, and corporate governance (ESG). Going forward, using the UN SDGs as the core framework for defining, monitoring, and evaluating ESG investment has great potential to redirect existing resources towards achieving the SDGs.

The second approach views the UN SDGs (particularly climate change, biodiversity, and poverty reduction) as relating to new sources of potential risk: for example, climate change is now identified by the global insurance industry as perhaps the greatest risk facing the industry going forward. This leads to policy changes and significant research into risk modelling, management, and mitigation, all resulting in substantial redirection of resources to support the SDGs.

The third approach involves thinking about how to restructure or even redesign the financial system, thereby transforming finance to support the UN SDGs. This third approach lies at the heart of the sustainable finance initiatives currently being developed in many places, but most prominently in the EU with its Sustainable Finance Action Plan (SFAP) of 2018 and successor strategies.[49]

---

[47] United Nations Educational, Scientific and Cultural Organization, 'A Global Framework of Reference on Digital Literacy Skills for Indicator 4.4.2' (Information Paper No 51, June 2018) <http://uis.unesco.org/sites/default/files/documents/ip51-global-framework-reference-digital-literacy-skills-2018-en.pdf>.

[48] See 'Kenyans Urged to Support the Digital Literacy Programme', *KenyaNews* (online, 8 March 2022) <www.kenyanews.go.ke/kenyans-urged-to-support-the-digital-literacy-programme/#:~:text=The%20 Digital%20Literacy%20programme%20which,of%20DLP%20devices%20to%20schools.>.

[49] See, for an overview, Dirk A Zetzsche and Linn Anker-Sørensen, 'Regulating Sustainable Finance in the Dark' (2022) 23 *European Business Organization Law Review* 47.

B. *Sustainability as a Driver of Datafication*

Each of these three regulatory approaches propel the datafication of finance. All approaches focus upon ESG and the UN SDGs as risk indicators and thus require data collection and analytics, in addition to traditional financial analysis. This is most obvious with regard to the 'double materiality' standard implemented in the EU SFAP, which requires firms to report on both how sustainability issues affect their business and their own impact on people and the environment.[50]

The number of datasets necessary for meeting the regulatory requirements in the EU exceeds what can be processed manually. For instance, Annex I of the Sustainable Finance Disclosures Delegated Regulation (EU) 2022/1288 of 6 April 2022 lists more than 30 environmental and social factors that require reporting. These data need to be collected for each 'economic activity', defined narrowly, for each firm, and for each 'sector' in which the firm is active, ranging from manufacturing to construction, consulting to sales. Data collection is challenging as the data sources are often external – even the most sustainability-oriented firms do not have access to all data necessary for meeting the regulatory requirements. In turn, complying with the EU SFAP requires, on the firm level, the creation of entirely new data sources and datasets, analytic models, and reporting standards and systems. None of this can be achieved without datafication and advanced IT-driven analytics.[51]

C. *Datafication as a Driver of Sustainability*

To the same extent that sustainability drives datafication, datafication drives sustainability.

Digital finance and FinTech play three core roles in achieving the SDGs.

The first is enhancing the allocation of existing financial resources by redirecting those resources globally and in individual countries to provide SDG-related finance. Examples include ESG and green investment strategies and the rapid growth in ESG-related financing in the EU, China, and Japan.

The second involves the expansion of resources in the financial system generally which can in turn support the SDGs. This takes place through financial inclusion and financial sector development, which together can increase the amount of financial resources available.

The third involves the use of digital finance and FinTech to directly achieve the SDGs themselves. This occurs through the use of new technologies and regulatory technology (RegTech) to design better financial and regulatory systems to achieve policy objectives.

Table 6.1 presents how FinTech can contribute directly or indirectly to the UN SDGs.

---

[50] 'Questions and Answers: Corporate Sustainability Reporting Directive Proposal', *European Commission* (Web Page, 21 April 2021) <https://ec.europa.eu/commission/presscorner/detail/en/QANDA_21_1806>.
[51] For a description of the complexities of the Sustainable Finance Action Plan, see Zetzsche and Anker-Sørensen (n 49).

TABLE 6.1 *How FT4FI could further the UN SDGs*

No.	Goals	Impact (Direct = D Indirect = I)	How FT4FI can further goal
1	No poverty	I	Allow for online financing, including credit and crowdfunding; create new income opportunities through online markets and payments; reduce impact of disasters, enable more longer-term thinking and planning
2	Zero hunger	I	Enhance financial stability; stabilise cash flows through saving and lending
3	Good health and well-being	I	Provide health insurance and financial stability
4	Quality education	I	Enable saving for school fees
5	Gender equality	D	Strengthen female entrepreneurship and financial control
6	Clean water and sanitation	I	Provide financing for development and maintenance of infrastructure; further education for local sustainability expertise
7	Affordable and clean energy	I	Ibid
8	Decent work and economic growth	D	Allow for online financing, including credit and crowdfunding; create new (online) income opportunities; ensure funding and use symmetry (long-term finance for long-term projects, short-term finance for short-term projects)
9	Industry, innovation, and infrastructure	D	Provide financing for development and maintenance of infrastructure
10	Reduced inequalities	D	See on gender at UN SDG 5. Education and savings provide the best opportunity for greater participation in most societies; with both furthered by FT4FI
11	Sustainable cities and communities	I	FT4FI assists the development of and investment in sustainable technology and transformation
12	Responsible production and consumption	I	Ibid
13	Climate action	I	Ibid
14	Life below water	I	Ibid
15	Life on land	I	Ibid
16	Peace, justice, and strong institutions	I	Robust economic development strengthens peace and civil institutions
17	Partnerships	D	FT4FI allows for engagement of private actors, multiplying assistance by public or state supported actors

The table draws on the authors' own research and experience. That digital financial services support the UN SDGs is very broadly accepted; see 'DFS and the SDGs', *UNCDF Mobile Money for the Poor* (Web Page) <www.uncdf.org/mm4p/dfs-and-the-sdgs>.

If financial markets are sufficiently mature, financial services supporting financial inclusion can contribute to *all* 17 UN SDGs. Financial inclusion through FinTech is thus perhaps *the most important* intermediate step economies should take on their journey to achieving the UN SDGs.

V. THE INTERRELATION BETWEEN EFFICIENCY, SUSTAINABILITY, AND INCLUSION

This section argues that all three drivers of change together must be present to achieve a well-balanced datafied financial system. We first argue that financial inclusion and sustainability are two sides of the same coin, before showing the relationship between efficiency and both sustainability and financial inclusion.

A. *Financial Inclusion and Sustainability: Two Sides of the Same Coin*

Financially excluded individuals lack tools to prepare for and manage the burden of life's challenges, including sickness, crime, poverty, etc. For instance, farmers without access to electronic payment systems worry about theft and may consume more immediately rather than risk saving. Yet, saving can fund children's education and provide for old age. Financial exclusion takes from people the opportunity to think, plan, and *act* in the long term. Risks that can be avoided, hedged, or socialised through the financial system can materialise at any time, yet financial exclusion forces the excluded to think and act in the *short* term, often unsustainably and inefficiently. Financial inclusion and sustainability are two sides of the same coin, with both aimed at the UN SDGs' core objective of promoting prosperity while balancing risks.

While financial inclusion is not a UN SDG per se, it facilitates achievement of all the SDGs and therefore should be seen as a key underlying objective in seeking balanced, long-term, and sustainable development (see Table 6.1).

B. *Efficiency versus Sustainability and Financial Inclusion: An Imperative Link*

Although often overlooked, there is an inherent link between efficiency, financial inclusion, and sustainability agendas: 'In a world where for the most part pension funds and other intermediaries serving retail beneficiaries provide the funding, only a *profitable* market-based sustainability strategy is truly sustainable.'[52]

This is so for four reasons. First, the sustainable transformation of the world's economy is costly. It requires development of more sustainable products and services as substitutes for less sustainable ones. This, in turn, requires investments

---

[52]   Zetzsche and Anker-Sørensen (n 49) 47, 80 (emphasis in original).

in research and development (R&D). Only profitable or potentially profitable firms will be able to finance these R&D expenses, regardless of whether they use retained earnings or projected future earnings (i.e., capital provided by investors) to finance R&D.

Second, unprofitable firms have a strong incentive to misreport their sustainability position to justify lesser financial performance. Unprofitability thus undermines the readiness to comply with stricter ESG requirements.

Third, the link between profitability and sustainability is to date uncertain. Despite high general interest in ESG-based investing, the sustainability agenda suffers from a lack of understanding and empirical data about sustainable investments needed to guide investor behaviour.[53] Every truly profitable *and* truly sustainable firm enhances investors' trust that the sustainable transformation of financial markets is possible.

Finally, the more money in the financial system, the faster it can finance any transformation. Higher firm profitability in the real economy generally attracts more capital to shift from financing the financial economy to financing the real economy. What is true, in general, is particularly true for the sustainability transformation.

Hence, the cost savings and efficiency gains that datafication and technology may provide are very welcome. The profits generated this way may well be used to finance the sustainability transformation. A large-scale, long-term unprofitable sustainable investment is in itself unsustainable in a business sense.

Furthermore, efficiency is informed by sustainability and financial inclusion perspectives. Where datafied technology negatively impacts financial inclusion and sustainability, it will prompt policy reactions. For instance, as part of the European Commission's Revised Sustainable Finance Agenda from July 2021,[54] the energy use of Bitcoin's blockchain is receiving great focus, making a restrictive regulatory response very likely. The same regulatory interference may well be seen in response to the exclusive effects of credit scoring[55] and taxi allocation algorithms,[56] with the EU's Artificial Intelligence regulation[57] providing a noteworthy example.

[53] Ibid 669.

[54] *Communication from the Commission to the European Parliament, the Council, the European Economic and Social Committee and the Committee of the Regions Strategy for Financing the Transition to a Sustainable Economy* [2021] COM(2021) 390, 8 <https://eur-lex.europa.eu/resource .html?uri=cellar:9f5e7e95-df06-11eb-895a-01aa75ed71a1.0001.02/DOC_1&format=PDF>.

[55] See European Commission, 'About This Initiative', *Sustainable Finance – Environmental, Social and Governance Ratings and Sustainability Risks in Credit Ratings* (Web Page, 2022) <https://ec.europa .eu/info/law/better-regulation/have-your-say/initiatives/13330-Sustainable-finance-environmental-social-and-governance-ratings-and-sustainability-risks-in-credit-ratings_en>.

[56] See European Commission, 'European Commission Adopts New Initiatives for Sustainable and Smart Mobility', *Mobility and Transport* (online, 2 February 2022) <https://transport.ec.europa.eu/ news/european-commission-adopts-new-initiatives-sustainable-and-smart-mobility-2022-02-02_en>.

[57] *Proposal for a Regulation of the European Parliament and of the Council Laying Down Harmonised Rules on Artificial Intelligence (Artificial Intelligence Act) and Amending Certain Union Legislative Acts* [2021] COM/2021/206 <https://eur-lex.europa.eu/legal-content/EN/TXT/?uri=celex%3A52021PC0206>.

In turn, a large, cost-efficient yet financially exclusive or unsustainable investment is as doomed to fail as a large-scale, long-term unprofitable sustainable investment.

Efficiency, financial inclusion, and sustainability are thus inherently intertwined.

VI. CONCLUSION

As we have argued in this chapter, the quest for efficiency, financial inclusion, and sustainability has driven the development of FinTech and datafication of financial services. None of these three factors alone will propel FinTech and datafication in the future. While efficiency gains originally drove FinTech, today the triangle of efficiency, financial inclusion, and sustainability together best explain the steps financial institutions are currently taking to datafy their economic activities.

PART II

Addressing the Challenges of Innovation in Finance

Since the 1960s, finance has undergone a long process of digital transformation and is today probably the most globalised segment of the world's economy and among the most digitised and datafied. This process is evident across four major axes: the emergence of global wholesale markets, an explosion of financial technology (FinTech) start-ups since 2008, an unprecedented digital financial transformation in developing countries (particularly China), and the increasing role of large technology companies (BigTechs) in financial services. This process of digital financial transformation brings structural changes with both benefits and risks. While finance and technology have always interacted and supported each other, since 2008 the extent and pace of change have been unprecedented, particularly in the new technologies summarised as the ABCD framework: (generative) Artificial Intelligence (AI), Blockchain, Cloud, and Data. We add Mobile Internet, Internet of Things (IoT), smart contracts, Regulatory Technology (RegTech), and digital identity to this framework of change enabling technologies. Together, these interacting factors underpin the FinTech revolution. This FinTech revolution has brought and will continue to bring new much-needed competition and efficiency and access to financial services in many countries.

In Part II, we consider some of the major new technologies employed in finance and the opportunities and challenges they raise.

To underpin our analysis, a brief account of the technologies discussed in Part II is useful at this stage.

The underlying idea of AI is software that mimics human cognitive functions, such as 'learning' and 'problem solving'.[1] AI puts data to use by drawing conclusions as to

---

[1] See Stuart J Russel and Peter Norvig, *Artificial Intelligence: A Modern Approach* (Pearson, 3rd ed, 2016). Russel and Norvig defined AI as devices that perceive their environment and take actions that maximise their chances of successfully achieving their task and describing the origin of the term AI in the Turing Test where 'a computer passes the test if a human interrogator, after posing some written questions, cannot tell whether the written responses come from a person or from a computer', and defining six core capabilities that together compose most of AI, including natural language processing, knowledge representation, automated reasoning, machine learning, computer vision, and robotics.

the probability of an event from prior knowledge of conditions related to the event; the greater the volume of data, the more insightful and accurate the inferences drawn from the data. Machine learning is a subset of AI that uses statistical, data-based methods to progressively improve the performance of computers on a given task, without humans reprogramming the computer system to achieve enhanced performance.[2] In practice, the learning is achieved through extensive 'practice' with multiple feedback rounds through which the machine is told whether it has passed or failed a task. The use of generative AI models that learn the patterns of their input data by applying neural network machine learning techniques, with a view to generating new data sets with similar characteristics, has dramatically increased access to and awareness of AI.

A distributed ledger is 'a database that is consensually shared and synchronised across networks spread across multiple sites, institutions or geographies, allowing a transaction to have [multiple private or] public "witnesses"'.[3] The sharing of data results in a database distributed across a network of servers all of which together function as a ledger. Distributed ledgers are characterised by an absence of, or minimal, central administration and no centralised data storage. They are, hence, 'distributed', in the sense that the authorisation for the recording of a given piece of information results from the software-driven interaction of multiple participants. Coupled with cryptographic solutions, such features (decentralisation and distribution across a network of computers) curtail the risk of data manipulation, thereby solving the problem of having to trust third parties, specifically data storage service providers as this is the point where the data are stored and can most easily be manipulated.[4]

The modus operandi of distributed ledgers are best understood by looking at their counterpart, the concentrated ledger. Let us assume that a centralised register administered by a single entity contains all relevant data, and let us further assume that, contrary to present practice, the centralised register is not secured and thus 'semi-distributed' through a myriad of back-ups stored on multiple servers. That arrangement entails a number of risks. First, if the hardware where the register is 'located' is destroyed, the information content, as well as the authority to ascertain that they are correct, is lost. Second, disloyal employees of the database administrator

---

 The seminal work on AI is of course Alan M Turing, 'Computer Machinery and Intelligence' (1950) 49 *Mind* 433.

2 Russel and Norvig (n 1) 693–859 (describing the training methods).

3 'Innovation-Driven Cyber-Risk to Customer Data in Financial Services' (White Paper No 5, World Economic Forum, 2017) 6.

4 See Sinclair Davidson, Primavera De Filippi and Jason Potts, 'Blockchains and the Economic Institutions of Capitalism' (2018) 14(4) *Journal of Institutional Economics* 639 (arguing that blockchain technology is a new governance institution that competes with other economic institutions of capitalism, namely firms, markets, networks, and even governments); Primavera De Filippi and Aaron Wright, *Blockchain and the Law: The Rule of Code* (Harvard University Press, 2018) 55, 136–40 (arguing that widespread deployment of blockchain will lead to tech-based business practices that could prompt a decline in importance of centralized authorities, such as governments, and urging a more active regulatory approach).

or an unfaithful administrator may manipulate the information content of the register. Third, a cyber-attack may result in manipulations and data losses.[5]

Distributed ledgers address these problems by raising the barrier for manipulation. The underlying technology requires consensus of many data storage points ('nodes'). If there are n nodes (instead of one concentrated ledger) and e describes the effort necessary to break into any single server, all other conditions being equal (safety per server etc.), the effort necessary to manipulate all the linked servers will be n × e rather than 1 × e.

Distributed ledgers are usually paired with a blockchain protocol. Blockchain refers to the storage of data in data bundles (the 'blocks') in a strict time-related series with each block linked through a timestamp as well as a number of protocols providing evidence of a user's authority to amend the data stored,[6] to the previous and subsequent blocks. The blockchain renders data corruption even harder, because a successful cyberattack would have to simultaneously corrupt not just one set of data but all subsequent datasets (i.e., the whole blockchain) as well as the timestamps simultaneously.

Distributed ledgers have provided fertile ground for the application of another innovation that seeks to address the problem of trust in human interactions (in particular relating to compliance with and enforcement of contracts) while at the same enhancing efficiency: smart contracts.[7] While neither smart, nor contracts in a legal sense, they are self-executing software protocols that reflect some of the terms of an agreement between two parties.[8] The conditions of the agreement are directly written into lines of code. Smart contracts permit the execution of transactions between disparate, anonymous parties without the need for an external enforcement mechanism (such as a court, an arbitrator, or a central clearing facility). They render transactions traceable, transparent, and irreversible. Processes driven by smart contracts may take place via and be recorded on distributed ledgers secured via blockchain. This particular combination is at the core of most discussions relating to DeFi.

Cloud computing[9] refers to the decentralisation of server capacity. Rather than using one server at one server centre, datasets can be distributed over many server

[5] Any server can be manipulated with unlimited computing power and time (even if no other weakness in an encryption system is known to the attackers). See generally Jean-Philippe Aumasson, *Serious Cryptography: A Practical Introduction to Modern Encryption* (No Starch Press, 2017) 10–18, 40–8.

[6] These protocols seek to address the risk that the timestamp may be unreliable, or open to easy manipulation.

[7] See Kevin Werbach and Nicolas Cornell, 'Contracts Ex Machina' (2017) 67(2) *Duke Law Journal* 313.

[8] Smart contracts can implement and execute contractual conditions and, in this sense, certainly have legal effect, but smart contracts cannot yet typically in practice embody all the terms of an enforceable legal contract purely in code: UK LawTech Delivery Panel, 'Legal Statement on Cryptoassets and Smart Contracts: UK Jurisdiction Taskforce' (Legal Statement, November 2019) 8.

[9] For an overview of cloud computing in the regulated financial sector, see Hal S Scott, John Gulliver and Hillel Nadler, 'Cloud Computing in the Financial Sector: A Global Perspective' (Research Paper, Program on International Financial Systems, July 2019).

centres accessible by many users located around the globe through the Internet more or less simultaneously.

Cloud computing refers to the on-demand availability of data storage and processing power without the users owning or controlling the servers providing these services. Cloud computing relies on data centres operated by commercial providers that rent capacity to customers who access the capacity over the Internet.

In order to provide for cloud stability in the light of volatile demand and energy supply, to diversify against demand peaks, and ensure economic operations where energy costs fluctuate through the day, cloud service providers typically link server centres across different time zones, countries, and economic regions and channel excess demand to servers where data processing capacity is cheaper, due to lower demand and energy costs.

Data are at the core of all these innovations, resulting from the digitisation of an ever-increasing range of processes: the idea of the 'digitisation of everything' that underlies theories of the Fourth Industrial Revolution.[10] The ever-greater volume of data supports both traditional data analytics and 'Big Data' approaches. BigData analytics refers to the collection and processing of datasets that are too large or too complex for traditional data processing applications. BigData applications look at massive numbers of data points and apply advanced data analytics methods to detect unexpected correlations, test expected correlations for causation, or determine the probability of a pre-defined pattern.[11]

We consider these in turn:

Chapter 7 addresses the use of AI and machine learning in finance, while Chapter 8 considers blockchain and DLT.

Chapter 9 considers the evolution of decentralised finance (DeFi) and embedded regulation and supervision, new forms of RegTech.

Chapter 10 considers the role of data and data regulation.

Chapter 11 presents a framework for a balanced proportional approach to supporting innovation, focusing on the role of innovation hubs and regulatory sandboxes.

---

[10] See Klaus Schwab, *Fourth Industrial Revolution* (World Economic Forum, 2016) 9–14 (predicting profound and systemic change due to physical, digital, and biological megatrends driving the renewal of industrial production).

[11] See Viktor Mayer-Schönberger and Kenneth Cukier, *Big Data: A Revolution that Will Transform How We Live, Work, and Think* (Harper Business, 2014) 6 (stating that the volume of information has outpaced IT engineers' manual data handling capacity so that they need to reinvent data analysis tools; the latter will result in new forms of value creation that will affect markets, organizations, and other institutions).

7

Regulating Artificial Intelligence in Finance

SUMMARY

This chapter develops a framework for understanding and addressing the increasing role of artificial intelligence (AI) in finance. It focuses on human responsibility as central to addressing the AI 'black box' problem – that is, the risk of undesirable results that are unrecognised or unanticipated due to people's difficulties in understanding the internal workings of an AI or as a result of the AI's independent operation outside human supervision or involvement.

I. INTRODUCTION

AI covers a series of technologies and approaches ranging from less-sophisticated 'if-then' rule-based expert systems[1] to natural language processing, to the marriage of algorithms and data known as machine learning. In this chapter, we focus on algorithmically driven, not rule-based, systems. One such system is machine learning, a subset of AI, which involves pattern recognition and inference trained by data rather than explicit human instructions. Machine learning progressively reduces the role of humans as AI systems expand from supervised learning to unsupervised deep learning neural networks.

AI is used heavily in finance.[2] In addition to the financial industry, regulators regularly use AI to identify insider trading, market abuse, fraudulent websites, and unlicensed solicitation of clients, among an increasing range of areas. Central to this is the rise of Big Data and datafication at large – the manipulation of digitised data through quantitative data analytics, including AI.[3]

---

[1] In rule-based expert systems, knowledge is represented as a set of rules. For example, *if* 'traffic light' is 'green', *then* the action is go; see Jiri Panyr, 'Information Retrieval Techniques in Rule-based Expert Systems' in Hans-Hermann Bock and Peter Ihm (eds), *Classification, Data Analysis, and Knowledge Organization* (Springer, 1991) 196.

[2] European Central Bank, 'Algorithmic Trading: Trends and Existing Regulation' (Media Release, 13 February 2019).

[3] United Kingdom Finance and Microsoft, *Artificial Intelligence in Financial Services* (Report, June 2019) 5.

In most sectors, AI is expected to contribute to problem solving and development. Cost savings, enhanced efficiency, entirely new opportunities, and business models explain why financial services companies' spending on AI will double from US$50.1 billion in 2020 to more than US$110 billion in 2024,[4] and why European spending on AI systems alone is projected to jump from US$17.3 billion in 2021 to more than US$50 billion in 2025, with financial solutions comprising the majority of these investments.[5] At the same time, AI and automation raise concerns, ranging from AI-specific issues, such as AI explainability, systemic risk, AI biases, and algorithmic collusion, to widespread job losses and 'the singularity' – when the capacities of AI surpass those of humans. These concerns have triggered many analyses of the ethical[6] and legal implications of AI, and yet few from the perspective we take here of AI's impact in finance. The prominence of these issues has dramatically increased as a result of the emergence of 'generative AI' systems from the second half of 2022.

Central to many of these concerns is the role of humans in the evolution of AI: the necessity of involving people in using, monitoring, and supervising AI. This chapter develops a framework for understanding and addressing the increasing role of AI in finance. It focuses on human responsibility, the 'human in the loop', as central to tackling the risk that AI generates processes and operations unknown to and uncontrolled by human beings, producing undesirable results. This we term the AI 'black box' problem. We propose herein our solution to the black box problem: bringing humans into the loop to enhance internal governance where financial supervision as external governance is ineffective. In particular, we propose addressing AI-related issues by requiring (1) AI due diligence, (2) AI explainability, (3) algorithmic assurance, and (4) AI review committees.

II. AI AND FINANCE

A. *AI in Financial Services*

Financial services are a fertile field for the application of AI for two reasons.

First, a major pillar of the process of digital financial transformation is the large-scale use of data underpinned by ever-falling data storage prices, cloud ubiquity,

---

[4]   *OECD Business and Finance Outlook in 2021: AI in Business and Finance* (Report, 24 September 2021) ch 2; World Economic Forum, *The New Physics of Financial Services: Understanding How Artificial Intelligence Is Transforming the Financial Ecosystem* (Report, 15 August 2018) 18.

[5]   See 'European Spending on Artificial Intelligence Will Reach $22 Billion in 2022, Supported by Strong Investments across Banking and Manufacturing, Says IDC' *IDC* (Web Page, 7 October 2021) <www.idc.com/getdoc.jsp?containerId=prEUR148297521>.

[6]   See generally Dirk Helbing, 'Societal, Economic, Ethical and Legal Challenges of the Digital Revolution: From Big Data to Deep Learning, Artificial Intelligence, and Manipulative Technologies' in Dirk Helbing (ed), *Towards Digital Enlightenment: Essays on the Dark and Light Sides of the Digital Revolution* (Springer, 2018) 47.

telecommunications linkages, ever-increasing computing power, and innovative algorithmic and analytical developments.

Second, AI tends to perform best in rule-constrained environments, such as games like chess or Go, where there are finite ways of achieving specified objectives. This is often the environment in finance. For example, stock market investment involves specific objectives (maximising profit), fixed parameters of action (trading rules and systems), and massive amounts of data.

AI's potential to process data is central to its utility. Correctly programmed AI treats all data objectively, while humans tend to discriminate among datapoints based on their experience, values, and other non-rational judgements.

B. *AI Use Cases*

Due to ever-improving performance in data gathering, processing, and analytics, AI increasingly affects all operational and internal control matters of financial intermediaries, from strategy setting,[7] to compliance,[8] to risk management, and beyond.[9]

AI use cases span operations and risk management, trading and portfolio management, payments and infrastructure, data security and monetisation, and regulatory and monetary oversight and compliance, in addition to a range of customer processes from onboarding to instant responses to credit applications.

Skyrocketing costs of compliance and sanctions have induced financial institutions to focus on back-office AI solutions, in the form of RegTech (as we discussed in Chapter 4). AI also drives the trend to seek alternative data for investment and lending decisions, prompting the mantra 'all data is credit data'.[10]

III. RISKS: AI IN FINANCE

No innovation is without risk, and AI is no exception. Analysed in terms of traditional financial regulatory objectives, major AI-related risks arise in data, financial stability, cybersecurity, law, and ethics. We deal with each in turn.

A. *Data Risks*

The centrality of data to the deployment of an AI model cannot be overstated: AI's key functions generally include data collection, data analysis, decision-making,

---

[7] John Armour and Horst Eidenmüller, 'Self-driving Corporations?' (2020) 10(1) *Harvard Business Law Review* 87, 96–7.

[8] Kenneth A Bamberger, 'Technologies of Compliance: Risk and Regulation in a Digital Age' (2010) 88(4) *Texas Law Review* 669, 690–3, 701–2.

[9] Saqib Aziz and Michael Dowling, 'Machine Learning and AI for Risk Management' in Theo Lynn et al (eds), *Disrupting Finance: FinTech and Strategy in the 21st Century* (Palgrave, 2019) 33.

[10] Mikella Hurley and Julius Adebayo, 'Credit Scoring in the Era of Big Data' (2016) 18(1) *Yale Journal of Law and Technology* 148, 151.

and the execution of those decisions.[11] Data collection has long been a major bottleneck in machine learning because it is expensive and hard to obtain, as large providers of data collection and analysis services may be unwilling to share data they have with other providers. Although AI adoption in many areas of financial services has increased significantly over time due to the availability of highly structured machine-readable data, challenges remain. First, data quality may be poor making it essential for regulators to focus on the development of widely used and well-designed data standards.[12] Second, the data may be biased, either from data selection issues ('dashboard myopia') or simply because data drawn from society will embody society's biases. For this reason, understanding the context of the data – when, where, and how they were generated – is critical to understanding its utility and potential risks. Combined with inappropriately or suboptimally selected AI model architecture and parameters, bad data will lead to bad AI analysis exposing financial services organisations to competitive harm, legal liability, or reputational damage.[13] Similar risks arise from different AI systems performing similar calculations simultaneously and one AI's decisions influencing the tasks performed by another, as illustrated by 'flash crashes' and worldwide regulatory attempts to address algorithmic trading.[14]

B. *Financial Stability Risks*

There are many financial stability implications of AI.[15] One AI-related risk is that oligopolistic or monopolistic players may dominate the markets as a result of additional third-party dependencies caused by network effects and scalability of new technologies. Some of these new market participants are currently unregulated and unsupervised, making the build-up of systemic risks difficult to monitor. Further, the difficulty of interpretability or 'auditability' of AI, particularly machine learning methods, has the potential to contribute to macroeconomic risk unless regulators find ways to supervise the AI.

[11] Henri Arslanian and Fabrice Fischer, *The Future of Finance: The Impact of FinTech, AI, and Crypto on Financial Services* (Springer, 2019) 167, 177; Accenture Federal Services, *AI: All about the Data* (Report, 2020) 4.

[12] Richard Berner and Kathryn Judge, 'The Data Standardization Challenge' in Douglas W Arner et al (eds), *Systemic Risk in the Financial Sector: Ten Years after the Great Crash* (McGill-Queen's University Press, 2019) 135, 148–9.

[13] Fernanda Torre, Robin Teigland, and Liselotte Engstam, 'AI Leadership and the Future of Corporate Governance: Changing Demands for Board Competence' in Anthony Larsson and Robin Teigland (eds), *The Digital Transformation of Labor: Automation, the Gig Economy and Welfare* (Routledge, 2020) 116, 127.

[14] Bonnie G Buchanan, *Artificial Intelligence in Finance* (The Alan Turing Institute, Report, April 2019) 6; Andrei A Kirilenko and Andrew W Lo, 'Moore's Law versus Murphy's Law: Algorithmic Trading and Its Discontents' (2013) 27(2) *Journal of Economic Perspectives* 51, 53–5.

[15] Financial Stability Board, *Artificial Intelligence and Machine Learning in Financial Services* (Report, November 2017) 15.

C. *Cybersecurity*

AI could be used to attack, manipulate, or otherwise harm an economy and threaten national security either directly through its financial system and/or by effecting its wider economy.[16] Algorithms could be manipulated to undermine economies to create unrest or to send wrong signals to trading units to seek to trigger a systemic crisis. The cybersecurity dimension is more serious as many financial services firms rely on a small group of technology providers, creating a new form of risk we term 'TechRisk' and discuss in Part IV. That many AI-enabled systems have not been tested in financial crisis scenarios further amplifies this risk.

D. *Legal Risks*

Ensuring fairness, transparency, and accountability in AI employment is challenging. In particular, existing accountability regimes, such as product liability, tort and vicarious liability, are not easily applied to AI and its corporate and individual creators.[17]

RegTech is increasingly seen as a way to address legal and regulatory requirements, and many solution providers are *using* AI and machine learning in areas such as onboarding, anti-money laundering, and fraud detection. Still, failures, including large-scale ones, such as inaptitude to deal with systemic risks due to defective technology and poor management, occur.[18] As more financial institutions, FinTechs, and crypto-asset service providers incorporate AI into their systems, including their RegTech infrastructure, the legal risks for such regulated entities are likely to increase.

E. *Ethics and Financial Services*

With regard to ethics, three areas are of particular concern in the context of AI: (1) AI as a non-ethical actor, (2) AI's influence on humans, and (3) artificial stupidity and maleficence.

First, code is a non-ethical actor that needs human monitoring and guidance for ethical decision-making.[19] Even though some ethical concerns, such as banning interest under Shariah law, can be codified in ways that suit algorithms, training AI

---

[16] Tom CW Lin, 'Artificial Intelligence, Finance, and the Law' (2019) 88(2) *Fordham Law Review* 531, 538–9.
[17] See, for example, European Commission Report from the Expert Group on Liability and New Technologies, *Liability for Artificial Intelligence and Other Emerging Digital Technologies* (Report, 27 November 2019) 24–9. <https://ec.europa.eu/transparency/regexpert/index.cfm?do=groupDetail.groupMeetingDoc&docid=36608>.
[18] *Chief Executive Officer of the Australian Transaction Reports and Analysis Centre v Westpac Banking Corporation* [2020] FCA 1538. See also section V(C)(4).
[19] Luca Enriques and Dirk A Zetzsche, 'Corporate Technologies and the Tech Nirvana Fallacy' (2020) 72(1) *Hastings Law Journal* 55, 78.

in values is difficult, since humans often cannot say why they act as they do. Drivers of most human actions are subtle and contextual. The risks, if unaddressed, are significant. AI's lack of ethical foundations could seriously harm portfolio values of financial assets if, for example, the AI misprices reputational risk. Moreover, the more data an AI has about a certain person, the greater the risk that the AI may nudge the person into unwanted behaviour, such as buying an unsuitable financial product. The advent and rise of unsupervised learning, generative adversarial networks that generate their own data and powerful autoregressive language models such as Generative Pre-trained Transformer 3 (GPT-3) increase the potential negative impact of AI operating with limited human control.

Second, AI can enhance or diminish human capacity. It can correct human biases in investment decisions (e.g., confirmation bias, optimism bias, and negativity bias) and turn an unskilled person into a skilled investor.[20] Conversely, it can de-skill humans. As the need to develop advanced maths and other sophisticated data analytical capacities decreases with appropriate programmes being widely available, human financial talent risks are being eroded.[21] Research into how people respond to computer-generated incentives suggests that we tend to over-rely on technology and give its outcomes undue weight.[22] AI developers thus bear a high level of responsibility, and there is a strong need for ethical restrictions through rules and internal controls of financial institutions and their management.

Third, protection against AI mistakes and unethical behaviour is a major concern. Errors and unethical behaviour can arise from poor or criminally motivated programming, or from inadequate datasets, or correlations with other events resulting in harmful unforeseen consequences. Another example could arise where certain conduct results in liability for which consumers are more likely to sue than institutional clients, as an algorithm could avoid such consumer relationships, thereby financially excluding them.

F. *Risk Typology: Framework of Analysis*

The risks of AI in finance fall into three major categories: (1) information asymmetry, (2) data dependency, and (3) interdependency.[23]

First, AI increases information asymmetry about the functions and limits of certain algorithms. Third-party vendors often understand the algorithms far better than the

---

[20] Chau Duong, Gioia Pescetto, and Daniel Santamaria, 'How Value-Glamour Investors Use Financial Information: UK Evidence of Investors' *Confirmation Bias*' (2014) 20(6) *European Journal of Finance* 524.

[21] World Economic Forum, *Navigating Uncharted Waters: A Roadmap to Responsible Innovation with AI in Financial Services* (Report, 23 October 2019) 69–71.

[22] See Andrea Ferrario, Michele Loi, and Eleonora Viganò, 'In AI We Trust Incrementally: A Multilayer Model of Trust to Analyze Human-Artificial Intelligence Interactions' (2020) 33(3) *Philosophy and Technology* 523; Omri Gillath et al, 'Attachment and Trust in Artificial Intelligence' (2021) 115 *Computers in Human Behavior* 106607.

[23] Enriques and Zetzsche (n 19) 55, 75–90.

financial institutions or supervisors that buy and use them. However, for proprietary and competitive reasons, technology vendors traditionally fail to fully explain how their creations work. Increased transparency through explainability and interpretability needs to be demanded by users, financial institutions, and regulators alike.

Second, AI increases data dependency as data sources are critical for its operation. The effects and potentially discriminatory impact of AI may change with a different data pool.

Third, AI increases interdependency. One AI model can interact with another AI model with unexpected consequences and enhance or diminish outcomes in finance.

IV. REGULATING AI IN FINANCE: CHALLENGES FOR EXTERNAL GOVERNANCE

The use of AI in finance has become a focus of regulatory attention. We summarise major general regulatory frameworks before turning to financial regulators' approaches to AI. We then argue that traditional regulatory approaches to financial supervision, such as external governance frameworks, are not likely to be effective in this context. Instead, external governance must require internal governance, in particular personal responsibility.

A. General AI Frameworks

General frameworks addressing degrees of human responsibility in developing and dealing with AI have been evolving worldwide since late 2017[24] with the most influential being the AI Recommendation and its five principles adopted by the Organisation for Economic Co-operation and Development (OECD) and the G20 AI principles.[25] Data protection and privacy commissioners have equally increasingly viewed the governance of AI as within their purview. Article 22 of the *European General Data Protection Regulation* (*GDPR*) also requires ethical AI performance by stipulating that a data subject has 'the right to not be subject to a decision based solely on automated processing, including profiling, which produces legal effects'.

Sometimes the scope of these general frameworks does not extend to finance. For instance, the EU is implementing general legislation specifically addressing 'high-risk AI systems' through risk management, data governance, documentation,

---

[24] Select Committee on Artificial Intelligence, 'AI in the UK: Ready, Willing and Able?' (House of Lords Paper No 100, Session 2017–19) 125 [417].

[25] Organisation for Economic Co-operation and Development, 'Recommendation of the Council on Artificial Intelligence' (OECD/LEGAL/0449, 22 May 2019) paras 1.1–1.5 <https://legalinstruments .oecd.org/en/instruments/OECD-LEGAL-0449> ('OECD AI Recommendation'); G20, 'G20 AI Principles' in annex to G20 *Ministerial Statement on Trade and Digital Economy* (8–9 June 2019) <www.g20-insights.org/wp-content/uploads/2019/07/G20-Japan-AI-Principles.pdf>.

transparency, and human oversight requirements; yet within finance to date only AI credit scoring systems fall into the scope of the incoming AI Act.[26] However, the European Commission is entitled to expand the scope in the years to come and may use its powers to include other aspects of AI in financial services.

B. *Financial Regulation and AI*

Globally, regulators have started considering how AI impacts financial services and issuing regulatory guidance. For example, the European Supervisory Authorities (ESAs) (European Banking Authority, European Securities and Markets Authority, and European Insurance and Occupational Pensions Authority) considered AI in the context of Big Data risks for the financial sector. It found that Big Data risks are best addressed by the existing legislation on data protection, cybersecurity, and consumer protection even though such legislation may not have been written specifically to address Big Data risks.[27] This legislation includes: the GDPR, the second *Payment Services Directive (PSD2)*, the second *Markets in Financial Instruments Directive (MiFID II)*, and the *Insurance Distribution Directive (IDD)*. The EU's *Digital Operational Resilience Act (DORA)* also aims to provide a framework that allows financial sectors in Europe to remain operational during severe disruptions (e.g., cyberattacks).

Other financial regulators, such as the Monetary Authority of Singapore, de Nederlandsche Bank, the Bank of England, the Financial Conduct Authority, and the Hong Kong Monetary Authority, are likewise increasingly engaging with AI. In particular, Singapore's Fairness, Ethics, Accountability, and Transparency principles, updated in 2019 and 2020, stipulate two guiding principles: (i) that organisations must ensure that decision-making using AI is explainable, transparent, and fair, and (ii) that AI solutions should be human-centric.[28]

C. *The Inadequacy of External Governance*

Financial supervisory authorities find it increasingly difficult to tackle AI-related risks through traditional means of financial supervision, that is, external governance. Five examples strongly suggest that external governance regimes are inadequate in

---

[26] See *Proposal for a Regulation of the European Parliament and of the Council Laying Down Harmonised Rules on Artificial Intelligence (Artificial Intelligence Act) and Amending Certain Union Legislative Acts* [2021] COM/2021/206 <https://eur-lex.europa.eu/legal-content/EN/TXT/?uri=celex%3A52021PC0206>.

[27] Joint Committee of the European Supervisory Authorities, *Joint Committee Final Report on Big Data* (JC/2018/04, 15 March 2018) 23.

[28] Singapore Personal Data Protection Commission, *A Proposed Artificial Intelligence Governance Model* (Report, January 2019); Singapore Info-Communications Media Development Authority and Personal Data Protection Commission, *Model Artificial Intelligence Governance Framework: Second Edition* (Report, January 2020).

addressing the risks of AI in finance: (1) the authorisation of AI, (2) the outsourcing of rules and e-personhood, (3) the role of AI with regard to key functions, (4) the qualifications of core personnel, and (5) sanctioning rules.

1. The Authorisation of AI

AI use influences the conditions for its authorisation. Devising appropriate authorisation requirements is challenging and compliance likely to be cumbersome. Generally, if a business model seeking authorisation relies on AI, the business and operations plan should detail the functioning of the AI, the client protection features, the regulatory capital assigned to financial and operational risks for the AI-performed services, and the back-up structure in case the AI fails. Regulatory frameworks across the globe already require IT contingency plans and multiple data storage and cybersecurity strategies. These regulatory approaches are unlikely to change fundamentally but will become even more important over time.

For financial institutions, one potential response to AI-based threats is a licensing requirement for AI use.[29] A mandatory AI insurance scheme is another.

To ensure that authorisation frameworks remain up to date, financial services authorities worldwide are increasingly seeking to upskill and introduce technology to perform AI reviews. However, the value of such technology depends squarely on it passing the established testing standards. Testing, in turn, depends on the available data pools. If the test pool for AI review technology differs from the real-use case data pools, the results of testing may be of little value and the AI review technology itself of little help.

Crucially, the requirement of authorisation may stifle innovation or be quite unnecessary. Authorisation is generally slow and in the case of AI those responsible for establishing rules would struggle to cope with the (often, almost daily) minor amendments and improvements to AI programmes. Authorisation is also expensive. In particular, where even minor changes to the code would require re-authorisation, they may be uneconomic, even though the cumulative effect of a number of minor amendments may be significant. Finally, for unsupervised self-learning AI, authorisation is ineffective as by definition such 'self-learning AI' develops while performing its services. Thus, authorisations will always be outdated.[30]

2. Regulatory Outsourcing of Rules and e-Personhood

In regulatory rulebooks worldwide, 'crucial supplier frameworks' apply for AI owned and operated by, or outsourced to, a separate services provider. The crucial supplier is subject to additional monitoring by the outsourcing financial institution. However, financial services AI may increasingly be owned and operated in-house by

---

[29] Andrew Tutt, 'An FDA for Algorithms' (2017) 69(1) *Administrative Law Review* 83, 111.
[30] Enriques and A Zetzsche (n 19) 55, 76.

the financial intermediary's own staff. This raises questions around the adequacy of the AI legal framework.

One option for regulating in-house AI is the granting of limited legal personality to the algorithm itself, similar to a partial license, paired with a self-executing 'kill switch' linked to minimum requirements as to the capital available for potential liability claims. If the capital is depleted, for example due to liabilities or regulatory sanctions, the algorithm will stop operating. The arguments against such limited e-personhood are similar to those against authorising AI: the calculation of capital requires a clear delineation of risks created by the AI. If the limits of AI functions are vague, as with self-learning algorithms, regulatory capital will most likely be set too low or too high. Further, authorities have cheaper ways to restrict AI use, without a financial institution AI's own regulatory capital. These include reporting requirements for AI deployment and losses and damage resulting from such deployment, and responding to such reporting by issuing orders limiting, or prohibiting, such AI applications as deemed appropriate.

3. AI as a Key Function Holder?

Can an AI serve as an executive or a board member of the financial institution? Here, legality and practicality differ.

In some jurisdictions, executive functions can be assigned to legal entities, or the law may be silent on the issue. In those jurisdictions, it may be lawful to appoint an AI as a board member, if necessary, by embedding the AI in a special purpose vehicle (i.e., a subsidiary with a very limited business objective) as its sole activity. In other jurisdictions, these functions must be fulfilled by people.

Regarding practicality, an AI may function as a board member for certain routine tasks (e.g., securitisation vehicles in a corporate group), and for procedural monitoring, but a human board majority may be required to ensure continuing operations when challenges exceed the AI's programmed limits.

Notwithstanding this, rules allowing AI to assume functions within a financial institution must respect the existing limits of AI, especially for compliance monitoring. AI alone is poorly adapted to handle compliance matters because it lacks ethical screening abilities and because rules are incomplete on purpose. Financial services are heavily regulated by rules that do not always operate in yes/no terms. Rather, their meaning depends on context. For this reason, an 'AI as compliance officer' could well lead to inaccurate monitoring, widespread misreporting, and mispricing of risks.[31]

4. The Fit-and-Proper Test for Core Personnel

AI will likely influence regulatory practice in the fit-and-proper tests for key function holders (i.e., senior management or executives) and the board of directors, in

---

[31] Ibid 74–5.

two ways. First, some existing requirements may be redundant or need modification when AI is used. For instance, if AI is making decisions, a human executive's credentials may not require review.

Second, new requirements will reflect the greater reliance on AI, and some office holders may have new qualifications. EU authorities require executives of a financial intermediary to have at least three years of executive experience prior to appointment. This experience should demonstrate good standing, diligent handling of client matters, and cooperation with the financial supervisory authority. However, AI experts may have accumulated their AI experience outside the financial sector, for example, within a major e-commerce or software firm. Financial supervisors will need to modify some of their experience requirements as many have for licensing requirements for FinTechs.

5. Sanctioning AI

Financial regulation typically imposes sanctions on an institution for its overall conduct and/or that of individual staff. To do so, regulators usually must prove negligence or ill intent of the institution and/or staff. When harm occurs, deficiencies in risk management systems may attract sanctions. With AI, these cases will be increasingly hard to make. Where AI fails and supervisors are incapable of establishing the AI's processes and limits with certainty, determining the culpability standard and burden of proof to be applied while retaining incentives to innovate will be very challenging. Potential sanctions may exercise little steering effect, even if sanctions are possible under the broad 'failure of risk management' rationale.[32]

This brings us to the question of sanctioning AI. Withholding compensation, naming and shaming, and financial penalties have little meaning for AI. Similarly, director disqualification – the equivalent of a death penalty for individuals in corporate management – and civil and criminal liability will have a limited steering effect for AI in its current form.

Hence, any sanctioning system needs reconsidered incentives for AI creation and deployment. AI-adapted regulation could possibly:

1. Require blame-free remediation in which organisations are able to learn from failures and make improvements;
2. encourage collaboration to promote early detection and the avoidance of unexpected AI failures; and/or
3. employ fit-for-purpose explainability with frameworks that determine 'if explainability is required based on a risk and impact assessment in any particular circumstance (thereby assisting organisations to prioritise their AI's objectives) and 'how' explainability should be achieved.[33]

---

[32] Bamberger (n 8) 669, 676.
[33] World Economic Forum (n 21) 21.

V. PUTTING THE HUMAN IN THE LOOP IN FINANCE

While regulators expect financial institutions to deploy AI responsibly and develop and use new tools to safeguard the financial system, we have shown that, given the severe information asymmetry, data dependency, and interdependency that arise with AI, external governance is not well suited to ensuring the responsible use of AI in finance.

Given these black box challenges in AI for regulatory and supervisory authorities, measures focusing on personal responsibility requirements that put the human in the loop are central to regulating AI-enabled systems in finance.

Two approaches are gaining increasing currency. The first involves using technology (including AI) to monitor staff behaviour and identify issues before they arise (a form of RegTech, cf Chapter 4).

The second approach requires putting a human firmly in the responsibility loop. We argue below that regulators should utilise and strengthen external governance requirements in order to require human-in-the-loop systems for internal AI governance. AI risks and challenges should be externally governed primarily by mandating the quality and intensity of financial institutions' internal governance. AI-adjusted personal responsibility frameworks are vital.

To provide context, we begin with the fundamentals of personal responsibility frameworks in financial regulation. Then, we analyse how these frameworks can be utilised for addressing AI-related black box issues.

A. *Personal Responsibility Frameworks in Finance*

Over the last ten years, most major financial jurisdictions have imposed[34] director and manager responsibility frameworks for financial regulation. Moreover, the first measure of the *AI Consultation Report* published by the International Organization of Securities Commissions (IOSCO)[35] is that '[r]egulators should consider requiring firms to have designated senior management responsible for the oversight of the development, testing, deployment, monitoring and controls of AI and machine learning.'[36] If implemented at the national level, this guidance will help install a personal responsibility framework for securities regulators across the world precisely along the lines of that for which we argue here for all financial institutions.

---

[34] For example, Australia, the EU, the United Kingdom, Hong Kong, and Singapore.
[35] Board of the International Organization of Securities Commissions, *The Use of Artificial Intelligence and Machine Learning by Market Intermediaries and Asset Manager: Consultation Report* (Report CR02/2020, June 2020) ('*IOSCO AI Consultation Report*').
[36] Ibid 2, 18.

B. *Addressing the Knowledge Gap*

The trend is clearly towards ever-increasing personal responsibility for senior management and people responsible for regulated activities within financial institutions. We argue that such personal responsibility frameworks can address the three challenges of AI in finance: information asymmetry, data dependency, and interdependency.

1. AI Due Diligence

The first tool reinforcing and supporting manager responsibility is mandatory AI due diligence, which should include a full stocktake of all AI characteristics (including the AI explainability standard described in the following subsection). AI due diligence should be required before AI procurement, adoption, and deployment, while AI explainability is the standard to meet in using any AI. One part of AI due diligence is mapping the datasets used by the AI, including an analysis of dataset bias, data gaps, and data quality.[37]

AI due diligence is key to individual responsibility systems: individuals need to conduct sufficient due diligence in the exercise of their responsibilities to avoid liability for any failures, whether from internal governance systems, employees, third parties, or ICT systems.

2. AI Explainability

Explainability requirements are necessary minimum standards for humans in the loop – that is, AI's functions, limits, and risks must be able to be explained *to someone*. Debates exist relating to the level of granularity required and to whom such explanations should be made (e.g., a programmer/statistician, user, or regulator), and the term 'interpretability' is sometimes used in the context of more technical explainability.

From a regulatory approach, this 'someone' could be an appropriate senior manager and/or a member of the executive board responsible for the AI (relying on the manager's incentive to avoid sanctions) or an external institution, in particular regulators, supervisors, and courts.

Thus, we encourage financial regulators to introduce explainability requirements for responsible managers, including documentation and governance requirements, with clarification of the standards depending on a risk and impact assessment and to whom the explanation is required. Supervisory authorities should review

---

[37] Brian W Tang, 'The Chiron Imperative: A Framework of Six Human-in-the-Loop Paradigms to Create Wise and Just AI-Human Centaurs' in Susanne Chishti et al (eds), *The LEGALTECH Book: The Legal Technology Handbook for Investors, Entrepreneurs and Fintech Visionaries* (Wiley, 2020) 38.

compliance with explainability requirements. As with their other decisions, individual senior managers must be able to explain and take responsibility for their own direct or indirect decisions about technology, the actions of their employees and contractors, and critically, the decisions of their AI systems.

3. Algorithmic Assurance

'Algorithmic assurance' – a framework for testing whether machine learning algorithms conform to the design goals[38] – is another mechanism to buttress manager responsibility. Based on the idea of technology assisting humans in reviewing technology, such a framework involves, for example, developing an algorithm to review the performance of another algorithm. In particular, the 'reviewing' algorithm will be searching for protected factors in the performance outcomes of the 'reviewed' algorithm in or close to real time and report on compliance with those factors. For example, it will be verifying that, in determining creditworthiness, the reviewing algorithm is basing its decisions on complete economic and financial data, rather than upon protected factors such as race, gender, or mobile phone usage.

In this way, algorithmic assurance can complement due diligence and explainability and assist humans in managing 'risky' algorithms. Importantly, the human in charge of overseeing AI will have to verify that the algorithmic assurance is available for, and applied to, a given AI application and then use and act upon its findings.

4. AI Review Committees

In addition, financial regulators should create independent AI review committees to provide cross-disciplinary and impartial expertise. This is an important practice emerging in some non-financial companies.[39] Some of these committees have been quite impactful, such as in Axon's management and board accepting the recommendation of its AI and Policing Ethics Board to impose a moratorium on the use of facial recognition in Axon's body cameras. Other committees have had less impact or their impact remains to be seen. In any event, these committees should not detract from the ultimate responsibility being vested in management and the board regarding AI governance.

---

[38] Shivapratap Gopakumar et al, 'Algorithmic Assurance: An Active Approach to Algorithmic Testing Using Bayesian Optimisation' (Discussion Paper, 32nd Neural Information Processing Systems Foundation Conference, Montreal, 2018).

[39] Brian W Tang, 'Independent AI Ethics Committees and ESG Corporate Reporting on AI as Emerging Corporate and AI Governance Trends' in Susanne Chishti et al (eds), *The AI Book: The Artificial Intelligence Handbook for Investors, Entrepreneurs and FinTech Visionaries* (Wiley, 2020) 180, 183.

C. *Personal Responsibility in Financial Regulation: Challenges in Building Human-in-the-Loop Systems*

Several concerns arise about the personal responsibility model. These include: (1) inability to fully control AI using internal governance, (2) unwillingness to curtail highly profitable AI, (3) tacit collusion between AI systems, (4) over-deterrence of innovation, and (5) differing attitudes to AI and technology in financial services.

1. Inability to Fully Control AI Internally

If AI cannot be controlled by external monitors, such as financial supervisors, it may be argued that AI cannot be monitored and controlled effectively by senior management not directly involved in AI data gathering, coding, and operations.

Existing methods of internal control include: internal reporting, defining risk limits in terms of risk budgets, assigning budgets for code development and data pool acquisition, and setting adequate incentives through balanced compensation models. Personal responsibility/liability systems place the responsibility for regulated conduct areas upon specific individual senior managers. Thus, a senior manager who is directly responsible for regulatory breaches arising in their area of responsibility will have strong incentives to innovate and strengthen the existing governance tools to monitor and better understand their functional area, staff, third-party contractors and suppliers, and IT systems. A culture of due diligence, explainability, and algorithmic assurance should then evolve to address black box problems. Where it does not, the individual and board will nonetheless remain responsible for any harm caused. Naturally, the manager responsibility model requires those involved in AI development, procurement, and deployment to be included within the net of responsibility.

One concern often raised against a manager responsibility concept is where self-learning AI taps into unexpected or malicious data input and produces unexpected correlations or unacceptable outcomes. However, as in the case of Microsoft's Tay, this can be countered by the proverbial mandatory 'AI off switch' depending on the risk and impact assessment and an appropriate contingency or business continuity plan.[40]

2. Unwillingness to Curtail Highly Profitable AI

A common issue in financial institution governance is the unwillingness to curtail profitable, yet complex, conduct. It was difficult for senior managers in the lead up to the 2008 Global Financial Crisis to understand the true risks of tranched and

---

[40] See, for example, Board of the International Organization of Securities Commissions (n 35) 19–20, which mentions such a kill switch in the explanatory note.

structured finance, but they had little incentive to stop complex and opaque, but highly profitable, business models. This argument is especially relevant in the light of the recent growth of less-regulated tech companies which offer new financial services and products.

This manifestation of agency risk is perennial in corporate and financial governance. While our proposal does not change management's incentives from the standpoint of profit-making, the implementation of personal responsibility incentivises individual and managerial due diligence and efforts to ensure sustainability. AI review committees add another level of oversight and input, and another avenue through which explainability can be sought.

3. Tacit Collusion between AI Systems

The profitability of tacit collusion among AI systems poses particular challenges.[41]
The World Economic Forum[42] has suggested this be mitigated by:

1. Restricting AI-enabled systems communication with their environments to 'explicitly justifiable business purposes';
2. ensuring that their AI-enabled systems' decisions are explainable by 'valid, legal business reasons'; and
3. requiring humans to oversee decisions made by AI-enabled systems.

These are good suggestions but may not always be sufficient to fully mitigate this substantial risk, in particular when collusion is highly profitable. However, personal responsibility regimes should address this risk, particularly when supplemented by review committees, due diligence, explainability, and algorithmic assurance requirements. Each of these measures brings potential director and managerial disqualification, and other severe sanctions, in cases of lack of oversight.

4. Over-deterrence of Innovation

On the other hand, manager responsibility may be counterproductive. If the regulatory burden deters good managers from being involved in AI-based financial services, we may find a reduction in innovation in finance and corollary reductions in efficiency, access to justice and combatting of financial crime, and/or less thoughtful and reflective people serving as senior managers for financial services firms. Regulators must respond to this concern with proportional 'carrots' to incentivise and recognise good actors as well as 'sticks' for irresponsible conduct.

---

[41] Bundeskartellamt and Autorité de la Concurrence, *Algorithms and Competition* (Report, November 2019); United Kingdom Competition and Markets Authority, 'Pricing Algorithms: Economic Working Paper on the Use of Algorithms to Facilitate Collusion and Personalised Pricing' (Working Paper, October 2018).
[42] World Economic Forum (n 21) 118.

Personal responsibility liability systems should also include continuing education frameworks.

Individual responsibility could lead to decreased diligence in monitoring fellow key function holders. Conversely, collective responsibility could increase monitoring among key function holders but lead to over-deterrence. This debate is underscored by the Australian Westpac bank scandal – a potent example of the potential magnitude of techrisk.[43] The bank had developed its own software to implement and govern remittances, and a relatively innocuous looking piece of software, and poor oversight, permitted 23 million anti-money laundering breaches. The breaches attracted a massive financial penalty and arguably even more reputational damage to the bank.

To avoid or limit over-deterrence against innovation, a compromise would include defining some collective core duties, while also imposing individual responsibility. This should apply to both board and corporate responsibility.

Regulators usually require finance experience as a precondition for licensing a financial entity. Technology start-up founders often have little experience in running a regulated firm. If regulators require this expertise of all key function holders in a start-up, innovation will be severely impaired. One obvious response is for regulators to require sufficient expertise and experience from the fintech start-up's board and key executives as a group. Therefore, some board members and executives can contribute the IT/AI expertise,[44] while others contribute experience in running regulated financial services firms. Gradually, all board members and executives should be able to meet the standards for seasoned financial intermediaries.

For personal responsibility in given areas, specific area-related expertise is required as one aspect of the fit-and-proper test. While it may make sense in a fintech start-up to take a balanced and proportionate approach to board and key executive requirements as a group, specifically mandated individual responsibility requirements, expertise, and experience requirements would remain necessary in the licensing process.

5. Differing Attitudes to AI and Technology in Financial Services

Our final, and perhaps most important, recommendation goes to the cultural attitude of many in financial services towards AI and technology in general. There is much talk about the trust crisis in our modern world of fake news and low institutional credibility. But we do not need to trust AI more in financial services, or medical care, criminal sentencing, or other applications. We need AI to demonstrate its trustworthiness.[45]

---

43 Ross P Buckley et al, 'TechRisk' [2020] (March) *Singapore Journal of Legal Studies* 35.
44 Maria Lillà Montagnani and Maria Lucia Passador, 'Toward an Enhanced Level of Corporate Governance: Tech Committees as a Game Changer for the Board of Directors' (2022) 14(1) *Journal of Business, Entrepreneurship and the Law* (forthcoming).
45 See David Spiegelhalter, 'Should We Trust Algorithms?' (2020) 2(1) *Harvard Data Science Review* <https://hdsr.mitpress.mit.edu/pub/56lnenzj/release/1>.

We have seen senior finance professionals unwilling to insist on what their organisation really needs in its AI and accept instead assurances or explanations from AI developers that they would not accept from other service suppliers. The reason seems to be the apprehension or lack of understanding of many senior staff about AI and technology generally. In one of the most regulated of all industries, financial services, these attitudes are inappropriate.

What is needed at the most senior levels of major banks, and within their in-house legal departments, is a cultural shift. Instead of the hesitancy and apprehension that often characterise current approaches to AI and technology more generally, these tools need to be approached with confidence, humility, and the understanding that they can and must be held to perform at the required standards.

VI. CONCLUSION

The financial services sector globally is one of the leaders in AI use and development. However, AI comes with numerous technical, ethical, and legal challenges that can undermine the objectives of financial regulation with respect to data, cybersecurity, consumer protection, systemic risk, and ethics – in particular, relating to black box issues.

As shown, traditional financial supervision focused on external governance is unlikely to address sufficiently the risks created by AI, due to: (1) information asymmetry, (2) data dependency, and (3) interdependency. Accordingly, even where supervisors have exceptional resources and expertise, supervising the use of AI in finance by traditional means is extremely challenging.

To address these weaknesses, we suggest governance of financial institutions is strengthened to impose personal responsibility requirements that put a human in the loop. This approach is based on existing frameworks of managerial responsibility that evolved in the continuing stream of ethically questionable behaviour across the world in finance. These frameworks should be cognisant of and consistent with broader data privacy and human-in-the-loop approaches beyond finance. From a financial supervisor's perspective, internal governance can be strengthened largely through a renewed focus on senior managements' (or 'key function holders') personal responsibilities and accountability for regulated areas and activities, as designated for regulatory purposes. Under these rules, the key function holders or managers in charge are responsible for themselves, their area of supervision, their staff, their third-party contractors, and their technology, including AI.

This direct personal responsibility encourages due diligence in investigating new technologies, their uses and impact, employment of algorithmic assurance, and requiring fairness and explainability as part of any AI system, with attendant dire personal consequences for failure. For a financial services professional with direct responsibility, demonstrating appropriate due diligence, explainability, and use of algorithmic assurance will be key to a personal defence in the event of a regulatory action.

Importantly, this approach also has great potential for addressing AI concerns in any other regulated industry facing black box issues arising from AI. It will at least ensure that humans are central to the evolution of AI in already regulated industries. As it is inevitable that AI will increasingly become part of our lives and world, as can be seen with the advent and unprecedentedly rapid increase in use of generative AI systems from the second half of 2022, it is imperative that we put humans in the loop in this human–machine relationship.

8

Distributed Ledger Technology, Blockchain, and Finance

SUMMARY

This chapter considers how distributed ledger technologies and blockchain can contribute to the creation of new foundational infrastructure for financial services, including crypto assets and smart contracts as well as in the context of traditional finance, particularly debt capital markets. We classify the new business models, analyse the opportunities, and highlight the regulatory challenges.

I. INTRODUCTION

Distributed Ledger Technologies (DLTs), our collective term for distributed ledgers which often incorporate blockchains, as further defined below, can provide the technological underpinning of new foundational infrastructure in capital markets, payments, and finance more broadly. This chapter introduces the technology and then focuses on the opportunities and challenges associated with the use of DLTs for finance and financial infrastructure.

II. CLASSIFICATION AND TERMINOLOGY

We start by introducing the core technologies before describing the crypto-asset types which have been created using such technology.

A. *Technology*

1. Distributed Ledgers

A distributed ledger is 'a database that is consensually shared and synchronised across networks that are spread across multiple sites, institutions, or geographies, allowing

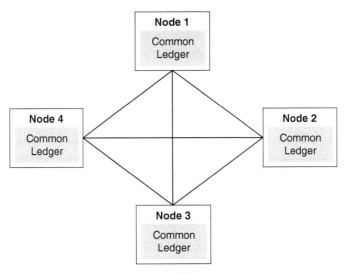

FIGURE 8.1 DLT set-up

transactions to have [multiple private or] public "witnesses"'.[1] Data sharing results in a sequential database distributed across a network of servers, which together function as a ledger. Distributed ledgers are characterised by the absence or minimal presence of central administration and data storage. They are, hence, 'distributed' in the sense that the authorisation for recording a given piece of information results from the software-driven consensus of many data-storage points ('nodes'). Coupled with cryptographic solutions, such features curtail the risk of data manipulation, thereby solving the problem of having to trust third-party data-storage service providers.[2] Furthermore, since all nodes run the same software code and store, in principle, the same data, all nodes have simultaneous access to the data stored, resulting in greatly enhanced transparency. Other nodes can observe if one tries to rewrite the data, and datasets can be amended only if the majority agree (usually by virtue of a pre-defined consensus mechanism) (Figure 8.1).

DLTs can be either permissionless (open) or permissioned (closed), and either public or private.[3] The first distinction (open/closed) reflects which entities can operate a node and thereby join in the consensus mechanism of *validating* transactions (referred to as 'miners' in Bitcoin terminology). The second distinction

---

[1] Oliver Wyman and World Economic Forum, *Innovation-Driven Cyber-Risk to Customer Data in Financial Services* (White Paper, 2017) 6 <www3.weforum.org/docs/WEF_Cyber_Risk_to_Customer_Data.pdf>.

[2] See Michèle Finck, *Blockchain Regulation and Governance in Europe* (Cambridge University Press, 2019) 12–14.

[3] See Evangelos Benos, Rodd Garret, and Pedro Gurrola Perez, 'The Economics of Distributed Ledger Technology for Securities Settlement' (2019) 4 *Ledger* 121, 126–27.

(public/private) reflects who can read the information on the ledger and initiate transactions on it (the owners of a 'wallet' in Bitcoin terminology). Upon this taxonomy, the Bitcoin ledger is permissionless (open) and public.

However, permissioned (closed) and private DLTs have the greatest potential in DLT market infrastructure since they avoid the environmentally scandalous energy consumption as well as the governance and accountability issues of Bitcoin-style 'public ledgers'. Compliance becomes difficult if anyone can take part in validating transactions. Public ledgers are difficult to reconcile with privacy, insider trading, and market abuse legislation. By contrast, permissioned systems require less extensive consensus mechanisms because the nodes are pre-approved (trusted), which enables faster and cheaper processing of transactions.

Indeed, a real obstacle to people understanding how DLTs will serve to underpin financial market infrastructure (FMI) arises because many of us assume most DLTs are like Bitcoins, which is simply not the case, and will not be the case with most DLTs used in finance.

2. Blockchain

Distributed ledgers are usually paired with a blockchain protocol. Blockchain refers to the storage of data in bundles ('blocks') in a strict time-sequenced series that links each block, through a time stamp, to previous and subsequent blocks. The blockchain renders data corruption more difficult, because a successful cyberattack will require simultaneously corrupting not just one set but multiple sets of data (i.e., the whole blockchain) and the time stamps.

3. Smart Contracts

Distributed ledgers have great potential to support another innovation that may remove the need for trust in many human interactions: smart contracts. While neither smart nor necessarily contracts, smart contracts are inaptly named self-executing software protocols that typically reflect some terms of a broader agreement between two parties.[4] Typically a smart contract will guarantee payment, or some other performance of a contract if this can be delivered digitally, upon the verified occurrence of a specific event. These conditions are directly written into code. A smart contract could, for instance, provide for payment upon receipt of a shipping container of components. After advanced scanners verify the contents of the container without needing to open it, the smart contract would pay the supplier. Smart contracts may render transactions traceable, transparent, and irreversible and reduce the need for an external enforcement mechanism such as a court, an arbitrator, or

---

[4] See Nick Szabo, 'Formalizing and Securing Relationships on Public Networks' (1997) 2(9) *First Monday* 548:469.

a central clearing facility. However, we do not believe smart contracts will in any sense be able to place themselves beyond the jurisdiction of courts, which for strong public policy reasons are closely guarded and preserved most everywhere.

The key impact of smart contracts is disintermediation, both in an institutional sense and a personal sense. If administrative processes exclusively depend on 'if–then' binary conditions, human intervention cannot wastefully delay or derail execution as the above example demonstrates. If the number and atomic composition of the components in the shipping container complies with the contract, payment occurs automatically. This reduces the need for trust and for security arrangements (such as payment mechanisms like letters of credit) to address human opportunism.

Although distributed ledgers and blockchains are information storage devices and smart contracts are information processing tools, we consider smart contracts here because they typically operate on distributed ledgers.

B. *Crypto-Assets and Offering Types*

1. Crypto-Assets

Based on DLTs, a new range of assets have evolved: crypto-assets. These crypto-assets are a bundle of data in a non-corruptible data block, called a 'token'. Digital tokens are well named in the sense that a token can represent almost any right or obligation, ranging from a financial interest in a company to purely non-financial rights to join an online community or play a game. There are well over 10,000 crypto-assets which differ widely by the rights (and obligations) the token represents. Academic analysis tends to place crypto-assets into one of three categories, adopting a functional approach which many regulators have followed.[5]

Utility tokens grant some sort of access or right(s) to use a company's ecosystem, goods or services. Utility tokens may also provide holders with governance rights in the issuing company, such as the right to vote for updates in the functional structure, and otherwise shape the future of issuing entities. These kinds of tokens often resemble the pre-payment of license fees or crowdfunding sales. A utility token falling into these schemes is not usually considered a security or financial product: it does not give rights to future cash flows but rather simply enables use of a blockchain-based ecosystem.

Security/financial/investment tokens are tied to an underlying asset and represent a fractional ownership of the asset or its value. Such tokens offer rights to future cash flow and are typically treated under financial regulatory regimes

---

[5] See Philipp Maume and Mathias Fromberger 'Regulations of Initial Coin Offerings: Reconciling U.S. and E.U. Securities Laws' (2019) 19 *Chicago Journal of International Law* 548, 558; Dirk Zetzsche et al, 'The ICO Gold Rush: It's a Scam, It's a Bubble, It's a Super Challenge for Regulators' (2019) 60(2) *Harvard International Law Journal* 267, 276.

as financial products, securities, financial instruments, derivatives, or collective investment schemes.

Currency/payment tokens in their pure form fulfil the economic roles of money, which are to serve as a means of exchange, store of value, and unit of account. Famously represented by Bitcoin, currency tokens have lately grown more diverse and now include stablecoins like Tether.

The three categories, though useful, can introduce uncertainty in legal systems, including in those with narrow definitions of 'security' or 'financial product' such as the EU and also in those with a comprehensive definition of 'security' or 'financial product' as in the United States with its Howey test, named after the leading case *SEC v Howey* of 1946.[6] The EU has now sought to resolve these uncertainties with its Markets in Crypto-Assets (MiCA) Regulation. The United States is likewise looking to reduce uncertainty by seeking to classify most tokens that are not innocuous utility tokens as securities under their Securities Acts regime.

While tokens are often characterised as 'utility' or 'currency' by their promoters, the reality of the particular transaction must be looked at carefully to deduce their actual nature, with tokens ranging from funding of early-stage research (similar to charitable crowdfunding), to pre-purchase of specific products, often blockchain-based, to investment structures of various forms (similar to equity or debt crowdfunding). The game in the Initial Coin Offering (ICO) boom of 2017 and 2018 was to assert the tokens being offered were utility tokens, and thus beyond the purview of financial regulation, while in reality buyers were buying the tokens in expectation of cash flows or capital appreciation or both. Once regulators in most major jurisdictions pushed back hard against this perspective, the ICO boom ended in 2019.[7]

2. Offering Types

Crypto-assets may be issued via, or included in trading at, crypto-exchanges, in various ways. We distinguish between issues with a centralised vehicle and those that are fully decentralised.

If crypto-assets are offered without a central issuer or an issuing vehicle, the issue is dubbed Initial Dex Offering, with 'DEX' the acronym for a decentralised exchange. Prominent examples include the initial trading of Bitcoin and Ether.

Often, however, an issuing vehicle is involved: a trust, foundation, or limited liability company; and the issue is then dubbed an 'Initial Coin Offering' (ICO) or, more recently and accurately, a 'Securities Token Offering' (STO) (Figure 8.2).

---

[6] *SEC v Howey Co*, 328 US 293 (1946) ('*Howey*'). See also *SEC v Edwards*, 540 US 389 (2004); *United Housing Found Inc v Forman*, 421 US 837 (1975) ('*Forman*'); *Tcherepnin v Knight*, 389 US 332 (1967) ('*Tcherepnin*'); *SEC v CM. Joiner Leasing Corp*, 320 US 344 (1943) ('*Joiner*').

[7] Zetzsche et al (n 5) 267.

the context of cybersecurity because a distributed ledger enables other nodes
inue operations even if one or more are compromised.

IV. REGULATORY CHALLENGES

the hype around DLT and blockchain, it is no panacea. DLT does not make
rate data accurate (irrespective of why the data were wrong in the first place),
not remove credit risk which remains between deal execution and settle-
and it does not extinguish the threat posed by cyberattacks on wallets and
providers. Indeed, it may even increase this threat if some of the nodes have
bersecurity than a traditional centralised ledger would.
ever, some of these issues of DLT can be remedied by law and regulation.
out these issues in the following subsection before we turn to the challenges
ulating DLT.

A. *Issues to Be Addressed*

1. Information Asymmetry

or issue requiring regulatory attention is information asymmetry. This became
bvious during the ICO bubble of 2017 to 2019, where many 'hot issues' would
received a cold reception if investors had been given all relevant information,
rospectus for a securities offering typically does.[12]
with all immature technologies, there will be both technical and regulatory
es that deliver unintended consequences. The speed of growth of the ICO
in 2017 is a good example of the scale of the challenge facing regulators. Here
his technologically new way of offering bundles of legal rights which were dif-
to classify or, at least, the character of which the offerors often tried diligently
scure. The demands upon regulators to be fully up to date, responsive, and
geous are high.[13]

2. Operational Risk

the standardisation and automatisation that form part of DLT mitigate – in
ciple – operational risk, an error once implemented in the code may easily
d over the whole system affecting a greater number of nodes and individuals

tzsche et al (n 5) 267.
nalogies with the 1980s to 2000s period are sobering, when the popular adoption of computers
arked innovations such as securitisation and credit default swaps. Policymakers supported these
bsequent developments, which eventually facilitated the global financial crisis of 2007–09. Cf
hris Brummer and Yesha Yadav, 'Fintech and the Innovation Trilemma' (2019) 107 *Georgetown
w Journal* 235, 254–58.

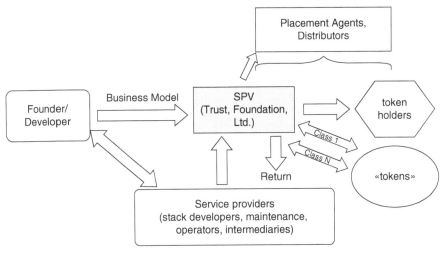

FIGURE 8.2 ICO set-up

ICOs/STOs often lead to cash flow streams that benefit the project financed and
the founder developers of the underlying technology.

C. *Financial infrastructure*

1. Financial Market Infrastructures

FMIs facilitate the clearing, settlement, and recording of payments, securities,
derivatives, and other financial transactions.[8] They include payment systems, central counterparty clearing houses, central securities depositories (CSDs), securities
settlement systems, and trade repositories.

Looking at FMIs in relation to securities and financial assets provides valuable context. A CSD, as a centralised ledger provider, holds the master ledger of all transactions
in a given security and performs the process of clearing, settlement, and recording.
Intermediaries with access to the CSD hold an account with the CSD and those
accounts constitute a copy of the master ledger. Once a transaction takes place, it
must be reconciled on all ledgers concerned. This typically happens after transactions
are settled individually on each ledger, for instance, daily at the close of business.

8   See CPMI, *Principles for Financial Market Infrastructures* (Report No 101, 16 April 2012) 7. For further
    guidance on the PMFI, see CPMI, *Resilience of Central Counterparties (CCPs): Further Guidance on
    the PFMI* (Report No 163, 5 July 2017); CPMI, *Recovery of Financial Market Infrastructures* (Report
    No 162, 5 July 2017); CPMI, *Guidance on Cyber Resilience for Financial Market Infrastructures*
    (Report No 146, 29 June 2016); CPMI, *Clearing of Deliverable FX Instruments* (Report No 143, 05
    February 2016); CPMI, *Application of the "Principles for financial market infrastructures" to Central
    Bank FMIs* (Report No 130, 19 August 2015); CPMI, *Public Quantitative Disclosure Standards for
    Central Counterparties* (Report No 125, 26 February 2015).

If financial securities are 'purchased' (i.e., exchanged for fiat currency), clearing and settlement take place both through a security leg and a payment leg. This process typically takes 1–3 days.[9] In the meantime, both securities and money are typically held as collateral and rendered unavailable for other economic purposes.

DLT-based market infrastructure can reduce the settlement time, under ideal circumstances, to almost real time: when settlement time is defined as the time of consensus in the ledger protocol, settlement time may be equal to the time necessary for rewriting the code across ledgers.

2 DeFi Stack

Upon individual DLT services, we often see a new *bundle* of individual services established, dubbed a 'Decentralised Finance Stack' (DeFi Stack). While the details of the DeFi Stack will be discussed in Chapter 9, as they form an integral part of decentralised finance, it is important to note that the stacking of individual applications may lead to an entirely new level of service: all functions of a given financial system may be replicated and provided within the financial ecosystem that serves the customers. Customers may not need to leave the DeFi stack, regardless of whether they seek services related to payments, lending, trading, asset management, or strategic advice. This makes the proper integration of the new foundational infrastructure into law and regulation, as we analyse here, of utmost importance.

3. Decentralised Autonomous Organisations

Both the DLT-based infrastructure and the DeFi stack may be related to a decentralised autonomous organisation (DAO). A DAO may be best understood as one form of collective body governing the new types of FMI. A DAO may take decisions on questions like fee setting, infrastructure design, or investment strategy. This is not the place to discuss DAOs in detail, as they pose separate questions from the perspective of corporate and private law and financial regulation.[10] However, in this context, it must be noted that the set-up, governance, and transparency of controls relating to DAOs feature thousands of variations, and some of these variations may prove problematic.

---

[9] Morten Bech et al, 'On the Future of Securities Settlement' [2020] (March) *BIS Quarterly Review* 67, 68.

[10] See on DAOs, Takeshi Nagai and Georges Ugeux, 'Regulating Digital Assets in the United States: Security Tokens, Utility Tokens and Stablecoins' (2021) 36(5) *Journal of International Banking Law and Regulation* 183; Shen Wei, 'When FinTech Meets Corporate Governance: Opportunities and Challenges of Using Blockchain and Artificial Intelligence in Corporate Optimisation' (2021) 36(2) *Journal of International Banking Law and Regulation* 53; Christopher M Brummer, 'Distributed Ledgers, Artificial Intelligence and the Purpose of the Corporation' (2020) 79(3) *Cambridge Law Journal* 431; Karsten Paetzmann, 'Challenges of Blockchain Technology in Financial Services: Use Cases, Smart Contracts and Governance' (2022) 37(8) *Journal of International Banking Law and Regulation* 294.

III. OPPORTUNITIES

In terms of financial infrastructure, DLTs proponents ho[...] opportunities. Of particular importance are increased lega[...] enhanced speed, and better risk management.

A. *Increasing Legal Certainty and Avoiding Dou[...]*

DLTs ensures the validity of datasets by spreading data over m[...] agree, via the consensus mechanism, to confirm data validity. [...] ter than other technologies that data are not manipulated w[...] also ensure that the party making a transfer has title on the le[...] transferred and is not able to transfer it twice.

B. *Disintermediation-Based Reduction of C[...]*

A synchronised and shared ledger potentially enables autor[...] ment, and recording of financial transactions without interr[...] at lower costs than hierarchical ledgers. This is because the lo[...] mediaries in DLT-based systems result in less fees for any giv[...] however, that systems development (in particular, through sma[...] a high degree of foresight and planning to work well, while ov[...] hidden costs charged within these networks is low; hence, the[...] presently quite open and undetermined.

C. *Enhancing Speed*

The use of smart contracts may speed up standard transaction[...] the fulfilment of specified conditions. For example, interest[...] may be automatically transferred to bondholders on the ledg[...] as we argued in the context of FMI, DLT is expected to reduc[...] Not only does this reduce counterparty risk and the need for c[...] settlement period, but DLT enhances trust because, once code[...] ledger, the parties can no longer interfere in contract executio[...] trust-enhancing, yet time-consuming, reconciliation diminishes[...]

D. *Improving Risk Management and Reducing Syste[...]*

A DLT-based transparency and accounting trail may enable b[...] ment[11] and enforcement, and its full potential to enhance resili[...]

---

[11] BIS Committee on Payments and Market Infrastructures, *Distributed Ledger T[...] Clearing and Settlement* (Report, February 2017) 19.

than with a concentrated ledger. Distributed ledgers rely on sophisticated software codes that are periodically rewritten to improve performance and security. As with all software, only IT experts fully understand the structure, and only IT experts are able to adapt it if and when weaknesses appear. This may create serious problems as 'there is no such thing as flawless software; there are always errors or "bugs" that negatively affect the performance of the software or make it vulnerable to attack by hackers.'[14]

In particular, poorly written, maintained, or outdated code can open the door for system hacks, such as those that occurred in the Mt. Gox and DAO cases. The governance deficiencies of permissionless ledgers may become real-world issues in the context of poor coding. For instance, the hard fork that occurred in the Bitcoin system in August 2017 was due to a lack of consensus as to whether a specific update improved the system or led to unfair benefits for some users.

3. Systemic Risk

Since we address tech-related systemic and other risks (dubbed 'TechRisk') in Part IV, it is sufficient here to stress the relevance of systemic risk in the context of DLT-based market infrastructure. Systemic risks stem both from the network character of DLT which results in technical interlinkages and from automation: if many smart contracts self-execute in response to an event, this could trigger contagion and adverse feedback loops.

4. Governance

Since some ledgers operated by DAOs spread governance rights and technical access to code across many participants (i.e., nodes), this creates a set of governance challenges. While some of these challenges are general issues that arise within decentralised finance and will be discussed in that context in Chapter 9, two challenges are peculiar to DLT: data and ledger governance.

First, as DLT relies on data storage across multiple nodes, each node operator has access to the data stored on the ledger;[15] this potentially raises concerns over data privacy, insider trading, and market abuse.[16]

Second, as to ledger governance, given that DLT relies on algorithms and a potentially large number of nodes, questions arise as to who is practically and legally accountable for its operations. This question of who controls the apparently

---

[14] See Angela Walch, 'The Bitcoin Blockchain as Financial Market Infrastructure: A Consideration of Operational Risk' (2015) 18 *The NYU Journal of Legislation and Public Policy* 837, 856.

[15] For example, the DLT supporting Bitcoin stores all data except the identity of the owners, which requires a private key.

[16] See Dirk Zetzsche, Ross Buckley, and Douglas Arner, 'The Distributed Liability of Distributed Ledgers' [2018] 4 *University of Illinois Law Review* 1361, 1375.

decentralised ledger is discussed in Chapter 9. If the servers are located in different jurisdictions with no central entity, there is also the question of which laws apply and which courts can rightfully assert jurisdiction which we discuss next.

B. *Applicable Law*

A key legal question that always arises is the law which applies. This question is particularly relevant in a cross-border setting, where the parties involved in a DLT-based infrastructure (the nodes, the ledger, or customers as the case may be) are located in more than one jurisdiction. The matter of applicable law is crucial from both financial regulation and private law perspectives.

1. Financial Regulation

Financial regulation recognises three types of conflict of law rules:

1. Incompatibility: Jurisdiction A prohibits conduct that is permitted in jurisdiction B. This configuration incurs the greatest costs for intermediaries, as they need to devise alternative solutions, typically involving separate legal entities licensed in different jurisdictions and connected by contract.
2. Restricted eligibility: A establishes additional requirements that may or may not be compatible with the institution's set-up and business model in B. This set-up requires an additional layer of law/regulation and oversight/enforcement in A that comes with additional costs.
3. Eligibility subject to mutual recognition, which is usually based on a substituted compliance/equivalence test: A recognises that the law/regulation and supervision/enforcement in B is, in substance, equivalent to and as effective as in A.

It is therefore important to determine which regulator has jurisdiction over the conduct.

Financial law has several ways to connect an institution to a regulator. One category often used for prudential regulation is the *headquarters and/or registered office* of the financial institution.

Distribution rules often ask where the institution offers or markets its services, while a third category asks where *the effects* of an institution's actions are felt. The latter arises with the so-called risk-based regulation, which seeks to identify where risks are likely to materialise, such as in market abuse, data protection and AML/CTF rules, and systemic risk oversight.

In turn, a given market infrastructure can be subject to the financial regulation of several different countries at the same time: the laws of the country's headquarters for prudential regulation and operational requirements, the laws of the countries where it offers its services (if only as a counterparty or settlement institution), and the laws of all those jurisdictions whose (a) citizens' data are stored, and (b) financial instruments are traded and/or settled and (c) currencies are booked in a payment institution's account.

2. Private Law

The applicable law issue is also crucial for private law, which follows different criteria than financial regulation. For the private law dimension it matters, in particular, who the parties are to the services contract, be it trading, clearing, settlement, lending, or asset management, and it may matter where the cloud servers on which the DLT operates are located. In terms of the DLT as a whole, conditions possibly arise in which the 'veil of the ledger' may be pierced so as to sheet liability home to other parties; and so, questions of governance arise: who is in charge, who has voting rights, and who can make decisions about ledger operations and technological revamps/updates?

Private law includes contracts, property and tort relationships between private actors, and also intra-corporate matters such as legal relationships between DLT nodes. However, we here consider only conflict of law rules for contracts.

As a matter of principle, entities involved in wholesale business can usually choose the jurisdiction the laws of which will apply and the courts which will have authority. However, some mandatory public law rules of a jurisdiction will apply even if the private law may otherwise be freely chosen. In addition, there are certain fundamental concepts of private law, such as *ordre public*, that always require recognition. In contrast, when it comes to retail clients and consumers, the mandatory consumer protection law of a country usually applies as a minimum, even if the law and courts of another country are chosen to govern the contract.

Institutions can thus among themselves be subject to the law and courts of one jurisdiction while the law applicable to, and courts governing, their relations with their customers may be that of another jurisdiction. If the law of the first jurisdiction is inconsistent with that of the second, no adjudicating body may be available to address the gap. To complicate matters further, in this fast-moving field, it will often be uncertain ex ante whether the second jurisdiction might award damage for certain conduct.

Hence, determining which private law will apply will really matter. Another approach to the applicable law matter is harmonisation which diminishes the differences in the legal systems thus harmonised. In fact, several expert bodies and working groups work on harmonisation of both the conflict of law rules and substantive law applicable to DLT.[17]

---

[17] Notable organisations that devote efforts to DLT include Unidroit and the European Law Institute. See, for example, 'Law & Technology', *Unidroit* (Web Page) <www.unidroit.org/law-technology>; Commission on International Trade Law and UNIDROIT, *Summary Report on the Joint UNICITRAL/UNIDROIT Workshop* (Report, 2019); Sjef van Erp et al, 'Blockchain Technology and Smart Contracts', *European Law Institute* (Web Page, 2021) <www.europeanlawinstitute.eu/projects-publications/current-projects/current-projects/blockchains>.

C. *Node or Ledger as Regulatory Access Point*

A major challenge of regulating DLT-based infrastructure stems from the fact that governance rights and influence over the ledger is, at least to some extent, distributed. This impacts on legal issues, not least the applicable law just discussed.

1. Node vs Ledger Perspective

Effective regulation will require, for legal, regulatory, contractual, and other issues, a decision as to whether the technical distribution of functions across ledgers should be acknowledged by law, that is, whether the law should adopt what we call 'the ledger perspective' or whether it should retain 'the node perspective' where the law requires each node to comply with applicable laws and regulations.

In principle, financial law generally assumes that ownership, governance, accountability, and responsibility for legal rights and obligations are all concentrated in one legal entity. In this way, the law looks at each node separately, establishing the duties and obligations of that node, in what we term the 'node perspective'. The perspective of the ledger – how it functions as a whole, and how all the nodes interact – is thus built up and derived from the individual rights and obligations of each node. A ledger, from the node perspective, is the product of multiple nodes interacting, and the law governing such interaction determines the conditions and outcomes of that interaction. Even when the law takes the node perspective, the ledger relationship must be considered, and this will not be simple. Typically, each ledger participant alone has no influence over the entire ledger's operation, given the very nature of a DLT is its distribution across various nodes. Allocating responsibility in a DLT-based payment scheme is thus difficult.

Furthermore, asking who among several participants issues a financial instrument if the instrument is issued via a DLT that is not controlled by any one entity leads to challenges in the application of the law.

Thus, as an alternative, the law could look at the DLT as a whole. Under this contrasting approach, the node perspective is replaced by the ledger perspective. Under the ledger perspective, the technical distribution of functions among ledgers is acknowledged by law, and rights and obligations are assigned to the ledger as a whole. From a legal standpoint, the ledger perspective in effect assigns entity status to the ledger, albeit – as we will show – not for all of the functions, rights, and obligations the law foresees. The node perspective applies the law as if any individual node were the sole subject of a given regulation – and so one looks at the exposure, costs, and risks of each node. In contrast, the ledger perspective considers the whole network as subject to regulation and each participating entity as subject to regulation through its participation in the network. Liability is intermediated through the network and responsibility is distributed among network participants. Here, one looks primarily to the network and to the participants only to the extent they are exposed as network participants.

As an example, let us assume there are two DLT participants: A (with an AAA rating) and B (with a below-investment grade rating). The node perspective would measure counterparty risk separately, resulting in one very good rating and one very poor rating. Third-party clients exposed to counterparty risk with respect to A will set aside less capital to cover the risk than clients exposed to B. Yet, from the perspective of the ledger, the rating mix of A and B would determine the outcome. If A is much larger and much stronger than B, the result may be much closer to A's rating than to B's, and vice versa if B's exposures exceed A's.

How we treat distributed ledgers is an issue that will fall for resolution legally in quite a range of contexts, and of course under different legal systems. How these issues are in time resolved will be fascinating to follow.

2. The Business Plan Approach

While most financial laws so far have retained the node perspective, seek to define the role of each type of intermediary, and make each explicitly accountable for their activities, some notable examples seek to find a legal solution more in line with the gist of DLT.

(A) PILOTR'S REQUIREMENTS In particular, the EU has enacted a pilot regime for market infrastructures based on distributed ledger technology known universally as PilotR.[18] This regime addresses the perennial issue of governance and accountability in distributed ledgers by requiring the appointment of *one operator*. It then takes a truly innovative approach to the rights, obligations, and accountability of DLT participants: it leaves the operator to determine how functions and obligations are distributed or whether they remain in the hands of the operator or other parties.

With regard to the substance of the DLT operations, the operator itself should define 'the rules under which the DLT market infrastructures and their operators are to operate, including the legal terms defining the rights, obligations, responsibilities and liabilities of operators of DLT market infrastructures, as well as those of the members, participants, issuers and clients using their DLT market infrastructure.'[19] All of these matters must be defined within the business plan.

Instead of defining and regulating the different roles and activities making up the FMI, the EU PilotR thus grants discretion to the operator (and in the real world, all DLT participants jointly) to determine these matters. Through what we call herein

---

[18] See *Regulation (EU) 2022/858 of the European Parliament and of the Council of 30 May 2022 on a Pilot Regime for Market Infrastructures Based on Distributed Ledger Technology, and Amending Regulations (EU) No 600/2014 and (EU) No 909/2014 and Directive 2014/65/EU* [2022] OJ L 151/1 ('PilotR').

[19] Ibid art 7(1).

the 'Business Plan Approach,' PilotR adopts an overall market infrastructure view as opposed to the conventional institutional perspective.[20]

(B) OPENNESS TO INNOVATION   The Business Plan Approach comes with obvious advantages with regard to openness to innovation. For instance, the operator can assign, and thus free itself of responsibility for, tasks to other participants, notably to the nodes in a distributed network. Given the decentralised nature of DLT, it would be highly impractical for one operator to be accountable for the actions of largely autonomous nodes. The operator is asked to set the rules, and to outline the sanctions and the enforcement mechanism in its application: PilotR requires the operator to 'specify the governing law, any pre-litigation dispute settlement mechanisms, any insolvency protection measures under [applicable EU law] and the jurisdictions in which legal action may be brought.'[21] Of course, a business plan cannot override mandatory law; hence, public intervention powers, administrative sanctions, and criminal law will continue to apply. At the same time, the arrangements will not affect legal rights granted to third parties not part of the DLT. Yet, with regard to intra-ledger rights and obligations, the business plan can stipulate rights and obligations, as a quasi-contractual tool.

As a safeguard against undesirable opportunism, the governance arrangements proposed by the operator will be reviewed by the competent authority and the European Securities and Markets Authority (ESMA) before specific permission is granted. Such an approach makes sense in a DLT environment where innovators may be better informed about the technical opportunities and about to best address the resulting challenges. Indeed, PilotR may serve as an example also for other areas where regulators lack the information and insights required to draft suitable legislation.

(C) CHALLENGES   Nonetheless, the Business Plan Approach comes with foreseeable challenges.

One issue will be the extent to which other DLT or market participants will be legally bound by the rules defined by the operator. Do we apply a contractual or public law perspective to determine the perimeter of the rules' effectiveness? Pertinently, do rights and obligations apply only to DLT or market participants that have signed up to them? Does involvement with the ledger as such imply the consent of participants to the rules, or do the rules apply as public law meaning consent is not required? Consent can only be assumed when arrangements are sufficiently transparent to be fully and informedly consented to. We doubt many, if any, business plans will be sufficiently detailed for third parties to fully understand all their obligations and rights, and these things will matter if anything goes wrong.

---

[20] Dirk A Zetzsche and Jannik Woxholth, 'The DLT Sandbox under the Pilot-Regulation' (2022) 17(2) *Capital Markets Law Journal* 212, 225.

[21] PilotR art 7(1).

In practice, we suggest the competent authority requires the operator to install a mechanism to ensure consent before market participants get involved with the ledger. For that purpose, *operational* details may be stipulated by way of contracts incorporating technical specification sheets. We further envisage the operator may set up a technical pilot where nodes test their operational rights and obligations under market conditions in an isolated environment before committing. The situation will be somewhat different with regard to *legal* details as legal complexity is often present in financial infrastructure contracts and, to some extent, can be remedied by applying the *contra proferentem* doctrine, that is, interpretation against the draftsman where doubts remain, taking into account the technical and financial expertise to be expected from all entities volunteering to function as nodes.

Another pressing issue is the extent to which the operator is entitled to impose sanctions and enforcement mechanisms upon third parties. Here, we draw an analogy to rules and sanctioning regimes prevalent at stock exchanges and other self-regulating financial infrastructure. By and large, if the competent authority and ESMA require the operator to install a mechanism to ensure consent before market participants get involved with the ledger, general contract law could govern sanctions and penalties assigned to participants for non-compliance.

Finally, we caution that public sanctioning usually requires some written legal text (*nulla poena sine lege scriptum*). This requirement has two implications. On the one hand, the regulators may be incompetent to enforce business plan duties vis-à-vis non-operator DLT participants. On the other hand, sanctioning the operator may be impossible because the operator was exempted from that very duty by way of the business plan approved by the competent authority, as the case may be, so that no one is held accountable by financial regulation.

3. Liability

Regulators need to determine to whom liability should be allocated to ensure proper incentives to comply with the law and avoid undesirable data distribution, data loss, or data manipulation. Further, assuming a distributed ledger promises certain security and processing standards to market participants so as to enhance market share, the question of who is responsible will arise if the ledger fails to meet the standards. Regulators in each of these cases need to allocate responsibility.

While few aspects of liability allocation can be answered with certainty to date, based on generally applicable principles of law, three principal criteria upon which to allocate liability may include:

- Which actors are best placed to avoid the harmful or non-compliant conduct (cheapest cost avoider)?
- Which actors contributed to the harmful or non-compliant conduct in question?

- Which actors created the sources of risk that eventually resulted in the harmful or non-compliant conduct, for instance, by programming a given server or process that brought with it cybersecurity risk?

Regulators are well advised to scrutinise, using the smart regulation tools laid out in Chapters 3 and 11, the details of the DLTs they govern, and set the right incentives considering the three above criteria. This may well result in node liability for some matters (such as updating cybersecurity protocols on a given server, and capital provisioning for risks specific to the clients of that node) and ledger liability for others (including AML/CTF and data protection across the whole ledger).

V. CONCLUSION

No blueprint has yet been developed for regulating DLT-based market and financial infrastructure, and we dare say any such blueprint would most likely fail, in the light of the thousands of variants of DLTs that may be used in the context of finance. Even if we look at niche use cases, such as cross-border payments among professional, well-connected financial institutions, only basic principles can be defined, while details must be left to the parties, as shown in the business plan approach above.

For every DLT use case in market infrastructure, effective regulation must address information asymmetry (through disclosure rules), ensure appropriate operational risk management (through operating requirements), deal with systemic risk supervision (through network analysis), and seek to ensure proper governance of the DLT in question. Seeking to address these issues, regulators must take particular care in defining the applicable financial regulation and private law and must clarify whether the nodes or the ledger are the point at which regulation attaches. Finally, the regulators will need to allocate liability in a fashion that reduces careless, and potentially criminal, conduct. In doing all of this, regulators will need to respect the immense speed of innovation in this field by developing a smart regulation approach that seeks to balance openness to new technologies (which necessitates leeway for innovators) with risk controls.

9

Decentralised Finance and Embedded Regulation

SUMMARY

This chapter analyses the meaning, legal implications, and policy consequences of Decentralised Finance (DeFi). Decentralisation has the potential to undermine traditional forms of accountability and erode the effectiveness of traditional financial regulation and enforcement. At the same time, where parts of financial services are decentralised, there will be a reconcentration in a different (but possibly less regulated, less visible, and less transparent) part of the financial services chain. DeFi regulation could and should focus on this reconcentrated portion to ensure effective oversight and risk control. In fact, DeFi requires regulation in order to achieve its core objective of decentralisation. Furthermore, DeFi may further the idea of 'embedded regulation' – building regulatory approaches into the design of decentralised infrastructure, potentially decentralising both finance and its regulation in the ultimate expression of RegTech.

I. INTRODUCTION

Decentralised Finance (DeFi) comprises, at its core, what its simple name suggests: the *decentralised* provision of financial services through a mix of infrastructure, markets, technology, methods, and applications. Beyond this pure meaning, DeFi is often associated with four elements: (1) decentralisation, (2) distributed ledger technology and blockchain, (3) smart contracts, and (4) disintermediation.[1] A decentralised system such as Bitcoin relies on these elements, but not all are essential to decentralised systems. In particular, decentralisation can be achieved by other means than distributed ledgers running blockchains. Decentralised provision of financial services means provision by multiple participants, intermediaries, and

---

[1] See Fabian Schär, 'Decentralised Finance: On Blockchain- and Smart Contract-based Financial Markets' (2021) 103(2) *Federal Reserve Bank of St Louis Review* 153; Yan Chen and Cristiano Bellavitis, 'Decentralised Finance: Blockchain Technology and the Quest for an Open Financial System' (2020) 13 *Journal of Business Venturing Insights* 1.

end-users spread over multiple jurisdictions, with interactions facilitated, and often initially enabled, by technology.

Many find the promise of decentralisation and its potential to displace the regulatory state with technology a seductive ideal. We take a different approach. Rather than arguing for the potential benefits of DeFi, we seek to identify what is actually taking place and the regulatory implications this may have. In other words, we analyse DeFi, not as a desired goal but as a real-world phenomenon, and seek to understand the growing challenges it poses for financial regulation. We suggest that decentralisation has the potential to undermine traditional forms of accountability and erode the effectiveness of traditional financial regulation and enforcement. We also predict some surprising effects: where parts of the financial services value chain are decentralised, we expect reconcentration in a different (but possibly less regulated, less visible, and less transparent) part of the value chain.

We argue that DeFi requires careful regulatory attention. In situations where DeFi produces new forms of technological reliance, regulation needs to focus on the re-concentrated portion of the value chain to ensure effective oversight and risk control: in this framework, regulation is necessary in order to support decentralisation, in much the same way that regulation is at the core of securities markets and other financial services.

Section II places DeFI in the context of the traditional financial economy and provides an overview of DeFI's technological foundation. Section III shows that DeFI brings an enforcement challenge, to which Section IV proposes a solution in the form of 'Embedded Regulation'. Section V concludes.

II. A DEFI PRIMER

A. *DeFi vs Traditional Finance*

1. Traditional Finance

Traditional finance is characterised by major intermediaries that centralise functions and financial resources. Intermediaries such as banks and exchanges bring disparate participants together so that capital supply (e.g., savers, lenders, and investors) can meet demand (e.g., borrowers and entrepreneurs). We typically think of the intermediary as being central in traditional market-based financial systems.

2. Hub-and-Spoke Conceptualisation of Finance

Traditional finance results in the hub-and-spoke conceptualisation of finance and financial centres. While customers have local access to payments, savings, investments, and insurance, these services are not typically provided at the point of access. Rather, financial markets and activities traditionally cluster in local, regional, and super-regional/

global access points ('hubs').[2] These services are in substance provided from a financial centre where sufficient concentration of transaction volumes and numbers in a given sector or service allows the development of expertise and resources. Depending on the sector/service, the required volumes and numbers may develop locally, regionally, or globally. For instance, a rarely traded currency issued by a developing country's central bank tends to be illiquid, as there is limited demand. In order to bring together sufficient supply and demand, and for transactions to take place at all, it may be necessary to look beyond the domestic market to regional or global markets.

Following this economic logic, financial centres have evolved, with local, regional, and global roles and significance. For instance, New York, London, and Hong Kong provide investment banking services around the globe, Luxembourg serves as the global investment fund hub, Switzerland and Singapore serve as global private banking centres, and Bermuda serves as a global insurance hub.

3. Decentralisation to Counter Structural Deficiencies

Financial centres depend on trust and confidence to function.[3] Trust and confidence are underpinned by law: rules, institutions, regulation, and courts.[4] While originally evolved forms of private ordering or self-regulatory frameworks prevailed, over time, the state has taken an increasing role as failures of private ordering and self-regulation culminated in varying kinds of financial crises. Market-based financial systems thus are usually seen as fundamentally unstable, with instability and other forms of market failures being addressed by crisis-inspired regulation, albeit never entirely successfully.[5] This weakness underlies the ideal of DeFi and its techno-utopian vision of finance without the dominance of concentrated intermediaries – and the too-big-to-fail risks they embody – and without the reliance on the weaknesses of governments and regulators. However, over time, DeFi has moved from this utopian vision to a simpler one in which technology replaces frail humans and their institutions, and potentially eliminates risks inherent in the concentrated systems of traditional finance.

4. DeFi: A Response and Challenge for Traditional Modes and Conceptions of Finance?

In the past, hubs were necessary since services were provided locally and booked on a single balance sheet, with the provider of that balance sheet usually headquartered

---

2   Douglas W Arner, 'The Competition of International Financial Centers and the Rule of Law' in K Meesen (ed), *Economic Law as an Economic Good* (Sellier 2009) 203.

3   Douglas W Arner, *Financial Stability, Economic Growth and the Role of Law* (Cambridge University Press, 2007).

4   See Katharina Pistor, *The Code of Capital: How the Law Creates Wealth and Inequality* (Princeton University Press, 2019).

5   Ross P Buckley and Douglas W Arner, *From Crisis to Crisis: The Global Financial System and Regulatory Failure* (Kluwer Law International, 2011).

in a hub, usually protected by high regulatory and supervisory standards reflecting the large quantity of risks from pooling and balance sheet concentration at the hub.

DeFi challenges this hub logic. Where scale can be created by technology rather than by bundling business in a hub, hubs make little sense, because a hub comes with downsides for clients. They need to adjust in terms of language and law, and subscribe to the high compliance standards reflecting the concentration of risks, information costs (for instance, for legal counsel), and penalties for non-compliance with laws implemented at the hub, but not (yet) the local level. Hub structures also create dependencies which may be unattractive from the political standpoint – for instance, if the Renminbi or Euro is settled in London or New York, the English and US regulators acquire influence over the currency, which may be used in the political context.

By contrast, in a decentralised setting, services can be tokenised and provided to the token holder regardless of the locations of provider and recipient, with Bitcoin being a prominent example: Bitcoin holders are linked through common technology rather than a massive balance sheet in a highly regulated payment hub.

B. *Technological Foundations*

Underlying DeFi are a series of technologies.

1. DeFi and the Patterns of Technological Evolution

DeFi emerges from three important patterns in technological evolution: Moore's law, Kryder's law, and one for which there is, to our knowledge, no term yet established. Moore's law refers to the assumption that the amount of data-processing power[6] grows exponentially. Kryder's law posits the same for data storage capacity.[7] The combination of ever-increasing processing power and ever-increasing data storage capacity leads to ever-lower costs for both. The third necessity for DeFi is the tremendous growth we have seen in communications bandwidth combined with decreasing costs – a phenomenon discussed since the late 1990s,[8] if not earlier. The underlying assumption of bandwidth growth at decreasing costs is supported by

---

[6] According to Intel's founder Gordon Moore's prediction in 1965 (referred to as Moore's law), the number of transistors that could be fixed per square inch on integrated circuits doubles every two years, while the costs are halved. Moore's law predicted an enormous increase in data-processing capacity. See Gordon E Moore, 'Cramming More Components onto Integrated Circuits' (1965) 38(8) *Electronics* 114.

[7] Mark Kryder was Seagate Corp's senior vice president of research and chief technology officer who focused on information storage throughout his life. Former CNN journalist Chip Walter honoured Mark Kryder's lifetime achievement in an article highlighting the rising hard-disk capacity against the background of rising processor capacity. See Chip Walter, 'Kryder's Law' (2005) 239(2) *Scientific American* 32.

[8] See CA Eldering, M LSylla, and JA Eisenach, 'Is There a Moore's Law for Bandwidth?' (1999) 37(10) *IEEE Communications Magazine* 117; KG Coffman and AM Odlyzko, 'Internet Growth: Is There a "Moore's Law" for Data Traffic?' in James Abello, Panos M Pardalos, and Mauricio G C Resende (eds), *Handbook of Massive Data Sets* (Springer, 2002).

increasing network efficiencies, which lead to more bandwidth per dollar invested. This may arise, inter alia, from lower production costs of network components, higher-bandwidth Network Interface Cards, higher utilisation and integrated photonics, or the use of higher-frequency microwaves requiring smaller cells using multiple frequency bands (with 5G as an example).

These three evolutionary patterns enable hardware virtualisation: software is hosted, updated, and run at decentralised servers rather than on each workstation. Only data that need to be processed locally (under conditions of instant online connection and abundant bandwidth) tend to remain processed locally. Hardware virtualisation allows for the creation and set-up of the service-oriented architecture ('software as a service') which is at the heart of DeFi. This combination also empowers AI and datafication, which we considered in Chapter 7.

2. The Interrelations between DeFi and ABCD

At the core of DeFi stand a number of new technologies best summarised with the acronym ABCD – for the four technologies identified in this book as drivers of FinTech and which are the focus of this part (Part II): AI, Blockchain (including distributed ledgers and smart contracts), Cloud, and Data (big and small); or in another iteration, AI, Big Data, Cloud, and DLT (including blockchain and smart contracts).

These four rapidly evolving technologies are each typically central to, because applied in the pursuit of, the decentralisation of finance. Many decentralised financial functions utilise: (1) the powerful efficiencies and cost savings offered by AI, (2) the superior record-keeping and efficiencies of smart contracts operating on distributed ledgers secured via blockchain, (3) the potentially decisive power of the algorithmic analysis of data, and (4) cloud systems to host virtually all decentralised financial functions.[9] Each of these four technologies benefit from the 'laws' of technology, since each of these technologies individually over time become less expensive and more convenient and efficient to use – and thus enable cooperation among the multiple participants that together provide the financial services in a decentralised manner.

3. DeFi Stack

Decentralised finance is often provided through 'DeFi stacks'. A DeFi stack is equivalent to an entirely independent financial ecosystem relying on multiple layers of applications, ranging from clearing to settlement up to applications where institutional clients hold assets,[10] as further shown in Figure 9.1.

---

[9] Data stored 'in the cloud' are data stored on servers accessible from various points across the world that can be accessed and stored by many users distributed across the globe.

[10] See Schär (n 1).

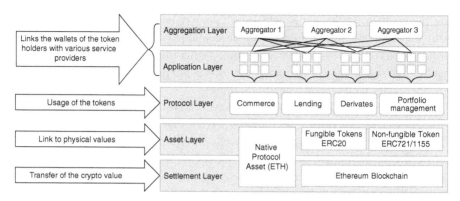

FIGURE 9.1 DeFI stack (based on Fabian Schär, 'Decentralised Finance: On Blockchainand Smart Contract-based Financial Markets' (2021) 103(2) Federal Reserve Bank of St Louis Review)

In this DeFi stack, some of the stack's functions are decentralised while others remain centralised. For instance, while the stack as such is governed in a decentralised manner, the lending function may be provided by a single lending intermediary (i.e., a bank). Further, what is understood as the substance of decentralisation varies. Often financial services marketed as DeFi are not 'DeFi' *stricto sensu*, that is, not fully decentralised, with all nodes having equal access to data *and* equal governance rights (or technical equivalents of governance rights).[11]

C. 'Democratisation' of Finance

DeFi enthusiasts go beyond technical decentralisation. For them, DeFi offers governance structures that represent the 'democratisation' of finance, while incumbents might view such structures as barely controlled 'anarchy'.

At the core of this claim lies a positive connotation of disintermediation (understood as disrupting incumbent financial institutions, particularly those that are very large: the 'too-big-to-fail' problem at the heart of the 2008 financial crisis) and of decreasing state influence and control of the financial system.

At a first look, such an idea seems very attractive, not least from the standpoint of financial inclusion as discussed in Chapter 6. Decentralisation of finance could enable embedding of local compliance standards and customs. The DeFi vision, however, is more than this. The objective is to develop systems that use technology to eliminate borders, jurisdiction, and the necessity of centralised control including governments. However, further analysis reveals that much larger challenges are likely to arise (discussed infra in Section III), which leads us to challenge whether DeFi, certainly in its purest form, is in fact desirable, without even addressing the limited likelihood of it coming to pass.

---

[11] See especially Linn Anker-Sørensen and Dirk A Zetzsche, 'From CEFI to DEFI: The Issue of Fake DeFI' (Working Paper 12, University of Luxembourg, 2021).

III. DEFI CHALLENGES: ENFORCEMENT AND TECHRISK

A. *The Challenges of Jurisdiction, Enforcement,*
and Data Protection and Privacy

In terms of the Rule of Law, DeFi poses a direct challenge to state-based systems: in its purest expression, DeFi is the ultimate form of 'code is law' with technology replacing state-based legal systems.[12] But beyond the obvious challenge of the strong form of DeFi, weaker forms of DeFi (in which some control remains with system operators) nonetheless pose major challenges for traditional geographically based, nation-state legal systems.

Three examples highlight how DeFi may be seen to undermine the Rule of Law: legal jurisdiction and applicable law, enforcement, and data protection and privacy.

1. Jurisdiction and Applicable Law

In a DeFi world of whatever form, anywhere along the spectrum from fully centralised to fully decentralised, determining the jurisdiction of courts and applicable law becomes increasingly difficult. Take for instance an unincorporated distributed ledger system, such as those used for Bitcoin or Ether. Private international law and civil procedural law look at the substantive claim to determine a court's jurisdiction and the applicable law. The substantive claim regarding distributed ledgers can be based on entirely different legal concepts in different jurisdictions, including but not limited to contracts, torts, joint venture and partnership law, antitrust law, and in some jurisdictions blockchain-specific legislation. Decentralisation results in uncertainty as to which courts and laws apply, if any.[13]

The same concern – determining jurisdiction – also extends to matters of financial regulation. While we think of finance as global, as is logical given the hub structure outlined *infra*, the reality is a world of individual legal jurisdictions and regulators, coordinated through a range of soft law systems. Established approaches tend to look at the entity that provides the service, the client to whom the product is sold, or services provided, or the market in which it is traded. Each of these is problematic in the age of DeFi: in a network economy multiple entities provide parts of a service, customers are similarly spread around the globe, and markets and individual providers lose importance as supervisory access and control points.

Further, technology allowing decentralisation may render entity-based approaches generally less effective.[14] The often-discussed alternative – a focus on functions – may be less than convincing where the services are performed by a set of algorithms

---

[12]   See Lawrence Lessig, *Code: And Other Laws of Cyberspace, Version 2.0* (Basic Books, 2nd ed, 2006) ch 1.
[13]   See Matthias Lehmann, 'Who Owns Bitcoin? Private Law Facing the Blockchain' (2019) 21(1) *Minnesota Journal of Law, Science & Technology* 93.
[14]   Karen Yeung, 'Regulation by Blockchain: The Emerging Battle for Supremacy between the Code of Law and Code as Law' (2019) 82 *Modern Law Review* 207.

in a permissionless system, for two reasons: first, where decentralisation is advanced, it will require the supervision of a myriad of small contributors to the services, some of which may lack the size and financial resources to pay supervision fees and many of which will contribute only partially to the overall service; and second, the functions performed will be transformed by machine learning. DeFi may force us to look beyond the entities involved and concentrate supervisory efforts on the underlying technological infrastructure that ties all contributors together. In fact, more and more of the risks in DeFi projects will come from the technology connecting all relevant entities rather than the entities themselves.

Take the example of BlackRock's risk management platform, Aladdin.[15] While Aladdin is discussed in detail in Chapters 6 and 19, suffice here to say that despite trillions of US\$ of assets managed, thousands of developers and investment professionals working with it, and more than 200 financial institutions relying on it, Aladdin as such has neither entity status nor license nor headquarters, and thus is not directly subject to financial regulation and supervision. Aladdin is a mere set of algorithms with a server and massive volumes of data available to be processed. Aladdin is connected globally, yet owned by the asset management giant BlackRock. Technically decentralised in connecting hundreds of entities, Aladdin is economically and technologically centralised. BlackRock accordingly has control over, and accountability for, all of Aladdin's functions.

Imagine now a DeFi Aladdin *not* controlled by BlackRock: an independent data framework on which market participants could operate, developing their own applications and frameworks without any control by any dominant single firm. For instance, envisage an open risk management platform whose code and functions are written by multiple individual programmers (instructed by multiple risk managers) developing multiple new platform functions and efficiencies.[16] This would have the advantage of generating a variety of niche risk management models – in addition to the standard ones Aladdin offers – thereby potentially reducing the systemic dimensions of model risk.[17]

In case of need, today regulators have jurisdiction over Aladdin indirectly, through the regulated entity BlackRock, as well as through the asset managers employing Aladdin. A fully decentralised, self-directing Aladdin, however, would

---

[15] See Dirk A Zetzsche et al, 'Digital Finance Platforms: Towards a New Regulatory Paradigm' (2020) 23(1) *University of Pennsylvania Journal of Business Law* 273.

[16] Readers may doubt whether such a decentralised giant could develop scale *and* work and operate efficiently. Yet, the global applications of some open domain software challenge this doubt, with Linux's usage in most web servers and supercomputers worldwide, and LibreOffice, as two notable examples.

[17] Model risk refers to the risk that a model does not reflect reality and potentially leads to misallocation of funds and losses if the parts of reality not reflected in the model become manifest. If all risk managers use the same model, model risk increases and can undermine financial stability. We do not claim that the open platform model erases model risk; the niche models may have their own problems, and BlackRock's expertise and reputation may function as gatekeeper against poor modelling, but a diversity of models should at least work to reduce the *systemic* dimension of model risk.

be very difficult to regulate, as it would be difficult to determine (a) which regulator or supervisory authority had jurisdiction and (b) over what they would have jurisdiction. A fully DeFi Aladdin would, most likely, be located everywhere and nowhere – which makes it very difficult to ascertain jurisdiction, assign responsibility and liability rules, and penalise misconduct. Even if we rely on indirect regulation and supervision, the regulated entities will have little means to comply with the regulators' demands: if it is a truly independent system, regulators will struggle to influence its operation. Supervisory requirements in relation to organisation, governance, legal structure, management, and employees may be impossible to impose if there are no staff. If there is no 'traditional' firm, entity, or headquarters to which financial regulation can apply, regulatory agencies will likely struggle to exert control and the salient, risk-reducing effect of law and regulation will thus be much diminished.

It has frequently been argued that DLT is not subject to law anywhere. We make the counter-argument that it is likely subject to law *everywhere* it operates or has consequences with every major participant and developer potentially at risk of liability.[18] It is this separation between liability and economic benefit that makes it so difficult to develop *true* DeFi frameworks. For that reason, in practice, Fake-DeFi examples often prevail in which crucial governance functions remain concentrated, albeit in an often non-transparent way apparent only to DLT expert coders.[19]

2. Enforcement

Enforcement becomes problematic in the context of DeFi. For instance, financial regulation on outsourcing and delegation, as a general principle, seeks to ensure that one entity is liable for compliance with all laws and regulations applicable to that entity even when that entity relies on external service providers, and regulation generally requires entities to manage legal, concentration, and reputation risks relating to outsourcing. In short, these rules create a hierarchy of liability and accountability, based on contractual rather than technical or financial relationships, where the supervised entity needs to ensure compliance from all service providers connected to it. How, in the world of DeFi, could a supervised entity enforce its oversight requirements vis-a-vis multiple, dispersed network participants that are spread around the world and subject to entirely different rules, ethics, and reputational concerns?

The core concern is not that the network participants reside in different countries, but that they are dispersed and decentralised. Non-compliance with rules

---

[18] Dirk A Zetzsche, Ross P Buckley, and Douglas W Arner, 'The Distributed Liability of Distributed Ledgers: Legal Risks of Blockchain' (2018) 4 *University of Illinois Law Review* 1361.
[19] See Anker-Sørensen and Zetzsche (n 11)

in a network setting is best understood if considered in terms of incentives. The service-integrating entity internalises all risks from services further down in the financial services value chain. As the entity is most likely to be sanctioned and held liable, and in the absence of under-capitalisation, it has a general interest in compliance to avoid sanctions and liability. The interests of the providers of the services that are integrated are not necessarily the same: to the extent the provider is too financially insignificant to be sanctioned and held liable, they fear neither sanctions nor liability. In a DeFi setting, many different providers contribute to the end product, and in the absence of collusion among network participants, issues of causation may well practically limit liability and sanctions since the burden is on the claimant or sanctioning entity to show that the non-compliance of a minor contributor caused the problems at issue. For this reason, where compliance is costly, the many small contributors each have a strong incentive to deviate from the integrator's general interest in complying with law, regulations, and contractual provisions. This risk increases with the number of parties involved and decreases with the benefits generated by compliance for each party.

In the cross-border world of DeFi, this incentive structure creates additional difficulties. The costs of complying only with one's own rules are lower than complying with one's own rules plus those of one or more foreign jurisdictions, due to information costs and the necessity of duplicative processes internally and externally. Regardless of how expensive or inexpensive one's own rules and regulation are, where the delegate complies with its own and the outsourcing entity's rules, the compliance costs of the outsourcing entity are always lower than the compliance costs of the delegate.[20]

One may wonder whether scale effects in compliance offset the non-compliance effect of decentralisation. If a service provider serves clients primarily from one jurisdiction governed by one set of financial regulation, we would expect the provider to adjust its own organisation to the regulatory environment of its clients. Yet, this is not the DeFi world: DeFi means cooperation *on a cross-border basis*; for small firms, cross-border regulatory harmonisation is even less likely than for large financial institutions, further reducing scale effects in compliance.[21]

3. Data Protection and Privacy

Decentralisation in the datafied world means that data are accessible at many points rather than one. Given the cloud and DLT operate on arrays of servers rather than

---

[20] Note that the delegate's *other* costs are most likely lower than the outsourcing entity's costs, otherwise outsourcing should not happen.

[21] Take the example of the United States: small financial firms are often subject to state rather than federal regulation, resulting in 50 different legal environments. The same is true for other large markets, notably the European Union, where due to proportionality as a regulatory maxim, small financial firms are often exempted from the single European rulebook.

individual single servers, saving data in the cloud or on a DLT means spreading data over multiple servers. Data protection and privacy violations are potentially very costly to institutions relying on DeFi. The argument that arises is that regardless of what data protection principles apply, any data generated will be 'decentralised' this way, rendering nugatory concepts of 'effective data control'. Even if there is legal standing to sue to enforce data protection or data deletion, some data particles will remain – in this sense, the Internet does not forget.

At the same time, today, as a result of jurisdictional data requirements and data localisation rules such as the EU's GDPR, we observe jurisdictional (re-)concentration of data. The major cloud service providers (Amazon, Microsoft, IBM, Alibaba, Google, and Apple) increasingly locate data in data centres in an ever-wider range of individual jurisdictions. Any of these data centres 'contains' the data of a given client, such as a large financial institution or a tech company. The end result of this interaction of technology, law, and economic incentives is not as envisaged by DeFi proponents: centralisation is often at the heart of decentralisation as a result of this interaction.

B. *Increasing TechRisk*

In addition, the very centrality of technology as the foundation of DeFi brings entirely new risks: DeFi in whatever form increases technological security risks due to tech dependency and connectivity. This is the case regardless of whether one considers 'strong form' DeFi or 'weak' DeFi, or DeFi built on centralisation (e.g., cloud).

While we discuss details in Part IV, suffice here to say that the interdependence created by the decentralisation of finance means a technical error or cyberattack is likely to affect all participants in a DeFi network, and may thus render participants more exposed than in a centralised system.

DeFi connects many servers around the globe – servers owned, operated, updated, and otherwise influenced by many different entities. While the network structure can reduce the risk of manipulation, as with distributed ledgers, it also enhances two other types of cyber risks. First, the number of access points to the network have multiplied. Each access point provides a cyber risk that needs to be managed. Second, many servers are connected, and new risks may come from this connectivity. At the end of the day, any extensive DeFi system provides a huge potential vulnerability: imagine a world in which a widely used, fully decentralised cryptocurrency that provides the monetary instrument and payment system for a major DeFi system is hacked.

If a tech operation providing material financial infrastructure experiences difficulties, it is much more difficult to organise meaningful support for a decentralised network than for a concentrated system where technical or financial support of one entity means that it has the technical or financial means to address the operational difficulties until a long-term solution is worked out.[22] This is particularly important in crises where systems and rescue schemes are stressed. For instance, if a network function depends on a myriad of small entities cooperating across the globe and all relying on crucial spare parts – where global supply is severely impaired – it is easier to direct spare parts to a few firms than to dispersed network partners.

All of these issues suggest that realisation of the DeFi ideal is unlikely in the near future.

IV. TOWARDS EMBEDDED REGULATION

Central to DeFi is a reaction to risks of concentration and dominance. Can DeFi render regulators superfluous? This is part of the DeFi vision but is not easily realised.[23] Hence, we consider how to best address the main risks identified above – that is, enforcement of laws, including risk-related requirements.

A. *Open Finance as Antitrust*

While evolving from different sources, the objectives of DeFi and 'Open Banking'/ 'Open Finance' overlap. Essentially, 'Open Finance' is based on decentralised rather than centralised control of data, in particular the data relating to individuals and their potential for use in finance.

Open Finance addresses market efficiency and antitrust concerns stemming from economies of scale and networks effects in the data economy, where the size of the data pool determines competitive strength[24] and where the BigTechs which we discuss more in detail in Part IV have foregone profits for years to build platforms with over-whelmingly dominant market share. As we discussed in Chapter 6, data-driven industries often naturally gravitate towards 'winner takes all outcomes', with the potential for significant benefits followed by significant negative externalities. For that reason, tech and data markets have tended towards oligopoly or monopoly over time.[25] The core assets of those commerce and financial platforms are the pools of shoppers' and merchants' data. Once these data pools are assembled they can be used for targeting

---

[22] See, for an overview of privileges granted to the 'incumbent' payment system, and the risks to clients and financial stability resulting from their absence for new variants of payment systems, Dan Awrey and Kerstin van Zwieten, 'The Shadow Payment System' (2018) 43 *Journal of Corporation Law* 776, 794–5 and 796–808.

[23] See, for the same argument in the context of Corporate Technologies, Luca Enriques and Dirk Zetzsche, 'Corporate Technologies and the Tech Nirvana Fallacy' (2020) 72(1) *Hastings Law Journal* 55.

[24] See Alberto Fraile Carmona et al, Policy Department for Economic, Scientific and Quality of Life Policies: Competition Issues in the Area of Financial Technology (Fintech) (Study PE 619.027, July 2018) 103–4.

[25] See Tim Wu, *The Master Switch: The Rise and Fall of Information Empires* (Vintage, 2011); Ariel Ezrachi and Maurice E Stucke, *Virtual Competition: The Promise and Perils of the Algorithm-Driven Economy* (Harvard University Press, 2016).

advertising, undercutting prices, offering new tailored services faster to more clients, or data analysis in all markets where superior information benefits profits.

Legal competition and antitrust scholars argue that where investors reward growth over profit, predatory pricing becomes highly rational and, even when costly, is worthwhile since it ensures monopoly rents from control of the essential infrastructure on which their rivals depend: 'This dual role also enables a platform to exploit information collected on companies using its services to undermine them as competitors.'[26] This has prompted the policy demand to treat data as a product, since information and data – although different from traditional goods and services – pose problems familiar to antitrust law, such as monopolistic behaviour and collusion.[27] Treating data as a product becomes a particular consideration in avoiding potential reductions in innovation and therefore in long-term growth and development.

Can these issues be addressed with Open Finance and DeFi? In essence, open banking facilitates greatly increased levels of democratisation of finance by enabling participants to simply, swiftly, and safely provide their raw financial data to competitors of their current financial services provider.[28] Open banking should result in a far greater range of product offerings and ecosystem participants. These new participants will not be burdened with legacy systems, and many will utilise more cost-efficient decentralised systems. As part of DeFi, DLT in particular could be used to decentralise and democratise access to data, thereby reducing concentration and control of the data both by the state and by BigTech firms. We will discuss further details in Part IV.

B. *Countering Pro-Concentration Effects*

DeFi relies, to a large extent, on data, processing and storage power distributed across the globe over many servers and re-concentrated for purposes such as bundling liquidity and Big Data applications. Promoting DeFi in general may thus be too simple an approach. Rather, we need to ask *which parts* of the financial services chain should be decentralised and which parts may (re)concentrate as a result.

The three data-related factors we discussed in Chapter 6 may lead to friction in the market for financial services that prevents private ordering from leading to socially optimal outcomes. These factors are traditional economies of scale, data-driven economics of scale, and network effects. The argument is that DeFi is different because it is decentralised, with core infrastructure neither owned nor controlled by any participant.

---

[26] See Lina M Khan, 'Amazon's Antitrust Paradox' (2017) 126 *The Yale Law Journal* 710; K Sabeel Rahman and Lina Khan, 'Restoring Competition in the U.S. Economy' in Nell Abernathy, Mike Konczal, and Kathy Milani (eds), *Untamed: How to Check Corporate, Financial, and Monopoly Power* (Roosevelt Institute, 2016).

[27] See Mark R Patterson, *Antitrust Law in the New Economy: Google, Yelp, LIBOR and the Control of Information* (Harvard University Press, 2017).

[28] See Christopher C Nicholls, 'Open Banking and the Rise of FinTech: Innovative Finance and Functional Regulation' (2019) 35(1) *Banking and Finance Law Review* 121, 123.

In this regard, Open Data (or Open Finance) is a two-edged sword. While the EU (with GDPR and PSD2) has required the financial industry to develop appropriate systems for data management and limited the use the industry can make of pooled data (thereby reducing the advantages of traditional financial institutions through their data pools), it has also driven the standardisation of data processes outside of finance – potentially making for a larger data pool and enabling new entrants to potentially access more data of their individual customers. In other words, data are now more freely accessible and transferable than ever before. Large technology companies know well how to make use of the new rights to data transfer – much more so than do new entrants with access to customers limited by budgets and resources. As we discuss more in detail in Chapter 15, this could prompt utterly unexpected results. While PSD2 and GDPR were originally designed to curtail the power of data behemoths, the eventual outcome of these two groundbreaking initiatives may well be less competition from the greater concentration of data in the hands of the few. We discuss a potential regulatory response in Part IV.

C. *Nationalisation of Core Infrastructure*

Government development, provision, control, or even nationalisation of core DeFi infrastructure may be necessary, utterly upending the claims of decentralisation. First, nationalisation may lead to informational advantages as to what data and financial streams are processed via the network. Second, the public stakeholder can force the cybersecurity measures upon the network it deems necessary. Third, setting and enforcing data and reserve localisation by legal means and supervisory tools become less important – the public stakeholder could simply (re-)arrange the system's architecture to meet its localisation requirements. Finally, the public stakeholder could apply all tools available to address pro-concentration effects, given that public stakeholders are less driven by the need to make profits.

Naturally, nationalisation can take various forms, ranging from stakes, co-management, and public coordination by a regulator or central bank to full ownership. The range of potential structures ranges from something like SWIFT to domestic RTGS systems to faster payment systems to property registries to central bank digital currencies (which we discuss in Chapter 14). For DeFi, the first variant – a public–private partnership where a public authority assumes a node function – is probably advisable in many cases, given that full ownership would require re-concentration and create a new single point of failure, thereby removing key benefits of decentralisation.

While national operation or control of crucial financial market infrastructure sounds radical, it is, in fact, not. For example, the US Federal Reserve currently functions as operator of the National Settlement Service (NSS), the Fedwire® Funds Service and real-time payment and settlement service FedNow Service, and – together with the Electronic Payments Network (EPN) – the Automated

Clearing House (ACH) system, through which depository institutions send each other batches of electronic credit and debit transfers.[29] Other examples include the European Central Bank's payment-vs-delivery system Target-2-Securities, which ensures that the transfer of securities and derivatives can occur among local and global custodians and central securities depositaries, as well as the Bank of England's CHAPS system.[30]

In the DeFi space, we observe a number of initiatives that are nationalisations in function, if not in name. For one, the Unified Payments Interface (UPI) that introduced real-time settlement in inter-bank payments in India was developed by the National Payments Corporation of India and regulated by the Reserve Bank of India as infrastructure supporting direct payments. In the second quarter of 2022 alone, the UPI processed over 20 billion transactions and recorded steeply rising transaction numbers.[31] India's UPI has become the role model for networked mobile finance. With the UPI, the Indian central bank has acquired control over the technological link between payment providers and customers. New institutions link to the network by using the UPI, thereby breaking the control of incumbent financial institutions and enabling innovation.

Another example is provided by the People's Bank of China's e-CNY project that we discuss in Chapter 14. Other examples under development are an increasing range of DLT-based corporate, securities, secured transactions and other forms of property registries that provide the decentralised infrastructure for wide ranges of financial and economic activity under public supervision. Thus, despite the anti-government ideal, it may well be that a role for government is necessary to achieve real decentralisation.

D. *Embedded Regulation*

Finally, DeFi may provide a major opportunity for RegTech (cf Chapter 4). In order to strengthen supervision and enforcement in the context of decentralisation, competent authorities can require or design *technology-based* regulatory systems and systems of supervision. Regulatory requirements can be embedded *technically* into DeFi systems to achieve regulatory objectives.

This could take the form, for instance, of 'embedded supervision', that is 'a regulatory framework that provides for compliance in tokenised markets to be automatically monitored by reading the market's ledger, thus reducing the need for firms to

---

[29] See Federal Reserve Board, 'Automated Clearinghouse Services', Federal Reserve (Web Page, 28 September 2020) <www.federalreserve.gov/paymentsystems/fedach_about.htm>.

[30] See Bank of England, A Brief Introduction to RTGS and CHAPS (Document, December 2021) <www.bankofengland.co.uk/-/media/boe/files/payments/rtgs-chaps-brief-intro.pdf>.

[31] ETBFSI, 'India Digital Payments Cross 20 Billion Mark in Q2, Led by UPI' *The Economic Times* (online 6 October 2022) <https://bfsi.economictimes.indiatimes.com/news/financial-services/india-digital-payments-cross-20-billion-mark-in-q2-led-by-upi/94680119>.

actively collect, verify and deliver data.'[32] Embedded supervision can thus be seen as an automated form of compliance, monitoring and supervision, using the system itself to implement, monitor, and enforce compliance requirements.

For DeFi, we suggest an expansion of this idea: 'embedded regulation'.[33] Under an 'embedded regulation' approach, the key regulatory objectives of market integrity, market conduct, and financial stability are included in the design of the DeFi system. Regulators can adjust the requirements based on algorithms setting risk limits and adjust granularity of regulatory reporting in certain products (e.g., derivatives, traditional currencies, and cryptocurrencies) under stress by 'zooming in' on details through their direct access to the financial institutions' trading and credit data.

A system of embedded supervision will rest upon an architecture of transparency and compliance. A properly designed DeFi system may thus be required to implement such features as part of its own automated structures, requiring assurances of data quality and other traditional forms of gatekeeping necessary for proper market functioning. In particular, compliance comes, naturally, with limited ability to override the systems' limitations. For instance, we could envisage that certain types of conduct, and certain combinations of conduct are impossible, while others are possible only with the regulators' consent – which in the DeFi world potentially means the consent of many supervisors – a high barrier.

At the same time, certain risk factors may be modified by supervisors while the system is running so as to manage systemic risk. Embedded regulation could also serve as the basis for addressing a range of cross-border collaboration issues. If data spread over many nodes of a given DLT are accumulated, sorted, and pooled by several supervisory authorities across several countries, re-concentration on the side of supervisors, collaborating in an embedded regulation platform, could offset some of the disadvantages with regard to determining jurisdiction and enforcing financial and data regulations. The objective of decentralisation may require an external guarantor of the platform within which regulation is embedded and supervisory cooperation is facilitated. In other words, the DeFi stack – the ledger as such – would function as the key regulatory access point in lieu of the various nodes attached to it.[34]

---

[32] Arguing that embedded supervision would reduce costs of both supervisors and supervised entities, see Raphael Auer, 'Embedded Supervision: How to Build Regulation into Decentralized Finance' (2022) 2(1) *Cryptoeconomic Systems*.

[33] This is an argument we have made previously in the context of ICOs; see Dirk A Zetzsche et al, 'The ICO Gold Rush: It's a Scam, It's a Bubble, It's a Super Challenge for Regulators' (2019) 60(2) *Harvard International Law Journal* 267.

[34] In such a system, regulators would adopt the ledger perspective, in contrast to the prevailing focus on the individual nodes so far. For that model, see Dirk A Zetzsche et al, 'DLT-Based Enhancement of Cross-Border Payment Efficiency – A Legal and Regulatory Perspective' (2022) 15(1–2) *Law and Financial Markets Review* 70–115.

V. CONCLUSION

Ever increasing processing, storage, and bandwidth capacity are enabling the potential of DeFi, while AI, blockchain, cloud, and data are providing the technological support for DeFi.

At the same time, decentralisation may facilitate the creation of efficient scale with regard to data and liquidity pools through connecting multiple small actors that in the past have justified the regional or global clustering of data services in financial centres and the pooling of liquidity through large balance sheets. Decentralisation may thus undermine some of the bundling activity performed by intermediaries. Decentralisation will lead to diverse and competitive financial services ecosystems and reduce the centrality of the role of financial hubs but not the role of digital finance platforms such as Aladdin's BlackRock in the United States or Ant Financial in China.

DeFi, in its purest form, cannot meaningfully exist within a properly regulated setting. The problem of pure DeFi is 'the tragedy of the commons'.[35] As Aristotle said about the education of children, adapted by Milton Friedman for the overall economy, 'when everybody owns something, nobody owns it, and nobody has a direct interest in maintaining or improving its condition.'[36] Wherever technical and economic decentralisation is taking place, incentives to invest in the sustainable development of the technology or business model potentially vanish: this is a core focus of the economics which is increasingly developing around theories of design of such systems.

DeFi also raises accountability and enforcement challenges around issues of public and private ordering. Most notably, difficulties of establishing standing to sue and of determining the applicable law and jurisdiction of regulators, supervisory authorities and courts, and the difficulties of establishing how many clients or counterparties are located in a given jurisdiction, all undermine the rule of law in financial services. But then again, to some extent, doing precisely this is one of the objectives of DeFi.

It is highly likely that both economic and legal factors explain why DeFi will never be fully decentralised, and at best partial: where parts of the financial services value chain are decentralised, there will be a re-concentration of a different (but possibly less regulated, less visible, and less transparent) part of the value chain. Cloud computing and BigData pools provide vivid examples of this re-concentration, yet also inside the DeFi stack true and full decentralisation will rarely be found. In this sense, real-world DeFi potentially increases concentration effects elsewhere and introduces further dimensions of cyber risk from tech dependency and interconnectivity.

---

[35] On the original concept, see William Forster Lloyd, *Two Lectures on the Checks to Population* (S Collingwood, 1833). The concept became widely known after it was used by Garrette Hardin, 'The Tragedy of the Commons' (1968) 162(3859) *Science* 1243.
[36] See Milton Friedman and Rose Friedman, *Free to Choose – A Personal Statement* (Mariner Books, 1990) 24.

Law thus faces real challenges from DeFi. If DeFi is to work in its ultimate expression, the rules governing it will need to be embedded in the system, as Embedded Regulation. Beyond this, law must adapt to the challenges of DeFI. Relevant tools will include those designed to enhance cooperation of competent authorities, enhance tech risk management, require data and reserve localisation, facilitate the use of RegTech to strengthen financial supervision and enforcement, and mandate open data and open access to services. These tools may well require a central role for government in monitoring and potentially controlling the central underlying systems: ironically, realisation of the DeFi dream may require government intervention. Given that DeFi will likely come with re-concentration *somewhere* in the value chain, this re-concentration *enables, justifies, and requires* DeFi supervision to focus on these new points of failure.

10

Data Regulation and Financial Regulation

SUMMARY

The fourth letter in the acronym ABCD stands for Data. This chapter discusses the relationship between data and financial regulation. We argue that data regulation is a crucial cornerstone that underpins how FinTech infrastructure can be designed, built, and operated, and thus influences the emergence of FinTech ecosystems. For FinTech, data regulation is a new form of financial regulation.

I. DATA AND BIG DATA

In Chapter 9, we discussed Kryder's law, which posits that data storage capacity grows exponentially, and Moore's law, which posits the same for data processing, as preconditions for the decentralisation of finance. Kryder's law and Moore's law also explain another major trend which drives the emergence of FinTech: Datafication and Big Data.[1]

When data storage capacity grows exponentially, storing vast amounts of data becomes far less expensive, which leads to storage of data even when its present usefulness is uncertain. These data may well prove valuable in time as data processing costs later fall, and algorithms (discussed in Chapter 7) are developed that link the various stored data and put them to use to identify peoples' preferences and characteristics and to detect yet unseen correlations. These data firms store data from all types of social, business, and financial environments, in an effort to identify correlations, and sometimes also causations, between various data points. Big Data brings scale and combines structured data (such as securities trading data and other forms of collected data) with unstructured data (such as news reports and the huge range of information of all forms that is available).

---

[1] See Salon Barocas and Andrew D Selbst, 'Big Data's Disparate Impact' (2016) 104(3) *California Law Review* 671; Sanra Wachter and Brent Mittelstadt, 'A Right to Reasonable Inferences: Re-Thinking Data Protection Law in the Age of Big Data and AI' (2019) 2 *Columbia Business Law Review* 671; Caryn Devins et al, 'The Law and Big Data' (2017) 27(2) *Journal of Law and Public Policy* 357.

In a BigData world, the customer becomes a combination of data points. Their preference for, let us say, organic, sustainably farmed food in groceries may be used to offer them sustainable green investments when they search for financial and other products.

In turn, the amount of data the firms hold in their data vaults has become the key asset determining their value, with Google being the archetypal BigData firm. Google does not charge people directly for searching information on the Internet. The search function is the teaser service that has people identify their preferences through searches. Google's clients pay for access to these people, by paying Google for advertisements to be placed within, or next to, the search results. Many firms like Apple, Amazon, and large retailers mimic Google's business model today through their customer loyalty programmes. All build up databases of their clients, and steer services directly to them, bypassing the random television and print media advertising that prevailed before the age of BigData.

When data storage becomes inexpensive, and firms tailor their business model towards datafication, the overall amount of data stored rises dramatically. In the 1960s, relatively tiny amounts of data were stored by businesses. By 2010, firms stored about 2 zettabytes of data globally, and by 2020 this amount had increased to some 64.2 zettabytes – a remarkable growth of over 3,000% in one decade. The large global firms have shown the way and now smaller ones are following suit. Hence, we expect the stored volume of BigData to continue to accelerate. Datafication in business and in finance is the new normal. It is estimated that 175 zettabytes of data will be stored in 2025.[2]

Finance leads this trend. All financial firms collect data on their clients to use in assessing credit risk and suitability of financial products for their clients. The credit scores that need to be assigned to clients under the Basel Accord[3] are evaluated sets of structured data aggregated on clients' (expected) financial performance. Financial laws also require financial institutions to ask for their clients' financial and, increasingly so in Europe, non-financial (i.e. sustainability) preferences,[4] as a precondition for offering or selecting investment products to or for their clients.

Some financial firms, like Robinhood, have taken a further step, and, like Google, trade in their customers' data. Robinhood may apparently not charge commissions to customers because they derive their income from selling their customers' data to brokers like Citadel.[5] Likewise, the massive firms like Ant Group or the large US brokerage houses are essentially data driven, with control of their clients' data and liquidity being their principal assets in the financial services value chain.

---

[2] Martin Hilbert and Priscila López, 'The World's Technological Capacity to Store, Communicate, and Compute Information' (2011) 332(6025) *Nature* 60.

[3] See Article 79 CRR.

[4] See Article 25 (2), (3) MiFID II.

[5] See Jason Aten, 'Robinhood Is the Facebook of Investing. You're the Data, Not the Customer', Inc. (Web Page, 28 January 2021) archived at <https://perma.cc/SH6E-SSL3>.

In data-driven business models the size of the data pool determines competitive strength.[6] This is why technology behemoths like Amazon, Google, and others forewent profits for years to build dominant platforms that could generate massive data pools. The core assets of these platforms are the data pool – that combines both shoppers' and merchants' data – and can be used for advertising, undercutting prices, offering new products and services faster to targeted customers, and data analysis in all markets where superior information promotes profits.

Data are key, because – as we have argued in Chapter 6 – they exhibit their own network effects, and economies of scope and scale, which combined lead to industry concentration and dominance. For this reason, data-driven industries are subject to 'winner takes all outcomes' and tend to generate huge benefits and huge negative externalities. Even when costly, striving for dominance is extremely worthwhile since it ensures monopoly rents from the essential infrastructure on which rivals depend. In Lina Khan's words, '[t]his dual role also enables a platform to exploit information collected on companies using its services to undermine them as competitors.'[7] This has prompted the policy demand to treat data as a product, since information and data – although different from traditional goods and services – pose problems familiar to competition/antitrust law, such as monopolistic behaviour and collusion.[8]

We discuss the issues related to concentration and dominance, including in the context of competition and antitrust policy, in Part IV. This chapter focuses upon how data collecting and analysis is, and should be, regulated in finance. This is of particular importance because while historically bank-lending decisions were based upon the unique, experience-based dataset of the bank manager about each customer, today this decision is made by data-driven algorithms, for which the quality and reliability of the data they use are key.

II. EVOLVING APPROACHES TO DATA-DRIVEN FINANCE

In the light of the datafication of business, and finance in particular, one of the larger challenges facing the financial industry globally is the at times conflicting requirements of data regulation and financial regulation. As demonstrated by the latest US Federal Trade Commission's (FTC) policy initiative requiring financial institutions to protect the privacy and security of customer data,[9] the role that finance, data, and technology play in both the digital economy and society are pressing issues of our time.

---

[6] See Simonetta Vezzoso, 'Fintech, Access to Data, and the Role of Competition Policy' in V Bagnoli (ed), *Competition and Innovation* (Scortecci, 2018).

[7] See Lina M Khan, 'Amazon's Antitrust Paradox' (2017) 126(3) *Yale Law Journal* 710.

[8] See Mark R Patterson, *Antitrust Law in the New Economy: Google, Yelp, LIBOR, and the Control of Information* (Harvard University Press, 2017).

[9] See Federal Trade Commission (FTC), 'FTC Strengthens Security Safeguards for Consumer Financial Information Following Widespread Data Breaches' (Press Release, 27 October 2021) archived at <https://archive.ph/Y7LCh>.

Many regulators globally are working hard to support and promote FinTech in pursuit of the competition and better service it tends to bring to finance. The world is thus currently providing a laboratory of different data regulation approaches that influence how data-driven finance can evolve. This chapter compares developments in the European Union (EU) with those in the United States, China, and India. These four massive markets are at very different stages of development, but all are evolving rapidly. Going forward, these are the markets others will look to when determining their own approaches to questions of financial and data regulation. A closer look at these respective regulatory approaches provides the context for how data, as the fourth pillar of ABCD, can be utilised by emerging FinTech businesses.

III. EUROPEAN UNION: OPEN BANKING WITH STRICT DATA PROTECTION

A. *Data Protection: GDPR*

The EU General Data Protection Regulation (GDPR) is the most important change in data regulation globally since the first Data Protection Directive of 1995: it has been a game changer for data collection and processing in the EU and, due to its exterritorial effect,[10] worldwide.[11]

As financial regulation drove the digitisation of data, the GDPR has driven spending on data-management systems aiding digitisation and datafication in the regulated financial industry and economy-wide. We analyse the GDPR in the light of its role as a key driver of data-driven finance.

1. Consent and Portability

Article 8(1) of the European Convention on Human Rights (ECHR), Article 8(1) of the Charter of Fundamental Rights of the European Union (the Charter), and

---

[10] See *Regulation (EU) 2016/679 of the European Parliament and of the Council of 27 April 2016 on the Protection of Natural Persons with Regard to the Processing of Personal Data and on the Free Movement of Such Data, and Repealing Directive 95/46/EC (General Data Protection Regulation)* [2016] OJ L 119/1, art 3(2) and recital 24 ("The processing of personal data of data subjects who are in the Union by a controller or processor not established in the Union should also be subject to this Regulation when it is related to the monitoring of the behaviour of such data subjects in so far as their behaviour takes place within the Union."). See also ibid, recital 25 and art 3(2). In particular, "[t]his Regulation applies to the processing of personal data of data subjects who are in the Union by a controller or processor not established in the Union, where the processing activities are related to: (a) the offering of goods or services … to such data subjects in the Union; or (b) the monitoring of their behaviour as far as their behaviour takes place within the Union."

[11] The interpretation of this notion has been clarified by the European Data Protection Board (EDPB): EDPB, *Guidelines 3/2018 on the Territorial Scope of the GDPR (Article 3)* (Guidelines Version 1.0, 16 Nov 2018).

Article 16(1) of the Treaty on the Functioning of the European Union (TFEU) provide that everyone has the right to the protection of their personal data.[12] An extensive regulatory framework has been developed around these fundamental guarantees, with the GDPR the major instrument. Specifically, the GDPR gives natural persons, but not legal persons, control of their personal data.[13]

The approach embedded in the consent requirement is taken a step further with the data subject's right to data portability stipulated in Article 20 of the GDPR: any natural person can ask the current data controller to transfer the data gathered, stored, and processed to another controller in a structured, commonly used and machine-readable format without hindrance from the current controller. This right is driven by antitrust law considerations and is applicable irrespective of the data controller's position in the market.

The GDPR requires data portability across the entire economy. Article 20 of the GDPR includes names, addresses, and personal data gathered while observing an individual's activities, such as a user's browsing history, movement and location data, and raw data delivered by wearable devices. However, Article 20 of the GDPR does not extend to additional information created based on the information provided, such as a user profile. Further, the right to data portability doesn't apply if the data are (1) pseudonymised and (2) processed to pursue legitimate interests or the public interest. For data in the context of payments, PSD2 introduces a bespoke regime to which we return subsequently.

2. Data Governance: Management and Compliance

In addition to the fundamental principles of consent and portability, the GDPR contains certain data organisation and compliance requirements, herein referred to as Data Governance.

The GDPR encourages pseudonymisation of personal data to 'reduce the risks to the data subjects and help controllers and processors to meet their data-protection obligations.'[14] It also regulates the use of online identifiers and imposes rules on tracing and profiling of users. In particular, natural persons have the right to be subject to a decision by a human (as opposed to a decision based solely on automated

---

[12] *Convention for the Protection of Human Rights and Fundamental Freedoms*, opened for signature 4 November 1950, 213 UNTS 221 (entered into force 3 September 1953), as amended by *Protocol Nos 11 and 14*, opened for signature 4 November 1950, ETS No 5 (entered into force 1 November 1998); *Charter of Fundamental Rights of the European Union* [2012] OJ C 326/391; *Consolidated Version of the Treaty on the Functioning of the European Union* [2012] OJ C 326/47 art 16.

[13] See *Regulation (EU) 2016/679 of the European Parliament* (n 10) art 4(1).

[14] See *Regulation (EU) 2016/679 of the European Parliament* (n 10) recital 28; see also *Regulation (EU) 2016/679 of the European Parliament* (n 10) recital 29.

processing, including profiling) where the decision has legal effects, such as entering or terminating a contract, or a denial of rights.[15]

Article 25 of the GDPR also introduces the requirements of 'privacy by design' (i.e., an obligation to ensure data protection through the design of technology) and 'privacy by default' (i.e., an obligation to only process personal data necessary for a specific purpose in compliance with the law and transparently communicated to the individuals concerned).[16]

3. Driving Data-Driven Finance

By establishing data processing rules, the GDPR has interfered in the internal organisation of data-intensive businesses, such as social media, health and financial institutions. GDPR did not directly aim to regulate the financial sector; yet there is no doubt the sector falls within the GDPR's scope and has been impacted profoundly by it. This impact flows from the GDPR's requirement on financial intermediaries to reorganise their data processing and customer data policies in line with the GDPR. The extensive requirements around individuals' personal data also require data categorisation tools that allow for data to be amended or deleted after a certain period or upon the individual's request.

(A) COMPREHENSIVE SYSTEMS, INFRASTRUCTURE Over time, financial intermediaries collect large amounts of data about their customers. However, in many cases, these data are not used effectively, and are siloed in business units or lines within firms.[17] Financial intermediaries now must build comprehensive systems to bring the collection, storage, use, and protection of data in line with the GDPR.

In fact, as we discuss further in Chapter 15, the process of digitisation and systemisation of data to meet the requirements of the GDPR is one aspect of a revolution in the financial industry's treatment of customer data which has been particularly effective in supporting the growth of data-driven finance.

(B) STRUCTURED DATA Notably, the GDPR has driven the standardisation of data processes across the economy which has generated larger data pools, furthered the structuring and coding of data from all aspects of social and economic activity, and enabled new market entrants to access and analyse more customer data.

---

[15] See *Regulation (EU) 2016/679 of the European Parliament* (n 10) art 22(2). Three exemptions apply when the decision is (a) necessary for entering into, or performance of, a contract between the data subject and a data controller, (b) authorized by Union or Member State law, or (c) is based on the data subject's explicit consent.

[16] European Data Protection Supervisor, *Preliminary Opinion on Privacy by Design* (Opinion 5/2018, 31 May 2018) [23]-[33].

[17] See Luiz Awazu Pereira da Silva and Goetz von Peter, 'Financial Instability: Can Big Data Help Connect the Dots?' (Speech, European Central Bank Statistics Conference, 29 Nov 2018).

(c) BARRIERS TO STRAIGHT-THROUGH DATA PROCESSING However, contrary to EU financial law reforms that drive datafication through generating colossal amounts of data (which we discuss in Chapter 16), the GDPR also creates barriers to centralisation of individual customer data and its use, requiring the financial industry to develop new systems of data management and shifting control of many aspects of their data from the financial and data intermediaries which have collected it to the individual customers who are its subject.

Arguably, this may impair fully data-driven business models. For instance, financial institutions cannot contact new clients for distribution or sales purposes after acquiring data pools from third parties unless the clients are legal persons, have consented to be contacted ex ante, or the data pools were assembled from web-based user data.[18] Furthermore, older data pools become increasingly unreliable for data analysis or risk management purposes triggering the GDPR's deletion requirements and removing some benefits from greater data-gathering activity. These deficiencies could be remedied in the risk models, for instance, by adding further security margins to 'old' or clearly deficient data pools, by mixing data from different sources, or by applying filters. Yet, all of this requires further sophistication in data gathering and processing methodology, prompting the EU's push towards data-driven finance and RegTech discussed in Chapter 16.

B. *Open Banking: PSD2*

1. The Advent of 'Open Banking'

The Second Payments Services Directive (PSD2) mandates that banks transfer customer data to third parties – FinTechs, TechFins, and traditional competitors – when directed to do so by their customers. Such data will need to be collected and digitised, repackaged for delivery to regulators and/or internal use, and managed by new purpose-built systems. PSD2 thereby sets the stage for the next level in the evolution of data-driven finance: active competition among incumbent and new participants.[19]

---

[18] See *Directive 2002/58/EC of the European Parliament and of the Council of 12 July 2002 Concerning the Processing of Personal Data and the Protection of Privacy in the Electronic Communications Sector* [2002] OJ L 201/37 art 13(1). This Directive is expected to be replaced by a so-called E-Privacy Regulation, coordinated with and simultaneously with the implementation of the GDPR. See *Proposal for a Regulation of the European Parliament and of the Council Concerning the Respect for Private Life and the Protection of Personal Data in Electronic Communications and Repealing Directive 2002/58/EC*, COM(2017) 10. However, political objections, particularly in respect of the proposed cookies rules, have caused a major delay and it is not year clear when this Directive will come into force.

[19] See Oscar Borgogno and Giuseppe Colangelo, 'Data, Innovation and Competition in Finance: The Case of the Access to Account Rule' (2020) 31(4) *European Business Law Review* 573; Benjamin Geva, 'Payment Transactions under the E.U. Second Payment Services Directive (PSD2) – An Outsider's View' (2019) 54(2) *Texas International Law Journal* 211.

By giving financial service providers access to client financial data, PSD2 paves the way for development of new banking products and services and facilitates customer transfer from one service provider to another. With the EU as the first mover in open banking, many jurisdictions are now following, with Australia and the UK taking leading roles.[20]

Open Banking is a regulatory response to the anti-competitive trends of the data economy laid out in Section I. The EU has answered the question of whether data should be treated as a product to avoid potential decline in innovation and long-term growth, in the positive. The EU's PSD2 establishes open banking for payment services, by loosening the holder of client data's control over the client data. In the past, this control of client data impeded clients' access to new services and hindered new entrants from developing scale to offer innovative services at competitive terms.

2. PSD2 and Open Banking

The first Payment Services Directive (PSD1) and its complementary legislation established the common European market in payment services with the Single Euro Payments Area (SEPA) framework. PSD1 was a success in harmonising payment transactions throughout Europe and achieving significant market integration in the commercial and consumer payment sectors.

Following the adoption of PSD1, there was 'rapid growth in the number of electronic and mobile payments and the emergence of new types of payment services in the market place.'[21] This offered the opportunity to further progress payments regulation. The process began with a strategic Green Paper by the European Commission in 2012[22] which explored what would be required to enable providers to 'launch innovative, safe and easy-to-use digital payment services.'[23]

The outcome was PSD2 which built a functional framework for the sharing of payments data while also addressing the security risks relating to electronic payments and extraterritorial payment transactions.

To treat equivalent transactions equally – regardless of the technology, legal form, or number of parties involved – PSD2 introduced a neutral definition of payment transactions and applied a single license prudential framework to all 'payment institutions', that is, providers of payment services not connected to taking deposits or issuing electronic money.[24]

---

[20] The Treasury, 'Statutory Review of the Consumer Data Right' (Report, September 2022) 20.
[21] See *Directive (EU) 2015/2366 of the European Parliament and of the Council of 25 November 2015 on payment services in the internal market, amending Directives 2002/65/EC, 2009/110/EC and 2013/36/EU and Regulation (EU) No 1093/2010, and repealing Directive 2007/64/EC* [2015] OJ L 337/35 recital 3.
[22] See European Commission, *GREEN PAPER Towards an Integrated European Market for Card, Internet and Mobile Payments* [2012] COM(2011) 941.
[23] See *Directive (EU) 2015/2366 of the European Parliament* (n 21) recital 4.
[24] See Ibid art 4(4).

In particular, PSD2 responded to new developments regarding internet payment services, such as payment initiation services (PIS) and account information services (AIS). PIS play an important part in e-commerce payments by establishing a software bridge between the consumer's financial institution and a merchant so that the consumer could initiate a payment from their bank account without having to use the bank's own payment interface each time they make an online purchase. AIS provide consolidated information on the consumer's multiple bank accounts in a single place allowing them to analyse spending patterns and financial needs in a user-friendly manner.

3. Driving Data-Driven Finance

PSD2 has played a central role in advancing the transition to data-driven finance. It has enabled technology firms to enter the payment markets by requiring payment institutions to provide data interfaces for new entrants from which the latter can extract client data to provide value-added services. This increases competitive pressures: the banks' only rational response is to enhance service levels and so avoid their clients seeking such value-added services elsewhere. The costs for such services need to be kept low. The only way to do so is to rely more heavily on technology, that is, advanced analytical tools and models that underpin the evolution towards data-driven finance. This process is reinforced through PSD2's reporting obligations, which have expanded the market for RegTech reporting software.

Nonetheless, we are yet to see PSD2 play out in full. PSD2's objective is to enhance competition. Due to the data portability rights under PSD2, the door is open for large technology firms that know best how to use these data portability rights to enter financial services markets. While aiming at increased competition, the outcome may well be the opposite: the concentration of data-driven services in the hands of a few technology firms that provide financial services as one aspect of their data-driven business models.

IV. CONTRASTING APPROACHES

In this section, we will compare the EU's approach with alternative approaches in the United States, China, and India.

A. *The United States: Free Market and Anti-government Sentiments*

The United States has led the world – at least until recently – in the evolution of data-driven finance and in data industries more broadly, because of the size and competitiveness of US markets and pro-market policy choices embedded in its legal and regulatory framework.

The United States has historically had a highly market-oriented approach to both finance and data. The overriding concern has been to support individual choice. US policy has generally been driven by a fear of the potential for government over-reach and a strong desire to maximise individual freedom of choice.

Until recently, this has led to data protection being largely driven by freedom of contract, allowing individuals and others to freely transfer ('alienate') data while simultaneously seeking to restrict its use by government. This has facilitated the emergence of massive data firms such as Google, Meta, and Amazon.

Simultaneously, distrust of large financial firms, especially since 2008, has led to a generally restrictive regulatory environment for financial institutions. The evolution of RegTech in the United States, where regulators have used technology to enhance their performance since the 1980s, has been underpinned by the disclosure-based financial system, technology innovation, and free alienability of data.

Since 2008, the approach of the US regulators to disclosure has been largely similar to that of Europe, except for the EU's extensive focus on organisational and operating requirements for intermediaries. Focusing on enhanced reporting obligations, this has driven the use of RegTech in compliance and is now driving RegTech's use by regulators, building on the fairly high degree of digitisation and datafication already present in many US regulators, particularly the SEC, the CFTC, the OCC, and FINRA. For instance, the US OCC – contrary to their European counterparts – calculates banks' capital requirements based on operational data reported by the banks, requiring very granular data on each business operation and the exchange of trillions of datasets.

US approaches to client data have been far more laissez-faire than those in Europe, even before Europe adopted the GDPR. As data acquisition and analytics became central to many aspects of the US economy, this relaxed regulatory environment supported the rapid evolution of datafication in finance and across the economy generally. Unlike the EU's general framework for data protection, the United States has developed sector-specific approaches, including for finance. To date, US financial regulation has disincentivised BigTechs from evolving into TechFins by entering into financial services. The regulatory and compliance burdens have driven US BigTechs to seek entry into finance in the areas of least regulation, eventually, perhaps, raising issues of shadow banking and regulatory arbitrage. A light touch regime for data and a heavy touch one for finance have so far provided a real disincentive for BigTechs to become TechFins.

Despite this historical trajectory, troublesome issues with large tech companies (particularly Meta) and data protection are beginning to trigger a process of rethinking in the United States which may lead to new legislation on data protection (which could potentially be influenced by the GDPR). Efforts are already underway to revise data protection frameworks specifically addressing finance, including at least partially from the need to meet EU equivalence tests to support ongoing cross-border data sharing and usage.

B. *China: Leading the World in Data-Driven Finance*

From a very low base a decade ago, today China has emerged as the world's leading example of digital financial transformation, data-driven finance and large data-driven technology firms in finance which we discuss further in Part IV as TechFins.

The Chinese rapid evolution has occurred in the context of a historically inefficient traditional financial industry and relaxed regulation of data acquisition and use by the private sector and the state. In conjunction with the size and growth rate of China's economy, this has allowed a few data firms to increasingly lead, if not dominate, the Chinese economy and financial system. These firms are now actively expanding outside China, in Asia, Europe, the United States, and beyond.

In China, however, certain factors are gradually constraining these trends. First, stock market and currency turmoil in 2015–2016 led to an increased focus on prudential and other forms of financial regulation. As a result, tech firms – both small and large – faced higher regulatory burdens. Second, the rapid growth of data-driven finance and the role of new entrants, large and small, forced regulators to use RegTech to deal with data on hundreds of millions of transactions and forced tech firms to adopt RegTech to meet their increasing regulatory compliance burdens. Third, abuses of data by private sector participants drove calls to reform data protection. In 2021, these calls were addressed by the adoption of the Personal Information Protection Law (PIPL) and the Data Security Law (DSL). The former serves to primarily regulate the relationship between large technology companies and consumers and address cybercrime; it does not create meaningful constraints on data collection and use by the state.[25] In contrast, the DSL creates a comprehensive protection framework for all data, personal or otherwise, to promote national security and the public interest.[26]

Two aspects of China's experience with finance and data stand out. The first is the widespread social acceptance of the extensive use of data by the state, in ways that would be culturally and politically untenable in the United States, EU, or India. The second is a broad acceptance of private acquisition and use of data, akin in many ways to that in the United States. This social tolerance has allowed and encouraged the state to take an active role in data acquisition and use, including in the context of facial recognition systems and social credit programmes. It has also promoted – as in the United States – the growth of data oligopolies.

Unlike the United States, however, there has already been a significant confluence of the finance and data industries in China. The Chinese government and public are concerned with potential abuses of personal data by the private sector and negative consequences for innovation and development. This has led to the

---

[25] See Rogier Creemers, 'China's Emerging Data Protection Framework' (2022) 8(1) *Journal of Cybersecurity* 1, 6, 8.
[26] See ibid 6–7.

adoption of PIPL: a general data protection framework that has derived some inspiration from the GDPR but reflects a very different cultural environment, and has a specialised framework for financial services as in the United States. In the words of Rogier Creemers, PIPL

> misses the generality of the European approach: where China has recreated the consumer protection aspect of the GDPR to a significant degree, it has not emulated the European foundational principle that privacy is a fundamental right. Most importantly, the PIPL largely leaves the power of government bodies untouched, as it does not impose any meaningful constraints on their ability to collect and process data.[27]

C. *India Stack: Infrastructure to Support Data-driven Finance*

India lagged well behind the United States, Europe, and China in finance generally and in the evolution of data-driven finance and RegTech in particular, until the roll-out of 'India Stack'[28] – a comprehensive strategy that combines a national system of digital identification, a national digital payments system supporting interoperability across traditional and new payments technologies and providers, an eKYC system to support account opening and use, and the commitment to use this infrastructure for a range of government and other services such as tax and salary payments.[29] At the centre of the India Stack stands 'Aadhaar', a government-driven, national biometric database and identification system that has transformed financial inclusion.[30]

This strategy, which we discuss and present as a role model for building financial infrastructure in Chapter 12, has triggered massive digitisation and datafication, enabled new entrants to compete with incumbents, and promoted financial inclusion, digital financial transformation and innovation, and the emergence of data-driven finance.[31] It has also benefited from RegTech at the core of its design (e.g., eKYC and digital ID systems[32]) and supported revolutionising the use of RegTech for compliance and regulatory purposes, particularly in securities and payments markets.

Aadhaar is operated by the Unique Identification Authority of India that issues a 12-digit randomised number to all residents on a voluntary basis.[33] Since its initiation, almost the entire population (1.31 billion of approximately 1.38 billion people)

---

[27] See Creemers (n 25) 1, 8.
[28] See 'Index', *India Stack* (Web Page, 10 December 2022) <www.indiastack.org/index.html>. See also Yan Carrière-Swallow, Vikram Haksar, and Manasa Patnam, 'India's Approach to Open Banking: Some Implications for Financial Inclusion' (IMF Working Paper WP/21/52, February 2021) 4.
[29] 'Index', *India Stack* (Web Page, 10 December 2022) <www.indiastack.org/index.html>.
[30] See 'What Is Aadhaar', *Unique Identification Authority India* (Web Page, 9 December 2022) archived at <https://archive.vn/BJ2eR>.
[31] See Carrière-Swallow, Haksar, and Patnam (28) 4.
[32] See Unique Identification Authority of India, 'Aadhaar E-KYC API Specification – Version 2.0' (May 2016).
[33] See 'What Is Aadhaar' (n 30).

has enrolled to benefit from access to social benefits, banking and insurance, and other services.[34]

Notwithstanding the huge success, there have been a range of real problems in Aadhaar's implementation, including its availability to certain minorities and problems around correcting misinformation.[35] Most notably, Aadhaar has been described as 'mass surveillance technology'[36] and challenged before the Supreme Court of India as violating the right to privacy – a fundamental constitutional right in India – for failing to establish checks on the power of the government to use biometric data.[37] While the Supreme Court confirmed that the right to privacy constitutes a fundamental right which the Aadhaar Act did not violate,[38] it nonetheless imposed restrictions on the mandatory use of digital ID (finding, e.g., that disbursement of pension payments or certain welfare benefits for children cannot be made contingent on the possession of an Aadhaar number).[39] Amendments to the Aadhaar Act and Rules (which now allow 'voluntary' use of Aadhaar by non-state entities) have been criticised for violating the court's decision. There is now a case before the Supreme Court challenging those amendments as unconstitutional. A first version of a data privacy bill to reflect the Court's findings has recently been withdrawn by the government after over three years pending in the Parliament due to a significant backlash over the state assuming excessive powers over personal data.[40] As of August 2023, India has enacted the Digital Personal Data Protection Act.[41] No prior draft was made available for consultation, and the bill was directly introduced in Parliament, and passed without significant deliberations.

However, practical impediments and legal controversies aside, Aadhaar has overall proven highly beneficial. When linked with a bank account, Aadhaar becomes the 'financial address' of an individual, eliminating the need to supply further information, such as the bank account or branch details. As of March 2021, over 730 million Aadhaar numbers have been uniquely linked with bank accounts on the National Payment Corporation of India mapper.[42]

---

[34] Ibid. See also 'Identity', *India Stack* (Web Page, 9 December 2022) <www.indiastack.org/identity.html>.

[35] 'Top 10 Insights', *State of Aadhaar* (Web Page, 9 December 2022) archived at <https://archive.ph/CVa3b>.

[36] See Sunil Abraham, R S Sharma and Baijayant Jay Panda, 'Is Aadhaar a Breach of Privacy?', The Hindu (Web Page, 31 March 2017) archived at <https://archive.vn/fHFcF>.

[37] See *Justice K. Puttaswamy (Retd) v Union of India* AIR 2017 SC 4161.

[38] Ibid 165–6, 301 [84].

[39] *Justice KS Puttaswamy (Retd) v Union of India* AIR 2017 SC 4161, 390–1, 402.

[40] See *Personal Data Protection Bill, 2019* (India). See also Sameer Yasir and Karan Deep Singh, 'India Withdraws a Proposed Law on Data Protection', *The New York Times* (Web Page, 4 August 2022) archived at <https://archive.ph/oiuYe>.

[41] See *Digital Personal Data Protection Act, 2023* (India). See also Sanjay Notani et al, 'India: Overview Of The Digital Personal Data Protection (DPDP) Bill, 2022', *Mondaq* (Web Page, 28 November 2022) archived at <https://archive.ph/tc4Xl>; John Reed, 'India releases more tech friendly data protection bill after backlash', *Financial Times* (Web Page, 22 November 2022) archived at <https://archive.ph/z9r1E>.

[42] Unique Identification Authority of India, Annual Report 2020–21 (Report, 31 March 2021) 44.

India – despite the size of its rapidly evolving market – has not yet seen the emergence of BigTechs, TechFins, or even the massive financial conglomerates common in the United States or Europe. One reason may be that, with India Stack, various state arms play a particularly strong role in financial market infrastructure. Private actors have tended to offer new services, in particular in the field of collateral applications, rather than be involved in financial core infrastructure, such as digital identity and bank accounts. Alternately, it may be that India is simply at a lower stage of financial and economic development and that developments there will move very rapidly as has been the case in China, now that the core elements necessary to support digital financial transformation are in place.

V. COMPARATIVE LESSONS

In the United States, a uniquely relaxed approach to privacy and data protection provides fertile ground for the use of customer data by businesses. Coupled with an overriding distrust of state use of personal data, this has empowered many data applications that are increasingly worrisome, particularly with the emergence of dominant data players such as Google, Meta, and Amazon.

In the EU, we see the converse with the GDPR representing, so far, the global high point of data protection and rigorous information reporting requirements. As a result, the demand for RegTech in the EU is currently outstripping the capacity to generate the IT needed. Europe's systems designed to ensure individual control of data combined with Europe's distrust of private sector use of consumer data present a very different possible future to that in the United States. We will lay out this trajectory which is further influenced by significant policy approaches to foster financial data infrastructure, in Chapter 16.

China's path to data-driven finance has been entirely different to other nations and emerged from the largely unfettered market activities of a small number of major tech firms, often with close state relations but without any overriding national strategy prior to 2016.[43] Ironically, given China's history, the private sector, in the form of Tencent and Alibaba, has led the evolution of data amalgamation and use. These firms have built identification systems that underpin payments, e-commerce, and other systems, and increasingly support the burgeoning superstructure of RegTech and other financial services applications.

In both the United States and China, free transferability of data enabled acquisition of large data pools, which reflected in the emergence of a small number of very large firms based on network effects and economies of scope and scale for data. Both jurisdictions, however, have experienced both the positives and negatives of this approach and are considering alternatives, including a more EU-like approach to data protection.

---

[43] See Weihuan Zhou, Douglas W Arner, and Ross P Buckley, 'Regulation of Digital Financial Services in China: Last Mover Advantage' (2015) 8(1) *Tsinghua China Law Review* 25.

India is characterised by its comprehensive, official, and – as we show in Chapter 12 – most successful strategy around digital transformation and to create financial infrastructure (which we discuss in Chapter 12). In many ways, India's top-down, state-led approach to designing digital infrastructure sharply contrasts with the market-driven, more laissez-faire approaches of the United States and China. In fact, Indian law largely followed EU data protection policy prior to the GDPR.

In each of Europe, China, and India, the state has had central, but very different, roles in data regulation and use. In Europe, the state regulates strictly the use of data by governments and the private sector. In China, prior to 2020, the state had a far more laissez-faire approach to data protection, which is reminiscent of that in the United States. This approach however changed rapidly in 2020–2022 with the introduction of a range of new data related legislation. China widely uses data about its citizens in ways the EU or US body politics would never tolerate. In India, the state has provided the essential underpinnings of a digital financial system, in the form of digital ID, which is now encouraging digitisation and datafication.

The approaches to data in each of these four massive jurisdictions reflect the cultural values and aspirations of their peoples and governments.

VI. DATA REGULATION AS FINANCIAL REGULATION

The interaction between data regulation and financial regulation influences in which way datafied finance *can* emerge. To date, the laissez-faire approaches to data regulation in the United States and China have resulted in a handful of participants dominating their data sectors. This has arguably been facilitated by few limits on individuals transferring control of data to BigTech firms, which in turn have benefited from network effects and economies of scope and scale in the amalgamation and use of data.

Repercussions follow for financial law's objectives and hence the remits of supervisors. We recommend financial regulators in such jurisdictions accept that a new systemic risk arises from the concentration of data in the hands of a few technology firms which mirrors the more familiar forms of systemic risk around banks that were too big to fail or too connected to fail. In turn, we strongly support (i) market structure-related interventions which aim to maintain the independence of, and choice among, critical infrastructure providers and (ii) data portability rights in favour of financial customers. Data regulation and financial regulation now dance together in ways not hitherto seen, and the resulting challenge for regulators calls for a particularly clear-sighted overview of how they interact.

We will provide a framework to address these issues in Part IV, after discussing the needs and means to build financial infrastructure in Part III.

11

Enabling a Balanced Proportional
Approach to Innovation

Regulatory Sandboxes, Innovation Hubs, and Beyond

SUMMARY

We saw in Chapter 3 how the attitude of regulators towards regulating innovation is moving from a cautionary to a balanced proportionate approach. This chapter explores the two main tools that regulators and policymakers are using to support this transition: regulatory sandboxes and innovation hubs. Regulatory sandboxes are dedicated testing environments that temporarily exempt admitted FinTech companies from certain regulatory requirements. Innovation hubs are portals through which innovative firms can interact with regulators and receive guidance on navigating the regulatory regime, and regulators in turn learn about current developments. This chapter argues that innovation hubs provide most of the benefits that the policy discussion associates with regulatory sandboxes, while avoiding most of the downsides of formal regulatory sandboxes. Consequently, regulators should focus their resources on developing effective innovation hubs, including, in appropriate cases, a sandbox as part of the hub.

I. BALANCING THE RISKS AND OPPORTUNITIES OF NEW TECHNOLOGIES AND INNOVATION

In the light of the changing attitude towards regulating innovation laid out in Chapter 3, where we described efforts towards a balanced, proportionate approach to regulating innovation under the rubric of 'Smart Regulation', the question remains: how can policymakers best support the development of an innovative financial technology ecosystem in the context of the emergence of new technologies, business models, and their application to finance? Two regulatory tools dominate the policy discussions on appropriate regulatory approaches to supporting innovation while balancing risks.

Since 2016, an increasing number of financial regulatory and supervisory authorities have announced the establishment of 'regulatory sandboxes'. Regulators typically seek to use a sandbox to bring more competition into their financial services sector through more diverse and affordable product offerings for consumers. Sandboxes have proven very popular with financial regulators worldwide since their introduction in the United Kingdom by the Financial Conduct Authority (FCA) in 2016. Regulators in other jurisdictions quickly followed, including Australia, Hong Kong, Abu Dhabi, Canada, Denmark, Malaysia, and Singapore. In 2020, the World Bank found 73 sandboxes in 57 jurisdictions.[1]

Yet, for all the interest the FCA's regulatory sandbox has generated, it has included only a tiny portion of the total number of financial services firms in the United Kingdom and significantly fewer firms than the FCA has assisted through its innovation hub.[2] More importantly, a significant share of young firms previously in the regulatory sandbox are now insolvent.[3] In other jurisdictions, like Australia, sandboxes have proven unattractive.[4] At the same time, some important financial systems – including most regulatory agencies in the United States, Germany, and Luxembourg – have refrained from introducing regulatory sandboxes.

In view of these experiences, another tool to further innovation explored in Chapter 3 comes into focus: 'innovation hubs'.

As we argued in Chapter 3, a regulatory sandbox is commonly a tightly defined safe space in which FinTech start-ups and other innovative enterprises can develop and test their innovations without being subject to the full extent of financial regulation: the sandbox comes with automatic relief from certain regulatory requirements for those entities that meet the entry tests. In contrast, an innovation hub is simply a portal: a means by which industry can readily access regulators to discuss their proposed FinTech innovations, gain some guidance on navigating regulatory requirements, and potentially seek dispensations from or adjustments to the specific regulations which they will be subject to.

We will argue in this chapter, although sandboxes tend to attract headlines and attention, that the real work of promoting and facilitating innovation in financial services tends to be done, in virtually all jurisdictions where it does occur, by some form of innovation hub. Regulators who genuinely wish to promote innovation need to make staff available to interact with industry, assist with advice and guidance to FinTech start-ups seeking to navigate the regulatory maze, and where necessary, issue bespoke waivers or other forms of dispensation of some of the regulatory requirements.

---

[1] 'Key Data from Regulatory Sandboxes across the Globe', *World Bank* (Web Page, 1 November 2020) <www.worldbank.org/en/topic/fintech/brief/key-data-from-regulatory-sandboxes-across-the-globe>.

[2] See Lev Bromberg, Andrew Godwin, and Ian Ramsay, 'Fintech Sandboxes: Achieving a Balance between Regulation and Innovation' (2017) 28(4) *Journal of Banking and Finance Law and Practice* 314.

[3] See Ross P Buckley et al, 'Building Fintech Ecosystems: Regulatory Sandboxes, Innovation Hubs and Beyond' (2020) 61(1) *Washington University Journal of Law & Policy* 55, 57.

[4] See 'Regulatory Sandbox: License Exemption Users' *ASIC* (2 November 2022) <https://asic.gov.au/for-business/innovation-hub/fintech-regulatory-sandbox/regulatory-sandbox-licence-exemption-users>.

This is not to say regulatory sandboxes serve no purpose. For the relatively small number of entities that qualify, sandboxes do assist in the development process. And more importantly, because it is sandboxes that have been attracting the attention, having a sandbox sends a strong and important message to the market that the regulator is flexible and accessible.

This chapter begins by analysing the typical entry conditions and elements of sandboxes in Section II. Section III outlines their potential benefits, and Section IV considers some of their risks and ways to address them. Section V concludes with a series of policy lessons for regulators seeking to support the development of innovation and innovation ecosystems in their own jurisdictions.

II. FINANCIAL REGULATORY SANDBOXES: ENTRY CONDITIONS AND ELEMENTS

A. *Entry Test*

Regulators around the world generally set up an entry test to determine whether a firm is qualified to 'play in the sandbox'. This test typically has three general elements.[5]

First, the test will ask whether the intended product or service is appropriate for the sandbox. For example, proposed products or services often must support (a) the financial services industry, (b) provide genuine innovation (i.e., new solutions to existing or new problems), and (c) benefit consumers. The adequacy of the innovation requirement and its assessment by the competent authorities is debatable, given that it requires regulators to assess innovation.[6] This task is arguably beyond their skill set, and is one that the Australian Securities and Investments Commission (ASIC) in Australia initially expressly chose not to undertake.[7] Sandbox rules will also often require regulators to assess whether the product or service enhances market stability, transparency, and consumer protection, or otherwise serves the broader financial system. This is not a simple task for regulators.

Second, regulators are often required to assess whether there is a need for the sandbox or whether the technology, service, or activity is already appropriately covered by existing law and regulation.

Third, regulators require adequate preparation from participants for them to enter the sandbox. They usually need to have entered the development stage (and have graduated from the project stage), understand laws and regulations governing their conduct, and engage in appropriate risk management.

---

[5] For references, see Buckley et al (n 3).
[6] See Bromberg, Godwin, and Ramsay (n 2) 314, 1329.
[7] ASIC, 'Testing Fintech Products and Services without Holding an AFS or Credit Licence' (Regulatory Guide 257, August 2017).

Other sandboxes, such as that of the Hong Kong Monetary Authority (HKMA),[8] have much less formal entry requirements and operations. This illustrates that, despite commonalities, the differences between sandboxes in different markets can be very great indeed – to the extent that what is labelled a sandbox may in fact operate as an innovation hub.

B. *Scope*

The scope of coverage of individual sandboxes varies considerably.[9]

1. Sectoral Restrictions

While Australia, the Netherlands, Singapore, and the United Kingdom do not limit the scope of sandboxes to certain sectors, Switzerland and Hong Kong restrict their sandboxes to authorised financial institutions working with or without FinTech firms, and Arizona limits its scope to the three categories of money transmission, consumer lending, and investment advice, thereby excluding Insurance Technology (InsurTech) firms from participation.

Sectoral restrictions do little for FinTechs and innovation and should, if possible, be avoided. Such restrictions may only be appropriate for highly specialised sandboxes being operated to address shortcomings of the regulatory framework regarding certain innovations, like robo-advice.[10] Restrictions entrench existing silos. In many cases, such as in risk management, technology initially developed for banks (FinTech) may be of more use for insurance (InsurTech). Hence, allowing expansion into InsurTech is crucial. Sectoral restrictions are also counterproductive in that they reduce economies of scale and thus the value of an innovation.

At the same time, while sectoral restrictions are undesirable, a regulator-sponsored sandbox may, of necessity, be limited by the respective regulators' scope of jurisdiction. In Hong Kong for example, the HKMA only has regulatory authority over banks and banking activities and its sandbox is therefore so limited. The same applies to the sandboxes of the Hong Kong Securities and Futures Commission and the Hong Kong Insurance Authority – each are limited to participants within the jurisdiction of the respective regulators. In such cases, cooperation between the banking and market-conduct regulators may show the way forward. Such cooperation is established among Hong Kong regulators so there is a 'single point of entry, if needed, for pilot trials of cross-sector

---

[8] For further detail on the procedures of sandbox, see 'Fintech Supervisory Sandbox' (FSS), Hong Kong Monetary Authority (Web Page, 18 November 2019) <www.hkma.gov.hk/eng/key-functions/international-financial-centre/fintech/fintech-supervisory-sandbox-fss>.
[9] Buckley et al (n 3) 55, 64–8.
[10] See generally Wolf-Georg Ringe and Christopher Ruof, 'A Regulatory Sandbox for Robo Advice' (Working Paper No 26, European Banking Institute, 2 May 2018).

FinTech products.'[11] South Africa's sandbox, announced in 2019, is another example which expressly covers all sectors but can only do so by involving all the financial regulators (in a n 'Intergovernmental FinTech Working Group' established in 2019).

2. Regulated-Entity Restrictions

Treatment of existing regulated entities varies. While some regulators do not allow elements of existing entities into the sandbox, others do. For instance, the HKMA opens participation only to authorised institutions (though potentially in conjunction with FinTech firms), whereas others (namely Brunei, the Netherlands, and Mauritius) only permit newer firms to enter. Existing authorised firms may benefit from no-action letters (which are not standard practice in some other countries, notably the United Kingdom), informal individual guidance on how to read the law, and waivers from certain mandatory requirements.

3. Limits in Targeting Customers

There are limits regarding the customers the sandbox participant is allowed to target. These limits typically vest discretion in regulators. For instance, the HKMA's sandbox is open for services targeting 'staff members or focus groups of selected customers',[12] while the Monetary Authority of Singapore (MAS) allows the applicant to choose the type of customer. This is only one side of the story however, as all regulators retain the rights to impose additional restrictions. The more that retail clients comprise the focus of FinTech, the more restrictions regulators will typically impose. This aspect is emphasised by the UK FCA,[13] which requires that the 'type of customers should be appropriate for the type of innovation and the intended market, but also to the type of risks,' while Bank Negara Malaysia may restrict 'the participation of customers to a certain segment or profile of customers.'[14]

Proportionality should underlie the sandbox approach. If wholesale clients are sufficiently sophisticated and skilled to understand the risks they take, it may suffice if FinTechs serving those clients are simply required to disclose their regulatory status. However, FinTechs targeting retail clients should typically incur a higher degree of regulation.

The client type does not obviate systemic risk concerns however, and we may expect those concerns to be aired more often when FinTechs target large, typically wholesale,

---

[11] 'Fintech Supervisory Sandbox' (FSS) (n 8).
[12] See Letter from Arthur Yuen, Deputy Chief Executive of Hong Kong Monetary Authority, to All Authorized Institutions, 6 September 2016.
[13] See Financial Conduct Authority, Default standards for sandbox testing parameters (Policy Statement, 5 August 2016).
[14] See Bank Negara Malaysia, Financial Technology Regulatory Sandbox Framework (Policy Document 030–1, 18 October 2016) 5.

clients. For instance, a FinTech delivering an entirely new risk calculation algorithm to most of the major banks in a market could well give rise to systemic concerns.

4. Time and Size

The period in which a FinTech is allowed to play in the sandbox is typically limited by a rule or on a case-by-case basis. Periods range, in the first instance, from 6 to 24 months. Extensions are generally available. Other limits may include, for instance, a threshold relating to the number of deposits from the public. However, such limits may not suit specific risks and opportunities, or may neglect systemic implications. In some cases, regulators should consider other thresholds, depending on the business model, including the number and type of clients.

C. *Mandatory Provisions Subject to Waiver*

Most sandbox rules do not specify which mandatory provisions may be lifted, but some regulators do disclose the minimum level of compliance required inside the sandbox.[15] For example, Singapore's MAS is flexible regarding licensing fees, an entity's capital requirements, leadership requirements, credit rating and relative size, and the organisation of the entity relating to supervisory standards of financial soundness, risk management, and outsourcing. However, MAS rules are, appropriately in our view, strict on confidentiality of customer information, the fitness of management (i.e., their honesty and integrity), handling of customers' monies and assets by intermediaries, as well as anti-money laundering, and countering terrorism financing (AML/CTF) measures.

The Ontario Securities Commission, upon conditions that certain investors access only certain services, has granted relief in respect to audit requirements regarding financial statements, know-your-client requirements, suitability requirements, dispute resolution requirements, certain disclosure and reporting requirements, and prospectus requirements. On the other hand, the HKMA requirements that may be waived in the sandbox are security-related requirements for electronic banking services and the timing of independent assessment prior to launching new technology services. Most authorities sensibly refrain from stipulating an exhaustive list of requirements that may potentially be relaxed within the regulatory sandbox, preferring to retain flexibility.

D. *Removing the Privilege*

Sandbox rules typically specify grounds upon which the regulators may withdraw the privilege.[16] Reasons for dismissal from the sandbox include: the risks of the venture exceeding the benefits, non-compliance with laws or regulatory impositions, and the purpose of the sandbox not being achieved.

---

[15] For references, see Buckley et al (n 3) 55, 69–70.
[16] See ibid.

The first reason reflects the objectives of the sandbox. The regulatory sandbox is made available *because* the regulator expects benefits to outweigh risks. Thus, the privilege should be removed as soon as it is established that the risks outweigh the benefits. Regulatory risks may come from the FinTech's conduct, so non-compliance is a natural reason to reconsider regulatory leniency. Likewise, if the regulator believes that granting privileges has not furthered innovation, it should 'pull the privilege'. Finally, of course, firms should have the right to opt out by shutting down the business or moving into the fully regulated sphere.

III. POTENTIAL BENEFITS OF SANDBOXES

There are three principal potential market benefits of implementing a regulatory sandbox. The first is the message the establishment of a sandbox sends. The second is the boost to innovation. The third is how much the regulator stands to learn about innovations.

Interestingly, while all the focus globally seems to have been on sandboxes, Australia's experience clearly suggests that an innovation hub may well be a far more important regulatory reform and a far better way of achieving these three ends. However, it also remains true that terms like 'Innovation Hub' or 'Project Innovate' do not serve as effective messaging the way the image of toys in a sandpit does. Perhaps one day a psychologist will identify some failure of maturation in childhood development shared by many FinTech entrepreneurs – but not scholars, who are too grown up for their own good. Or perhaps the term *sandbox* is simply fun, somewhat paradoxical, and memorable? Thus, if one must call an innovation hub a *sandbox* to make it happen, we are not adverse. But it is important to make sure that it is the innovation hub elements which are included in order to maximise developmental benefits.

A. *Market Message of Having a Sandbox*

A regulatory sandbox signals a regulator's propensity to support innovation. Even if, as initially in Australia's ASIC sandbox, the number of firms participating is in fact very small, regulators may see such sandbox projects as successful precisely because they send a message to the industry and market that the relevant regulator is flexible and approachable in dealing with innovative enterprises.

The number of entities in a regulator's sandbox is typically very small. For instance, in the pioneering sandbox established by the UK FCA, there were 18 participants in Cohort 1 – a number that has remained a guideline in all following cohorts. In 2022, only 13 firms were accepted into the sandbox.[17]

---

[17] 'Regulatory Sandbox Accepted Firms – Cohort 1', *Financial Conduct Authority* (Web Page, 18 August 2022) <www.fca.org.uk/firms/regulatory-sandbox/cohort-1>.

Our research suggests that sandboxes play two far more important roles than supervising the small number of sandboxed entities, and both should appeal to developing countries' regulators. First is the strong message sent to FinTechs that the regulator is open to innovation. The strength of this message, however, is diluted in a world where more than 70 sandboxes have been created or announced globally. Nonetheless, the World Bank's sandbox data indicate that sandboxes have a great appeal for emerging and developing economies.[18]

Second, sandboxes provide an important learning opportunity for regulators, especially when coupled with an innovation hub. An innovation hub that integrates with a sandbox can change traditional dynamics, as the industry comes to see the regulator as an entity they can approach for assistance with regulatory challenges, rather than a distant policeman to be avoided. ASIC, in a series of proactive moves, has managed to achieve this cultural shift with a combination of an innovation hub, a regulatory sandbox, and its Digital Finance Advisory Panel, which meets quarterly and includes representatives from industry, industry associations, and relevant regulatory agencies. South Africa's sandbox is similar and is explicitly envisaged as a way for the regulator to learn about innovations in technology and business models to best develop proportional regulatory responses.

While an innovation hub is admittedly far more demanding of seasoned regulatory expertise and riskier to regulatory reputation – due to the need to issue an immediate assessment – than a sandbox, this demand on regulator time is also a major advantage of a hub as it facilitates more interactive two-way knowledge exchange. This is vital for regulators in this field as it keeps them right at the cutting edge of developments in technology. The previous literature has accredited those 'bidirectional educational benefits' to sandboxes alone.[19] In fact, innovation hubs are doing the same work, and we would suggest doing it much better.

In Australia, ASIC has long been a flexible regulator willing to work one on one with industry participants, so in one sense its innovation hub is merely a continuation and formalisation of past practices. The important thing, however, is that their sandbox and hub have served to announce to FinTechs outside Australia, in particular, that ASIC is open for business.

If the pro-innovation message is the sandbox's principal objective, there should be little reason to create one in financial centres known for their openness to innovation. This is particularly true if the pro-innovation message can be sent without a sandbox, as Luxembourg's regulator (the CSSF) did by creating the world's first innovation hub in 2014. In due course, the CSSF issued licences to companies like Bitstamp Europe, BitFlyer Europe, Finologee, PPRO, and SnapSwap International,

---

[18] 'Key Data from Regulatory Sandboxes across the Globe' (n 1).
[19] See Michael Wechsler, Leon Perlman, and Nora Gurung, 'The State of Regulatory Sandboxes in Developing Countries' 25 [2018] (December) *SSRN Electronic Journal*; Chris Brummer and Yesha Yadav, 'Fintech and the Innovation Trilemma' (2019) 107 *Georgetown Law Journal* 235, 291.

in the process turning Luxembourg into a cryptocurrency and payments centre. Since 2018, the Luxembourg House of Financial Technology (LHoFT), a public–private partnership, has provided the functions of an innovation hub in cooperation with the CSSF.[20]

The US landscape is different and currently does not have an active federal regulatory sandbox[21] (although various private initiatives adopt the name, such as in the context of the Digital Dollar Project).[22] This is partly because of the view that, while the promotion of innovation matters, doing so may not be the proper role of the regulator.[23] There is also a view that many of the federal securities laws are not amenable to being waived. However, some efforts have gone into promoting innovation on a federal level, including the creation of innovation hubs, proposing a federal sandbox through a body other than the US Securities and Exchange Commission (SEC), and sandboxes being implemented at the state level, with Arizona[24] and Wyoming[25] leading and some 11 US states following suit.

The SEC includes the Strategic Hub for Innovation and Financial Technology (FinHub). The FinHub seeks to facilitate the SEC's 'active engagement with innovators, developers and entrepreneurs', as the financial technology sector quickly evolves.[26] The FinHub does not include a sandbox, with the SEC stating that its 'role is not to hand out permission slips for innovation.'[27] Rather, the FinHub seeks to promote innovation through activities such as providing advice on digital marketplace financing and automating investment advice.

However, the view of the SEC regarding sandboxes was not uniform in the United States. The US Consumer Financial Protection Bureau's (CFPB) innovation department had a 'Product Sandbox' which gave firms regulatory relief when testing new financial products and services and included the sharing of data with the CFPB. However, the CFPB announced in June 2022 that this sandbox would be discontinued due to lack of broad usage and the increasing risks to consumers from the regulatory relief provided.[28]

---

[20] The non-exhaustive list on LHoFT's website details more than one hundred firms, including Ripple and LendInvest: 'Our Innovators', *The LHoFT* (Web Page, 2022) <www.lhoft.com/en/our-startups>.

[21] See Hilary J Allen, 'Regulatory Sandboxes' (2019) 87 *The George Washington Law Review* 579, 623–24.

[22] Luke Huigsloot, 'Think Tank Launches "technical sandbox" Exploring United States CBDCs', *Cointelegraph* (Web Page, 2 September 2022) <https://cointelegraph.com/news/think-tank-launches-technical-sandbox-exploring-united-states-cbdcs>.

[23] Hester M Peirce, 'Beaches and Bitcoin: Remarks before the Medici Conference' (Speech, US Securities and Exchange Commission, 2 May 2018).

[24] See Paul Watkins, Evan Daniels, and Stuart Slayton, 'First in the Nation: Arizona's Regulatory Sandbox' (2018) 29 *Stanford Law & Policy Review* 1.

[25] See *Financial Technology Sandbox Act*, HB 57, 65th Leg. (Wyo 2019).

[26] FinHub, 'Strategic Hub for Innovation and Financial Technology (FinHub)', SEC (Web Page, 1 August 2022) <www.sec.gov/finhub>.

[27] Peirce (n 23).

[28] Ryan Deffenbaugh, 'The CFPB Doesn't Want to Play in the Fintech Sandbox Anymore', Protocol (Web Page, 2 June 2022) <www.protocol.com/fintech/cfpb-fintech-sandbox>.

B. *Boost to Innovation and Competition*

Sandboxes and innovation hubs are designed to promote innovation and competition.[29] First, the hope is that they will incentivise financial services firms to accelerate their digital transformation. Second, at the global level, sandboxes have added to the competition among financial centres to become pre-eminent FinTech hubs. The sandbox, as an institution, challenges reluctant regulators without sandboxes and pushes them to publish and possibly review their dispensation policies.

Both of these impacts can be seen in the 'global sandbox' programme established by the Global Financial Innovation Network (GFIN), an FCA-inspired coalition of regulators and related organisations from around the world. GFIN 'was created to provide a more efficient way for innovative firms to interact with regulators, helping them navigate between countries as they look to scale and test new ideas.'[30] The programme also seeks to increase the appeal of the participating jurisdictions to incoming financial services firms with their broad network.

While sandbox conditions could lead to a race-to-the-bottom competition, on balance, the more likely outcomes from sandboxes at this stage will be beneficial, as most countries are in dire need of more competition within their financial services sectors.

C. *Regulatory Learning*

In a regulatory sandbox, regulators learn from FinTech start-ups due to their freedom to operate and communicate openly. This allows entrepreneurs to freely discuss their concerns without fear of putting their licence at risk and allows regulators to learn before major risks materialise. In the context of the GFIN, this learning occurs on an international level, with the network functioning as a forum for collaborative knowledge sharing between firms and regulators. Within the sandbox, dispensation efficiency is less curtailed by regulators being criticised for being too lenient, and when the conditions of the sandbox are specified clearly, entrepreneurs are assisted in arguing for dispensations.

On the other hand, an innovation hub does not deliver the same certainty for regulatory lenience. So, entrepreneurs may be more reluctant to share all details of their business. However, seasoned regulators with a pro-innovation reputation will share information in an innovation hub that immediately assists firms to draft an adequate business plan. This results in a faster track to market with a full licence, something that regulatory sandboxes cannot promise. This fast track to market requires a quid pro quo as to the details of the technology employed. Hence, in

---

[29] See Wechsler, Perlman, and Gurung (n 19) 11–14, 24.
[30] 'The Global Financial Innovation Network (GFIN)', *GFIN* (Web Page, 2021) <www.thegfin.com>.

practice, an innovation hub prompts mutual learning as does, and probably more so than, a regulatory sandbox.

IV. RISKS OF SANDBOXES AND ALTERNATIVE APPROACHES

A. *Maintaining a Level Playing Field*

In designing a regulatory sandbox, maintaining a level playing field between regulated and unregulated entities may matter because otherwise, in the longer term, banks, insurers, and asset managers may suffer from a shortage of human and financial capital *and* of innovation that migrates to FinTech start-ups. However, limitations on time and money imposed on most firms in sandboxes at least diminish that risk. Regulators must strike a balance between encouraging innovation and protecting clients and the financial system. *Regulated* financial institutions must be supported to innovate in using their advantageous datasets, expertise, and experience. Existing institutions should enjoy the supervisory free space to support the development of innovative products and services that is extended to FinTech start-ups.

Accordingly, regulators are well advised to pair a regulatory sandbox with an appropriate approach to testing, piloting, adequate dispensation, and no-action policies for established regulated institutions. Sandbox rules and other practices should enable licensed und unlicensed institutions to benefit equally if they seek to develop innovative products or services.

Sandboxes are not necessarily appropriate in all circumstances. Sandboxes are but one way to enhance communication between regulators and innovative firms. Other approaches include class-waivers, piloting, and sandbox umbrellas.

B. *Alternatives and Complementary Measures to a Sandbox*

The principal complement to a sandbox, and the one we recommend, is an innovation hub. It supports the message of regulatory openness and flexibility that the sandbox sends. It also achieves the second and third benefits of a sandbox – the boost to innovation and competition and the facilitation of regulatory learning – better than any sandbox, and it offers a further benefit because it will typically benefit a much wider array of Fintech Firms than will fall within the relatively strict limits of any sandbox. The reason a hub may not achieve the first benefit of sending a message as effectively to the market is the present interest and hype around sandboxes. This is the principal reason for a regulator to have both a hub and a sandbox. The hub does the heavy lifting of promoting innovation and competition (and it is heavy lifting because it will consume substantial regulator time), while the sandbox does the advertising role of promoting the jurisdiction as being open and receptive to FinTech business. Both roles matter. In Australia's case, the innovation hub preceded the sandbox by over a year, and experience has shown it to be a far more effective regulatory innovation.[31] This likely explains why some sandboxes seem to resemble innovation hubs more than they do sandboxes as described in this chapter.

C. *A Brief View on Alternatives to Sandboxes and Innovation Hubs*

There are other alternatives to a sandbox of course, including class waivers and a testing and piloting regime. While the class waiver provides notable certainty, the experimental space it creates is limited. Any successful FinTech operation will outgrow these limits quite quickly, which raises the question of whether regulators may grant an additional sandbox arrangement beyond these limits or grant a restricted licence to class-waiver beneficiaries that exceeds the waiver limits following a case-by-case assessment. To retain the pro-competitive effects of the class waiver, the possibility of combining several arrangements or licences seems preferable. Notwithstanding the former, the main difference between the class waiver and a normal regulatory sandbox is that in the former case, a regulator does not engage with innovative firms prior to granting the privilege – the waiver is granted as a matter of law to those qualified for it, rather than upon application. Innovation is not a prerequisite, nor does knowledge exchange necessarily occur at all between privileged firms and the regulator.

The other oft-used alternatives include regulators' guidance on testing and piloting. An exemption for testing and piloting is particularly useful for authorised financial institutions. They can test new technology and business models without filing for regulatory approval. The point where testing and piloting ends and regular activity starts can be challenging to identify. One characteristic for determining the perimeter of regular activity, however, will be an intention to permanently remain active in the market. A test lacks this feature; it is a one-time event, and whether the process is continued depends on the outcome of the test, which is entirely open. A pilot is a test where the organisational and financial resources have been devoted to a business intended to be ongoing and only some data for the decision are missing, which the pilot is designed to provide. Where customers consent, FinTech could justify testing and piloting for some time. For this reason, the clarity of a sandbox's rules may well be attractive from a regulator's point of view.

V. CONCLUSION

We began this chapter with a question about the most effective way to support the development of an innovative FinTech ecosystem. We have argued that much of what regulatory sandboxes promise is being delivered by innovation hubs, often

---

[31] See Australian Securities and Investments Commission, Australian Securities and Investments Commission Corporations (Concept Validation Licensing Exemption) (Cth) (Instrument 2016/1175, 15 December 2018) s 6.

established by regulators simultaneously with the sandbox. If we define sandboxes narrowly, they are a set of entry requirements, compliance with which entitles FinTechs to participate in a safe harbour freed of many regulatory requirements. Among the many advantages commonly associated with sandboxes the only one uniquely attributable to them is the easier, cheaper, and faster regulatory compliance delivered through a tailored process of restricted authorisation. The many other potential advantages of sandboxes are delivered at least as well by innovation hubs. These advantages include:

- the potential for the regulator to issue informal advice and directions regarding regulatory compliance;
- guidance on how to interpret requirements for a firm's specific situation;
- waiver or modification of any 'unduly burdensome rule' for the purpose of the test; and
- 'no-action' letters where individual guidance or waivers are not possible, which provide an indication that disciplinary action will not be pursued for a finite time if certain conditions are met (but which typically do not offer protection against liabilities to consumers).

At the same time, the data so far available do not justify the statement that regulatory sandboxes, alone, are the most effective means to further FinTech innovation. Given regulatory sandboxes require significant financial contributions, and sometimes new legislation, we suggest regulators should initially focus their resources on developing effective innovation hubs.

In time, in most cases, the maximum benefit will be achieved by integrating an innovation hub and a sandbox together to support the evolution of an innovative FinTech ecosystem. We see distinctive benefits for innovation hubs – perhaps combined with a sandbox – in jurisdictions where there are few start-ups and limited innovation, as in many developing countries. In markets where there are many FinTechs, sandboxes as defined in this chapter may well prove more useful – even without an innovation hub.

We draw this distinction between sandbox and innovation hub because we believe that a narrowly conceived sandbox is particularly attractive to regulators, promising to be pro-innovation without drawing unduly on regulatory resources. Conversely, setting up both a sandbox and an innovation hub demands substantial regulatory resources and delivers pro-innovation benefits in line with this investment of resources. There is no such thing as a free lunch, even for regulators. Where resources are limited, regulators should focus their resources on developing innovation hubs to build FinTech ecosystems, rather than sandboxes. And where a sandbox is developed, in order to gain the greatest benefits to ecosystem development, it should be integrated as part of an innovation hub.

PART III

Building Better Financial Systems

Going forward, there is a major opportunity to use the impetus of the pandemic of 2020–22 to build better and more resilient financial systems that support future development. Financial technology is key to achieving financial inclusion and sustainable development as embodied in the UN Sustainable Development Goals (SDGs). As we have seen in the context of COVID and other sustainability crises, financial inclusion is important not only from the standpoint of empowerment and sustainable development.

The full potential of digital finance in all these respects will only be realised through an ecosystem approach, focusing on three levels: infrastructure, regulation, and the wider environment.

Infrastructure is fundamental and comprises four key elements. The first foundational element is digital inclusion, the key to digital finance and, in this, Asia offers many lessons. Generally, Asia is characterised by high smartphone penetration levels, providing an important foundation for ongoing and future digitisation. But hundreds of millions of people across the world still lack access to digital communications of any sort. This will be key going forward. The second, drawing on pandemic experiences, is open interoperable electronic payment systems. Experiences in China and India, while very different, had highlighted the significance of digital payments prior to COVID. Experiences across the world have since highlighted the power of electronic payments to enable crisis responses, economic and other activities, and new business models. The third entails digital identity, including simplified account opening and e-KYC systems. This infrastructure underpins the electronic provision of both government services and payments and private sector activity. India's experience with Aadhar has been pathbreaking, with an increasing range of countries worldwide now pursuing sovereign digital identity projects to support financial inclusion, bringing people into the formal economy, and enhancing market integrity. The fourth infrastructure element – digital financial markets and systems – broadens access to financial and investment opportunities. Implementing these four elements is a major journey for any economy, but is one with major potential to transform finance, economies, and societies through FinTech, financial inclusion, and sustainable development.

To truly maximise its potential, this infrastructure needs to be complemented and supported by a balanced proportional graduated approach to financial regulation. This will likely involve the strategic use of technology for regulation, and supervision in an environment that supports research and development, human capital development, and encourages innovation. In all these respects, data and related strategies are key.

Sustainable development has increasingly been accepted as a financial regulatory objective. This has global consequences for financial regulation generally, and Fintech regulation in particular, as we demonstrate in this part with financial inclusion. Financial inclusion relates to economic growth and sustainable development; it also relates to financial resilience and the role of finance in crisis response. Financial inclusion also has an independent basis in enabling financial empowerment.

While both FinTech and financial inclusion are important *tools* to support sustainable development, they are mutually connected. Digital finance supports financial inclusion where the distances and lack of infrastructure render traditional banking a challenge. At the same time, digital services are more effective the more customers can use them. FinTech and financial inclusion are mutually reinforcing. Promoting FinTech and financial inclusion thus follows from making sustainable development a financial regulatory objective.[1]

Digital financial transformation is one important way regulators and policymakers can support achievement of the SDGs. For financially excluded people who lack bank accounts, government-issued identification or other documentation, increased digitisation (through digital government-to-person (G2P) payments and cashless stores) can pose an additional barrier. The infrastructure developed, therefore, must be directed at enabling inclusion.

Based on India's experience and the other successful examples including Kenya, China, and Russia, we argued in our major study for AFI that countries must focus on four pillars of digital financial infrastructure to support digital financial transformation.[2] COVID has further demonstrated the need for digital finance in terms of crisis resilience, response, and recovery.

The role of digital finance, financial inclusion, and sustainable development come together dramatically in the context of sustainability and other crises.

In Part III, we move from questions around addressing new technologies to strategies for building better financial systems, in our view the true potential of FinTech, RegTech, and digital financial infrastructure.

---

[1]   Douglas W Arner et al, 'Sustainability, Fintech and Financial Inclusion' (2020) 21(1) *European Business Organization Law Review* 7, 17.
[2]   DW Arner, Ross P Buckley and Dirk A Zetzsche, 'Fintech for Financial Inclusion: A Framework for Digital Financial Transformation' (University of New South Wales Law Research Paper No. 18-87, 2018).

Chapter 12 presents the lessons of a decade and a half of digital financial transformation for policymakers, focusing on the role of digital inclusion, digital identity, open interoperable electronic payments, universal access to finance, and the development of digital infrastructures such as financial data repositories.

Chapter 13 focuses on the role of digital identity as a core enabling infrastructure.

Chapter 14 considers the digital transformation of payments and the emergence of central bank digital currencies.

Chapter 15 highlights the experience of the European Union in bringing these elements together to support digital financial transformation.

12

Building the Infrastructure for Digital Financial Transformation

SUMMARY

The full potential of FinTech may best be realised by a progressive approach to the development of the underlying infrastructure for digital financial transformation. Our research suggests the best way to think about such a strategy is to focus on four primary pillars. The first pillar requires the building of digital identity, simplified account opening, and e-KYC systems. The second pillar is open interoperable electronic payments systems. The third pillar involves using the infrastructure of the first and second pillars to underpin electronic provision of government services and payments. The fourth pillar is the design and development of digital financial markets and systems, which supports broader access to finance and investment. Implementing the four pillars is a major journey for any economy, but one with tremendous potential to transform financial systems, economies, and societies.

I. THE NEED FOR INFRASTRUCTURE

As shown in Part I of this book, FinTech may promote market efficiency, enhance service levels, facilitate crisis management, and further sustainable development. At the same time, financial regulators seeking to accelerate FinTech need to keep their other mandates in mind, including monetary and financial stability, financial integrity, and consumer protection. Part II considered the evolution of new technologies and regulatory approaches, arguing for a balanced approach incorporating facilitation as well as regulation.

We focus in this chapter on digital financial transformation in support of financial inclusion and sustainable financial development. Using finance for transformation rests on two preconditions: to develop technology that allows for the delivery of financial services (FinTech) and to assure people's access to these services (financial inclusion).[1] While we set out the interlinkage between sustainability, FinTech, and financial

---

[1] Kern Alexander, 'Financial Inclusion and Banking Regulation: The Role of Proportionality' (2021) 84(1) *Law and Contemporary Problems* 129.

inclusion in Chapter 6, we focus in this chapter on how to move from policy to practice (i.e., on what regulators can do to build inclusive financial digital infrastructure).

An ever-increasing range of international development organisations are focusing on the role of FinTech and digital financial transformation in supporting broader developmental objectives, including the Group of 20, the United Nations Secretary-General's Task Force on Digital Financing of the Sustainable Development Goals, the Alliance for Financial Inclusion, the World Bank, and Consultative Group to Assist the Poor (CGAP), many regional development banks, and a plethora of private or semi-private initiatives, including those of the Gates Foundation and the Green Digital Finance Alliance.

Given the many partly competing, partly complementary initiatives, we focus here on two questions:

1. Which among the various technologies considered in Part II are most likely to facilitate financial inclusion and sustainable development?
2. How can regulators further the types of FinTech most likely to advance these objectives?

While mobile money – the provision of e-money on mobile phones, with M-Pesa in Kenya as the paradigmatic example – is often the simple, immediate answer, the longer-term answer is more complex. The real opportunity of FinTech is to develop an entire infrastructure for a digital financial ecosystem underpinning sustainable financial development, inclusion, stability, and integrity.

Lessons can be taken from India's FinTech strategy, India Stack, implemented in recent decades. India Stack is a set of Application Programming Interfaces (APIs) which form a digital infrastructure used by the government, businesses, and other entities to provide paperless and cashless services.[2] India Stack involves four main levels. First is a national biometric identification system: a sovereign digital ID for individuals. Second is simple access to bank accounts and digital wallets. Third is a common payment API, enabling interoperable electronic payments across mobile and smart phones into accounts and wallets. Fourth is a series of electronic KYC initiatives allowing individuals to provide their financial details to financial services and other providers, designed to reduce barriers to customer acquisition and financial access. These eKYC utility platforms demonstrate how RegTech – regulatory technology – can improve the integrity of financial markets and reduce risks while at the same time supporting financial inclusion and sustainable development.

Building on India's experience, and other successful examples including those of Kenya and China, we show in Section II that digital financial transformation rests on four policy pillars. We develop these four pillars into a comprehensive regulatory strategy in Section III. Section IV concludes with an analysis of the potential impact of such a policy approach on financial inclusion and sustainable development.

---

[2] 'India Stack Is', *India Stack* (Web Page) <https://indiastack.org>.

II. FOUR PILLARS OF DIGITAL FINANCIAL TRANSFORMATION

The track records of successful developing and emerging economies support our view that countries need to focus on four pillars of digital financial infrastructure to support digital financial transformation.[3] These four pillars are:

1. Pillar I: Digital ID and eKYC for identification and simplified account opening.
2. Pillar II: Interoperable electronic payment systems, infrastructure, and an enabling regulatory and policy environment that facilitates the digital flow of funds from traditional financial intermediaries and new market entrants.
3. Pillar III: Account opening initiatives and electronic provision of government services, providing vital tools to access services, save, and invest.
4. Pillar IV: Design of digital financial market infrastructure and systems that support value-added financial services and deepen access, usage, and stability.

These four pillars are examined in the following subsections.

A. *Pillar I: Digital ID and eKYC – Establishing the Foundation*

1. Base ID as Foundation

As we analyse next in Chapter 13, digital identity is central to the transformation process. This is particularly challenging in developing countries where many people often lack formal identification documents.

India's Aadhaar system, analysed in detail in Chapter 10, is the first level of India Stack and involves issuing a 12-digit randomised number to all residents to underpin a digital identity system.[4] Aadhaar had its difficulties in implementation and around data protection, but these should not be allowed to detract from the potential of a national biometrically based identification system to underpin a digital financial ecosystem. Digital ID – particularly sovereign digital ID – is a necessary foundation for all subsequent aspects of a digital financial ecosystem.

A good example is IrisGuard, a project implemented by the United Nations and Jordan focusing on digital identity solutions for refugees.[5] IrisGuard is iris recognition technology that converts an iris image into a unique code which is then used to identify the individual. Since 2016, IrisGuard's EyePay platform has been used by the United Nations to deliver financial aid. The technology provides sufficient digital identity for beneficiaries to receive food vouchers, withdraw cash, and transfer

---

3 Douglas W Arner et al, 'Sustainability, FinTech and Financial Inclusion' (2020) 21(1) *European Business Organization Law Review* 7.
4 'About Aadhaar', *Unique Identification Authority of India* (Web Page) <https://uidai.gov.in/en/?option=com_content&view=article&id=14>.
5 As of 2022, see 'About Us', *irisguard* (Web Page) <www.irisguard.com/who-we-are/about-us/>.

funds without a bank account. EyePay, in conjunction with the Ethereum block-chain, has been used to promote financial inclusion of Syrian refugees in Jordan by processing supermarket and ATM transactions in real time. IrisGuard states that more than 2.8 million refugees in regions neighbouring Syria have been enrolled using their iris scanners.[6] Users reported that IrisGuard improved their freedom of choice and ability to access food and services with ease. Like Aadhaar, however, IrisGuard's implementation has come under scrutiny. Users have raised concerns about consent and confidentiality. While there remain real concerns about IrisGuard's implementation, its infrastructure is nonetheless an illustrative example of the power of digital ID infrastructure.[7]

IrisGuard offers what we call Base ID infrastructure: a link between the physical person and the digital service. While IrisGuard uses physical features, Base ID can also be developed from multiple sources, including business-specific e-identities, such as customer accounts with e-commerce platforms.

Base ID provides the fundamental element of the KYC process. It needs to extend as broadly as possible to maximise efficiencies. Particularly when linked electronically with other golden source data (e.g., tax information), Base ID underpins a simple eKYC system. The core objective is to make opening accounts for most people and entities simple and cheap, thereby allowing resources to be focused on protection of market integrity and the analysis of higher-risk customers.

2. Interconnecting ID Technologies

Technology enables the interconnection of various existing systems so as to balance market integrity, financial inclusion, and economic growth while meeting international financial standards. For instance, as part of its Aadhaar system, India has developed a paperless eKYC service to instantly establish the identity of prospective customers.[8] The digitisation of identity authentication streamlines account opening and allows easy access to both digital and traditional financial services. Axis Bank was the first Indian bank to offer an eKYC facility in 2013, reducing the turnaround time for opening bank accounts from between 7 and 10 days to just 1 day.[9] Today, many traditional banks and licensed payment banks in India offer accounts which can be opened and used instantly with eKYC.

[6] 'Humanitarian Aid', *irisguard* (Web Page) <www.irisguard.com/industry-sectors/humanitarian-aid/>.

[7] Beata Paragi and Ahmad Altamimi, 'Caring Control or Controlling Care? Double Bind Facilitated by Biometrics between UNHCR and Syrian Refugees in Jordan' (2022) 44(2) *Society and Economy* 206.

[8] 'How to Get Aadhaar Paperless e-KYC Document for Offline Verification', *India Today Web Desk* (online, 19 December 2021) <www.indiatoday.in/information/story/how-to-get-aadhaar-paperless-ekyc-document-for-offline-verification-1889588-2021-12-19>.

[9] 'Axis Bank Introduces a Paperless, eKYC Based A/C Opening', *India Infoline News Service* (online, 26 February 2014) <www.indiainfoline.com/article/news-top-story/axis-bank-introduces-a-paperless-ekyc-based-a-c-opening-114030300116_1.html>.

The European eIDAS system interconnects the ID systems in 27 EU member states. For instance, Italian students can identify themselves for public services (e.g., enrolment at universities) through eIDAS at the University of Luxembourg, and convey all data linked to their eIDAS ID under their national legislation to the receiving university. Previous exam results and certificates are provided in this way, which considerably shortens the registration process. eIDAS enables a bank account to be opened without physical attendance while maintaining rigorous identification standards.[10] Further use cases in the field of finance include storage of customer financial criteria under the respective ID, so financial institutions have strong starting points from which to identify their customers' needs and preferences.

To allow for such a wide range of services, electronic identification is needed as the foundation from which entities can meet customer due diligence requirements.

The interconnection of ID systems – while technically feasible – may not always be politically feasible. Further, data protection and cybersecurity concerns may undercut support for a mandatory, all-encompassing system for all members of society. Systems of optional digital identity, based on, but separate from, sovereign identification systems, may hold greater transformative potential in some countries.

We consider related issues in more detail in Chapter 13.

B. *Pillar II: Open, Interoperable Electronic Payment Systems – Building Connectivity*

After developing an eID system, the next stage is ensuring access to payments. Payment systems provide the fundamental infrastructure for money to flow through any economy. As was shown in the context of the COVID pandemic, access to payment is the precondition for financial inclusion, sustainable development, *and* the functioning of the real economy.

1. Mobile Money

Facilitating a mobile money (e-money) ecosystem is one way FinTech can help. E-money is typically defined as a stored value instrument or product that: (i) is issued on receipt of funds, (ii) consists of electronically recorded value stored on a device such as a mobile phone, (iii) may be accepted as a means of payment by parties other than the issuer, and (iv) is convertible back into cash.[11] Mobile money

---

[10] 'eIDAS: The Digital Identification Regulation for Europe', *ElectronicID* (Blog Post, 12 May 2022) <www.electronicid.eu/en/blog/post/eidas-regulation-electronic-signature/en>.

[11] See Jacek Binda, 'Cryptocurrencies: Problems of the High-Risk Instrument Definition' (2020) 17(1) *Investment Management and Financial Innovations* 227, 228–9.

enables mobile phones to be used to pay bills, remit funds, deposit cash, make withdrawals, and save, using e-money that is occasionally issued by banks but mostly by telecommunication companies ('telcos'). Even poorer members of society and SMEs can then access the services they need to flourish.

In this manner, technology can enable developing countries to leapfrog the stage of having bricks-and-mortar bank branches to a digital financial ecosystem, as is currently happening in almost 100 countries and growing rapidly.[12]

M-Pesa is the paradigmatic mobile money success story. Today, it provides financial services to some 55 per cent of Kenya's population.[13] However, the success of mobile money schemes has not been consistent across countries. This is due to the differing needs of consumers in different countries, the inability of service providers to adapt to different markets,[14] a tendency of central banks to over-regulate these services,[15] a lack of trained payment professionals in many markets,[16] and cultural and anthropological reasons.

Mobile money services, especially those offered by telcos, are key to defeating financial exclusion in poorer countries and in responding to crises (see Chapters 5 and 6) but often pose real challenges for regulators. Initially, such services typically do not present systemic stability concerns nor require traditional levels of banking regulation.[17] At the same time, successful services tend to grow rapidly, particularly when introduced by a dominant mobile telecoms provider, meaning that risks and the consequent need for regulation can arise very quickly in some cases. Service providers benefit from a central bank that encourages innovation and understands local customer needs: a major shift from the traditional role of central banks.[18]

---

[12] Mike McCaffrey, 'Where in the World Is Mobile Money Prominent?', UNCDF Impact Capital for Development (Blog Post, 6 September 2022) <uncdf.org/article/7904/where-in-the-world-is-mobile-money-prominent>.

[13] M-Pesa crossed the 30 million active user mark in Kenya in March 2022. See Otiato Guguyu, 'Safaricom's M-Pesa Crosses 30 Million Active Users in Kenya', *The East African* (online, 10 March 2022) <www.theeastafrican.co.ke/tea/business/safaricom-m-pesa-crosses-30-million-active-users-in-kenya-3743258#:~:text=Mobile%20money%20transfer%20platform%20M,digital%20transactions%20in%20the%20country>.

[14] RP Buckley and S Webster, 'FinTech in Developing Countries: Charting New Customer Journeys' (2016) 44 *Journal of Financial Transformation* 151, 151.

[15] For example, the Central Bank of Kenya applied a 'light-touch' approach from the outset, which many believe assisted the provision of these services.

[16] See McKinsey and Company, *Fintech in Africa: The End of the Beginning* (Report, August 2022); Ross P Buckley and Ignacio Mas, 'The Coming of Age of Digital Payments as a Field of Expertise' (2016) 2016(1) *Journal of Law, Technology and Policy* 71.

[17] Douglas W Arner, Ross P Buckley, and Dirk A Zetzsche, *Fintech for Financial Inclusion: A Framework for Digital Financial Transformation* (Report, 2018) 12. For the impact on financial stability, see also Global System for Mobile Communications Association, *State of the Industry Report on Mobile Money* (Report, 2022).

[18] Buckley and Webster (n 14).

2. Designing Regulatory Infrastructure for an
Open Electronic Payments System

In China, Alipay and WeChat Pay show the power of facilitating new entrants and the digitisation of the traditional payments system among banks.

As we have discussed in Chapter 2, Alibaba established Alipay in 2004 as a payment method for its ecommerce business. It is now the second largest mobile wallet provider in the world, behind PayPal.[19] The Yu'e Bao money market fund was established by Alipay in 2013, providing the opportunity to make small investments, and quickly became the world's largest money market fund.[20] Yu'e Bao's fund size has since shrunk to 55 per cent of its 2018 peak following strengthened 'regulatory oversight and capital requirements'.[21]

WeChat was established as a messaging platform by Tencent in 2011. Cash transfers and in-store cashless payments became possible using the WeChat wallet by 2014.[22] By 2021, 64 per cent of the Chinese population had adopted mobile payment, with WePay and Alipay comprising 91 per cent of all digital payments made in China.[23]

The People's Bank of China (PBoC) has since 2017 subjected mobile wallet services to increasing regulation. Mobile payment institutions are now required to channel payments through a new centralised clearing house, the China NetsUnion Clearing Corporation. The PBoC has also raised payment platforms' reserve funds ratios.[24]

These Chinese experiences highlight how payment providers should be subject to appropriate proportional regulation to address risks and provide a level playing field.

Interoperability to bring together traditional and new forms of payments is central to making such systems attractive. Governments are increasingly mandating interoperability as a licensing condition for payment providers; and, in many cases, governments are involved in the development of switches to provide the supporting infrastructure for such interoperability across different systems.

---

[19] Tom Phillips, 'PayPal and Alipay Top Digital Wallet Leaderboard', NFCW (Web Pge, 27 April 2022) <www.nfcw.com/2022/04/27/376968/paypal-and-alipay-top-digital-wallet-leaderboard/>.

[20] Quan Yue and Denise Jia Caixin, 'China Curbs Money Market Funds, among Them Ant's Yu'e Bao', *NikkeiAsia* (online, 18 January 2022) <https://asia.nikkei.com/Spotlight/Caixin/China-curbs-money-market-funds-among-them-Ant-s-Yu-e-Bao>.

[21] Samuel Shen and Andrew Galbraith, 'Ant Group's Money Market Fund Yu'e Bao Shrinks One-Fifth in Q2', *Reuters* (online, 21 July 2021) <www.reuters.com/business/ant-groups-money-market-fund-yue-bao-shrinks-one-fifth-q2-2021-07-21/>; Yue and Caixin (n 20).

[22] See Aaron Klein, 'China's Digital Payments Revolution' (Research Paper, April 2020).

[23] Alexandra Schirmer, 'Payment Methods in China: How China Became a Mobile-First Nation', *Daxue Consulting* (Web Page, 3 August 2022) <https://daxueconsulting.com/payment-methods-in-china/>.

[24] Robin Hui Huang et al, 'The Development and Regulation of Mobile Payment: Chinese Experiences and Comparative Perspectives' (2021) 20(1) *Washington University Global Studies Law Review* 1, 21.

C. *Pillar III: Electronic Government Provision of Services – Expanding Usage*

As a third step, government use of the open electronic payments infrastructure (Pillars I and II) is vitally important for digital transformation.

1. Electronic Payment: Government Salaries and Transfers to Those in Need

For the poor, state support payments are vital. This pre-pandemic need was exacerbated when the poor were deprived of their daily income due to lockdowns and the slowdown of economies during COVID-19.

Long before the COVID-19 pandemic (where most countries utilised e-payments for crisis support, see Chapter 5), the Indian government provided government salaries and services electronically through bank accounts based on India Stack. By these means, it promoted financial inclusion, empowerment, savings, and dramatically reduced leakage and corruption.

Digital Government-to-Person (G2P) payments achieve three beneficial outcomes. First, digital payments enable governments to shift from in-kind assistance (such as supply of food and water) to inexpensive cash transfers. Second, accounts established for government support payments are available for non-government payments. Third, the need to use the technology to receive government payments forces people to learn how to use it and tends to break down the cultural attachment to cash.

There are many notable examples of G2P payment programmes aimed at financially including the unbanked as well as enhancing the efficiency and effectiveness of government services, transfers, and payments. The use of such programmes expanded significantly during the COVID-19 pandemic, with 60 low-and-middle income countries utilising digital assets or payments to deliver social assistance programmes.[25] Tunisia delivered its first emergency COVID-19 payment through post offices. By the second round of payments, users could register for their payments digitally and select a digital payment method. Jordan leveraged its existing digitised government payments system to identify and reach out to individuals to deliver COVID-19 supplementary payments to mobile wallets. South Africa's online portal allowed it to process around 13 million digital applications for financial relief while the Thai government used its PromptPay to target around 24 million people for digital cash transfers.[26] Many of these projects, however, are at best half-digital. There remain barriers to access, including limited network coverage and restrictions on the providers and ways in which G2P payments can be spent.

---

[25] Identification for Development and G2P, Annual Report (Annual Report, 2021) 51.
[26] The Economist Group, *Rethinking the Global Microscope for Financial Inclusion: 2021 Key Findings Report* (Report, 2021).

In Pakistan, in a G2P women's programme, only 53 per cent of transactions were initiated by women; the rest were initiated allegedly for them by male representatives. Consequently, the Pakistan government adopted biometric technology, ensuring women received cash transfers directly, and thereby hopefully empowering them to decide how to use the money.[27]

G2P payments can further financial inclusion and sustainable development, *if properly designed*. Well-designed G2P payments have three characteristics:

1. Account procedures should later facilitate unrestricted payments.
2. The digital-to-real gap must be bridged well. When digital transaction partners are few, individuals will prefer cash. If merchants cannot do business without accepting e-money, they will provide devices to accept e-money efficiently, with or without incentives. Hence, it all starts with e-liquidity on the customer side.
3. Functionality must be simple. The learning required to receive government support must enable one to make and receive other transfers. A customised set-up could assist, for instance, by providing customers with the account information of their most important payers and payees.

2. Advancing e-Government

Government-driven e-payments may prompt a number of positive side effects, such as the furtherance of e-commerce, with significant benefits for SMEs, as more money is available, and thus can be spent, digitally. Governments can support digital transformation by highlighting the advantages of e-money, setting limits for cash transactions in the real economy, and requiring merchants to accept digital payments at low or no cost to customers.

Integrated strategies have the potential to transform government revenue, delivery of services, and trust and confidence, when digital payments are followed by digital accounting. G2P payments may improve tax collection, as SMEs grow within the formal financial system instead of outside it, and may support the development of national pension systems over time, which enhance the financial safety net and provide additional financial resources to support growth.

D. *Pillar IV: Enabling New Activities, Business, and Wider Development*

Innovative forms of financial services can be built on the digital infrastructure created in Pillars I–III.

---

[27] See Iftikhar Cheema et al, *Benazir Income Support Program's Impact Evaluation Report, Oxford Policy Management* (Report, March 2020).

1. Transforming Credit Provision: From Collateral and Microfinance to Cashflow

Historically, credit risk analysis was conducted only by specialised banks. The expense meant it was uncommercial for most individuals and SMEs. The traditional solution was to rely on collateral, which may well be very difficult in developing countries where property rights are weak or nonexistent, and enforcement of contracts are largely a theoretical option.

Digitalisation has changed this. Providers with accurate customer data are able to price credit through datafication (i.e., the process of using and analysing data). Superior data may derive from social media services, search engines, e-commerce platforms, and telcos.[28] The big data approach applied by TechFins (which we discuss in Chapter 16) potentially improves business decisions by providing a better picture of a customer's financial position using these superior datasets. While not without their problems, TechFins can play a crucial role by re-personalising the financial relationship with clients by adjusting credit rates based on individuals' real risk profiles. Transaction costs per client are greatly reduced due to the economies of scale inherent in the tech platforms used (see Chapter 6). This provision of 'personalised' services at a much lower cost per customer enables the delivery of financial services for small amounts of money, resulting in enhanced financial inclusion.

Notwithstanding the huge benefits, the emergence of TechFins also brings new challenges at the intersection of data regulation and financial regulation. As with G2P payments, much depends on the appropriate regulatory framework, which we discuss in Part IV.

2. Adding Insurance and Investments Services

The argument laid out above, that digitalisation can increase access and reduce transaction costs for financial services, also facilitates the expansion of service range, level, and quality in insurance and investment, and furthermore supports the development of technologies such as AI discussed in Part II. This expansion and development have the potential to bring new financial resources into the financial system which can in turn support innovation, business development, and infrastructure, as savings rates increase and are redirected through the financial system.

III. DEVELOPING A COMPREHENSIVE STRATEGY

The power of pillars I to IV is greatest when all are pursued and become mutually reinforcing in a comprehensive strategy.

---

[28] Dirk A Zetzsche et al, 'From FinTech to TechFin: The Regulatory Challenges of Data-Driven Finance' (2018) 14(2) *New York University Journal of Law and Business* 393, 406.

A. *The Challenge of Technology*

Any FinTech-based approach must accept that technology is not perfect. Three consequences follow.

First, technology may operate beyond its developers' intentions. Self-learning algorithms may enhance biases existing in the data.[29] Providers must constantly test, and regulators supervise, the outcomes of algorithmic data interpretation.

Second, technology may do exactly what the developers intend, and the problem is the developers. Financial history is replete with fraud. Every new technology will be abused by some. FinTech examples include the use of initial coin offerings for defrauding investors/participants,[30] and potential theft in the context of highly valued tech start-ups.

Third, ever-accelerating technology facilitates ever more new entrants, making regulators' roles ever more challenging. This will most likely require regulators to respond with (regulatory) technology as explored in Chapter 4.

B. *Building Innovation Ecosystems: Facilitating Financial Innovation and RegTech*

Probably most important are the need for policymakers and regulators to develop methods to understand new technologies and the related risks and opportunities, and the increasing necessity for regulators to consider how they can better use technology in redesigning their regulatory systems for digital finance and FinTech. We have discussed the regulatory options including innovation hubs, sandboxes, no-action letters, waiver programmes, testing, and piloting in Chapters 3 and 11.

One way forward will be for regulators to mandate the use of technology. Regulators can require supervised firms to report digitally to supervisors, and supervisors to receive and process reported information by digital means, thereby driving a RegTech cycle that will propel both supervised firms and supervisors into the digital age (see Chapter 4).

C. *Balancing Inclusion with Client Protection*

Client protection is key for digital financial inclusion and digital financial transformation more broadly. One promising option is regulation by design: regulatory restrictions embedded technologically in the product.[31] These restrictions would

---

[29] See, for example, Amazon's recent discontinuance of its AI recruitment system which taught itself to favor the word 'male': Jyh-An Lee, 'Algorithmic Bias and the New Chicago School' (2022) 14(1) *Law, Innovation and Technology* 95, 95.

[30] Dirk A Zetzsche, 'The ICO Goldrush: A Challenge for Regulators' (2019) 60 (2) *Harvard International Law Journal* 267.

[31] Karen Yeung, 'Towards an Understanding of Regulation by Design' in Roger Brownsword and Karen Yeung (eds), *Regulating Technologies* (Hart Publishing, 2008) 79; Pompeu Casanovasabc, Jorge González-Conejeroc, and Louis de Koker, 'Legal Compliance by Design (LCbD) and through Design (LCtD): Preliminary Survey' (Research Paper, 2018).

reflect client exposure and ability to bear risks and would substitute for today's restrictions on access to financial services.

It is unlikely a reasonable approach will seek full access for all of society to all financial services. To protect customers, any policy must be partially exclusive and restrict access to highly risky products for those with low financial literacy. The result will be an asymmetric paternalistic system in which people with greater financial sophistication have access to wider ranges of financial products. We envisage customers being categorised by income, education, experience, and wealth. Depending on their category, access to risky products may be controlled. This approach also allows preferred ethical restrictions. For instance, clients who wish to avoid leverage for religious reasons (as in Islamic finance) will be able to do so.

The FinTech aspect of this new legal, rather than de facto, customer segregation is that the criteria can be set, reviewed, and adjusted day to day, as its application follows data-driven rules, and its outcome can be supervised using RegTech.

IV. TOWARDS INCLUSIVE AND BALANCED SUSTAINABLE GROWTH

Digital financial transformation is *one* important answer to how regulators and government can support sustainable inclusive development. Digital financial transformation supports sustainable inclusive development in three key ways: first, by potentially generating additional financial resources; second, by more efficiently using existing and new financial resources; and third, in some cases, by directly supporting people.

A comprehensive digital financial transformation strategy based on the four pillars, including digital ID, open interoperable payment systems, FinTech for G2P programmes, and long-term development of sophisticated financial market infrastructure, is essential.

From the standpoint of transforming all aspects of society and development, the most powerful technology to have emerged is the mobile phone, particularly smartphones coupled to internet access. Major barriers remain though, particularly in the context of the last mile generally, and in regions where feature phones still prevail and internet access is mixed. Because of the digital access foundations provided by smart phones, phone sophistication and connectivity are core areas for focus in seeking rapid transformation.

Another transformational technology for digital inclusion in finance and beyond is digital identification. India's Aadhaar system, through which over a billion people have received digital biometric identification, has been transformative: it has shown the power of such systems for sustainable inclusive growth, including for increasing available financial resources. At the same time, the India Stack has highlighted the potential dangers for data protection and potential for other abuses.

Combining ID systems, open interoperable services platforms for payments and credit, G2P payments, and a potential openness to expansion into insurance and investment services, will gradually allow governments, businesses, and others to provide better and more inclusive financial services.

As digital financial transformation proceeds, digital finance increasingly enables individuals to save and invest small amounts of money, with customer acquisition costs made viable through foundational technologies of the sorts described here. This brings new money for sustainable growth and investments, as potentially billions of people join the financial system and are empowered to make investments that support wider social objectives.

Looking forward, the power of digital finance is greatest in those countries which are furthest behind and make policy choices to support foundational technologies. Such countries will be able to leapfrog to higher levels of development. While such a strategy will not solve all challenges – for instance, we may face a new digital divide between the technologically able and others particularly those lacking access to the internet or even mobile phones – it does provide the core elements of an enabling framework to support sustainable inclusive growth in the parts of the world that need it the most.

13

Digital Identity

SUMMARY

This chapter considers the various requirements for identification in the financial sector and the evolution in the nature of identity from analogue to digitised to digital. We argue that technology presents an opportunity to solve this challenge through the development of digital identity infrastructure and related utilities. The establishment of such utilities for digital or electronic identification requires addressing design questions such as registration methods, data availability, and cross-jurisdictional recognitions. As with any reform, a balance needs to be reached to ensure the objectives of efficiency and financial inclusion are not achieved at the cost of market integrity and financial stability.

I. THE IDENTITY CHALLENGE IN FINANCE

Identity is fundamental in finance. From a business standpoint, knowledge of client identities is essential to protect against fraud and crime, underpins all know-your-customer (KYC) obligations, and is critical to providing quality services. From a risk management and regulatory standpoint, identity is essential to market integrity and credit risk evaluation. Yet identification and KYC rules can be major barriers to accessing financial services, for individuals and small businesses specifically.

The rules for verifying customer identity and carrying out due diligence on new customers (onboarding) and on an ongoing basis comprise a wide range of anti-money laundering/countering the financing of terrorism/customer due diligence (AML/CFT/CDD) requirements, based on internationally agreed approaches.[1] Additionally, CDD underpins how customer needs are understood and is essential

---

[1] See the standards provided by the Financial Action Task Force (FATF), an intergovernmental body established to set standards and promote effective implementation of legal, regulatory, and operational measures for combating money laundering, terrorist financing, and other related threats to the integrity of the international financial system.

to providing appropriate financial services, a function often summarised under the general framework of suitability.[2]

Because of the sometimes conflicting objectives and regulatory frameworks of transparency, privacy, financial integrity, revenue collection, financial inclusion, economic growth, and financial stability, identification and identity pose particular challenges in finance. Where bigdata firms (which we discuss in Chapter 16) are moving into financial services, and therefore collecting or transferring customer money, a tension emerges as to which is the most effective method of customer identification and KYC. Should the solution be found in the reformulation of identity? Should it be found in the methodology of retrieving identification, including the sources and types of data drawn upon to establish identity? Or should it be found in both, or in other ways? This chapter addresses these and other questions around the interrelationship between identity and finance.

II. THE EVOLUTION OF IDENTIFICATION AND IDENTITY: ANALOGUE TO DIGITALISED TO DIGITAL

Identity can today be either analogue (passport), digitised (the scan of an ID document), or digital (online footprints). While any and all may be used for authentication purposes (such as accessing a social media or banking account), they are not universally compatible, nor acceptable, for all purposes. Anonymity is a feature, not necessarily a failing, of the Internet and directly conflicts with customer identification requirements in finance.

The rise of the Internet has transformed financial services. With e-banking and social media have come a series of unanswered questions: can a pin code plus mail address replace a 'wet signature' to identify a person and authenticate a transaction? If services can be rendered digitally and globally, what happens with remote onboarding of new customers? These questions became all the more important with the entry of the TechFins into financial services. The critical question becomes whether such new entrants should adapt to existing identity regimes, or be permitted to privatise the previously essentially sovereign function of identity verification.

In both digitised and digital forms, one's identification – and even identity – is converted into an electronic form, whether a digitised version of a passport (e-KYC) or a digital aggregation of one's online footprint (through analysis of browsing cookies). In some cases, these identities are collected and verified on a regular basis (for bank account maintenance) or transferred between entities (as social media credentials).

---

[2]   For the EU, see *Directive 2014/65/EU of the European Parliament and of the Council of 15 May 2014 on Markets in Financial Instruments* [2014] OJ L 173, 349–496, art 25.

TABLE 13.1 *Identity Topology*

State	Static Identities	Dynamic Identities
Form	Physical Legal	Electronic Behavioural

A. *Typology of Identification*

A person's identity can take one of four different forms and be in one of two states: static or dynamic (Table 13.1). The four different forms include:

1. *Physical identity* such as fingerprint, iris scans, or DNA.
2. *Legal identity* such as passports, national ID cards, or driving licence.
3. *Electronic identity* comprising social media accounts such as Twitter, WeChat, and so forth.
4. *Behavioural identity* comprising the unique way you walk, talk, or even hold and use your phone.

Static identification has been used historically to prove an individual's identity to, say, a bank. It is an *analogue* form of identification which requires physical documents, or physical markers (a fingerprint), and records to establish someone's individuality. By its nature, static identification changes minimally over time. *Digitised* forms of identity rely on the same limited kinds of information but put them into a digital format which can be readily used in different contexts, for example in opening a bank account over the Internet using scanned versions of otherwise analogue identification documents, or broadcasting one's features via the Internet to an identification clerk who performs background checks by asking questions the answers to which only that person could know. The next stage in the evolution of identity marks the shift to new forms of *digital* identity, in which the concept of 'identity' is broadened to include dynamic behavioural characteristics that reflect an individual's distinct personality, for example, by collecting data from social media profiles and analysing patterns of searching or other consumer behaviour on the Internet. The high number of data points thus assembled make it very likely that the user is the person she claims to be.[3]

These characterisations apply not only to individuals but also to legal entities, which generally require some form of legal authorisation (e.g., company registration) to exist. Their identity can be physical or digital, and often today it is mainly digital.

---

[3] International Bar Association, *Report of IBA Legal Practice Division Working Group: Digital Identity: Principles on Collection and Use of Information* (Report, 2015) 11 <www.ibanet.org/MediaHandler?id=2E931F85-C5D0-4952-A6E6-6EA48C593155>.

B. *Traditional vs Non-traditional KYC*

In finance, a bank performs its 'legal KYC' when a client opens an account and provides an identity document, such as a passport or company registration. Consequently, as the bank gets to know a customer from a transactional standpoint, this can be extended by capturing payment, insurance, or investment data. These touch points represent great opportunities for a bank to better understand its customers. While a passport provides identification data, transaction data create a profile of a person, including creditworthiness.

In this second stage of identity, banks seem disadvantaged relative to their more tech-driven and data-driven counterparts such as TechFins and FinTechs. Such entities capture behavioural and overall business data, and often use safer authentication options. For instance, a datafied firm can use how a person holds a phone, or brings it to their ear (using an in-built gyroscope) or how (and how often) they enter a password. Such things can act as second-factor authentication methods.

Similarly, online data can result in a better assessment of a customer risk profile. For instance, online devices, such as smart phones or fitness monitors and social media data may reveal whether a customer tends to cancel orders frequently, engage in risky activities (e.g., paragliding), or has a risky lifestyle (e.g. consumes a lot of fast food, owns dangerous dogs, or has relatives with infectious diseases).

Therefore, banks can be at a disadvantage, compared to tech companies, in having a comprehensive view of their client. An average person checks their online bank accounts less than 10 times per month, compared with the hundreds of visits to a social media platform or thousands of messages typically sent over the same period. Less data indicate less well-informed decisions, for example, in banks' capacity to assess customer credit.

Consumers do not necessarily have control over this wide-ranging digital identity. Individuals typically do not know who has access to what information about them, as privacy policies are routinely overly complex or totally unread. If our 'identity' is limited to what we know about our own personally identifiable information, then we will not fully appreciate or be able to manage our expanding digital identities which will likely include our behavioural data. It is important that control of this information lies with the person it is about, not the entity collecting it.[4] Dynamic information which a bank seeks to incorporate into its assessment of a prospective customer's identity must therefore be obtained with consent.

C. *The Case for Digital ID*

Rethinking and implementing new digital identity approaches will disproportionately benefit emerging markets precisely because many people there fail the first hurdle to

---

[4] Ibid 5–6.

access financial services: a valid ID document. Presently, some 1 billion individuals lack a formal, legal form of identity.[5] As a result, financial inclusion remains a problem. It comprises the capacity to have a bank account and access financial products that can smooth consumption (savings and micro-loans) or protect against unexpected unfortunate events (insurance). Yet, approximately one in eight people globally cannot access financial services. Even where users have bank accounts, they sometimes hardly use them. This lack of financial engagement can either be self-imposed (by cultural or geographical factors) or externally imposed (customer fails KYC or risk criteria).

Emerging markets present a stronger case for reforming approaches to identification. India, for example, where 15 years ago one in five people lacked formal ID documents, responded to calls for new methods of identification as part of the India Stack. Notably, while in developed countries, social media often only marginally enhances the datasets available to inform credit scoring decisions, in developing countries social media usage is often a primary way to start forming a customer profile.

D. *Three Concerns*

The benefits of reforming identity approaches in finance, from static identities (passports) to dynamic e-identities, are not limited to individuals. The consequences are economy-wide and include stakeholders ranging from banks to tech companies and from governments to supranational organisations.

However, the collection and use of dynamic identities, being behavioural or electronic, raise important issues.

First, there is the issue of fake IDs. National legal documents are assumed to be legitimate because they are state issued, administered on centralised ledgers, and have built-in security features. In contrast, existing electronic identities can be tampered with and non-existent ones invented. Stolen e-identities cannot readily be replaced, for example due to the fixed number of fingerprints, or the difficulty in reconstructing the previous social media account and accompanying data.

Given comprehensiveness of electronic identities, the second concern is privacy loss in the event of data breaches. In view of this, governments and non-governmental organisations have nominated principles to manage dynamic digital identities, such as the user control principle (individuals choose whether, and to what extent, to disclose their information), the transparency principle (data processors must justify why they are collecting data), and the data minimisation principle (only the minimum data required for a certain purpose is to be collected).[6]

---

[5] Calum Handforth and Kendrick Lee, 'How Digital Can Close the Identity Gap', *United Nations Development Programme* (Blog Post, 19 May 2022) <www.undp.org/blog/how-digital-can-close-identity-gap>.

[6] See for example International Bar Association (n 3); Mike Bracken, 'Identity and Privacy Principles', *UK Government Digital Service* (Blog Post, 24 April 2012) <https://gds.blog.gov.uk/2012/04/24/identityand-privacy-principles/>; 'The Principles', *Information Commissioner's Office* (Web Page, 2022) <https://

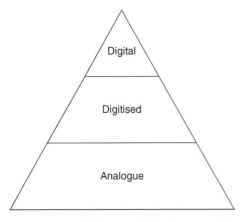

FIGURE 13.1 Evolution of identity pyramid

Third is the risk of monopolisation and misuse of market power. In the data business, size matters. The more data points a tech business holds on an individual, the better are its identification services as well as its risk assessments.

E. *From Analogue to Digital*

A *legal identity* is external and *summarises* who someone is personally. By contrast, a physical or *behavioural identity* is internal, interactive, and *defines* who someone is. Finally, *electronic identity*, while external, is increasingly shaped by time spent online and provides a relatively complete picture of one's persona and preferences. Indeed, most people are more willing to provide their passport details to a third party, than their social media credentials, as the latter are far more disclosive.

Two paths exist to solving the identity challenge found in financial markets: developed markets are likely to digitise pre-existing infrastructure while some more innovative emerging markets may leapfrog and adopt fully digital identities.[7]

The path of least resistance is to focus on digitising analogue identities. This triggers a broader and sequenced reform process of enhancing digitised identities to create a fully digital identity. The latter step transcends finance and entails rethinking privacy standards, achieving a consensus on existing notions, such as data sovereignty, and developing new frameworks that treat data as an economic right. For these reasons, it may be easier to focus on entities first at the international level and leave identification of individuals to domestic sovereigns (Figure 13.1).

---

ico.org.uk/for-organisations/guide-to-data-protection/guide-to-the-general-data-protection-regulation-gdpr/principles/>.

[7] This geographical distinction has likewise been seen in how FinTech has evolved differently in developed (i.e., a reaction to the crisis) and developing economies (i.e., a reform mechanism). See Chapter 2 on the evolution of FinTech.

F. *Windhover Principles*

The Windhover Principles articulate guidelines for managing online identities.[8] They provide that individuals should have control over their digital identities and personal data and argue that new and evolving digital technologies should protect the individual's privacy while providing government access to consumer identification. To illustrate, the Windhover Principles could be applied when a customer signs up with a digital currency exchange integrated with an open-source platform and creates an account. The open-source platform then sends the identity information to a trusted third party for independent verification. Regulators could access the information via an access token.[9]

Although largely aspirational, the Windhover Principles are supported by organisations like BitPay, Coinsetter, and Ripple Labs and have significantly influenced public policy such as New York's bitcoin regulation, the Bitlicence.

The optimal destination of this identity journey will probably embody elements of all approaches. Crucially, social welfare demands sharing *some* data among industry and the state. The question of where precisely the delineating line lies will be the most important question in the next decade and likely to be answered differently in the United States where data protection and privacy are of lesser importance than in the EU, and where state involvement in identification is also less politically acceptable than in the EU.

III. SOLVING THE IDENTITY CHALLENGE: DESIGNING INFRASTRUCTURE FOR DIGITAL IDENTIFICATION

Financial technology, particularly RegTech (which we discuss in Chapter 4) presents opportunities to build the necessary infrastructure to balance market integrity, financial inclusion, and sustainable economic growth while simultaneously meeting international financial standards, including those set by the Financial Action Task Force (FATF), Basel Committee, Financial Stability Board (FSB), and the UN. New forms of digital identification will be the foundation of this infrastructure.

One must differentiate between digital identification for people, legal entities, and other things. Within each category, the identification system can be regulated (and perhaps monopolised) by the sovereign, or be private in nature. Such systems can be mandatory by imposing a national identity card or voluntary, as passports

---

[8] 'HubID First to Deploy Windhover Principles and Framework for Digital Identity, Trust, and Open Data', *Hub Culture* (Web Page, 20 October 2014) <https://hubculture.com/hubs/47/news/689>.

[9] Dougla W. Amer et al, 'The Identity Challenge in Finance: From Analogue Identity to Digitized Identification to Digital KYC Utilities' (2019) 20 *European Business Organization Law Review* 55, citing John Clippinger, *A Proof of Concept Pilot for A Decentralised Autonomous Authority (DAA) For KYC Compliant Decentralised Identity and Authentication Services* (Research Paper ID3, MIT Media Lab).

are in many countries. Various measures may incentivise voluntary systems: for instance, registration is required for a company to acquire the entity's attributes, or legal entity identifiers may be mandated (as is the case for entities dealing with EU counterparties under MiFID2).

Equally important is to distinguish base identity (generally a sovereign function for individuals and corporates) and digital identity. Base and digital identities can be merged, as in Aadhar and Iris Guard, or separated, as in the electronic Identification, Authentication and trust Services (eIDAS) Regulation (eIDASR) in the EU and in systems developed by Alibaba and Tencent in China.

A. *Aadhaar in India*

As highlighted in Chapter 12, India's Aadhaar system is operated by the Unique Identification Authority of India (UIDAI) and involves issuing a 12-digit randomised number to all residents for use in accessing government services, subsidies, social benefits, banking, taxation, insurance, and other services. Enrolment is free, and the biometric de-duplication process seeks to ensure only one Aadhaar number is generated for each individual. The Aadhaar number acts as a proof of identity, but is unrelated to citizenship rights, and does not identify people's caste, religion, or income. To be issued with an Aadhaar number, an individual must satisfy the UIDAI verification process, which requires various demographic and biometric data, including the individual's name, date of birth, gender, address, mobile number, email address, ten fingerprints, two iris scans, and a facial photograph.[10]

Because the Aadhaar number can be linked to a growing number of services, a critical feature of the system is the numerous avenues for updating different kinds of data. Biometric data can, for example, be updated as children grow, in the event of accidents or diseases, or as the quality of technology improves. Such updates can be made online by logging in with the Aadhaar number and registered mobile number and uploading the requisite supporting identification documents, or by visiting an enrolment centre in person.

Criticisms of Aadhaar include that the *Aadhaar Authentication Regulations 2016* provide for transaction data to be archived for five years, leading to allegations of mass surveillance technology. However, Aadhaar has also proven highly beneficial. As of 2022, Aadhaar has reportedly saved the government about US$ 29 billion in welfare payments that would otherwise have been lost through fraud and corruption and have now reached the intended recipients.[11]

---

[10] Unique Identification Authority of India, *Annual Report 2020–2021* (Report, 5 April 2021), <https://uidai.gov.in/images/UIDAI%20Annual%20Report%202020-21_English_final.pdf.>.

[11] ENS Economic Buro, 'Amitabh Kant: Aadhaar Helped Govt Save over Rs 2 Lakh Crore', *The Indian Express* (online at 2 June 2022) <https://indianexpress.com/article/business/amitabh-kant-aadhaar-helped-govt-save-over-rs-2-lakh-crore-7948221/>

Aadhaar faced constitutional challenges leading to two decisions in the Supreme Court of India in September 2018 and January 2021.[12] The claimants argued Aadhaar breached privacy, and data were collected by third-party contractors hired by UIDAI without proper safeguards in place. It was also argued that the biometric identification techniques, fingerprinting, and iris scanning, were susceptible to misuse and fraud. In January 2021, the court, however, affirmed the verdict of September 2018 when the top court upheld the biometric identity system and Aadhaar being mandatory for recipients of government welfare benefits.[13]

There have been many problems in Aadhaar's implementation. However, difficulties and sloppiness in implementation do not detract from the potential of a national biometrically based identification system to underpin an entire, highly beneficial digital financial ecosystem.

B. *Digital Identification without a National ID: The Australian GovPass Project*

Australia lacks any form of national identity card, partly because earlier attempts to introduce such an initiative were politically fraught. Identity in Australia has historically been established through documents ranging from passports to drivers' licences, tax file numbers, or Medicare numbers. In 2015, the Australian Government initiated the Trusted Digital Identity Framework (TDIF) following the final report of the 2014 Financial System Inquiry, which highlighted the benefits of a national digital identity system for economic efficiency and public engagement.[14] Since 2017, the TDIF has undergone several iterations based on extensive community and industry consultation.[15] On 1 October 2021, the Australian Government released the exposure draft of the Trusted Digital Identity Bill 2021 and related legislative instruments,[16] which are a legal framework for two separate but related initiatives: the TDIF accreditation scheme and the expansion of GovPass.

The TDIF accreditation scheme imposes minimum standards and rules upon providers of digital identity services pertaining to accessibility and usability, privacy

---

[12] *Justice K.S. Puttaswamy (Retd) v. Union of India*, AIR 2017 SC 4161. See also 'Aadhaar Review', *Supreme Court Observer* (Blog Post) <www.scobserver.in/cases/beghar-foundation-ks-puttaswamy-aadhaar-review-case-background/>.

[13] See also Chapter 10, Section C(III).

[14] Australian Government, *Improving Australia's Financial System: Government Response to the Financial System Inquiry* (Treasury Report, 2015) <https://static.treasury.gov.au/uploads/sites/1/2017/06/Government_response_to_FSI_2015.pdf>.

[15] Trusted Digital Identity Bill 2021 (Cth), Exposure Draft, *Parliament of the Commonwealth of Australia*. <www.digitalidentity.gov.au/sites/default/files/2021-11/Digital%20Identity%20Legislation%20-%20what%20is%20it%20-%20factsheet.pdf>.

[16] *Draft Trusted Digital Identity Framework Accreditation Rules 202x* (Cth) <www.digitalidentity.gov.au/sites/default/files/2021-09/TDIF%20accreditation%20rules.pdf>; *Draft Trusted Digital Identity Rules 20XX* (Cth) <www.digitalidentity.gov.au/sites/default/files/2021-09/TDI%20rules.pdf>.

protection, security and fraud control, risk management, and technology integrity. The proposed legislation adopts the statutory contract model set out in the Consumer Data Right legislation,[17] where each accredited service provider is contractually bound to other accredited service providers.[18]

The Australian Government's Trusted Digital Identity System, 'GovPass', currently provides 'whole of government' digital identity credentials for Australians who choose to opt-in to access Australian Government services. GovPass allows individuals to merge identification information across a patchwork of discrete, service-specific verification systems into a single digital identity recognised by all accredited services and protected by baseline security and privacy standards. The draft Bill expands GovPass's ambit by allowing private sector and state and territory bodies to rely on digital identities provided by the system and establishes an independent authority to oversee onboarding, accreditation, and enforcement.[19]

Whilst this draft Bill was circulated in October 2021 by the Coalition government, the Labor government went into power in April 2022, before the Bill was introduced before Parliament.[20] The next stage of developing the System will depend on the Labor government's efforts to alleviate criticisms of the System.

C. *Interlinking Domestic Digital ID Systems in the EU*

In contrast to Australia, Canada, and the United States, identity cards embedded with chips and common security features, including biometrics, are ubiquitous in EU/EEA Member States.

1. E-Signature Directive (1999)

A 1999 EU Directive ensured that advanced electronic signatures based on a qualified certificate and created by a secure-signature-creation device were valid under the laws of each Member State, much like handwritten signatures. However, this initiative achieved little traction. Gaining an e-signature certificate was burdensome, few recipients had the technology to identify it, and in a decade the underlying technology was outdated. Further, the directive did not deal with authentication and trust services, two pillars of today's online markets.

---

[17] *Treasury Laws Amendment (Consumer Data Right) Act 2019* (Cth).
[18] Trusted Digital Identity Bill 2021 (Cth), Exposure Draft, chs 3–5.
[19] Ibid ch 6.
[20] Philip Hamilton, 'Digital Identity System', *Parliament of Australia* (Blog Post, 25 May 2022) <www .aph.gov.au/About_Parliament/Parliamentary_departments/Parliamentary_Library/FlagPost/2022/ May/Digital_Identity_system>.

2. EIDASR as Open Standard (2014)

In response, European regulators adopted the eIDASR[21] in 2014 to reduce the costs of transacting online and enhance competition.

The eIDASR provides a predictable regulatory environment to enable 'secure electronic interaction between citizens, businesses and public authorities.'[22] The underlying rationale is that legal certainty of eID services will greatly assist businesses and citizens in digital interactions.

Since a pan-European ID card system would have doubled the work for Member States, the eIDASR ensures that people and businesses can use their national eIDs to access public services in EU countries where eIDs are available. This creates a European internal market for eTrust Services by ensuring that eIDs work across borders and have the same legal status as traditional paper-based processes. Use cases include tax declarations, foreign university enrolments, remote bank account opening, and business establishment in other Member States.

Rather than harmonising various national standards of eIDs, the eIDASR focuses on the technical interoperability of existing eID standards. By mandating liability on Member States as well as the eID provider for meeting certain identification obligations (including that the personal identification data uniquely represents the person to which it is attributed and that online authentication is available),[23] the eIDASR creates trust in the eIDASR-based cross-border identification.

The eIDASR is a potential role model among eID projects since it provides an open standard not limited to EU jurisdictions. Every national ID system that wants to connect to eIDAS can do so by defining nodes (so-called eIDAS connectors) that provide the cross-border links between other countries' systems and one own's system.

3. The (Draft) EU Digital Identity Regulation

Under the impression of the COVID-19 pandemic, the EU Commission defined as targets[24] that by 2030, all key public services in the EU should be available online, all citizens will have access to electronic medical records, and 80 per cent of citizens should use an eID solution. Compared to India, where already in 2022 almost all citizens use such an eID, i.e. Aadhaar (see supra, at Section III(A)), these targets sound

---

[21] *Regulation (EU) No 910/2014 on Electronic Identification and Trust Services for Electronic Transactions in the Internal Market of 28 August 2014* [2014] OJ 257/73.

[22] Ibid preamble[2].

[23] See *Regulation (EU) No 910/2014 on Electronic Identification and Trust Services for Electronic Transactions in the Internal Market of 28 August 2014* [2014] OJ 257/73 art 11.

[24] European Commission, *2030 Digital Compass: The European Way for the Digital Decade* (COM/ 2021/118 Final, 9 March 2021) <https://eur-lex.europa.eu/legal-content/en/TXT/?uri=CELEX%3A5202 1DC0118>.

remarkably modest, yet they must be read in the light of a very well-functioning analogue ID system, with the entire population used to identifying themselves with paper-based identity cards. The European Commission seeks to achieve its goals by further developing eIDASR.

EIDAS lacked a requirement for EU Member States to develop a national eID and make it interoperable with those in other Member States. This has led to a digital divide between more advanced and less advanced EU Member States. By 2021, three years after recognition of notified eID became mandatory across the EU Member States, only 60 per cent of Europeans could benefit from the eIDAS cross-notification system. The remainder were residents of countries with lesser digital ambitions. At the same time, the European Commission found that take-up of the eIDAS cross-recognition scheme is low, their use is cumbersome, and business cases are limited.

In June 2021, the EU Commission's new (draft) European Regulation on Digital Identity[25] seeks to ensure that each EU citizen has access to eID to 'guarantee the unambiguous electronic identification of a person and ensure the right service is delivered to the person who is really entitled to it, for example for banking purposes.' In particular, the Digital ID Regulation extends the benefits of eIDASR to the private sector. EU Member States will be mandated to offer citizens and businesses digital wallets based on each Member State's ID system and issued by public or recognised private providers, to link various aspects of their national digital identities and facilitate the commercial use of the former. Consumers will have control over the data they share; they can use the digital wallet to access services online without having to use private platforms or unnecessarily sharing personal data with private providers that create, as a precondition for providing the services, a business ID collecting additional consumer data. The EU Commission also furthered the technical implementation through a recommendation on technical tools and standards.[26]

The EU bottom-up initiatives end where Aadhaar started top-down: by making a digital wallet mandatory for all citizens, they require nothing less than building a unique digital ID for each citizen.

---

[25] See European Commission, Proposal for a Regulation of the European Parliament and of the Council amending Regulation (EU) No 910/2014 as regards establishing a framework for a European Digital Identity (COM/2021/281 Final, 3 June 2021) <https://eur-lex.europa.eu/legal-content/EN/TXT/?uri=CELEX%3A52021PC0281>. See on the draft regulation: European Commission, Directorate-General for Financial Stability, Financial Services and Capital Markets Union and Stephane Mouy, *Developing a Digital Identity Solution for Use by the Financial Sector Based around eIDAS Trust Services* (Publications Office of the European Union, 2021); Steffen Schwalm, Daria Albrecht, and Ignacio Alamillo, 'eIDAS 2.0: Challenges, Perspectives and Proposals to Avoid Contradictions between eIDAS 2.0 and SSI' (2022) *Open Identity Summit 2022* 63–74. f

[26] *Commission Recommendation (EU) 2021/946 of 3 June 2021 on a Common Union Toolbox for a Coordinated Approach towards a European Digital Identity Framework* [2021] OJ L 210/51 <https://eur-lex.europa.eu/legal-content/GA/TXT/?uri=CELEX:32021H0946>.

4. Integrating Financial Services

The eIDASR laid the foundation for a *service-oriented ID base*. The European Commission's Consumer Financial Services Action Plan,[27] which aims at 'better products and more choice for European consumers', pledges to 'work with the private sector to explore how they could use electronic identification and trust services for checking the identity of customers.' Action Item 11 states: 'The Commission will facilitate the cross-border use of electronic identification and KYC portability based on eIDAS to enable banks to identify customers digitally.'

By facilitating online relations with customers and establishing fully digital customer relationships, the Action Plan abolishes offline 'in office' identification and the need for handwritten signatures on contracts. According to the European Commission,

> [t]he use of electronic identity schemes, as set out in eIDAS, would make it possible to open a bank account on-line while meeting the strong requirements for customer identity proofing and verification for know-your-customer or customer due diligence purposes. The legal certainty and validity of qualified eSignatures, as provided for under eIDAS, could also enhance the security of electronic transactions. This should work across borders and across sectors, and it should have the same legal effect as traditional paper based processes.[28]

The first steps have been undertaken by the European Fourth Anti-Money Laundering Directive in accepting electronic identification systems under eIDAS to meet customer due diligence requirements. Along with creating a common EU-wide identity repository for the public sector, the European Commission encourages Member States to ensure that the schemes they are preparing for notification under eIDAS are available for the private sector. Further, the European Commission opened the Connecting Europe Facility subsidy scheme for tests relating to cross-border use of electronic identification by financial institutions, and introduced an implementation plan and information system architecture to progressively achieve an eBanking foundation to remotely identify all bank customers.

The second step includes the (draft) EU Digital ID Regulation in combination with the (draft) AML Regulation that will alter client onboarding procedures with a wider impact on the financial sector's competitive landscape. In particular, the EU Digital Identity Wallets (EDIWs) will serve for customer onboarding and payment authorisation purposes, the expansion of electronically attested attributes, as well as the harmonisation of customer due diligence data (CDD data). As of today, the CDD data dealt with by financial institutions include identity attributes, status

---

[27] European Commission, *Communication from the Commission: Consumer Financial Services Action Plan: Better Products, More Choice* (COM/2017/0139 Final, 23 March 2017) <https://eur-lex.europa.eu/legal-content/EN/TXT/?uri=CELEX%3A52017DC0139>.

[28] Ibid [4.2.1].

attributes, and credit/risk-related attributes. Thus, it should be noted that the portability of identity attributes in isolation from other CDD data points may not yield
the desired results if the status and the credit/risk rating of the clients remain a mere
assessment of each individual service provider.

Regarding the CDD data storage, we can identify two possible solutions: a 'bank-
centric' and a 'user-centric' solution. While the bank-centric solution merely relies
on a financial institution which acts as a 'delegated custodian' of the CDD data and
provides the necessary information when needed, the user-centric approach is the
innovative solution of the eIDASR and entails a time-efficient and direct way to
provide the necessary data.

As far as the European digital identity wallets (EDIWs) are concerned, financial institutions can play an important role both in the CDD data receiving side
and in the providing side. On the receiving side, financial institutions will have to
accept the EDIWs for client onboarding and payment authorisation procedures, for
example, when a citizen opens a bank account or applies for a bank loan. On the
providing side, there is a discussion on whether financial institutions can be providers of identity attributes and of electronically attested attributes, which requires
a State approval, or if they can be 'Recognised Designated Intermediaries'. The
latter solution would require an official list of those entities held with the regulatory authorities. Additionally, it is important to involve the financial industry in the
EDIW specification developments and consider the idea of an open EDIW led by
financial institutions as well as recognise the role of a CDD data custodian and draft
a liability allocation framework.[29]

D. *Synthesising Lessons*

As seen during the pandemic, identification is the basis for all digital-only activities. Digital ID is necessary for a solid foundation for any digital financial ecosystem. As illustrated in Figure 13.2, all further parts of the ecosystem indispensable
for digital financial transformation (cf Chapter 13) build upon this foundation:
(1) sophisticated and advanced payments infrastructure, (2) streamlined account
opening procedures, (3) payment of government benefits, and (4) credit provision to individuals and SMEs based on credit scores compiled from diverse and
accurate data.

Such a comprehensive digital financial ecosystem provides many benefits. In
addition to the benefits we discussed in Chapter 6 – efficiency, financial inclusion,
and sustainability – such an ecosystem can enhance consumer protection and social

---

[29] For further details, please see European Commission, Directorate-General for Financial Stability,
Financial Services and Capital Markets Union and Stephane Mouy, *Developing a Digital Identity
Solution for Use by the Financial Sector Based around eIDAS Trust Services* (Publications Office of
the European Union, 2021) <https://data.europa.eu/doi/10.2874/600037>.

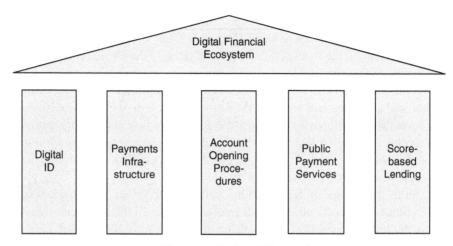

FIGURE 13.2 Elements of a digital financial ecosystem

welfare, transform government tax collection, and fund government investments in education, health, roads, and other infrastructure. It can also minimise losses in the payment of government benefits in developing countries beset with corruption and better allocate credit in a way that enables SMEs, the principal employers in most countries, to thrive.

Certain choices will have to be made in building such systems, such as embedding additional information for financial services providers into a customer's legal entity identifier (LEI) or a new smart ID card. These identifiers include information on links to exposed political persons and the range of financial services deemed suitable for the entity. These data would be machine readable and determine which client relationships would be subject to additional checks. The receiving financial institution would tap into the KYC utility only to check whether new information is available and such checks could be fully automated, superseding manual processes. Information embedded in the transaction code will not always be collected by the same entity. For instance, the first payment service provider to accept the client's money within a jurisdiction may review AML questions, while the first investment firm selling the client investment products may add information on suitability.

These ID systems are, from a sectoral perspective, neutral instruments. Financial services were not the centre of attention, nor was their necessity considered, when agreeing on standards and developing technologies. For instance, the European e-IDASR tackles the issue of ensuring that a person claiming an identity is the person they say they are, focusing on cross-border identification. No further information is forwarded and certified than that necessary for identification. Examples of information that are not forwarded include whether the person is a politically exposed person under money laundering legislation, or whether the person is a sophisticated investor.

IV. FROM DIGITAL IDENTIFICATION TO
DIGITAL IDENTITY AND KYC HUBS

A. *Balancing Objectives*

Different data are important for different use cases. A sole Business ID may work well for sectoral use even if it provides less, or entirely different, data than the Base ID. For instance, for financial services, it is irrelevant whether a client is born on 1 or 8 July 1965, or in Malawi or Mozambique. However, it is relevant that the identification features are unique and that data are stored through which the client can be identified and contacted today; and for AML/CFT purposes, business and private connections may also matter. The data points necessary for financial services may differ from those stored in the Base ID, and come from different sources (e.g., social media, shopping, and telco platforms).

When building infrastructure, it is critical to consider how Base ID can be extended to as much of the population as possible to maximise efficiencies in other systems. Beyond individuals, similar systems can be considered for corporates (e.g., based on the LEI system) and other types of entities, particularly as these interact with business registration and tax systems. From the international standpoint, corporate ID based on LEI combined with CRS (Common Reporting Standards for tax information sharing) and beneficial ownership requirements may be more politically acceptable than in systems focusing on individuals.

B. *Financial Law Prerequisites*

Base identity performs a fundamental function in the KYC process. Particularly when linked electronically to other golden source data (telephone, utility, tax, address, etc.), it provides the basis of a simple eKYC system while also addressing concerns regarding market integrity (e.g., AML and related considerations). The core objective is to make account opening by the vast majority of market participants, including SMEs, as simple and inexpensive as possible and focus resources on higher-risk customers, thus supporting financial inclusion and protecting market integrity. This may also reduce the role of the shadow or underground economy, with potentially wide-ranging benefits.

In some cases, however, financial law requirements restrict access to financial services and must be balanced against objectives of financial inclusion, overall customer experience, financial competitiveness, and economic growth.

C. *Towards KYC Hubs*

The COVID-19 crisis, social distancing restrictions, and closure of many physical banking branches significantly impeded face-to-face customer identification as part of the KYC process for financial institutions globally. Despite historical reliance by banks on hard copy documentation to verify customer identification, over 40 per cent of consumers in Europe reported that the pandemic heralded marked changes in the way they bank.[30] Unsurprisingly therefore, the idea of a sector-wide e-ID KYC utility ('KYC Hubs') – as a potential solution to the cost and infrastructure challenges in financial centres – has gained traction globally. Since standardising e-ID faces practical challenges, a network based on national identification systems similar to the European eIDASR but focused on Business IDs is most suitable.

One approach to KYC compliance that does not rely upon digital biometric identification has been taken in South Africa, following the imposition of a collective fine of 8 million EUR against the four largest banks for failure to implement adequate AML controls and risk measures in 2014. Three major financial institutions and Refinitiv[31] partnered to create a central web-based database of KYC information, provided to participating financial institutions free of charge. The service collects the KYC information from the customer, verifies it, and distributes it to all of the customer's chosen institutions. Customers control who can access and view their information, with service providers applying strict data privacy laws. The centralised database and standardised KYC information collection policies ensure efficiency by eliminating document duplication and streamlining account-opening procedures at no cost to the customer.[32]

Another example is the Aadhaar digital identity system, through which India has developed a paperless e-KYC service to instantly establish the identity of prospective banking customers. Provided customers expressly consent to their identity being made available by the e-KYC service, it provides a non-repudiable proof of identity to other service providers, including address, date of birth, gender, mobile number, and email address. The India Stack e-signature layer also interacts with e-KYC. This allows prospective banking customers to electronically sign contracts and other documentation. The digitisation of identity authentication streamlines the account-opening process for customers and allows all consenting customers to easily access both digital and traditional financial services. Axis Bank was the first bank to offer an e-KYC account-opening facility in late 2013, reducing the turnaround time for opening an account from 7–10 days to just 1 day. Today, many traditional banks in India offer accounts that can be opened and used instantly using e-KYC authentication. In 2020, the Reserve Bank of India (RBI) imposed uniform KYC compliance obligations upon all legal entities compelling the uploading of KYC data onto the Central KYC

---

[30] 'COVID-19 Drives Global Surge in Use of Digital Payments', *The World Bank* (Press Release, 29 June 2022) <www.worldbank.org/en/news/press-release/2022/06/29/covid-19-drives-global-surge-in-use-of-digital-payments>.

[31] Formerly known as the Financial and Risk (F&R) business of Thomson Reuters.

[32] Digital Innovation Network, *Diginno Cross-Border KYC Utility Feasibility Study* (Report, September 2019) 12 <https://likta.lv/wp-content/uploads/2019/10/DIGINNO-cross-border-KYC-utility-feasibility-study.pdf>.

Records Registry for all accounts opened prior to 1 April 2021. The amended directions promote KYC digitisation and reduce the cost of maintaining KYC documents for financial intermediaries.

V. DESIGNING EKYC INFRASTRUCTURE

A. *From Simple to Complex*

The costs savings expected from eKYC are greatest when most financial institutions participate. The most efficient, yet politically most unlikely, goal would be one global KYC utility with a full, up-to-date register of all clients within the regulated banking system.

Still, even small improvements matter. Assume, for instance, that five entities each invest three staff hours in onboarding the same client. If a KYC utility (in addition to one-time technical set-up costs) reduces the needed efforts to three hours invested by a single entity, the overall cost savings approach 80 per cent. With 10 members – putting the cost of the technology aside – the cost saving would be 90 per cent if a customer deals with all 10 entities, which is 10 per cent greater than those of the utility with 5 members. That additional 10 per cent will be partially offset by the additional costs of coordinating the additional five members. Importantly, the calculated savings materialise only when participating institutions serve the same client. Assuming all participants serve the same number of clients, the likelihood of this increases with the number of participants in the KYC utility. Given, however, that agreeing on governance features and standards is easier with fewer members, transaction costs may be a good reason to start small and grow over time.

Issues that will need to be addressed in building a KYC utility include the following:

1. Which technological platform will be used – centralised or distributed? Ensuring simultaneous access favours using (permissioned) distributed ledgers, while data privacy, governance concerns, and technical complexity may tip the balance towards more concentrated ledgers. These are not exclusive: best practice suggests centralised ledgers for individual forms of golden source data but a decentralised structure linking these together so that, for instance, a customer would only have to change their address once for it to be immediately confirmed for all other linked systems.
2. Who will participate and how?
3. What type of information will be shared? A sector-wide eKYC solution might first aim at digital identification of domestic licensed financial intermediaries, then extend to locally incorporated companies (relying on LEIs) and subsequently to non-face-to-face onboarding of individuals. Internationalisation,

including foreign legal entities, is the final step, as foreign entities are more difficult to integrate than domestic ones.

4. How often will it be updated, and by whom?
5. How will liability be shared if, and when, things go wrong? Options range from locating liability in one entity to joint liability. The answer depends on the response to question 2. The more reliable and financially stable the members, the more acceptable is joint liability.
6. Which standards will be used for data sharing? Options include an open standard or a standard designed specifically for participants.

Legal factors may influence complexity. For instance, regulated entities are easier to include than non-regulated ones and individuals raise different questions than legal entities.

B. *Responsibility*

One issue facing the one-stop-shop concept for eKYC is compliance responsibility. While financial institutions may use an intermediary to perform any part of the CDD process, the ultimate responsibility remains with the financial institution.[33] Crucially, the respective rules of each jurisdiction are burdensome. For instance, Article 27 of the European AML Directive requires that when financial institutions use information from a third party for CDD compliance, the financial institutions take 'adequate steps to ensure that the third party provides, immediately, upon request, relevant copies of identification and verification data and other relevant documentation on the identity of the customer or the beneficial owner'.

However, the restrictions are loosened, by one AML CDD being able to serve many banks, if certain funds circulate within a regulated banking system where all participants are subject to the same AML rules. Consider, for example, money that enters the EU banking system from a bank account in the Cayman Islands. The first EU bank needs to apply full CDD. Barring new information, banks that receive payments from that first EU bank can categorise those transactions as 'low risk', that is, they can, in principle, trust that the CDD applied by the first EU bank led to accurate findings that the money is 'clean'.[34] The same logic could be utilised for a sector-wide KYC utility working in closed systems.

---

[33] See, for instance, *Directive 2015/849 of the European Parliament and of the Council of 20 May 2015 on the Prevention of the Use of the Financial System for the Purposes of Money Laundering or Terrorist Financing* [2015] OJ L 141/73, art 25.

[34] See Joint Committee of the European Supervisory Authorities, *Joint Guidelines under Articles 17 and 18(4) of Directive (EU) 2015/849 on Simplified and Enhanced Customer Due Diligence and the Factors to be Considered When Assessing AML/CTF Risk in Individual Business Relationships and Occasional Transactions* (Report 2017/37 of 26 June 2017) 83.

C. *Governance*

Governance is key where knowledge means power, and concentrating knowledge concentrates power. Take, for instance, Luxembourg, the largest global distribution centre for investment funds offered in more than 70 countries. A sector-wide AML/KYC tool that truly covered all client relationships would provide enormous synergies but also pose new risks for clients globally. Regardless, an interlinked system of golden source company data from certified jurisdictions around the world based on LEIs would benefit all legitimate interests without the risks of centralising data in any single location.

Addressing these risks requires careful consideration of legal factors (such as property rights, liability, competition and antitrust concerns, applicable data privacy rules, such as the General Data Protection Regulation), non-legal factors (such as the technology used – with DLTs a natural candidate), cybersecurity risks, and the need to build a networked infrastructure to which thousands of entities can be linked.

From a governance perspective, the following legal questions are of particular importance:

1. Should the KYC utility be a *public or private enterprise?*
2. Should the KYC utility be a *for-profit entity or an association* acting on behalf of its members?
3. Who should run the day-to-day business of the utility?
4. Should the users or members have participation rights, and if so, how?
5. Who decides on membership applications?

We believe such utilities largely pose similar questions to stock exchanges in the nineteenth century, or payment systems today, since they all aim to reduce the costs of information asymmetries, and entail a degree of influence on market participants. The different rules for stock exchanges and payment systems around the world suggest that every jurisdiction interested in KYC utilities must answer these questions for itself, considering its traditions, legal structure, and the risks its members are willing to assume.

VI. CONCLUSION: ADDRESSING THE IDENTITY PROBLEM

In developing an e-ID strategy, three steps are of particular importance.

First, where an economy is implementing new digital identification solutions (a national ID card for individual digital identification purposes, or the LEI required under MiFID for financial transactions), it is advisable to plan ahead and link identity devices to AML/KYC checks, by ensuring that complementary technology is implemented on the user side and that sufficient data points exist in storage devices. The same applies if regulation focuses first on business IDs and remanufactures base IDs from the former, particularly through networking existing golden data sources.

Second, 100 per cent digital identification and eKYC coverage is neither feasible nor likely in the short term and will either increase the risk of disruption or delay any synergies from sector-wide eKYC systems in the foreseeable future. Thus, care should be taken with which steps are taken and in which order.

Third, from the beginning, attention needs be given to the governance of the sector-wide eKYC tool, particularly in global financial centres, where a sector-wide AML/KYC tool covering all client relationships will provide enormous synergies but also pose new risks which need to be addressed.

More importantly, to focus on only identification and ignore sector-specific needs and use cases may well miss many of the potential opportunities of an eKYC system. In an ideal digital financial services world, every step necessary for client onboarding and back-up checks would be done along with identification, and only once per client for all services and intermediaries. When this is achieved, financial intermediaries will benefit from the full potential of a sector-wide eKYC system.

14

Electronic Payments, Stablecoins, and Central Bank Digital Currencies

SUMMARY

Money and payment systems are being reshaped in unprecedented ways by technology. Catalysts include the launch of Bitcoin in 2009, the evolution of decentralised and centralised ledger technologies, the announcement of Libra in 2019, the ongoing live trials of China's 'digital Yuan' (eCNY), and the COVID-19 pandemic and the related move to presenceless payments.

This chapter considers the policy issues and choices associated with cryptocurrencies, stablecoins, and central bank digital currencies (CBDCs) and emphasises that there is no single model for CBDC design. The catalysts reshaping monetary and payment systems deeply challenge regulators. While Bitcoin and its thousands of progenies could be ignored safely by regulators, Facebook's proposal for Libra, a global stablecoin (GSC), brought an immediate and potent response from regulators globally. This proposal by the private sector to move into the traditional preserve of sovereigns – the creation of currency – was always likely both to trigger such a regulatory response and the development of CBDCs by central banks. China has moved first with its e-CNY – an initiative that may, in time, provoke a chain of CBDC issuance around the globe.

In the future, we expect domestic money and payment systems to involve public central banks cooperating with (old and possibly new) private entities, including commercial banks, to launch digital currencies which underpin better monetary and payment systems at the domestic and, especially, the international levels.

I. INTRODUCTION

At the core of all modern economic and financial systems are monetary and payment systems, with a central bank generally responsible for maintaining monetary stability and financial stability as public goods underpinning wider economic, social, and developmental objectives.[1] Historically, the state has played the key

---

[1] See Anton N Didenko and Ross P Buckley, 'The Evolution of Currency: Cash to Cryptos to Sovereign Digital Currencies' (2019) 42(4) *Fordham International Law Journal* 1041; Michael W Taylor et al, 'Central

role of authorising certain media of exchange as national currency and promoting demand for such media of exchange by requiring that certain payment obligations (e.g., taxes, duties and levies) be satisfied exclusively through its use. Payment systems – situated centrally in monetary and financial systems – form the key linkage between the economic and financial systems, with dependable and efficient payments an important public good, supporting monetary and financial stability.

In contemporary economic and financial systems, the state sets out the framework of the national payment system and oversees its implementation. Public entities (e.g., central banks) are frequently directly involved in setting up, or operating, retail and large value payment systems. Payment systems today generally operate either (i) intermediary-based payments with deferred net settlement, (ii) wholesale real-time gross settlement (RTGS), or (iii) 'fast' or 'instant' payment systems.[2]

The two broad policy objectives that dominate the payment system design are safety and efficiency. Safety encompasses stability, integrity, and customer and data protection. Efficiency encompasses cost efficiency, competition, and innovation.[3]

Developments in existing centralised technologies and new technologies, like distributed ledger technologies (DLTs) and blockchain, offer new ways to promote these policy objectives. Yet, while these technologies have attracted much regulator attention, with the exception of mobile payments (largely based on centralised systems to date), they have not yet substantially disrupted the money and payments landscape. Notwithstanding the immense hype around cryptocurrencies, they have never grown to be real competitors, or sources of fundamental disruption, to existing systems. This threatened to change with the announcement of Libra in 2019.

II. LIBRA

In June 2019, Facebook revealed plans to issue its own cryptocurrency – a global stablecoin (GSC) called Libra.[4] While some of the underlying technologies differed,

---

Banks' New Macroprudential Consensus' in David G Mayes, Pierre L Siklos, and Jan-Egbert Sturm (eds), *The Oxford Handbook of the Economics of Central Banking* (Oxford University Press, 2019) 482.

[2] For different approaches to the design of payment systems and the role of the central entity, see Taylor et al (n 1) 148. For the history of payment systems and the law governing them, see Benjamin Geva, *The Payment Order of Antiquity and the Middle Ages: A Legal History* (Bloomsbury Publishing, 2011); Benjamin Geva, 'Cryptocurrencies and the Evolution of Banking, Money and Payments' in Chris Brummer (ed), *Cryptoassets Legal, Regulatory and Monetary Perspectives* (Oxford University Press, 2019) 11.

[3] Bank for International Settlements and International Organization of Securities Commissions, 'Principles for Financial Market Infrastructures' (Committee on Payments and Market Infrastructures Paper No 101, April 2012); Bank for International Settlements and International Organization of Securities Commissions, *Recovery of Financial Market Infrastructures: Revised Report* (Report, July 2017); Bank for International Settlements and International Organization of Securities Commissions, 'Application of the Principles for Financial Market Infrastructures to Stablecoin Arrangements' (Committee on Payments and Market Infrastructures Paper No 198, October 2021).

[4] Financial Stability Board, *Addressing the Regulatory, Supervisory and Oversight Challenges Raised by 'Global Stablecoin' Arrangements* (Report, 14 April 2020).

in design terms, Libra was to be similar to a mobile money scheme of the kind made famous by M-Pesa in Kenya – parties would buy Libra 'coins' for fiat currency which would be deposited in the 'Libra Reserve' such that each Libra coin would be backed by deposited major fiat currency or short-term government securities denominated in such currencies.[5]

Libra was the first digital currency with the potential to become systemic – a characteristic Bitcoin and its progeny lacked. This potential scale led regulators to respond vigorously and central banks to rethink their approach to Central Bank Digital Currencies (CBDCs).[6]

A. *Libra's Impact*

A number of features of Libra – a combination of cryptocurrency, global electronic payment system, and framework of accounts and identification – gave it the potential to be particularly disruptive for payment systems and particularly sovereign fiat currencies:

1. Libra's role as an alternative payment system operated by private entities with massive resources and scale meant that a 'wait and see' regulatory strategy was never likely, since Libra had the potential to become systemic virtually upon launch.

2. Libra's goal to promote low-cost movement of money and payment networks was highly attractive and posed a major challenge to existing payment systems, characterised, as they are, by high costs and poor access to payment infrastructure.

3. Libra forced central banks to reconsider their own monetary offerings in order to better meet the needs of the economy and financial system, and resist potential competitors, be they private, public–private, or state sponsored.

B. *Global Stablecoins*

The impact of Libra, as the first proposed GSC, arose because of its potential for near-instantaneous scale, reach, and impact. Like most forms of systemically important financial market infrastructure or systemically important financial institutions, precise definition can be difficult.[7] The elements of a GSC, however, include size,

---

5   For a discussion about the differences between electronic money and various digital currencies (including stablecoins), see Didenko and Buckley (n 1) 1041,1082–5.

6   See Christian Barontini and Henry Holden, 'Proceeding with Caution: A Survey on Central Bank Digital Currency' (BIS Paper No 101, January 2019).

7   'Global Systemically Important Banks: Assessment Methodology and the Additional Loss Absorbency Requirement', *Bank for International Settlements* (Web Page, 21 November 2022) <www.bis.org/bcbs/gsib/>; Douglas Arner et al, 'Stablecoins: Risks, Potential and Regulation' (BIS Working Paper No 905, November 2020).

scale, and interconnectedness. These economies of scope and scale combined with network effects tend to suggest systemic significance in financial systems.

The first stage in dealing with GSCs is to identify them. This can be difficult in practice because offerings by non-traditional participants in finance, the so-called BigTechs, have the potential to scale very quickly.[8] The second stage in dealing with GSCs is to develop appropriate regulatory and supervisory tools in advance – tools that can be activated when a GSC is identified. Third, there could be a variety of approaches which could be activity, institutional, or infrastructure based depending on the nature of the specific GSC.

The key point is that the Libra experience should be used as a catalyst to develop global systems through the Financial Stability Board (FSB) to identify GSCs, to put in place appropriate supervisory arrangements, and to monitor their activities and impact.

C. *Libra 2.0*

Reacting to the remarkably strong pushback from regulators, the parameters of Libra 2.0 were announced in a new whitepaper in April 2020, at which time the Libra Association (an organisation responsible for the development of the Libra project) also formally applied for supervision by the Swiss Financial Market Supervisory Authority (FINMA).[9] These two events coincided with the launch of the FSB's consultation on regulatory and supervisory approaches to GSCs.[10]

Libra 2.0 saw the GSC renamed as Diem. The Libra Association dramatically scaled back the original ambition of Libra 1.0 to create a global digital currency. Instead, Diem was a series of domestic currency stablecoins linked in a global basket.

Despite the scaling back of its ambitions from Libra 1.0 to 2.0, the Libra/Diem journey nonetheless highlighted how, for the first time, the technology, capital, and scale now exist to potentially challenge the paradigm dominant since the beginning of the twentieth century that central banks issue and control currencies. Libra also forced central banks to consider how they might use technology to build better monetary and payment systems as the foundation of economic and financial activities to address potential challengers, while at the same time enhancing the performance of their own core objectives of monetary and financial stability, particularly through public good provision of robust monetary and payment systems.

---

[8] See Dirk A Zetzsche et al, 'Digital Finance Platforms: Toward a New Regulatory Paradigm' (2020) 23(1) *University of Pennsylvania Journal of Business Law* 273.

[9] Swiss Financial Market Supervisory Agency, 'Libra Association: FINMA Licensing Process Initiated' (Press Release, 16 April 2020) <https://finma.ch/en/news/2020/04/20200416-mm-libra>.

[10] Financial Stability Board, 'FSB Consults on Regulatory, Supervisory and Oversight Recommendations for "Global Stablecoin" Arrangements' (Press Release, 14 April 2020) <www.fsb.org/2020/04/fsb-consults-on-regulatory-supervisory-and-oversight-recommendations-for-global-stablecoin-arrangements>.

The combination of technological developments, the expression of its possibilities in the context of Libra, and the COVID-19 pandemic have together pushed forward a revolution in monetary and payment systems.

III. COVID-19 AND THE ADVENT OF MAJOR CURRENCY CBDCS

The immediate impetus, across 2020, for governments and central banks to review and redesign existing electronic payment systems was provided by the COVID-19 crisis, as a result of the need to efficiently and swiftly channel financial support to individuals, firms, and healthcare systems, and to ensure that national payment systems were capable of dealing with the far higher levels of online and electronic payments in the crisis. These factors also drove China to launch its e-CNY in a series of trials as well as discussions in both the European Union (EU) and the United States. While major economy developments will have implications for the rest of the world, most countries will need to focus on their own individual contexts when considering options, with particular variations depending on levels of local monetary, payment, financial, and technological development.

A. *China's Digital Currency/Electronic Payment Project*

China had been researching the implications of blockchain for its monetary and payment systems, including the possibility of developing a CBDC since 2014.[11] Following the launch of Libra in 2019, China announced that it would launch its 'Digital Currency/Electronic Payment' (DCEP) Project to create a 'Digital Yuan', potentially making it the first major economy to launch a CBDC.[12] The People's Bank of China (PBoC) moved to live trials of the CBDC in 2020.

DCEP is now termed the e-CNY. It is shaped by China's monetary, financial, economic, and political context and aims to provide a true CBDC as well as a payment system. In 2022, the PBoC released its new digital yuan app for iOS and Android, available for download by residents in the 23 Chinese cities currently in the pilot programme, with more to come.

The e-CNY operates in a two-tiered system.[13] The top level is a network of top tier intermediaries (TTIs), including major banks and large technology firms such as Ant (Alipay) and Tencent (WeChatPay), connected to the central bank RTGS. These entities, in turn, make the digital yuan available to individuals through digital wallets. This dual nature gave the system its original name – DCEP – digital

---

[11] We have used the best sources available to us for this section, but our analysis may be influenced by their reliability or the quality of their translation into English.

[12] We predicted this response in an article first posted online on 11 July 2019, see Dirk A Zetzsche et al, 'Regulating Libra' (2021) 41 *Oxford Journal of Legal Studies* 80.

[13] Working Group on E-CNY Research and Development of the People's Bank of China, *Progress of Research and Development of E-CNY in China* (Report, July 2021) 3–4.

currency/electronic payments. The design seems to be that the e-CNY will become Mo, eventually replacing all other monetary instruments. WeChatPay and Alipay have integrated the e-CNY into their payment systems, allowing consumers to use the e-CNY, and at the time of writing seven Chinese commercial banks have been authorised to provide e-CNY.

The e-CNY is a hybrid system (as elaborated upon in Section IV): the tokens issued by the PBoC to TTIs can then be transferred to retail or wholesale accounts.[14] It is fundamentally a monetary system designed to underpin the existing electronic payment systems, including traditional bank-intermediated systems and the ecosystems of Alipay and WeChatPay, both of which are currently non-interoperable closed-loop private systems. Using e-CNY is functionally very similar to using Alipay and WeChatPay.

The e-CNY will not replace cash in the immediate future, and it is interoperable with existing domestic payment systems but not foreign systems, although foreign participants in China will eventually be able to use it. Competition from private entities or instruments is prohibited. In addition to preventing the emergence of alternatives in China, the e-CNY will provide much improved sources of data to the government for monitoring the economy and market integrity (especially if it eventually replaces cash) and will centralise control of the underlying monetary instrument across all payment systems.

B. *Sweden and Canada: Developed Open Economies but Not Major Financial Centres*

Sweden is generally accepted as leading the world in the move towards going cashless, and its central bank has produced a series of substantial reports that, if one reads between the lines, imply clearly that the central bank will issue a centralised CBDC before it stops printing cash.[15] The central bank has completed two pilot phases on the possibility of issuing a digital complement to cash (the e-krona).

During Phase One, a network for the distribution and use of the e-krona was created on a DLT-based blockchain platform, where tokens represented the e-krona.[16] During Phase Two, the technical framework of the e-krona pilot was tested and a possible legal framework was considered.[17] The Phase Two report states that the central bank has not yet decided whether to launch an e-krona, nor the technology and legal framework to be adopted. The purpose of the pilot was to consider how the e-krona could work in practice. The project has now entered Phrase Three,

---

[14] Ibid 7.
[15] This is only implied in the two reports: Sveriges Riksbank, *The Riksbank's E-krona Project Report No 1* (Report, September 2017); Sveriges Riksbank. *The Riksbank's E-krona Project Report No 2* (Report, October 2018).
[16] Sveriges Riksbank, *E-krona Pilot Phase 1* (Report, April 2021).
[17] Sveriges Riksbank, *E-krona Pilot Phase 2* (Report, April 2022).

where further technical work and legal issues identified during Phrase Two are being addressed.[18]

In September 2022, the Swedish central bank also began Project Icebreaker, in partnership with the central banks of Israel and Norway and the Bank for International Settlements (BIS).[19] The current e-krona platform is being used in conjunction with Israel and Norway's digital currencies to test cross-border retail CBDC payments. The project will finish at the end of 2022, with a final report anticipated in early 2023.

Likewise, based on a series of previous projects, in February 2020, the Bank of Canada issued a laudably clear document analysing its contingency planning for a CBDC.[20] This document made clear that the Bank of Canada had no plans to launch a CBDC but was building capacity to do so, if it became necessary. The Bank of Canada envisaged two scenarios in which such a need could arise.

The first scenario is if Canada is moving to being a cashless society. Should the move away from cash necessitate Canada issuing a CBDC, its February 2020 report envisages that this CBDC would be 'cash-like' (i.e., 'earn no interest and be universally accessible').[21] It also envisages that it would offer a 'great deal of privacy'[22] but not anonymity. The usage of cash in Canada has been in decline, as it has in most major economies. By 2021, only 22 per cent of transactions at the point of sale were completed using cash, down from about 54 per cent in 2009.[23] This compares with cash being used in some 27 per cent of transactions in Australia in 2019 and only 9 per cent of respondents in the Sverige Riksbank's 2020 survey using cash for their most recent transaction in Sweden.[24]

The second scenario would arise if Canada's monetary sovereignty is threatened by 'a private digital currency not denominated in Canadian dollars'.[25] This is an obvious reference to Libra or some similar initiative.

The Bank of Canada's report is interesting in that it focuses very much on the loss of monetary sovereignty whereas the reports of the Sverige Riksbank in Sweden

---

[18] At the time of writing, Phase Three had commenced but there was no published report.

[19] Bank for International Settlements, 'Project Icebreaker: Central Banks of Israel, Norway and Sweden Team up with the BIS to Explore Retail CBDC for International Payments' (Press Release, 2022) <www.bis.org/about/bisih/topics/cbdc/icebreaker.htm>; Sveriges Riksbank, 'The Riksbank Tests Cross-Border Payments with the E-krona' (Press Release, 28 September 2022) <www.riksbank.se/en-gb/press-and-published/notices-and-press-releases/press-releases/2022/the-riksbank-tests-cross-border-payments-with-the-e-krona>.

[20] Bank of Canada, *Contingency Planning for a Central Bank Digital Currency* (Report, 25 February 2020).

[21] Ibid.

[22] Ibid.

[23] Ron Morrow, 'Preparing for Payments Supervision' (Speech, Bank of Canada, 2 November 2022) citing Christopher Henry, Matthew Shimoda and Julia Zhu, '2021 Methods-of-Payment Survey Report' (Bank of Canada Discussion Paper, 27 February 2023).

[24] Luc Delaney et al, 'Cash Use in Australia: Results from the 2019 Consumer Payments Survey' (RBA Bulletin, June 2020); Sveriges Riksbank, *Payments in Sweden* (Report, 2020).

[25] Bank of Canada (n 20).

consider the loss of monetary sovereignty but are more concerned about the impacts on the poor and those living remotely of only having commercially provided payment mechanisms.

The experience of these two countries is likely to be the most relevant in the context of countries with well-developed existing financial systems, particularly those faced with the challenges of evolution away from cash.

C. *Singapore, Hong Kong SAR, and the UK: Major International Financial Centres*

The approaches of the United Kingdom (UK), Singapore, and Hong Kong Special Administrative Region (Hong Kong SAR) will also be watched closely given their leading roles as financial centres, particularly for FinTech and RegTech. All three have carefully focused on their positions and the role that CBDCs – particularly in the wholesale and trade contexts – could have going forward.

These jurisdictions are particularly focused on their potential to be intermediaries: how to be a node between major digital currencies going forward? This is an issue which of course is central to Hong Kong's future most clearly, given how it could emerge as the major point of exchange for transactions between the e-CNY area and the rest of the world.[26]

D. *The Digital Euro*

The Eurosystem's *Report on a Digital Euro*,[27] published in October 2020 (the Report), is intended as the starting point for broader discussion and sets out how the European Central Bank (ECB) intends to consider possible approaches to issuing a CBDC for Europe based on three critical elements. First, a Digital Euro must comply with the Eurosystem's core principles, mandates, and policies. Second, the Report considers the scenario-driven prerequisites necessary to balance the issuance of a Digital Euro with the needs of users and the Eurosystem's core principles and aims. Finally, a set of general requirements is identified with the purpose of ensuring that the EU economy is protected against any risks arising from the issuance of a Digital Euro.

The Report also considers the possible functional designs, technical and organisational approaches to a Digital Euro in line with the scenario-driven prerequisites and general requirements set out above. While this discussion does not provide any concrete decisions for the basic design features of a Digital Euro, it does set out the initial thoughts of the ECB. Overall, restricted usage through synchronised

---

[26] Andy Mukherjee, 'Crypto Yuan Will Meet the Dollar: In Hong Kong', *Bloomberg* (online, 23 August 2022) <www.bloomberg.com/opinion/articles/2020-08-23/china-s-crypto-currency-may-challenge-u-s-dollar-peg-in-hong-kong?leadSource=uverify%20wall>.

[27] European Central Bank, *Report on a Digital Euro* (Report, October 2020).

functionality offline (physical devices such as smart cards) and online (web-based services) provided through supervised intermediaries seems plausible. Whether an account-based or token-based instrument is preferable depends on the choice of the underlying back-end infrastructure.

In July 2021, the Governing Council of the ECB launched its two-year investigative phase of the Digital Euro Project.[28] In September 2022, the Governing Council approved further consideration of both an online system with third-party validation and an offline peer-to-peer validated solution.[29] At the time of writing, the next phase of the investigation will explore design and distribution options, including analysis of the front-end services that financial intermediaries could provide, distribution of the digital euro, and settlement of payments.[30] In the third quarter of 2023, the Governing Council is expected to decide upon possibly launching a realisation phase.[31]

E. *The Digital Dollar*

President Biden released an Executive Order on 'Ensuring Responsible Development of Digital Assets' in March 2022, which prioritised the importance of researching, and developing deployment options of, a United States (US) 'digital dollar'.[32] Policy objectives outlined in the Executive Order include to protect consumers, investors, and businesses, improve the payments system, and ensure transparency, connectivity, and architecture interoperability within the global financial system.[33]

In response, the Office of Science and Technology Policy conducted a technical analysis on the development of a US CBDC system, concluding that, among other things, the Federal Reserve should continue researching and experimenting on CBDC systems.[34] The Department of the Treasury's Report similarly encouraged the Federal Reserve to continue researching and experimenting, noting that considerable time and effort will be required to research and develop the technology for a US CBDC system.[35] The Digital Dollar Project, a partnership between Accenture and the Digital Dollar Foundation, is also researching challenges and opportunities

---

[28] European Central Bank, 'Eurosystem Launches Digital Euro Project' (Press Release, 14 July 2021) <www.ecb.europa.eu/press/pr/date/2021/html/ecb.pr210714~d99198ea23.en.html>.

[29] European Central Bank, *Progress on the Investigation Phase of a Digital Euro* (Report, 29 September 2022).

[30] Ibid.

[31] European Central Bank, 'Digital Euro: Our Future Money' (Presentation, 11 October 2022) <www.ecb.europa.eu/paym/digital_euro/investigation/profuse/shared/files/dedocs/ecb.dedocs221017_ecbatsibos.en.pdf?447523fb3a77c4c58413c7f3870340da>.

[32] The White House, *Ensuring Responsible Development of Digital Assets* (Executive Order 14067, 87 FR 14143, 9 March 2022) <www.federalregister.gov/documents/2022/03/14/2022-05471/ensuring-responsible-development-of-digital-assets>.

[33] Ibid.

[34] The White House, *Technical Evaluation for a U.S. Central Bank Digital Currency System* (Report, September 2022).

[35] United States Department of the Treasury, *The Future of Money and Payments: Report Pursuant to Section 4(b) of Executive Order 14067* (Report, September 2022).

of a US CBDC.[36] As with the Digital Euro, the development of a Digital Dollar remains very much in its early stages.

In the absence of a Digital Dollar, the Digital Yuan, once eventually allowed off-shore,[37] will potentially undercut the dominant role of the US dollar in the denomination of international trade, such that it will threaten the many, major benefits the United States currently receives from minting the world's global reserve currency.[38] For this reason alone, it is difficult to see the United States not launching a digital dollar as a defensive measure, should the prospect of the e-CNY being allowed to be used in trade become imminent. China faces major challenges, principally around trust and political non-interference, in promoting its e-CNY for use in international trade. However, the geopolitical benefits of at least partially dethroning the dollar are such that we expect China to make every possible effort to promote the e-CNY for use in trade.

F. *The Bahamian Sand Dollar*

The digital Bahamian currency, referred to as the Sand Dollar, was launched on 20 October 2020 as the first nationwide CBDC in the world.[39] Opening personal accounts, in the form of low-value digital wallets, to access these services is subject to reduced Know-Your-Customer (KYC) requirements with transaction limit restrictions. Business accounts are subjected to stricter KYC requirements with higher transaction limits. The Sand Dollar digital wallets themselves incorporate multi-factored authorisation and data encryption functionality. Each transaction is integrated into an Anti-Money Laundering and Counter-Terrorism Financing (AML/CFT) platform for regulatory compliance and governance risk management checks. Overall, the launch of the Sand Dollar forms part of the government's broader financial inclusion strategy to increase financial literacy awareness and access to payment services across the archipelago with the aim of driving down delivery costs, increasing efficiency, and promoting financial inclusion overall.[40]

In 2021, the Bahamian Central Bank began increasing public education efforts about the Sand Dollar, including the launch of the Sand Dollar website. The website sets out the enrolment steps, which includes the selection of one of the listed

---

[36] 'About', *The Digital Dollar* (Web Page) <https://digitaldollarproject.org>.

[37] See Gunter Dufey and Linda Li, 'China's Digital Currency Getting More Buzz Than Warranted', *The Straits Times* (online, 1 June 2020) <www.straitstimes.com/opinion/chinas-digital-currency-getting-more-buzz-than-warranted> (highlighting limited RMB internationalisation to date).

[38] Barry Eichengreen, *Exorbitant Privilege: The Rise and Fall of the Dollar and the Future of the International Monetary System* (Oxford University Press, 2012).

[39] Central Bank of the Bahamas, 'The Sand Dollar Is on Schedule for Gradual National Release to the Bahamas in Mid-October 2020' (Press Release, 25 September 2020) <www.centralbankbahamas.com/news/public-notices/the-sand-dollar-is-on-schedule-for-gradual-national-release-to-the-bahamas-in-mid-october-2020?N=C&page=2>.

[40] Ibid; AFI's Digital Financial Services Working Group, *Leveraging Digital Financial Services to Advance Inclusive Green Finance Policies* (Report, September 2022).

authorised financial institutions and a link to download the Sand Dollar App.[41] However, adoption of the digital currency remains low, with only some 300,000 Sand Dollars in circulation at the end of 2021.[42] In May 2022, the Central Bank was recommended by the International Monetary Fund (IMF) to 'accelerate its education campaigns', as well as to 'continue strengthening internal capacity and oversight'.[43]

IV. REDESIGNING MONEY AND PAYMENTS

Technological evolution combined with geopolitics and the COVID-19 crisis have driven new thinking and approaches to money and payments. In looking at the potential to design better money and payment systems, design choices must be based on the specific circumstances of individual economic and financial systems rather than on any single model or technology. In this section, we set out our CBDC taxonomy and discuss the opportunities and challenges that come with design choices relating to CBDCs.

A. *CBDC Taxonomy*

CBDC projects typically differ across four major design parameters: (1) users, (2) architecture, (3) technology, and (4) scope.

1. Users

The range of potential users is very broad. Some CBDC projects include TTIs only, some include all intermediaries (TTIs and non-TTI PSPs), while others seek to include all wholesale or even all retail transactions. At first sight, opening CBDCs for all (retail and wholesale) users seems a major leap. But central banks do have a long history of opening direct accounts for non-financial institutions and individuals.[44] For example, the Bank of England allowed members of the public to open accounts from its founding until well into the twentieth century, and continued this for employees up to 2016, as did the Banque de France.[45] In addition, some central banks offer direct accounts for governmental agencies.[46]

---

[41] 'Home', *Sand Dollar* (Web Page) <www.sanddollar.bs/>.

[42] The Central Bank of the Bahamas, *2021 Annual Report* (Report, 25 April 2022).

[43] International Monetary Fund, 'IMF Executive Board Concludes 2022 Article IV Consultation with The Bahamas' (Press Release No 22/141, 9 May 2022) <www.imf.org/en/News/Articles/2022/05/09/pr22141-the-bahamas-imf-executive-board-concludes-2022-article-iv-consultation-with-the-bahamas>.

[44] JP Koning, *Fedcoin: A Central Bank-Issued Cryptocurrency* (Report, 2016) 13.

[45] See Gwyn Topham, 'Bank of England to Close Personal Banking Service for Employees', *The Guardian* (online, 18 July 2016) <www.theguardian.com/business/2016/jul/17/bank-of-england-closing-personal-banking-service-employees>. See also Jon Frost et al, 'An Early Stablecoin? The Bank of Amsterdam and the Governance of Money' (BIS Working Paper No 902, November 2020).

[46] See, for example, 'About Treasury Direct', *TreasuryDirect* (Web page) <www.treasurydirect.gov>. The website is 'the first and only financial services website that lets [users] buy and redeem securities directly from the US Department of the Treasury in paperless electronic form'.

As with any settlement system, however, the efficiency of central bank access for non-banks and individuals depends on demand: disintermediation is only achievable when both parties to a payment transaction have an account with the central bank. This is ensured where *all* transactions are settled with the central bank. At the same time, partial central bank access could be less efficient than the current TTI oligopoly, which leads us to the second question: the choice of architecture.

2. Architecture

As to architecture, we distinguish between three different kinds of CBDCs.[47]

(A) CENTRALISED CBDCS In essence, each user has an account with the central bank where their units of value are stored and available for all transactions. Such a design is necessarily account based, which means verification is required to access and spend the currency based on the identity of the currency owner, similar to identification of bank account holders.[48] It essentially resembles so-called 'electronic money' systems that are based on exchange of official currency for a matching balance (generally at par value) with the issuer (such as a telecoms operator). By design, centralised CBDCs are permissioned systems and tend to lack cash-like qualities, in particular anonymous exchange.[49]

(B) DECENTRALISED CBDCS A *decentralised* CBDC bears the closest resemblance to Bitcoin and other decentralised digital Accreting Principal Swaps (APS). One such concept, Fedcoin,[50] is, at its core, a variation of the Bitcoin protocol that nonetheless enjoys a guaranteed exchange rate into the official currency (USD). In this system, mining is still required to produce a record of transactions, but alternative consensus algorithms can be implemented.[51] Crucially, a truly decentralised CBDC offers cash-like features and does not necessarily require identification and KYC checks for each user. Technically, full decentralisation is achievable through tokenisation.

---

[47] Our taxonomy is equivalent to that proposed by Raphael Auer and Rainer Böhme, 'The Technology of Retail Central Bank Digital Currency' (BIS Quarterly Review, March 2020), but understands the design choice 'account' or 'token' as inherent to the degree of centralisation or decentralisation. Full decentralisation requires some kind of token, while full centralisation will require some kind of account.

[48] This is in contrast to token-based verification that is based on the validity of the actual units of currency (similar to the operation of cash, but in a digital format). For more detail, see Committee on Payments and Market Infrastructures, *Central Bank Digital Currencies* (Report, March 2018) 4.

[49] In its second report on the E-krona project, Swedish Riksbank concludes that the 'focus of this programme should be on developing an e-krona that constitutes a *prepaid value* (electronic money) without interest and with *traceable transactions.*' See Sveriges Riksbank. *The Riksbank's E-krona Project Report No 2* (Report, October 2018). See also Dave Birch, 'Britcoin or Brit-PESA?', *Consult Hyperion* (Web Page, 4 January 2016) <www.chyp.com/britcoin-or-brit-pesa>.

[50] See Koning (n 44).

[51] Jaemin Son et al, 'Consumer Choices under New Payment Methods' (2022) 8 *Financial Innovation* 82.

(c) HYBRID CBDCs A *hybrid* CBDC is a blend of a centralised and decentralised CBDC. While it may use central bank accounts, not all users need to have such an account: intermediaries may link users to the central bank with each intermediary running its own DLT-based system. Design options are many. One involves several levels of interoperable blockchains. The first is operated by authorised (private) payment system operators (which produce blocks that may reference not only their own previous blocks but also the previous blocks of each other – thus creating a cross-referenced chain). The second is maintained by the central bank that produces the 'main blockchain' containing the authoritative record of transactions. Within each distributed ledger, tokenisation may lead to cash-like characteristics such as anonymity. If each of the distributed ledgers is an enclosed system, AML/CFT and KYC checks can be performed at the initial stage. The risk of intermediary default can be mitigated by legal means, for instance by appointing the intermediary as the central bank's agent, turning all tokens substantively into drawing rights on the funds stored in the central bank accounts.

Some proposals suggest an intermediated approach where central banks through qualified counterparties provide access to central bank accounts. These operators would be prohibited from lending or taking on any new risks on client funds. In addition, a multiplicity of operators would create competition and reduce the administrative burden and operational risks on central banks and avoid their needing to deal with millions (and perhaps even a billion) accounts simultaneously. Alternatively, in Ketterer and Andrade's model, private firms 'provide all the transactional and customer services related to CBM [central bank money] accounts', while maintaining a 100 per cent reserve for each deposit at all times.[52]

Intermediation of central bank accounts can take various forms: from new types of commercial bank accounts to accounts with (non-bank) trusted intermediaries fully guaranteed by the central bank. In each case, however, users of the new currency should have direct recourse to central bank accounts. This would require introducing the technology while preserving the current TTIs' oligopoly of central bank deposits and at the same time ensuring the corresponding benefits to end-users (in particular, insolvency remoteness).

3. Technology

Technology remains an evolving choice, with some systems centralised using traditional payments processing technologies (e.g., RTGS, FPS) and others based on DLT/blockchain (albeit so far centralised permissioned systems rather than decentralised permissionless structures), an issue we return to in the next section.

---

[52] Juan Antonio Ketterer and Gabriela Andrade, 'Digital Central Bank Money and the Unbundling of the Banking Function' (Inter-American Development Bank Discussion Paper No IDB-DP-449, April 2016) 7.

4. Scope

The system may extend only to monetary arrangements or to payment arrangements or it may include elements of both. We return to this issue in the next section as well.

B. *Benefits, Opportunities, and Challenges*

1. Benefits and Opportunities

A CBDC is often an attempt to marry the benefits of APS and central bank money. The dream is to ensure universal acceptance within the formal payment system while eliminating, or greatly reducing the role of, costly intermediaries. Such a design would bring a number of benefits, including:

1. Central banks could act as the ultimate trusted, bankruptcy-proof intermediary, replacing commercial banks, and use CBDC as a vehicle for critical national expenditure to bypass commercial banks completely, potentially reducing systemic risks associated with commercial banks.

2. Central banks and governments could modernise their ageing wholesale payment systems with advanced functionality including support for smart contracts (the idea of 'programmable money').[53]

3. CBDCs could also be used for raising money by the state – a feature of Venezuela's Petro, an asset-backed cryptocurrency which was designed to supplement Venezuela's ailing economy, raise capital, and attract investment by circumventing US sanctions – a feature that remains possible notwithstanding that for other reasons the Petro failed.

2. Challenges

Regulatory challenges relating to CBDCs include:

1. Technical issues involved in setting up a CBDC, particularly in the absence of accepted international standards on DLT and blockchain. Regulators are faced with a multitude of possible design choices, yet may have inadequate resources or limited access to the required expertise to answer the many technical questions required.

2. Concerns about the impact of CBDCs on the payment system, financial markets, and economy:

---

[53] Morten Bech and Rodney Garratt, 'Central Bank Cryptocurrencies' (BIS Quarterly Review, September 2017) 66–7.

a.　Regulators should perform a comprehensive ex ante analysis of the system, identifying entities that may end up in direct competition with the state once it implements a CBDC (e.g., commercial banks, electronic money issuers).

b.　Alternately, regulators may seek to level the playing field by artificially making CBDCs less attractive by placing limits on interest or other features (at least initially).

c.　Regulators must also consider implications for money supply and whether the new currency will be issued via an initial coin offering (ICO) or in exchange for other forms of sovereign money (e.g., cash) or commercial bank money (or both) and design corresponding conversion mechanisms.

3.　Legal issues around the need to introduce the concept of CBDC into the national regulatory system will need to be resolved. This may, in turn, alter the existing approach to regulation of non-sovereign cryptocurrencies. In particular, many central banks still lack full authority to regulate and supervise payment systems and providers and many central bank laws also limit the forms in which currency may be issued (e.g., notes and coins).[54]

C. *Technology: Departure from DLT*

An oft-discussed aspect of CBDCs is technology.[55] Although the examination of the option of issuing a CBDC may flow from consideration of the opportunities offered by the technologies underlying Bitcoin against the recurring challenges facing payment systems, implemented CBDCs may well use neither DLT nor blockchain. In the words of a recent Bank of England discussion paper, '[a]lthough CBDC is often associated with Distributed Ledger Technology (DLT), we do not presume any CBDC must be built using DLT, and there is no inherent reason it could not be built using more conventional centralised technology'.[56]

Fully decentralised systems would need to use permissionless DLTs (most likely with blockchain), while the far more likely centralised and hybrid CBDCs would use permissioned DLT if they use DLT at all. In terms of issuance control, the system is likely to be centralised. For example, in the mBridge Project, a multi-CBDC platform was built as a private permissioned fit-for-purpose blockchain 'built by central banks,

---

54　See Wouter Bossu et al, 'Legal Aspects of Central Bank Digital Currency: Central Bank and Monetary Law Considerations' (IMF Working Paper No 2020/254, 20 November 2020).

55　For discussion of related issues, see Matthieu Bouchaud et al, 'Central Banks and the Future of Digital Money: A Practical Proposal for Central Bank Digital Currencies on the Ethereum Blockchain' (ConsenSys White Paper, 20 January 2020).

56　See Bank of England, 'Central Bank Digital Currency: Opportunities, Challenges and Design' (Discussion Paper, March 2020) 6.

for central banks'.[57] Yet DLT often suffers from performance, data protection/privacy, liability, and other difficulties. System designers seem to prefer DLT for token-based systems, while account-based systems mostly rely on conventional infrastructure.[58]

Further design choices made more difficult to address by a DLT environment relate to cybersecurity, the rectification of mistakes and erroneous payments, and user identification. In the light of all these factors, we expect most CBDCs not to use DLT or blockchain.[59]

D. *Central Bank Access: Efficiency vs Financial Inclusion*

The four major design parameters of users, architecture, technology, and scope lie at the heart of a CBDC and interrelate: if user groups are strictly limited, efficiency can be the guiding rationale. That is because most TTIs, as large financial intermediaries, can withstand short-term shocks and periods of non-operation. If absolutely necessary, TTIs can refinance themselves in the capital markets and discuss compensation with the central banks. All this can occur internally without threatening public trust.

But the same is not true for most retail and many wholesale users – any service interruption would immediately erode trust in the financial system. The more user groups in a system, the more the focus of necessity shifts from efficiency to safety. Given that intermediation isolates some operational risk in the organisation of one intermediary, where central banks follow the safety paradigm, a hybrid (semi-decentralised) model is most likely.

For developing countries, however, the main concern will be *creating* an *inclusive* infrastructure: a stable system that includes, in particular, rural residents and the poor.[60] Here, full disintermediation may be favoured since intermediary-based coverage may not currently exist. However, a developing country choice in favour of a centralised CBDC may only be temporary. Once additional services are provided by the private sector, the respective central banks may return to a hybrid CBDC model with gradually receding *optional* central bank access replaced by the private sector.

---

[57] Bank for International Settlements Innovation Hub, *Project mBridge: Connecting Economies through CBDC* (Report, October 2022). The mBridge Ledger is being built by the Hong Kong Monetary Authority, the Bank of Thailand, the Digital Currency Institute of the People's Bank of China, and the Central Bank of the United Arab Emirates.

[58] See Raphael Auer and Rainer Böhme, 'The Technology of Retail Central Bank Digital Currency' (BIS Quarterly Review, March 2020).

[59] DLT has been criticised by some central banks as lacking adequate scalability, offering no fundamental advantages over existing systems, or failing to ensure cash-like resilience during blackouts. See Auer and Böhme (n 58).

[60] See, for example, Edil Corneille, 'Cambodian Central Bank Implements First Retail Payments System in the World Using Blockchain Technology', *IBS Intelligence* (Web Page, 19 August 2020) <https:// ibsintelligence.com/ibsi-news/cambodian-central-bank-implements-first-retail-payments-system-in-the-world-using-blockchain-technologycambodian-bank-implements-first-retail-payments-system-in-the-world-using-blockchain-technology/#:~:text=Bakong%20is%20said%20to%20be,with%20a%20 simple%20smartphone%20app>.

Another factor involves the operational resilience of the issuing central bank. If a central bank is reliable, tech savvy, and capable, and seeks to enhance financial inclusion, a centralised architecture will probably be more suitable, and where it is unreliable or unable to operate retail accounts well, a decentralised architecture will, in principle, be advisable.

From this design choice will follow who has access. Where efficiency is paramount, access will be limited to TTIs. Where financial inclusion matters most, central banks may prefer retail access.

E. Towards Public–Private Partnerships

Within this framework, we envisage three dominant alternative approaches: (i) central bank accounts with general access, (ii) central bank accounts with intermediated access, and (iii) new digital forms of fiat currency.[61]

Within these three approaches, option (i), a *fully* disintermediated CBDC, while conceivable in theory and desirable from a financial inclusion perspective, is unlikely to be maintained by central banks in the long run. With a fully disintermediated architecture, operational malfunctions of the system (in the event, for instance, of a cyberattack or a deficient software update) will impact directly on the economy, without intermediaries diversifying the risk and partially mitigating its impact. There is little evidence that central banks could handle efficiently day-to-day operations with millions of retail clients and even less evidence to suggest they have any appetite to do so. Central banks tend to lack both the infrastructure and expertise for such a role. Full disintermediation would require central banks to significantly enhance their operational capacities,[62] entering, inter alia, into (1) credit scoring, (2) AML/CTF and KYC checks, (3) rebooking of erroneous transactions, and (4) building large-scale retail infrastructure equivalent to ATMs and payment terminals for CBDCs. At the same time, 'monobank' structures in centrally planned systems were never known for their efficiency although technological advances may be altering this.[63]

Finally, while CBDC mining and destruction could be monopolised in the hands of the central bank to ensure monetary stability, a truly decentralised CBDC would likely come with reduced enforcement of AML/CTF and KYC standards and reduced information flow to the respective central bank.

For these reasons, central banks and regulators will most likely collaborate with commercial banks, payment system operators, TechFins, and FinTechs to utilise their existing infrastructure. To our minds, successful CBDCs will most likely be public–private partnerships (PPPs), with the central banks providing the definitions,

---

[61] For a more detailed discussion of available approaches, see Didenko and Buckley (n 1) 1041, 1085–93.
[62] See also Auer and Böhme (n 58) 90.
[63] See Agustín Carstens, 'The Future of Money and Payments' (Speech, Whitaker Lecture, Central Bank of Ireland, 22 March 2019).

interfaces, and accounts, and the private sector offering the applications and operational interface to service mass clients.

Such systems will most likely be complemented by a range of CBDCs, in many cases combined with new forms of fast payment systems, potentially eliminating traditional intermediated structures in some cases, and being operated by them in others. Hence, the most likely outcome is a mix of central bank accounts with intermediated access and new digital forms of fiat currency.

Regardless of the benefits, a PPP may also come with downsides: partnership with private entities may require more information sharing with the private sector (as the latter needs to build interfaces), and if proprietary information needs to be shared, this could offset the beneficial effect created by the additional resources available to private entities.

F. *Money versus Payment?*

A real opportunity in particular exists to address the separation between transactions (such as securities or derivatives) and payment for those transactions, particularly at the wholesale level.[64] Rather than issuing a CBDC, a central bank might allow the creation of a stablecoin, backed by deposits of fiat currency with the central bank – what the IMF has called a 'synthetic stablecoin'.[65] A synthetic stablecoin could effectively serve as sovereign currency in specific DLT-based systems – even where the rest of the monetary system is not using DLT.

Fundamentally, regulators must determine whether they want to build a monetary or a payment system. The word *currency* implies building the former. But this is only achievable if the CBDC is designed to substitute for (or replace) cash, that is, with anonymous transactions (though it is almost certain that many will in fact collect a variety of information for central banks and other authorities) and payment finality. As we have shown, both the decentralised and the hybrid CBDC models are able to have these features. If these features are implemented, the distinction between payment and monetary systems – previously so important due to credit, transactional and operational risk – ceases to exist.

We suggest that the hybrid model will prove to be the most widely adopted but that the greatest benefit in many cases may come not from a digital monetary instrument alone but rather from a merger of monetary and payment arrangements as highlighted in the context of the Digital Dollar. A DCEP approach is likely to be the most effective where comprehensive electronic payment arrangements (such as in China or the EU) currently exist. In jurisdictions where there are substantial numbers of people without

---

[64] See, for example, Societe Generale 'Societe Generale Performs the First Financial Transaction Settled with a Central Bank Digital Currency' (Press Release, 20 May 2020) <www.societegenerale.com/en/news/newsroom/societe-generale-performs-first-financial-transaction-settled-central-bank-digital>.

[65] Tobias Adrian and Tommaso Mancini-Griffoli, *The Rise of Digital Money. FinTech Notes* No 19/01 (IMF Report, 2019).

access to accounts (including the US, UK, and most developing countries), a centralised account structure (albeit providing minimal services) may well prove more efficacious.

V. CONCLUSION

The catalysts of technological development, Libra, COVID-19, and the increasingly likely implementation of one or more major currency CBDCs are driving new approaches to payment systems and money itself.

Looking forward, the advent of one or more major currency CBDCs will trigger the need to address questions not only of competition but also of external use and interoperability. If and when the eCNY fully launches, it will most likely be the first major-currency CBDC. Its full launch across China may trigger the activation, acceleration, or development of a number of similar projects around the world. Its launch for use in international trade will certainly trigger such a response from other nations because, at the least, no major economy will want the real-time data related to its trade with China being available exclusively to China.

The eCNY should provide a means of controlling currency inflows and outflows into the RMB area, initially mainland China. One intention is that it will be gradually opened to foreign participation, albeit not necessarily to be used outside of China's Internet and blockchain environment. In time, its geographic reach could well be expanded, so as to serve as a potential dollar alternative outside the reach of the United States but fully under the oversight of China. Once opened to foreign use, it will provide a potential means of internationalising the RMB – a stated major goal of China since the 2008 Global Financial Crisis.

The expected eventual full launch of the eCNY is having a similar catalytic effect to that which Libra had: central banks around the world are increasing their own developmental efforts. In addition, the launch of a major currency CBDC will force countries around the world to carefully consider how they will build systems to interact. Likewise, the development of one major currency CBDC is forcing other major currency issuers to consider the implications for the competitiveness of their own offerings, with major discussions about a 'Digital Dollar' and 'Digital Euro'. The technological revolution in money and payments is thus now moving beyond the theoretical, and as a result monetary and payment professionals around the world are increasingly grappling with how to improve their own systems and to interact with the new systems being created, particularly those which will eventually emanate from the major currency issuers.

As we have shown, there is no single model for CBDCs and we have argued that the key parameters of design choices are, in fact, largely determined by the efficiency versus safety paradigm that shapes most central banks' and regulators' decisions. Ultimately, highly *robust* and *efficient* digital monetary and payment systems will most likely be neither fully 'public' nor 'private' but rather arise from public private partnership.

15

Digital Financial Transformation

Lessons from the EU

SUMMARY

Europe's path to digitisation and datafication in finance has rested upon four apparently unrelated pillars: (1) extensive reporting requirements imposed after the Global Financial Crisis (GFC) to control systemic risk and change financial sector behaviour; (2) strict data protection rules; (3) the facilitation of 'Open Banking' to enhance competition in banking and particularly payments; and (4) a legislative framework for digital identification imposed to further the European Single Market.

This chapter suggests that together these seemingly unrelated pillars have driven a transition to data-driven finance. The emerging ecosystem based on these pillars aims to promote a balance among a range of sometimes conflicting objectives, including systemic risk, data security and privacy, efficiency, and customer protection. Furthermore, we argue Europe's financial services and data protection regulatory reforms have unintentionally driven the use of regulatory technologies (RegTech), thereby laying the foundations for the digital transformation of European Union (EU) financial services and financial regulation. The EU experiences provide insights for other countries in developing regulatory approaches to the intersection of data, finance, and technology.

I. INTRODUCTION

As in other parts of the world, the EU reforms after the 2008 GFC focused on reducing risk-taking and systemic risk in the financial sector. At the same time, and unrelated to the 2008 crisis, European legislators adopted extensive reforms around data protection, furthered Open Banking, and developed digital identification regimes. This chapter explores how these four areas of regulatory reform, each introduced for their own discrete reasons, are interacting today in the EU to drive and support the development and adoption of digital finance.

As we argued in Chapter 6, FinTech often has the potential to reduce transaction costs, either outright due to the economies of scale inherent in software, data, and liquidity, or due to disintermediation. As we will discuss in more detail in Part IV, FinTech also creates new risks. The volume of data facilitates identification of correlations rather than causations, and correlations can lead to unintended, and socially regressive, consequences. Yet the methods to properly control and supervise self-learning algorithms are still being developed. Cybersecurity risks and tech-based complexity challenge supervisors and regulators trained to deal with traditional financial services. FinTech does not abolish risks. It alters the form of some existing risks and adds new risks.

These risks compel thinking through how law, regulation, and in particular regulatory technologies may counter the risks of FinTech, and in this way provide a new distinctive reason for the development of RegTech.

This chapter deals with how technological ecosystems can be designed to support financial efficiency, integrity, and stability. We analyse the four EU regulatory frameworks that, with the benefit of hindsight, have empowered digital financial transformation in Europe: the post-2008 reforms aiming at enhancing financial stability, the rigorous data protection of the General Data Protection Regulation (GDPR), the imposition of Open Banking by the second Payment Services Directive (PSD2), and, finally, the pan-European digital identity framework built pursuant to Electronic Identification, Authentication, and Trust Services (eIDAS) (discussed in Chapter 13).

We argue that the four legislative measures analysed here were each implemented for separate reasons, but their combined effect has been to give an extraordinary, unanticipated impetus to the rapid evolution of digital finance and a RegTech ecosystem in the EU.

II. FOUR DRIVERS OF CHANGE

A. *Extensive Digital Regulatory Reporting Obligations: From AIFMD to CRR and MIFID II*

Since the 2008 financial crisis, in tandem with the post-crisis international regulatory approaches described in Chapter 2, European regulators have imposed ever more extensive reporting obligations on financial intermediaries in an effort to combat systemic risk and address the range of integrity risks emerging from money laundering, terrorism financing, and other scandals (in particular those around London Inter-Bank Offered Rate (LIBOR) and foreign exchange trading). The most important regulatory initiatives in this regard include: for the banking sector CRR/ CRD IV (effective in 2014), for the asset management sector the AIFMD (effective in 2013), for financial markets MiFID II/MiFIR (devised in 2014 and in effect from 2018), for market infrastructure the EMIR (effective in 2013), for payment services PSD2 (devised in 2015 and in effect from 2018), and for money laundering the AMLD 5 (Anti-Money Laundering Directive devised in 2018 and in effect in 2020).

These frameworks share a common focus on international financial regulatory standards and impose extensive reporting requirements upon the financial services industry. Regulators in the EU, by requiring financial intermediaries to report far more data on their decisions, activities, and exposures, have triggered a digital transformation of Europe's financial industry as well as the evolution of a RegTech ecosystem. When faced with a proposed regulation, the financial services industry routinely demands sufficient time within which to build the necessary IT systems to implement it. The need to respond to regulatory reporting requirements by technology has forced intermediaries and their service providers to continually invest in the development of their IT systems to ensure that sufficient data are collected within their organisation to meet reporting requirements, that these data are packaged and reported in the necessary structure and form, and that they flow from the supervised entities to the supervisors in the required manner at the required times.

This has also forced regulators and supervisors to develop data management systems capable of receiving and processing the volume of data being generated and delivered by industry.

In addition, as the industry has digitised and standardised the data being collected across the global operations of individual firms, it has begun to focus on better using the data being collected, to both reduce compliance costs and generate new opportunities. This is the process of datafication: the application of analytics tools to digital data. Datafication is the fundamental process that underpins digital financial transformation and the evolution of data-driven finance in the traditional financial services industry.

In addition, as supervisors have been deluged with ever-increasing volumes of data, supervisors have had to enhance their data analytics tools. Once their analytics tools are enhanced, supervisors can handle even more data and tend, in turn, to ask supervised entities to collect and transmit even more of it, triggering another RegTech cycle.

A clear example comes from a United Kingdom (UK) Financial Conduct Authority (FCA) enforcement action against Merrill Lynch in October 2017, in which the firm was fined just over GBP 34.5 million for failing to report some 68.5 million exchange-traded derivatives transactions between 12 February 2014 and 6 February 2016,[1] as required under European Market Infrastructure Reporting (EMIR) and Markets in Financial Instruments Directive (MiFID). The case highlights the role of EU financial regulatory requirements in driving RegTech in financial services: for only through the use of technology could Merrill Lynch ever report such a volume of transactions at the frequency required. The market conduct that gave rise to this enforcement action also highlights the role of RegTech in supervision (often termed 'SupTech') for otherwise the chances of the FCA knowing of the

---

[1] See 'FCA Fines Merrill Lynch £34.5 Million for Failing to Report Transactions', *Financial Conduct Authority* (Web Page, 23 October 2017) <https://archive.ph/KEtzx>.

failure would be low, as it could not first receive the necessary digital reports and then subject them to appropriate analytics.

This development, part of a wider process examined in Chapter 4, is central to the process of Europe's digital financial transformation because this regulatory evolution has forced the financial services industry to digitise and standardise data collection and regulatory reporting comprehensively.

B. *Data Protection: GDPR*

As analysed in detail in Chapter 10, the EU GDPR is the most important change in data regulation since the first Data Protection Directive of 1995 in the EU and, to a large extent, globally. Due to its exterritorial effect, the GDPR has been a game changer for many businesses that collect and process data worldwide.

Unlike the financial regulatory reforms that have driven digitisation and datafication of massive amounts of data, the GDPR has created barriers to the centralisation of individual customer data and its use and required the financial industry to develop new systems of data management. These consequences arise because the GDPR has shifted control of much data from the financial and data intermediaries which collect it to the individual customers who are its subject.[2]

Arguably, these aspects of the GDPR may impair fully data-driven business models. For instance, financial institutions cannot contact new clients for distribution or sales purposes after acquisition of data pools from third parties unless the clients are legal, not natural, persons or the clients have consented ex ante, or the data pools were assembled through web-based gathering of user data.[3] Furthermore, older data pools become increasingly unreliable for data analysis or risk management purposes to the extent the GDPR's deletion requirements apply, removing some benefits from earlier major data gathering activity. These deficiencies could be considered and remedied in the risk models, for instance, by adding further security margins to 'old' or deficient data pools, by mixing data from different sources, or by applying filters. However, all of these measures require high levels of sophistication in data gathering and processing methodology.

C. *Open Banking: PSD2*

Besides extensive and purely digital reporting to regulators (which further reinforces the RegTech cycle), PSD2 imposes to a certain degree 'Open Banking' requirements, whereby incumbent financial intermediaries must share client data with third parties,

---

[2] See *Regulation (EU) 2016/679 of the European Parliament and of the Council of 27 April 2016 on the Protection of Natural Persons with Regard to the Processing of Personal Data and on the Free Movement of Such Data, and Repealing Directive 95/46/EC (General Data Protection Regulation)* [2016] OJ L 119/1, recital 1 ('GDPR').

[3] See GDPR [2016] OJ L 119/1, recitals 6, 32, 42, 46, 47.

including potentially innovative new competitors. By giving providers access to client financial information, PSD2 paves the way for new banking products and services and facilitates the change of customers from one bank or service provider to another. With the EU as first mover, many other nations are now working to establish Open Banking regimes. Australia is pursuing the most ambitious programme, working to extend consumer-directed data-sharing beyond banking to the energy and telecommunications sectors, all of finance, pensions, insurance, and, in time, other sectors of the economy.[4] In time, the EU PSD2 experiment is proving in other countries to be seminal.

Furthermore, PSD2 is playing a central role in supporting both digital financial transformation and the evolution of RegTech in the EU Single Financial Market.

On the one hand, it allows technology firms to enter the payments business.[5] Given incumbents' control of client data, which can only be shared with certain other qualified service providers, these new entrants will seek to keep their costs down and respond to regulatory requirements by technological means, furthering the evolution of RegTech.

On the other hand, payment institutions must respond to PSD2 by providing data interfaces for third-party providers from which those providers can extract data from customers. As analysed in Chapter 10, this forces banks to defend what is becoming their most valuable asset – customer data – by reconsidering their business models to either enhance service levels to retain their customers or become platform infra-structure providers and serve other providers.

The only way to achieve these reforms will be to rely more heavily on technology, through advanced analytical tools. This process is then reinforced through the reporting obligations contained in PSD2 and elsewhere, thereby driving the next stage of the evolution of Europe's RegTech ecosystem. This entire evolution in Europe's financial systems is built upon digital identity, to which we next turn.

D. *Digital Identity: eIDAS and Beyond*

As discussed in Chapter 13, digital identification is central to the future evolution of digital financial ecosystems. In the EU, this began for companies with the require-ment of Legal Entity Identifiers (LEIs) for all counterparties under MiFID II, which has in its turn been core in underpinning the role of digital reporting in the EU. The next level addresses individual digital identification which can be tied to personal

---

[4] Ross P Buckley and Natalia Jevglevskaja, 'Australia's Consumer Data Right: How to Realise this World-Leading Reform' (2022) 45(4) *University of New South Wales Law Journal* 1325; Ross P Buckley, Natalia Jevglevskaja and Scott Farrell, 'Australia's Data-Sharing Regime: Six Lessons for Europe' (2022) 33(1) *King's Law Journal* 61.

[5] See *Directive (EU) 2015/2366 of the European Parliament and of the Council of 25 November 2015 on Payment Services in the Internal Market, Amending Directives 2002/65/EC, 2009/110/EC and 2013/36/ EU and Regulation (EU) No 1093/2010, and Repealing Directive 2007/64/EC* [2015] OJ L 337/35, recitals 3, 6.

data collected and processed under MiFID II/GDPR/PSD2. The eIDAS regulation (discussed at length in Chapter 13) was adopted in 2014 to provide mutually recognised digital identity for cross-border electronic interactions between European citizens, companies, and government institutions. Member states can notify the European Commission of their national form of eID. Other member states have been able to recognise these voluntarily since 2015 and have been required to do so since September 2018. When an eID is ultimately recognised throughout the EU, an individual will be able to use it in any member state. The eID is assigned a certain level of assurance based on its security specifications, and this allows states to determine the services in relation to which it may be used.

The eIDAS regulation lays the foundation for a service-oriented ID base tying all individual personal data to a single identity, which is the core for both the GDPR and PSD2. It also supports the establishment of electronic know-your-customer (eKYC) utilities in Europe, particularly when used in tandem with LEIs (required under MiFID II), tax information sharing requirements under the Organisation for Economic Co-operation and Development (OECD) Common Reporting Standard (CRS) and post-Panama Papers requirements relating to transparency of beneficial ownership and control of legal entities under the respective Money Laundering Directives. The European Commission's Consumer Financial Services Action Plan[6] aims to 'work with the private sector to explore how they could use electronic identification and trust services for checking the identity of customers.'[7] In particular, action item 11 states: 'The Commission will facilitate the cross-border use of electronic identification and know-your-customer portability based on eIDAS to enable banks to identify customers digitally'.[8] Such eKYC utilities are a major RegTech innovation that promise substantial reductions in customer onboarding costs for providers, and substantial increases in the integrity of onboarding processes as nefarious customers are limited in their capacity to shop around for a friendly and compliant, or perhaps inept, financial services provider. It is thus eID (combined in particular with LEIs, tax information sharing, and beneficial ownership transparency) which will complete the foundations of Europe's datafied financial ecosystem.

E. *Digital Financial Transformation and the EU RegTech Revolution*

Individually and in combination, it is clear that these four separate EU initiatives – financial regulation, data protection, payments, and digital ID – all independently

---

[6] *Communication From the Commission to the European Parliament, the Council, the European Central Bank, the European Economic and Social Committee and the Committee of the Regions Consumer Financial Services Action Plan: Better Products, More Choice* [2017] COM(2017) 139 ('*Financial Services Action Plan*').

[7] European Commission, 'Consumer Financial Services Action Plan: Better Products and More Choice for European Consumers' (Press Release IP/17/609, 23 March 2017).

[8] *Financial Services Action Plan* [2017] COM(2017) 139, action 11.

have driven forward the evolution and growth of digital finance and RegTech in the EU Single Market. Taken together, they provide the core elements of a digitised and datafied regulatory European ecosystem.

In addition to their impact within the EU, aspects of these discrete legal and regulatory initiatives apply extraterritorially for firms and others engaging in financial services with EU customers or dealing with EU customer data. Thus, the combination of initiatives in the EU is requiring global action, driving digital financial transformation elsewhere, and spending on RegTech.

It is also clear that the policy concerns that have driven the development of the four EU pillars discussed herein are driving an increasing range of other jurisdictions around the world to consider how best to approach the intersection of data, finance, and regulation. The EU experience in driving (even if inadvertently) digital financial transformation and building a RegTech ecosystem has already had global implications.

III. EVOLVING REGTECH ECOSYSTEMS IN THE UNITED STATES AND INDIA

The EU initiatives came at a time when the world was providing a laboratory of different environments in which RegTech could operate and evolve. To show the unique EU features we next compare the differing approaches in the US and India to that of the EU and the potential lessons from these jurisdictions.

A. *The United States: Free Market and Anti-government*

The United States has led the world in both digital finance and the evolution of RegTech, highlighted in particular in the context of US securities markets since the 1970s. It is a major competitor for European finance and was the major example to which others looked prior to 2008.

The US approach to finance and data can be summarised for our purposes as a highly market-oriented approach, favouring individual choice. Until very recently, this approach was largely driven by freedom of contract, allowing individuals to freely transfer ('alienate') data while imposing restrictions on its use by government.

At the same time, distrust of large financial firms has led to a generally restrictive regulatory environment for financial institutions, albeit one focused mainly on correcting market failures through disclosure.[9] The combination of a disclosure-based financial system, technology innovation, and free alienability of data has underpinned the evolution of RegTech in the United States, where technology has been used by financial regulators to enhance their own performance since at least the 1980s.

---

[9] See, for example, *Dodd-Frank Wall Street Reform and Consumer Protection Act*, 12 USC (2010).

In comparing the United States to Europe, since 2008, and disregarding the EU's extensive focus on organisational and operating requirements for intermediaries for reasons of simplicity, financial regulatory approaches to disclosure have been largely similar and focused on enhanced reporting obligations which in turn have driven the use of RegTech in compliance. The use of RegTech in compliance is beginning to drive its use by regulators to a new level, building on the fairly high level of digitisation and datafication already present in many US regulators, particularly the Securities and Exchange Commission, the Commodities Futures Trading Commission, the Options Clearing Corporation (OCC), and Financial Industry Regulatory Authority. For instance, the US OCC – contrary to their European counterparts – calculates banks' capital requirements based on operational data reported by the banks.[10] This necessitates very granular data on each and every business operation, and hence trillions of datasets need to be exchanged.

Similar to the EU, legal and regulatory approaches in the United States have been one of the major driving factors in the evolution of its RegTech ecosystem.

B. *India Stack: Designing the Infrastructure to Support Digital Financial Transformation and a RegTech Ecosystem*

The India Stack – described at length in Chapter 13 – is the leading example to date of the rapid development and implementation of a comprehensive strategy to provide the infrastructure to support digital financial transformation. The India Stack is a combination of a national system of digital identification, a national digital payments system supporting interoperability across traditional and new payments technologies and providers, an eKYC system to support account opening and use, and a national strategy to use this infrastructure for a range of government and other services such as tax payments, salary payments, etc. The combination – as intended – has triggered massive digitisation and datafication as well as enabled new entrants and competition, resulting in great increases in financial inclusion and digital financial transformation and innovation.

In particular, since its initiation, almost the entire population (of some 1.3 billion people) has been enrolled in the Aadhaar system, the first level of the India Stack. Aadhaar has made access to financial accounts much easier, thus supporting financial inclusion, and it has enabled digitisation of government payments and services, thereby increasing efficiency, decreasing costs and losses due to corruption, and providing a pressing reason for consumers to engage with digital finance.

Such a comprehensive digital financial ecosystem has the potential to transform governance and delivery of services and result in economic gains that can be used to fund investments in education, health, roads, and other infrastructure.

---

[10] Office of the Comptroller of the Currency, *Capital and Dividends* (Handbook, July 2018) 2.

Unlike the United States, India – despite the size of its rapidly evolving market – has not yet seen the emergence of BigTech, TechFin, or even massive financial conglomerates of the sort common in the United States or Europe (see Chapter 16). One reason may be that, in implementing the centralised strategy of an India Stack, various state arms play a particularly strong role in financial market infrastructure. In turn, private actors tend to provide new services in and around collateral applications, rather than in core financial infrastructure such as digital identity and bank account services. Or it may simply be that India is at an earlier stage of financial and economic development and that developments in India will move very rapidly now that the core elements necessary to support digital financial transformation are in place. The truth perhaps lies in the middle: regulators were concerned with WhatsApp Pay's impact on the emerging FinTech ecosystem in India and thus limited the initial approval for Meta's payment services to 40 million users in 2020. In the second stage from April 2022 onwards, India's payment regulator, the National Payments Corporation of India (NPCI), allowed the roll-out of services to 100 million users which is well below the 400 million users of WhatsApp in India.[11] We agree with NPCI that there may well be good reasons for concern about undue market concentration in the payments market, which could potentially remove some of the benefits through India Stack, and we discuss these reasons in Part IV.

C. *Comparative Lessons*

India's strong centralised agenda to drive digital financial transformation through digital financial infrastructure as the core of a RegTech ecosystem is certainly demonstrating the truly transformative potential of FinTech and RegTech. In comparison, the rise of digital finance and RegTech in the United States and the EU can be attributed initially to the post-Crisis legislative focus on risk management and reporting obligations. The RegTech ecosystem in the United States had developed ahead of that in the EU due to the earlier existence of large volumes of data, arising because of earlier policy reforms. This appears to be changing rapidly in Europe, with the intersection of the four pillars we describe underpinning the rapid emergence of a new datafied financial ecosystem.

IV. BUILDING REGTECH ECOSYSTEMS

The EU experience highlights how, as financial systems digitise, it is necessary to carefully consider approaches to financial regulation, cybersecurity, data protection, digital identity, and competition. The approaches taken in different

---

[11] See Manish Singh, 'WhatsApp Permitted to Extend Payments Service to 100 Million Users in India', *TechCrunch* (Web Page, 13 April 2022) <https://techcrunch.com/2022/04/13/whatsapp-permitted-to-extend-payments-service-to-100-million-users-in-india>.

jurisdictions – and the resulting role of RegTech – will be driving forces in financial and economic development and innovation in the twenty-first century. We argue that these must be based on policy and legislative strategies designed explicitly to build RegTech ecosystems.

A. *Transformative Role of Data*

The interaction between data and financial regulation is clearly one of the most significant issues facing finance and its regulation in coming years. As we argued in Chapter 2, finance has always been an information industry, but financial regulation and data regulation have evolved over time in distinctive non-interactive legal silos, based on very different underlying principles and policy objectives.

Limitations on pooling and restrictions on cross-border storage and use of data are also encouraging significant research and spending on new systems of data aggregation and analysis which do not require individual data access, but rather are based on query-only or decentralised structures. These are driving innovation in data systems and analytics, with important implications for RegTech.

Thus, while regulation places limits on RegTech, it also drives it forward in new ways through its focus on the use, collection, storage, transfer, and protection of data.

The transformative role of FinTech around the world highlights how finance, data, and technology are now all tethered one to the other. As such, regulatory approaches in each area will interact with approaches taken in other areas. This poses particular challenges for regulators. The EU provides a vivid example of this through the interaction of key legislations such as MiFID II, GDPR, PSD2, and eIDAS. It is this combination of regulatory approaches and policies which are and will continue to push RegTech forward in the EU.

As other jurisdictions around the world are increasingly forced to consider the interaction of financial regulation with technology, data protection, and cybersecurity in the context of their own cultural and political environments, the experience of the EU will provide major policy and regulatory lessons. This will also be the case as jurisdictions consider the relationship of financial regulation, data protection, and cybersecurity with competition/antitrust policy and regulation. We address this latter topic in Part IV.

B. *Initial Conclusions from the EU Experience*

We suggest that the EU's regulatory reforms prompt six initial conclusions in relation to the future evolution of RegTech.

First, RegTech is not, and should not be, a simple transposition of existing analogue processes into a digital context, but instead requires a reinvention of these processes. The datafication of processes requires a Digital Due Diligence approach which divides processes into tiny steps that can be captured in a binary and check-the-box fashion. This then facilitates default and override hierarchies that need to be carefully considered and implemented.

Second, the adoption of RegTech will require a readjustment of accountability and liability rules. Where the lines are to be drawn is neither obvious nor simple. An overly friendly approach to technology exposes clients and the financial system to the risk of tech vulnerabilities, while an overly strict approach renders unnecessarily difficult and expensive the management of financial intermediaries. A possible approach may be one that assesses decisions around software and data use, management and processing, and treats leniently those arising from care and diligence – something akin to the business judgement rule regarding the liability of corporate directors. While a very large amount of financial regulation is objective (such as reporting requirements) and therefore subject to digitisation, datafication, and potential automation, a significant amount (such as culture, ethics, and 'fit-and-proper' standards) are subjective and not suitable for RegTech processes.

Third, the nature of supervision will change as a result of RegTech. Data-driven supervision is a somewhat different skill from more traditional paper-based approaches. Accordingly, while the judgement calls may be similar, the information these will be based on will be far more granular and up to date, and thus a different skill set may well be necessary for RegTech-based financial supervision. Overall, we expect more statistical approaches to supervision where decisions are taken based on empirically based probability assumptions rather than case-by-case scrutiny of files. At the same time, there will necessarily be a differentiation between processes which can be automated (and are largely objective in their application and compliance) and those which are more subjective and require substantial human input.

Fourth, the rise of RegTech will lead to fewer human resources needed in banks for client contact and account management, and more bank staff with technological, risk assessment, and trouble shooting skills. This will mean fewer less skilled, lower paid jobs and more highly skilled, better-paid jobs. Most jurisdictions face human resources shortages in these specific fields. Implementing a RegTech strategy thus requires a comprehensive approach starting from educational programmes. At the same time, management will have to consider very carefully how to build cultures within institutions – in particular what sort of culture to build and the role of technology in supporting that culture, without dehumanising it.

Fifth, RegTech does not abolish risks. Rather, some risks to which we are well accustomed will be replaced by new risks. For instance, human-based operational risk, one of the major capital costs since the 2008 GFC, should decrease, whereas cybersecurity and tech risks will increase. Further, in our view, antitrust risks and the risks for markets resulting from extremely swift transmission of information will increase and require further investigation and regulation.

Sixth, as RegTech develops, financial intermediaries will need to re-consider their risk budgets and capital allocations. Reviewing risk models has long been a challenge. Unique risk models have created information asymmetries, leading some capital markets to penalise banks with advanced risk models by imposing discounts on the disclosed book values. For this reason, standardisation of risk models is on the regulatory agenda. However, this standardisation may bring with it a loss of innovation and increased systemic risk since standardisation of risk models will likely lead to standardised business models and strategies, as arguably occurred in the lead up to the 2008 GFC and which has since become a core focus of macroprudential regulation. However, RegTech enables supervisors to assess, for the first time, the impact of firm-specific risk models by transferring the underlying datasets into the supervisor's risk modelling systems and then stress testing against certain occurrences. So RegTech should improve supervision and reduce market concerns about advanced, bespoke risk models.

V. CONCLUSION

In this chapter, we consider how a series of clearly motivated but uncoordinated projects played a crucial role in shaping Europe's financial ecosystem by building the foundation of a digital finance ecosystem, making EU finance more open to innovation by data-driven financial services providers – of an increasing range of forms – than ever before. However, what the EU did without an overarching roadmap, other jurisdictions may – and we argue should – impose purposefully through careful development of coordinated legal and regulatory approaches to finance, data, and their interaction. In this regard, the EU presents an interesting, and still rapidly evolving, case study, relevant to every other jurisdiction in the world. In the EU, the road to a digital financial ecosystem has been paved by a robust rule of law environment (that ensures the viability of long-term investments), a willingness to use regulation to drive evolution of markets and societies, and an approach aiming at 'controlled' rather than 'cutthroat' capitalism.

Based on experiences to date, we would suggest two central lessons. The first is that finance, data, and technology are now intertwined as a result of a long-term process of digitisation and datafication of finance in developed markets – a process that is likewise happening rapidly in emerging and developing markets. As a result, the use of technology for compliance, monitoring, enforcement, and system design in financial regulation – RegTech in short – will continue to increase. There will be particular challenges for regulators and supervisors in managing the process but also opportunities to design RegTech ecosystems to better achieve regulatory objectives. Jurisdictions are already considering how to shape the evolution of RegTech through digitisation, datafication, and systems design in a process that will only increase in importance going forward. In addition to the important benefits, the transition to data-driven finance also brings new risks, in particular in the context of cybersecurity, technology, and data protection, requiring careful consideration of the design of an appropriate RegTech ecosystem to balance benefits and risks.

The second lesson is that because of the integration of data and finance, when designing financial regulatory systems (particularly those with a clear RegTech strategy) and seeking to regulate data, it is necessary to consider – during the design process – the implications of the interaction of data and finance. As can be seen from the EU experience, conflicts between objectives and rules should be considered ex ante. One area where this is particularly important is in choices about whether to pursue open banking and digital ID strategies. At this point, the EU experience is at an early stage but it will determine the approach taken in many other jurisdictions: success or failure will echo around the world. We argue that most jurisdictions will need both a general data regulation framework and one that operates specifically in the context of finance, where societal differences are likely to be less important and financial regulatory objectives around transparency, information sharing, consumer protection, and systemic risk are likely to dominate.

PART IV

From FinTech to TechFin to BigTech to FinTech 4.0

Balancing the Opportunities and Risks of Scale and Concentration in Digital Finance

Over the past five decades, finance has undergone a process of digital transformation, encompassing digitisation and datafication. Today, finance is not only the most globalised segment of the world's economy but also among the most digitised and datafied.

In Part I, we considered the evolution of finance, technology, and regulation.

In Part II, the book addressed the main new technologies that have emerged in the past two decades and their application to finance. We presented both the opportunities and challenges, arguing for a balanced proportional risk-based approach to regulation including support for innovation.

In Part III, the book framed an overall strategic approach to building the infrastructure for digital finance and the appropriate regulatory systems and ecosystems to support digital financial transformation and inclusive sustainable development.

This part focuses on the darker aspects of digital financial transformation: the risks of FinTech 4.0.

Finance is an industry characterised by strong economies of scope and scale. These effects have led over time to the emergence of large financial groups and conglomerates. Finance is also characterised by the generation of strong positive and negative externalities: finance has benefits that extend well beyond its direct participants in the form of greater economic growth and development and also causes instability and crises. Extensive regulation has therefore emerged to control the industry and reduce the likelihood of failure, with the object of increasing positive externalities and reducing negative ones.

Over time, this combination of factors has inexorably resulted in concentration within the financial sector, posing risks to competition, efficiency, and financial stability especially in the context of systemically significant financial institutions. These factors were core to the 2008 Global Financial Crisis and the focus of post-crisis regulatory reforms.

At the same time, while technology and finance have always developed together, digitisation and the application of new technologies have transformed finance, as now embodied in the term FinTech. Much of the focus of the 2010s was on the opportunities and challenges posed by new entrants, in particular FinTech start-ups using technology to challenge incumbent approaches and models. The business model of these FinTechs (perhaps with certain exceptions in decentralised finance) was to focus on achieving scale.

Like finance, technology benefits from network effects, which manifest with increasing numbers of customers, interconnections, and data. Network effects in technology inexorably led to the emergence of dominant technology platforms as we have seen in both the United States and China.

In this part, we highlight this process in the context of the entry of technology firms into finance (TechFins) and the emergence of digital platforms in traditional finance (particularly asset management), and explain this emergence of concentration from a technological perspective. We argue that technology, and in particular the resulting access to customer data and liquidity, allows for utterly unprecedented economies of scale in finance. In fact, very large firms that combine features of both finance and technology have developed from the combination of technological evolution, conducive regulatory approaches, and the pro-concentration effects that characterise both data *and* financial industries.

We also see this in the context of the entry of BigTech platforms into finance and the scaling of FinTechs as some move quickly from being too small for regulators to care about to being too big to fail. These trends characterise the current period in the evolution of FinTech, which we characterise as FinTech 4.0. We foresee the decade of the 2020s in finance to be dominated by a massive battle between centralisation and decentralisation, of seeking the positive externalities of data aggregation and finance while seeking to reduce the negative externalities of change at a pace that at times bewilders regulators.

Conventional economies of scale, data-driven economies of scale, and network effects explain why FinTech markets can increase efficiencies in processes such as client onboarding, compliance, and reporting, and facilitate algorithm-based investment and trading that use market information at a greater pace than humans ever could.

The same technological advances that account for cost reduction and increased efficiencies also potentially contribute to decreasing competition in FinTech markets. On the one hand, conventional FinTechs (including trading platform Robinhood and the archetypal FinTech firms Aladdin and Ant Group) have been able to collect massive amounts of assets and numbers of customers. On the other hand, these very same forces have enabled new entrants into financial services like Meta (formerly Facebook), Apple, Google, Microsoft, and Amazon ("MAGMA") in the United States, and Baidu, Alibaba, and Tencent ("BATs") in China, to extend broadly across most aspects of the society and economy within their respective countries and beyond.

The data-driven finance business is often a platform industry. In the digital finance context, the term "platform" refers to a systems architecture where multiple applications are linked to and through one technical infrastructure so that users can use one major integrating software system to run all applications written for that system. One outcome of platformisation is financial ecosystems with multiple services linked to clients via one platform, with the platform serving as the indispensable technical core that ties all services and clients together, but also provides some services itself.

We present here a framework of analysis of these issues and highlight the challenges to existing regulatory silos in finance, competition/antitrust, data, and technology regulation. We argue the need for a balanced proportional approach, enabling and encouraging competition and innovation while also carefully monitoring emerging scale, concentration, and dominance issues. Key to this approach is data regulation and the necessity of focussing on building systems to enable data aggregation while limiting the extraction of monopoly rents by dominant private players, whether in finance, in tech, or in FinTech/TechFin markets.

While the resulting concentration and dominance of these "BigTechs" have long been of concern in the European Union, they have now also emerged as major social, political, regulatory, and legal foci of attention elsewhere, with the corporate governance dimension relating to the might of institutional investors particularly pronounced among US corporates, and the public concerns at the heart of the Chinese response to Ant.

The evolution of financial ecosystems can bring many advantages. Yet, the rapid emergence of concentration and dominance in digital finance via platformisation can pose great risks; the corporate governance aspects discussed in recent ECGI scholarship being only one of them. Financial regulators worldwide must step up to the difficult challenge of dealing with these transformative contemporary market structures in a sufficiently firm, yet balanced and proportionate, manner.

This part thus focuses on the challenges of scale, concentration, and dominance to innovation and competition, whether in the form of BigTechs or traditional financial intermediaries in the context of FinTech 4.0. Chapter 16 first considers the evolution of TechFins and digital finance platforms and the opportunities they present. Chapter 17 presents a framework of analysis of new risks of scale, focusing on cybersecurity and data. Chapter 18 discusses regulatory approaches to the range of new entrants such as TechFins and digital financial infrastructure. Chapter 19 focuses on data and concentration risks while also arguing for the need for coordinated approaches at domestic and international levels and suggesting a set of principles which may serve as the basis of a framework to address these sorts of risks going forward.

16

Of TechFins, Digital Financial Platforms, BigTechs, and FinTech 4.0

SUMMARY

This chapter focuses on the evolution of non-financial businesses such as technology, e-commerce, and telecommunications companies (tech companies) entering the financial services sector: TechFins. China has been at the forefront of this change, with Alibaba establishing the online financial conglomerate Ant Group, which we have discussed in previous chapters. The global tech behemoths of Amazon, Apple, Google, and Facebook have also all entered the financial services sector in various ways: BigTechs. The chapter considers the emergence of digital finance platforms in the context of traditional finance and then considers the entry of BigTech firms into finance. Together, these processes constitute the expression of the combination of the economies of scope and scale of finance combined with the network effects of data and technology. Together, they embody one of the major trends we characterise as at the heart of the current era of FinTech 4.0: a natural process of concentration, with many benefits, as well as many risks and challenges, which are the subject of Chapters 17–19.

I. INTRODUCTION

This chapter is structured as follows. Section II analyses the TechFin phenomenon. Sections III and IV describe the features of, and opportunities offered by, TechFins and financial platforms, and explain how these combine in the era of FinTech 4.0. Section V highlights the opportunities and how they differ from those of FinTech.

II. FINTECHS AND TECHFINS, DIGITISATION AND DATAFICATION

While most discussions of FinTech across the 2010s focused on the opportunity for new FinTech entrants to disrupt traditional finance, as a general matter, this has not happened. Rather, the key challenge has arisen from established technology companies entering finance, first in the context of TechFin and then in the form of BigTechs.

A. *TechFins*

The critical distinctions between a technology company offering financial services (a TechFin), a FinTech start-up, and a traditional financial institution are clear: TechFins use technology to lever data they typically already possess so as to provide financial services. A TechFin has existing customer relationships in a non-financial services setting through which they collect large amounts of data that can then be monetised by offering, among other things, financial services. FinTechs, on the other hand, are typically start-ups that identify a 'pain point' in financial services, devise a technological fix for the problem, and then seek to sell that solution directly to customers or to incumbent institutions, and, in doing so, themselves become an acquisition target. FinTechs do not enter the financial services sector from the same starting point as a TechFin. FinTechs were mostly start-ups responding to various consequences of, and opportunities generated by, the 2008 Global Financial Crisis (GFC), as we have considered in Chapter 2. TechFins are established tech companies seeking to use their pre-existing data to underpin a move into financial services. In contrast, traditional financial institutions, such as banks, have historically focused on customer relationships, not data. Banks have only recently begun to consider supplementing customer risk analysis with more broadly derived data.

The provider with the most accurate, detailed, and extensive customer information will be best placed to price credit and insurance through 'datafication' (i.e., the process of analysing and using data).[1] In the past, this was a customer's bank. Banks relied on detailed customer questionnaires to garner information on income and expenses. Objectives, experience, and risk tolerance were collated over time from the bank's knowledge of the customer's financial history. This data advantage that banks once enjoyed is diminishing fast.

TechFins' data superiority is derived from information collected from several sources, which when combined, provide a comprehensive profile of the customers' preferences and behaviours. The data can be derived from:

1. Software companies (e.g., Microsoft and Google) aggregating information about users' activities;
2. hardware companies (e.g., Huawei, Tesla and Apple) and 'Internet of Things' companies utilising sensors which continually monitor usage behaviour and location;
3. social media services (e.g., Facebook and Tencent) and search engines (e.g., Google and Baidu) providing insight into social preferences and activities;

---

[1] Jens-Erik Mai, 'Big Data Privacy: The Datafication of Personal Information' (2016) 32(3) *The Information Society* 193.

4. e-commerce companies (e.g., Amazon, Alibaba and major retail chains with large market shares, such as Walmart) providing insight into customers preferences and payment history; and

5. telecommunications services providers (e.g., Vodafone) providing data on mobile activities.

The data from such sources are typically expansive, covering a large population of the reference market and often deep in the number of data points for each customer.

TechFins can relatively efficiently collect financial information (comparable to information accumulated by a bank or an asset manager) to supplement their detailed knowledge of a customer's choices and preferences. This information is processed through algorithms that have established correlations between preferences and creditworthiness[2] to formulate a far more nuanced assessment of creditworthiness than traditional bank assessments. Once a client relationship is established, TechFins can seamlessly leverage existing levels of trust to expand service offerings.

To summarise, a FinTech is a 'financial' intermediary, while a TechFin is a 'data' intermediary. For TechFins, data accumulation and analytics are key and typically start with self-developed algorithms that find and measure data correlations and then progress to machine learning and artificial intelligence.

B. *TechFin Evolution*

TechFins push into financial services in typically three stages:

1. The first stage is when the TechFin aggregates data from its existing customer-focussed business and functions as a data broker. For example, aggregate data are licensed to incumbent financial institutions or FinTechs, to carry out data analytics (for lending or investment decisions) or to test and/or supplement datasets which may eventually be offered for sale. Buyers are typically financial institutions that use the data to formulate and then use customer correlations.

2. The second stage is when TechFins leverage existing customer relationships to facilitate the provision to them of financial services by regulated financial institutions, thereby functioning as the conduit between customer and financial services provider.

3. The third stage is when the TechFin begins to deliver its own financial services and thus becomes or establishes a financial institution.

When a tech company moves from a non-financial business model to the first stage, or moves from the first to second stage, the core issue from a regulator's perspective is: when should the technology company be regulated as a financial institution? Some activities clearly attract regulation, such as when client funds are taken on

---

[2]   Mikella Hurley and Julius Adebayo, 'Credit Scoring in the Era of Big Data' (2016) 18 *Yale Journal of Law and Technology* 148.

to the tech company's balance sheet, when discretion over client money is exercised, or when client assets are pooled. Yet such formal characteristics of banking and financial services may only materialise late in the evolutionary process. Many TechFins do not apply for a financial services license or authorisation until they are about to enter the third stage. It is not unusual for TechFins to provide credit or sophisticated payment services to individuals or small- and medium-sized enterprises (SMEs) without a financial services license.

Financial regulation normally requires intermediaries to be licensed when handling client funds (either from a bank account or a security deposit), and when soliciting clients and marketing or arranging financial services and products. In the TechFin world, clients often voluntarily contact the TechFin for services. For example, Standard Chartered partnered with Amazon Web Services (AWS) to run new digital banking applications on AWS cloud services.[3] Technically speaking, this may not constitute solicitation, marketing, or arranging, and thus may fall outside financial licensing requirements. This is because TechFins do not seek access to a client's assets but rather their data: from that all else follows. The critical distinction is that TechFins derive their capacities and profits from access to data, not access to money.

When TechFins have direct access to client funds, such as through Alipay's money market funds, they will (or at least should) be subject to mandatory regulation. Where the part of the business that must be licensed is quarantined in a subsidiary of the parent company, only a tiny fraction of the overall dataset and algorithms will be regulated. Accordingly, regulators will only supervise a small part of the tech company conglomerate and a fraction of its overall risk.

Development from the first to third stage to can occur rapidly. For example, Alipay introduced its online money market fund, Yu'e Bao, in June 2013 and by leveraging Alipay's user base of one billion customers it became the fourth largest fund worldwide in under a year.

C. *Over Time the Distinctions Disappear*

As noted, there are stark differences between traditional financial institutions, FinTech start-ups, and TechFins. As the importance of data analytics increases, these differences will diminish. For example, large international banks can buy more aggregated datasets to factor into their business decisions. Some TechFins may ultimately apply for full banking and financial services licenses and become global financial conglomerates. E-commerce provides an apt analogy: ten years ago, buying products online was engaging in e-commerce. Today it is shopping. Our focus is on how regulators will respond to the coming transition.

---

[3] See 'AWS Selected to Power Our Strategic Banking Systems and Workloads', *Standard Chartered* (Web Page, 12 November 2020) <www.sc.com/en/media/press-release/weve-selected-aws-to-power-our-strategic-banking-systems-and-workloads>.

III. DIGITAL FINANCE PLATFORMS

Scale has long been a major challenge for finance and financial regulation. Systemically important financial institutions (SIFIs), systemically important financial market infrastructures (FMIs), and the challenge of the evolution of too-big-to-fail, too-complex-to-fail, and too-big-to-save have been at the heart of finance and financial regulation for hundreds of years. Most recently, they were at the centre of the 2008 GFC.

As can be seen with TechFin, technology and data benefit from network effects. At the same time, finance is characterised by economies of scope and scale. The combination has also resulted in the evolution of ever-larger digital finance platforms in the context of traditional finance.

To develop a theoretical conceptualisation of financial platforms, digital finance platforms (DFPs), we first define them and then focus upon the critical distinctions between DFPs, 'traditional' FinTechs, and financial market utilities (FMUs).

A. *Digital Finance Platforms*

DFPs are multilateral IT systems that connect a network of participating institutions to one another and to the operator of the system for the purpose of conducting financial transactions. At first glance, they may appear similar to digital e-commerce platforms, but the distinctions really matter. Chief among these, the DFP is not a party to the financial transactions performed on it; rather with multiple applications connected to and run on it, each DFP facilitates and/or executes decisions for financial transactions taken by third parties (e.g., the payer, the investor, the broker) or separate entities related to the platform provider.

DFPs can take various legal and organisational forms.[4] Examples include bank or non-bank service entities (where all linked intermediaries are contracting partners to the service entity)[5] or mutual associations, typically of financial institutions.[6] The DFP can be owned and operated by one private entity where the entity is in sole[7] or dispersed ownership,[8] or mutualised, with the users as members;[9] we also see public

---

[4] See Committee on Payment and Settlement Systems, Bank for International Settlements, *Payment and Settlement Systems in Selected Countries* (April 2003) 7 <www.bis.org/cpmi/publ/d53.pdf>, detailing variety of financial market infrastructure.

[5] Visa is structured as a bank while SWIFT is not. See ibid 455–7, describing the structure of SWIFT.

[6] The stock exchanges as constituted until recent decades are the classic example.

[7] For example, the New York Stock Exchange (NYSE) today, with the trading conglomerate Intercontinental Exchange as sole owner. See 'The History of NYSE', NYSE (Web Page) <www.nyse.com/history-of-nyse>.

[8] For example, Nasdaq, Inc. and Euronext S.A. See 'Investor FAQs', NASDAQ (Web Page) <https://ir.nasdaq.com/resources/investor-faqs>; 'Corporate Governance at Euronex', *Euronex* (Web Page) <www.euronext.com/en/investor-relations/corporate-governance>.

[9] For example, the user-owned Depository Trust & Clearing Corporation, located in New York City, the world's largest financial value processor: 'DTCC's Businesses, Subsidiaries and Joint Ventures', *DTCC* (Web Page) <www.dtcc.com/about/businesses-and-subsidiaries>.

entities (such as central banks)[10] running systemically important DFPs (e.g., real-time gross settlement (RTGS) payment systems).

B. *Digital Financial Platforms vs Financial Market Utilities*

A 'financial market utility' (FMU), as encoded in various parts of US securities and banking regulation, is 'a person that manages or operates a multilateral system for the purpose of transferring, clearing, or settling payments, securities, or other financial transactions among financial institutions or between financial institutions and the person'.[11] FMU systems in the United States include the multilateral settlement service owned and operated by the Federal Reserve Banks (the National Settlement Service)[12] and Visa, which link banks executing payment transactions from payer to payee and connects to the central bank to ensure liquidity.[13] Nasdaq's systems, similarly, link brokerage firms with traded securities and their central clearing houses; and the electronic information exchange and messaging system, Swift, connects more than 11,000 financial institutions around the world.[14] The Depository Trust and Clearing Corporation ensures the transfer of securities and derivatives among local and global custodians and central securities depositaries.

Financial platforms may be a form of FMU, yet FMUs, in their classic incarnation, are too narrow, too mechanical, and too limited in scope to serve as fully fledged service platforms. In particular, FMUs have focussed on making markets and processes more efficient and secure by promoting trust and reducing transaction costs within the financial system, while generally avoiding direct contact with the retail client base. The FMU serves the intermediary so that the *intermediary* can offer better products less expensively; hence, profitability is not the main concern of FMUs.

---

[10] For example, the US Federal Reserve currently functions as an operator of the National Settlement Service, the Fedwire® Funds Service, the Electronic Payments Network, and the Automated Clearing House system, through which depository institutions send each other batches of electronic credit and debit transfers. The Federal Reserve has committed to develop and operate FedNow, a real-time payment and settlement service slated to start operations in 2023: Board of Governors of the Federal Reserve System, 'Federal Reserve Announces Plan to Develop a New Round-the-Clock Real-time Payment and Settlement Service to Support Faster Payments' (Press Release, 5 August 2019) <www.federalreserve.gov/newsevents/pressreleases/other20190805a.htm>. Other examples include the ECB's payment-vs-delivery system, TARGET2-Securities, and the Bank of England's CHAPS system. See 'What Is TARGET2-Securities (T2S)?', *European Central Bank* (Web Page) <www.ecb.europa.eu/paym/target/t2s/html/index.en.html>; 'CHAPS', *Bank of England* (Web Page) <www.bankofengland.co.uk/payment-and-settlement/chaps>.

[11] See Proposed Rules of the US Federal Reserve System: *Financial Market Utilities*, 87 Fed Reg 60314 (5 October 2022).

[12] See 'National Settlement Service', The Federal Reserve (Web Page, 2022) <www.frbservices.org/financial-services/national-settlement-service>.

[13] International Monetary Fund, *United States Financial Sector Assessment Program: Technical Note on Supervision of Financial Market Infrastructures, Resilience of Central Counterparties and Innovative Technologies* (IMF Country Report No. 20/249, August 2020).

[14] See 'About Us', SWIFT (Web Page) <www.swift.com/about-us>.

A DFP, by contrast, aims to provide an entire ecosystem with multiple services between clients and regulated intermediaries, either directly (where the client is a DFP client) or indirectly, in an effort to earn profits that can be considerable indeed.[15]

C. *Digital Financial Platforms vs FinTechs*

DFPs possess three critical differences from traditional FinTechs. First, FinTechs typically focus on disruption – challenging incumbents – which is in sharp contrast to the intense cooperation with incumbents which characterises the business model of DFPs.[16] Second, most FinTech applications link retail and small and medium enterprises to a FinTech firm. DFPs, by contrast, link multiple *financial intermediaries* together, in an effort to create an entire financial ecosystem. Third, in an effort to disintermediate, some high-profile FinTech businesses take the form of a marketplace, brokering various services and goods and taking a commission.[17] DFPs, by contrast, function as *innovation* platforms comprising 'a technology, product or service that serves as a foundation on top of which other firms (loosely organised into an innovative ecosystem) develop complementary technologies, products or services.'[18]

A DFP is at its core similar to Apple, Microsoft, SAP, Oracle, and Intel, each of which offer core innovation platforms on which various applications run. DFPs thus 'establish a core of tools and standards that serve as a foundation for third-party software or content,'[19] where content can include data of all kinds and data-analytic tools, as well as contracting, execution, and settlement systems.

IV. TECHFINS AND FINTECH 4.0: TOWARDS A NEW DIGITAL 'TOO-BIG-TO-FAIL' IN FINANCE

FinTech 4.0, the current period in the evolution of FinTech which commenced in about 2019, is characterised primarily by the emergence of scale in the platformisation of finance. This scale has come from TechFin and BigTech firms joining the

---

[15] Derryl D'Silva et al, 'The Design of Digital Financial Infrastructure: Lessons from India' (BIS Papers No. 106, Monetary and Economic Department, Bank for International Settlements, December 2019) <www.bis.org/publ/bppdf/bispap106.pdf>.

[16] Douglas W Arner, Jànos Barberis, and Ross P Buckley, 'FinTech, RegTech and the Reconceptualization of Financial Regulation' (2017) 37(3) *Northwestern Journal of International Law and Business* 371, 383–4.

[17] See Peter C Evans and Annabelle Gawer, 'The Rise of the Platform Enterprise: A Survey' (The Emerging Platform Economy Series, The Center for Global Enterprise, January 2016) <www .thecge.net/app/uploads/2016/01/PDF-WEB-Platform-Survey_01_12.pdf> 10, 14, stating that of the 176 platform firms that were surveyed in 2015 globally, 160 platforms were transaction platforms.

[18] Ibid 9.

[19] Daniel Haberly et al, 'Asset Management as a Digital Platform Industry: A Global Financial Network Perspective' (2019) 106 *Geoforum* 167, 168.

few Big Finance incumbents in the DFP market.[20] Our central point is that the digitisation and datafication of finance over decades, combined with network effects and economies of scope and scale, is resulting in an ever-greater concentration and dominance in technology and finance and the emergence of new 'too-big-to-fail' and possibly even 'too-big-to-regulate' phenomena.

BigTechs, which include Meta, Google, Amazon, Tencent, and Alibaba, to name a few, represent a broader group of firms in which technology has dramatically driven their growth, scale, diversification, and dominance. When these firms enter into the financial services industry in some capacity, we term them TechFins. Their entrance into finance is significant because of the scale at which they operate and the means through which they can engage with large numbers of people, including the unbanked, underbanked, and otherwise financially excluded persons.[21] In credit markets, for example, it is estimated that these firms lent nearly US$572 billion globally in 2019 and were important lenders in China, the United States, and an increasing number of emerging markets.[22] In 2020, the credit offered by these TechFins grew to a global total of over US$700 billion.[23] This is all the more staggering because TechFins are not traditional financial institutions. Rather, they are large companies whose primary activities encompass a broad array of more general digital services, including online search engines, social media, e-commerce, ride-hailing, and telecommunications. Data are their primary currency, and few suspected that platform-based models would be the medium through which these entities could become financial intermediaries, offering a growing range of digital financial services. This generally starts with payment, then moves to credit and investment, and from there to an ever-wider range of areas. Indeed, by leveraging their large customer bases, the troves of data from these customers, and sophisticated technology applications (such as artificial intelligence and cloud computing), TechFins have been able to provide payments, credit, insurance, and digital wallets in ways that traditional financial institutions have failed to do. This trend has been driven by several factors.[24]

---

[20] See Erik Feyen et al, 'FinTech and the Digital Transformation of Financial Services: Implications for Market Structure and Public Policy' (BIS Papers No. 117, Monetary and Economic Department, Bank for International Settlements, July 2021) <www.bis.org/publ/bppdf/bispap117.htm>.

[21] See Financial Stability Board, *BigTech Firms in Finance in Emerging Market and Developing Economies: Market Developments and Potential Financial Stability Implications* (Report, 12 October 2020) <www.fsb.org/wp-content/uploads/P121020-1.pdf>.

[22] Giulio Cornelli et al, 'FinTech and Big Tech Credit: A New Database' (BIS Papers No. 887, Monetary and Economic Department, Bank for International Settlements, September 2020) 1–2 <www.bis.org/publ/work887.htm>.

[23] Leonardo Gambacorta, Fahad Kalil, and Bruno M Parigi, 'Big Techs vs Banks' (BIS Papers No. 1037, Monetary and Economic Department, Bank for International Settlements, August 2022) 1 <www.bis.org/publ/work1037.htm>.

[24] Financial Stability Board, *BigTech in Finance: Market Developments and Potential Financial Stability Implications* (9 December 2019) 11–12 <www.fsb.org/wp-content/uploads/P091219-1.pdf>.

First, TechFins enjoy increasing numbers of users on their platforms as more people around the world gain smartphone and internet access. With user-friendly application programming interfaces (APIs), firms are able to offer a series of services through a platform-based model that connects users across a vast global network.[25] The connections vary depending on the type of digital platform. From social media apps to e-commerce websites, there are a variety of platforms that bring together buyers and sellers across a range of industries and enterprises. The use of these platforms increased significantly during the COVID-19 pandemic, as governments mandated lockdowns and forced people indoors to control the spread of the virus.[26] These changes supported the success of the BigTech business model.

The BigTech business model is founded upon the Data–Network–Activities model.[27] The DNA model is the second factor driving the entry of BigTechs into finance and into becoming TechFins. This is the reinforcing cycle of data analytics, network effects, and interwoven activities. As users realise that a platform offers a valuable product or service, over time they are likely to encourage or attract other users onto the platform. For example, sellers on an e-commerce site may realise that the platform provides an easy-to-use and secure site to sell merchandise to buyers in a global marketplace. This ease of business is likely, in turn, to attract more sellers onto the site. As the number of sellers or merchants increase, there is a concomitant increase in the number of buyers on the site, attracted by the diversity of merchants and the competitive prices. As this network of buyers and sellers increases, the platform begins to generate 'network effects', which arise whenever greater numbers of users participating on a platform render it more useful to all users. Rising numbers of participants in turn generate new troves of data for the platform. The data are a key input into the platforms' algorithms and data analytics, and allow them to create better products and services that are tailored more specifically to their users and consumers. As the products and services become better, they attract more users and enable the platform to create new services and products for those users–often termed 'interwoven activities'.[28] This cycle can lead to a platform's rapid growth and dominance within a particular sector and helps to explain how BigTechs came to dominate their respective categories in such relatively short periods of time.

---

[25] Bank for International Settlements, *Annual Economic Report 2019* (Report, June 2019) 62 <www.bis .org/publ/arpdf/ar2019e.htm>. See Chapter III, Big Tech in Finance: Opportunities and Risks.

[26] See, for example, Financial Times Editorial Board, 'The Big Tech Boom Marks a Lasting Change', *Financial Times* (online, 31 July 2021) <www.ft.com/content/36fd57a0-52bb-4bed-b9a9-46dfb69b2f52>; Laura LaBerge et al, 'How COVID-19 Has Pushed Companies over the Technology Tipping Point: And Transformed Business Forever', *McKinsey & Company* (Web Page, 5 October 2020) <www .mckinsey.com/business-functions/strategy-and-corporate-finance/our-insights/how-covid-19-has-pushed-companies-over-the-technology-tipping-point-and-transformed-business-forever>.

[27] See Bank for International Settlements (n 25).

[28] Ibid.

This DNA model also explains how BigTechs have been able to move into financial services. As they attract more users onto their platforms and analyse the increasing data from their activities, BigTechs are able to create and offer complementary
services, such as payments, in order to better facilitate interactions and transactions
across the network, which is particularly valuable in the context of e-commerce
and gaming, as well as enabling the monetisation of social media.[29] Ant's Alipay
and Tencent's TenPay are two prominent examples from China, emerging from
e-commerce and social media enterprises, respectively. Another notable example
was Meta's more daring proposal of a global stablecoin for its platform, introduced
as Libra and then termed Diem, analysed in detail in Chapter 14, which was to be
enabled by WhatsApp/Facebook/Instagram Pay, Novi digital wallets, and related
identification frameworks. BigTech firms, as TechFins, are expanding further into
other areas of economic interest for users, such as credit, insurance, and money
market funds by playing a matchmaking or an intermediary role for consumers and
various financial product vendors or by providing loans or investments directly,
enabled by automated analytics supported by their massive pools of data.[30]

The third enabling driver for BigTechs' expansion into financial services is the
application of relatively new technology and tools that have matured significantly in
recent years. These technologies consist primarily of artificial intelligence, big data,
cloud computing, and distributed ledger technologies, often shortened to 'ABCD'.[31]
Using a combination of these technologies, BigTechs can extend credit to individuals in ways beyond those available to traditional financial institutions.[32] Traditional
financial institutions typically determine whether to make a loan on the basis of collateral, earning potential, or business plans. BigTechs, on the other hand, are able
to use alternative and unconventional data sources amassed in large quantities from
activities on their platforms and other accessible sources (Big Data), and then process
these data using advanced analytical methods such as machine learning and network
analysis (artificial intelligence).[33] The Big Data used can include any combination
of: (i) transactions (sales volumes and average selling prices); (ii) reputation-related
information (claims ratio, handling time, reviews, and complaints); and (iii) industry-
specific characteristics (sales seasonality, demand trends, and macroeconomic sensi-
tivity). This can be enriched by using non-traditional data obtained via social media
and other channels, in addition to credit and payment history data.[34] These multiple

---

[29] See Financial Stability Board (n 24).
[30] Jon Frost et al, 'BigTech and the Changing Structure of Financial Intermediation' (BIS Papers No.
779, Monetary and Economic Department, Bank for International Settlements, April 2019) 7, 9
<www.bis.org/publ/work779.htm>.
[31] See Dirk A Zetzsche, Douglas W Arner, and Ross P Buckley, 'Decentralized Finance' (2020) 6(2)
Journal of Financial Regulation 172 <https://doi.org/10.1093/jfr/fjaa010>.
[32] Frost et al (n 30) 9–10.
[33] Ibid 14.
[34] See Bank for International Settlements (n 25) 66.

data points, taken together, can provide a better picture of a borrower's financial health and ability to repay a loan, and are applicable to both individuals and businesses.[35] These applications of technology can be far more efficient and effective than traditional methods. They are efficient as BigTechs can make quicker and more accurate determinations of credit allocation than traditional banks, and more effective because they are able to reach and service the large numbers of unbanked and underbanked people and businesses (particularly micro- and small-and-medium-sized enterprises, or 'MSMEs') typically neglected by traditional banks. These efficiencies can be further enhanced by cost savings using cloud computing and data servers which can reduce or remove the need for traditional brick-and-mortar branches and staff who meet individual customers in person. BigTechs simply invite individuals and institutions to log on to their platforms and interact with user-friendly APIs from the comfort of their smartphones or computers.

The entrance of BigTechs into financial services has been a boon for financial inclusion, particularly in emerging market and developing economies (EMDEs).[36] By acting as intermediaries, BigTech platforms have opened the door to digital payments, savings and investment opportunities, and alternative sources of finance. Some of these alternative finance models include platform-based lending (as described above), debt and equity crowdfunding, peer-to-peer (P2P) lending, and invoice-based lending. Further, by developing and deploying sophisticated payment tools and infrastructure, such as the Quick Response (QR) code-based systems, which have rapidly gained popularity in several Asian and Latin American countries,[37] BigTechs have contributed to economic growth and development.

The best examples are in China which we have discussed in Section II(B)(2) of Chapter 6. In 2004, Alibaba created Alipay, a payment service, to enable electronic payments that support e-commerce and spun it off into a separate affiliate in 2011 (renamed as Ant Financial in 2014).[38] By 2020, almost a billion people used Alipay, with similar numbers using TenPay. From payments, Ant expanded into money market funds (Yu'e Bao) in 2013 as an alternative saving and investment tool, and before its 2018 peak Yu'e Bao had become the largest such fund in the world in 2017.[39] Ant also branched into platform lending, becoming one of the largest consumer and MSME lenders in China and one of the largest issuers of asset-backed

---

[35] Frost et al (n 30) 14.

[36] Karen Croxson et al, 'Platform-based Business Models and Financial Inclusion' (BIS Papers No. 986, Monetary and Economic Department, Bank for International Settlements, January 2022) <www.bis .org/publ/work986.htm> 10–13; Financial Stability Board (n 21) 17–18.

[37] Financial Stability Board (n 21) 10.

[38] Aaron Klein, *China's Digital Payments Revolution* (Report, The Brookings Institution, April 2020) 7 <www.brookings.edu/research/chinas-digital-payments-revolution>.

[39] Ibid 8; Stella Yifan Xie, 'More Than a Third of China Is Now Invested in One Giant Mutual Fund', *The Wall Street Journal* (online, 27 March 2019) <www.wsj.com/articles/more-than-a-third-of-china-is-now-invested-in-one-giant-mutual-fund-11553682785>.

securities (to finance these lending operations) by 2018.[40] By 2020, Ant had expanded across payments, wealth management, lending, insurance, credit scoring, and data sales services.[41] Ant's only major competitor was fellow BigTech Tencent (which owns the dominant messaging and social network app WeChat), and the two firms accounted for 94 per cent of the payments market.[42] As seen in China, BigTechs are able to generate and command such significant economies of scope and scale as to existentially threaten traditional financial institutions.[43] At the same time, their dominance triggered a comprehensive regulatory response in China across 2020 and 2021 which continues to evolve and has curtailed the growth of Ant in particular.

The entrance of any new actor or activity in financial services can pose risks to financial stability, market integrity, competition, and consumer protection.[44] This is particularly so where the new actors do not operate primarily within the financial industry. As e-commerce, telecommunication, or social media platforms, the new actors typically engage a multitude of other regulatory issues, such as data privacy and cybersecurity. This is also the case as incumbents seek to pursue similar approaches and models on the basis of the digitalisation of finance.

Moreover, like global SIFIs but perhaps more so, the sheer size and global spread of BigTechs pose systemic and cross-border risks that can perplex and daunt regulators and policymakers. For example, regulators now have to grapple with BigTechs accumulating vast amounts of data in ways that raise barriers to entry, support anticompetitive practices, and present novel risks to consumers' data privacy and protection.[45] These issues arise from the DNA model, network effects, and economies of scope and scale that all combine to drive the emergence of concentration and dominance through the platformisation of finance.[46] Problems also stem from the pursuit of 'ecosystem' models, based on the exclusive acquisition and control of data, that seek to lock customers into corporate 'walled gardens'.[47] This approach is characteristic of MAGMA, BATs, and most tech firms engaging in financial services. Most FinTech start-ups seek to build ecosystems and platforms with the intention of growing into Big FinTechs, as occurred with earlier FinTechs such as Bloomberg, Visa, and PayPal. Financial institutions transforming into data platforms have followed

---

[40] Frost et al (n 30) 10.

[41] Financial Stability Board (n 21) 4.

[42] See 'Digital Disruption in Banking and its Impact on Competition', OECD (Web Page, 2020) <www.oecd.org/daf/competition/digital-disruption-in-financial-markets.htm>; Croxson et al (n 36) 16–17; Dennis Ferenzy, A New Kind of Conglomerate: BigTech in China (Institute of International Finance, November 2018) 12.

[43] See Financial Stability Board(n 21) 10.

[44] See Frost et al (n 30) 9–10; see Bank for International Settlements (n 25) 55.

[45] See Bank for International Settlements (n 25) 67–8.

[46] See also Croxson et al (n 36) 4–5.

[47] See, for example, Qian Tong, 'China's Assault on Big Tech's "Walled Gardens"', *Nikkei Asia* (online, 28 September 2021) <https://asia.nikkei.com/Spotlight/Caixin/China-s-assault-on-Big-Tech-s-walled-gardens>.

similar paths, such as BlackRock in asset management, Ping An in insurance, and Citadel and Robinhood in trading. This is the TechFin model of applying a data-centred approach to finance. It is even the approach of DLT platforms such as Ethereum, with decentralisation in time requiring platformisation.

This evolutionary growth results in a cycle of concentration and dominance. Yet still, according to a recent report by University College London's Institute for Innovation and Public Purpose, it is likely that we are underestimating the true extent of this dominance and its resulting wealth because of how disclosure frameworks are currently designed.[48] At present, reporting rules mandated by the US Securities and Exchange Commission give BigTech firms significant discretion as to which product financials they disclose and when. This enables them to keep large products, often with dominant user bases, hidden from investors and potential competitors, limiting the ability of regulators to police highly profitable digital platforms. These large user bases, typically generated from 'free' services, are a critical source for data aggregation, cross subsidisation, and further monetisation strategies. For example, Google Chrome and the Android mobile operating system both contribute significantly towards Google's user acquisition and retention, thus driving revenue generation on its other products including online ads, Google Search, and the Android App Store. Thus, data and technology businesses are often characterised as 'winner-takes-all' or 'winner-takes-most' industries in which oligopolies or even monopolies are a natural result[49] Consequently, while the platformisation of finance as an extension of BigTech ecosystems can deliver considerable benefits for consumers, the tendency towards concentration and dominance brings a range of risks and concerns. These can span from reductions in competition and innovation to security (both of personal data and in financial stability and national security) and eventually to inequality. This is the new 'too-big-to-fail'.

It is also potentially the catalyst for the emergence of firms which are 'too-big-to-regulate'. For example, a recent International Monetary Fund study found that firms with significant market power and cash reserves, such as Apple and Alphabet (parent of Google) with $200 billion and $150 billion of cash reserves, respectively, and market capitalisations over $1 trillion, are less sensitive to regulatory efforts through monetary policy change.[50] Consequently, policymakers and regulators need to respond thoughtfully, strategically, and with growing urgency. The benefits

---

[48] Ilan Strauss et al, *Crouching Tiger, Hidden Dragons: How 10-K Disclosure Rules Help Big Tech Conceal Market Power and Expand Platform Dominance* (Policy Report No. 2021/04, Institute for Innovation and Public Purpose, University College London) 4–5.

[49] Joost Rietveld and Melissa A Schilling, 'Platform Competition: A Systematic and Interdisciplinary Review of the Literature' (2021) 47(6) *Journal of Management* 1528 <https://doi.org/10.1177/0149206320969791>.

[50] Romain Duval et al, 'Market Power and Monetary Policy Transmission' (Working Paper No. 21/184, International Monetary Fund, July 2021) 2–3 <www.imf.org/en/Publications/WP/Issues/2021/07/09/Market-Power-and-Monetary-Policy-Transmission-461332>.

and challenges are such that governments are looking to develop their own digital finance platforms in response, such as CBDCs.[51]

In the next section, we consider the major regulatory issues applicable to BigTechs and other large digital finance platforms and their global operations, starting with the question of whether existing frameworks are sufficient to address the rising challenges and opportunities from the platformisation of finance.

V. OPPORTUNITIES FROM TECHFINS AND DIGITAL FINANCIAL PLATFORMS

The combination of economies of scope and scale of finance with the network effects of data and technology brings tremendous benefits and opportunities, particularly for consumers and for financial inclusion.

A. *Reducing Transaction Costs*

Technology and the data underlying TechFins can reduce transaction costs. Traditional financial institutions have fixed transaction costs for each contract. If technology can automate procedures, transaction costs should reduce once the initial investment in software and server set-up (i.e., sunk costs) has been recuperated. Reducing transaction costs is not unique to TechFins: this is the rationale for most FinTech and information technology innovations such as distributed ledger technologies or even interbank electronic payment systems.[52]

B. *Improved Business Decisions and Risk Management*

TechFins' big data approach should improve business decisions. This is because TechFins' datasets are typically more comprehensive and therefore of higher quality than those of incumbent financial institutions. Traditional banks only practice the 'back-end' of transactions: the cash flow processed from bank accounts, accompanied by qualitative statements from the client on projected income and expenses. The 'front-end' of transactions is the client relationship: customer product preferences, which network participants contacted the client and for what reasons, which contracts were entered into or terminated, and which goods were returned and why. This information enables a TechFin to form a far more accurate representation, in close to real time, of the actual financial position of an individual or a business when considering offering financial services.

---

[51] Bank for International Settlements, *Annual Economic Report 2021* (Report, June 2021) 65 <www.bis .org/publ/arpdf/ar2021e.htm>. See Chapter III, CBDCs: An Opportunity for the Monetary System.

[52] Kim Kaivanto and Daniel Prince, *Risks and Transaction Costs of Distributed-Ledger Fintech: Boundary Effects and Consequences* (Lancaster University, 2017) 2 <https://arxiv.org/pdf/1702.08478.pdf>.

TechFin datasets comprise a large cross section of society and the economy. This is because TechFins originate and leverage data derived from social media and e-commerce into financial services to an extent which is unattainable for traditional financial institutions. For example, correlations may indicate that the purchase of door stoppers to prevent doors from damaging walls correlates with conscientious homeowners who are slightly more creditworthy.[53] The challenge of the next decade is identifying which correlations are random and which function as appropriate bases for prudent business decisions.

C. *Financial Inclusion*

TechFins can also facilitate financial inclusion by replacing the need, common in traditional banking, for interpersonal relationships.

1. SMEs and Consumer Loans

In the past, relationship banking was characterised by a high level of personal trust from long-standing business relationships.[54] From a big data perspective, the relationship banker (located at a branch) collected an enormous number of client data points based on multiple transactions and information collected from, for example, discussions, business lunches, referrals from other clients, and so on. Relationship banking for small clients has been replaced by data analytics. Traditional financial institutions are now focusing on relationship services for large clients, while SMEs and small clients are offered either standardised services or excluded altogether.

In contrast, with TechFins, the costs of an automated contract are basically the same regardless of volume after sunk costs have been recuperated. Once automated (and in the absence of costly regulation), the risks associated with a transaction will determine business strategies and decisions.

From a risk perspective, big data should drive strategic change. The general assumption in the past has been that lending to small businesses is high risk,[55] whether due to a higher likelihood of failure or a lack of professional management. By compiling more comprehensive datasets and extracting more accurate data analytics, TechFins are in a better position to assess risk and the customer's credit rating, and to 'personalise' the financial relationship through algorithms. In fact,

---

[53] Example provided by Paul Schulte during the launch of his book, Paul Schulte, *The Next Revolution in Our Credit-Driven Economy: The Advent of Financial Technology* (Wiley, 1st ed, 2015), on 4 September 2015.

[54] Ross P Buckley, 'The Changing Nature of Banking and Why It Matters' in Ross P Buckley, Emilios Avgouleas and Douglas W Arner (eds) *Reconceptualising Global Finance and Its Regulation* (Cambridge University Press, 2016) 9–27.

[55] See, for example, 'Basel III: International Regulatory Framework for Banks', *Bank for International Settlements* (Web Page) <www.bis.org/bcbs/basel3.htm>.

MYbank, Alibaba's SME lending arm, was able to finance more than 16 million small businesses, with a default rate of only 1 per cent.[56] Data-based finance could simultaneously be more attuned to customers' real risk profile (only if the data-based methodology is sound) and more inclusive by providing affordable 'personalised' financial services.

2. Developing Countries

Lower transaction costs and better access to risk-related data also explain the remarkable tech-based financial inclusion prompted by TechFins in developing countries, such as through M-Pesa and M-KESHO.[57] While an in-depth examination is beyond the scope of this chapter, we note that technology has revolutionised access to financial services in many countries, especially in East Africa and parts of Asia, principally through mobile phone–based e-money services such as M-Pesa.

VI. CONCLUSION

The rise of TechFins and financial platforms will redefine the entire industry in years to come. These new market entrants into financial services represent a clear existential threat to traditional banks.

TechFins have not evolved from FinTechs but instead represent a new type of market participant. They originate in technology or e-commerce environments which are typically connected to a multitude of clients (both consumers and/or small businesses) and have access to very deep pools of data. TechFins can enter the world of finance by providing data, either raw or processed, to incumbent financial institutions and/or FinTech start-ups. Over time, the likelihood is that many TechFins will start providing financial services directly to their customers.

Efficient financial services can be provided by TechFins to society. In particular, TechFins can reduce transaction costs and improve decision-making by using a more comprehensive dataset than that of established financial intermediaries. These two advantages can lead to an increased level of financial inclusion for SMEs, consumers, and the underprivileged. But while scope, scale, and network effects bring benefits, they also result in the emergence of new SIFIs and FMIs. Size, concentration, and dominance bring new risks as well as new opportunities.

---

[56] See Bloomberg, 'Jack Ma's US$290 Billion Loan Machine at MYbank Is Changing Chinese Banking, in a Harbinger of the Financial Industry's Revolution', *South China Morning Post* (online, 29 July 2019) <www.scmp.com/business/banking-finance/article/3020457/jack-mas-us290-billion-loan-machine-mybank-changing>.

[57] See Ross P Buckley and Sarah Webster, 'FinTech in Developing Countries: Charting New Customer Journeys' (2016) 44 *Journal of Financial Transformation* 151–9; Ross P Buckley, Jonathan Greenacre and Louise Malady, 'The Regulation of Mobile Money in Malawi' (2015) 14(3) *Washington University Global Studies Law Review Global Studies Law Review* 435, 441–5.

17

The New Systemic Risks

Cybersecurity and Data Risks

SUMMARY

Since the 1960s, finance has undergone a long process of digital transformation and is today probably the most globalised segment of the world's economy and among the most digitised and datafied. This process is evident across four major axes: the emergence of global wholesale markets, an explosion of financial technology (FinTech) start-ups since 2008, an unprecedented digital financial transformation in developing countries (particularly China), and the increasing role of large technology companies (BigTechs) in financial services. This process of digital financial transformation brings structural changes with both benefits and risks. This chapter considers new risks, particularly new systemic risks which have emerged, focusing on cybersecurity and data.

I. FINANCE, TECHNOLOGY, AND FINANCE: FRAMEWORK OF ANALYSIS

As analysed in Chapter 14, in 2019 Facebook sought to create a new electronic payment system for its social media ecosystem based on a new payment instrument called Libra, allowing it to facilitate the financial interactions of its 3 billion users globally, particularly in developing countries without similar sorts of payments infrastructure.[1] Facebook wanted to be, like WeChat in China, the 'app for everything' – the app through which customers could conduct most of their online life – and an in-app payments system was essential to realising that vision.

While this proposal never came to pass, it highlights many of the key areas of concern raised by digital financial transformation: What if Libra was hacked and destroyed (cybersecurity risk)? What if Facebook had used the data acquired for its own purposes (data protection and privacy risk)? What if user data were stolen (data security risk)?

---

[1] See Dirk A Zetzsche, Ross P Buckley, and Douglas W Arner, 'Regulating Libra' (2021) 41(1) *Oxford Journal of Legal Studies* 80.

What if Facebook came to dominate the international financial system as a result of Libra (new systemically important financial institution risk)? What if Libra became the dominant international form of money (technological infrastructure risk, threats to competition)? These concerns, coupled with the potential loss of monetary sovereignty, explain the hostile response to Libra from regulators around the globe.[2]

These risks are key considerations for financial regulation. The objectives of financial regulation can be summarised in four major categories: (1) financial stability, (2) financial integrity, (3) customer protection, and (4) financial efficiency, development, and inclusion. Financial stability can be seen both negatively (as avoidance of crises) and positively (as appropriate functioning of the financial system). Financial integrity focuses on prevention of criminal activities and use of the financial markets for criminal activities, for instance money laundering, terrorist financing, international criminal organisations, and even state organised attacks. Customer protection focuses on systems to prevent abuses of users of financial services: consumers, savers, and investors. Financial efficiency, development, and inclusion focus on how to support and enhance the positive functioning and role of the financial system.

While FinTech raises concerns in all of these areas, our focus in this Part and Chapter is on financial stability, a core focus of regulators around the world particularly since 2008. Prior to 2008, the focus in terms of supporting financial stability and preventing crises was on the identification of major forms of risk and building appropriate regulatory and supervisory frameworks to address these, with the Basel II Capital Accord the state-of-the-art embodiment at an international level. Financial regulation in general focused on a 'microprudential' approach prior to 2008, in which regulators and supervisors placed the greatest emphasis on the safety and soundness of individual financial institutions through prudential regulatory standards such as Basel II.

This approach focused on five major categories of risk: credit/counterparty risk, market risk, payment risk, operational risk, and legal risk. Basel II included capital charges and related regulatory standards for the first four of these (with relatively little attention paid to legal risk).

In this framework, risks relating to technological and data issues were incorporated into the operational risk framework, thus incurring a relatively small cost in terms of capital charges and related risk management and compliance systems. Since 2008, financial stability regulation has focused very heavily on addressing 'macroprudential' risks: risks arising not just from the potential failure of individual institutions but from interdependencies in markets, which were at the heart of the 2008 financial crisis and thus have been central to post-crisis financial regulatory reform. Related analyses are now beginning to extend to a range of considerations and risks from FinTech.

We suggest that with digital financial transformation, this treatment is no longer sufficient nor appropriate to capture the full range of risks faced by the financial system.

---

[2] For a summary of countries' responses, see ibid.

In looking at digital financial transformation, an appropriate framework of analysis encompasses: (1) new sources of traditional forms of risk; (2) new forms of risk; and (3) entirely new markets and systems, including for regulation (such as regulatory technology: RegTech).

We develop this framework by discussing a number of key areas of concern that have emerged during the process of digital financial transformation, in particular cybersecurity and data protection (the focus of this chapter), the emergence of new systemically important financial institutions, and the emergence of new financial market infrastructures and dependencies (considered in detail in Chapters 18 and 19).

II. DIGITAL FINANCE AND SYSTEMIC RISK

Traditionally, issues relating to technology have been included in operational risk, which is recognised as one key form of financial risk along with credit risk, market risk, and legal risk.[3] As a result of the emergence of digitisation and datafication, we suggest that technology risks (including those relating to cybersecurity and data privacy) should be seen as a separate form of risk, beyond the traditional operational risk categorisation. Technology risks can arise in the context of individual institutions and in the interconnections among institutions. Even more fundamentally, technology risks have the potential to directly impact financial sector confidence and stability. As a result of digital financial transformation, cybersecurity has become one of the major sources of systemic risk in the financial system. This view is increasingly being expressed by the Basel Committee as well.[4]

Before we give a detailed view of the new tech-induced threats, some background on systemic risk is required to contextualise our analysis.

Systemic risk has long been a major focus in financial regulation, particularly banking regulation.[5] According to the G10:[6]

> [s]*ystemic financial* risk is the risk that an event will trigger a loss of economic value or confidence in, and attendant increases in uncertainty about, a substantial portion of the financial system that is serious enough to quite probably have significant adverse effects on the real economy.

[3] See Basel Committee on Banking Supervision, *Basel III: A Global Regulatory Framework for More Resilient Banking and Banking Systems* (Report, Bank for International Settlements, June 2011) <www.bis.org/publ/bcbs189.pdf>.

[4] Basel Committee on Banking Supervision, 'Basel Committee Issues Principles for Operational Resilience and Risk' (Press Release, Bank for International Settlements, 31 March 2021) <www.bis .org/press/p210331a.htm>.

[5] Steven L Schwarcz, 'Systematic Regulation of Systemic Risk' (2019) 2019(1) *Wisconsin Law Review* 1–53; see also Douglas W Arner et al (eds), *Systemic Risk in the Financial Sector: Ten Years after the Great Crash* (CIGI Press, 2019).

[6] Group of Ten, Report on Consolidation in the Financial Sector (Report, January 2001) 126 <www.bis .org/publ/gten05.pdf>.

Prior to the 2008 Global Financial Crisis (GFC), financial stability regulation was a core regulatory function, focusing on the identification, prevention, and management of systemic risk.[7] The focus was generally on banks – usually excluding non-bank financial institutions – and in particular on the larger individual institutions (the 'too big to fail' (TBTF) problem) and the payments system.

Yet despite decades of experience and effort, systemic risk was a core feature of the 2008 GFC, highlighting distinct failures in financial stability regulation.[8]

Following the 2008 GFC, there was a general consensus that systemic risk usually arises from the financial intermediary's size (TBTF) or from interrelationships between intermediaries ('too connected to fail': TCTF). Both TBTF and TCTF are now seen as core aspects of financial stability regulation, both from the microprudential (TBTF) and the macroprudential (TCTF) standpoint.

Since the 2008 financial crisis, large volumes of research have sharpened the understanding of systemic risk. As defined by former US Federal Reserve Chair Ben Bernanke, a systemically important financial institution (SIFI) 'is one whose size, complexity, interconnectedness, and critical functions are such that, should the firm go unexpectedly into liquidation, the rest of the financial system and the economy would face severe adverse consequences.'[9] SIFIs – particularly global SIFIs (G-SIFIs) – have thus become a central focus of the G20/Financial Stability Board post-crisis regulatory reform agenda, as well as a key focus of domestic and regional regulatory reforms since 2008.

In the context of the TBTF paradigm, systemic significance follows from the size of a financial institution.[10] Under the TCTF paradigm, systemic importance follows from the fact that other financial intermediaries are linked to the financial institution, and all of the linked institutions and intermediaries together are of critical importance for the financial system and cannot readily be replaced. The key post-crisis insight here is that interlinkages can take many forms, not just payment interlinkages, with a particular post-crisis focus on linkages from over-the-counter (OTC) derivatives and the related counterparty risk. In addition, interlinkages are now seen as arising from common business models (e.g., originate-to-distribute), contractual approaches (e.g., standardised documentation such as that of ISDA), and commonalities across risk-management systems.

---

[7] See Douglas W Arner, *Financial Stability, Economic Growth, and the Role of Law* (Cambridge University Press, 2007).

[8] See Steven L Schwarcz, 'Systemic Risk' (2008) 97(1) *Georgetown Law Journal* 193.

[9] Ben S Bernanke, 'Causes of the Recent Financial and Economic Crisis' (Testimony before the Financial Crisis Enquiry Commission, United States Congress, 2 September 2010) <www.federalreserve .gov/newsevents/testimony/bernanke20100902a.htm>.

[10] Luc Laeven, Lev Ratnovski, and Hui Tong, 'Bank Size and Systemic Risk' (International Monetary Fund Staff Discussion Note SDN/14/04, May 2014) <www.imf.org/external/pubs/ft/sdn/2014/ sdn1404.pdf>.

One consequence of systemic importance is that, for political reasons, governments are invariably pressed to provide massive support to systemically important financial institutions if they face financial problems.[11]

Much of the G20/FSB post-crisis regulatory agenda thus focuses on the prevention of systemic risk through a range of financial stability systems, including: (1) microprudential supervision of SIFIs, particularly G-SIFIs; (2) macroprudential supervision to identify interconnections and risks prior to any crisis trigger; and (3) strengthening core infrastructures, particularly in the context of systemically important infrastructures such as payment systems, securities settlement systems, and central counterparties.[12] These have been undertaken through a wide range of efforts: domestic, regional, and international, including regulatory changes and changes to the scope of regulatory mandates (in individual jurisdictions as well as through the Financial Stability Board) and the creation of new systemic risk supervisory structures (such as the European Systemic Risk Board in the EU and the Financial Stability Oversight Council in the United States).

III. CYBERSECURITY AND SYSTEMIC RISK

Cybersecurity has become one of the leading foci of financial regulators, governments, and financial and tech firms globally. We suggest cybersecurity is now the most significant source of systemic risk and one of the more significant national security issues. Cyberattacks are consistently increasing in severity and frequency.[13] The increasing digitalisation of critical infrastructure sectors and the growth of the industrial internet of things (IIoT) are exposing organisations to increasingly aggressive and sophisticated attacks.[14] Cyberattacks have been used as a geostrategic tool in the Indo-Pacific region and in military conflicts in Ukraine.[15] The period 2021–22 has seen further examples of ransomware groups targeting governments and critical infrastructure, including the energy, finance, and construction sectors globally.[16] Cybersecurity risk can thus be seen as a new source of

---

[11] See Bernanke (n 9).

[12] See, for example, Kern Alexander and Steven L Schwarcz, 'The Macroprudential Quandary: Unsystematic Efforts to Reform Financial Regulation' in Ross P Buckley, Emilios Avgouleas, and Douglas D Arner (eds) *Reconceptualising Global Finance and Its Regulation* (Cambridge University Press, 2016) 127–58.

[13] 'From Stricter Reporting Rules to a New Cyber Threat Hub, the EU Is Upgrading Its Cybersecurity Law', *World Economic Forum* (Web Page, 2 December 2022) <www.weforum.org/agenda/2022/12/cybersecurity-european-union-nis>.

[14] See World Economic Forum, 'European Commission's Cybersecurity Package: Commentary in Light of Recent Sophisticated Supply Chain Attacks' (European Commission Paper, June 2021) 11 <www3.weforum.org/docs/WEF_Commentary_in_light_of_recent_sophisticated_supply_chain_attacks_2021.pdf>.

[15] See Australian Cyber Security Center, July 2021 – June 2022 Annual Cyber Threat Report (Report, 2022) 30 <www.cyber.gov.au/sites/default/files/2022-11/ACSC-Annual-Cyber-Threat-Report-2022.pdf>.

[16] See Australian Cyber Security Center (n 15) 53–5.

traditional risk as well as an entirely new form of risk with potentially catastrophic consequences.

From the standpoint of SIFIs, which have almost entirely digitised their operations, hacking, cybertheft, cyberterrorism, cyberactivism, and cyberattacks all pose grave risks. While financial institutions have long focused on all forms of fraud and theft risk, digitisation and globalisation raise the potential for even simple fraud and theft to take on much greater scale: instead of robbing one account, office, or firm, an attacker can potentially rob or attack all accounts and offices of more than one firm in multiple jurisdictions at the same time. The challenge here is increased by the wide range of motivations of attackers.

While regulators – in individual jurisdictions, internationally, and regionally – are focusing attention on related issues, the wide range of actors and motivations are a challenge: though it is clearly appropriate and necessary for all financial institutions and infrastructure providers to focus significant resources and efforts on cybersecurity, the large role of state and state-supported actors highlights the difficulties of pushing the entire burden onto the financial sector. Concurrently, the shift towards FinTech exacerbates certain cybersecurity threats that are unique to the financial system. Vulnerabilities in the financial system stem from the high level of leverage, asset conversion chains, and procyclicality.[17] The growing dependence on complex digitalised information technology hubs without substitutes is contrasted by the growing amount of outwards facing FinTech, which tends to increase cyber exposure.[18] Cyberattacks can exploit these security gaps to, for example, disrupt payment systems, corrupt data at custodian banks or central securities depositories, or cripple infrastructure on which the financial system relies. While these may be low frequency events, their occurrence may have huge impacts that are capable of snowballing into systemic financial destabilisation if not contained.

As a result of the increased state presence in cyberactivities (including cyberwarfare), there is a clear need for states to take a leading role in building systems to monitor and support key sectors of the economy – such as the financial sector – in addition to private and regulatory attention to issues of cybersecurity.

We posit three factors that transform cybersecurity into a new form of risk, and one that is material to financial stability. These are: (1) the growing rate of technological development and adoption in finance, (2) the lag and divergence in international FinTech governance, and (3) the erosion of trust from the conflation of national security and financial stability in the cyber domain.

---

[17]   Martin Boer and Jaime Vazquez, '*Cyber Security and Financial Stability: How Cyber-Attacks Could Materially Impact the Global Financial System*' (Institute of International Finance, 2017) <www.iif .com/Portals/0/Files/IIF%20Cyber%20Financial%20Stability%20Paper%20Final%2009%2007%20 2017.pdf?ver=2019-02-19-150125-767>.

[18]   Artie W Ng and Benny KB Kwok, 'Emergence of Fintech and Cybersecurity in a Global Financial Centre' (2017) 25(4) *Journal of Financial Regulation and Compliance* <www.emerald.com/insight/ content/doi/10.1108/JFRC-01-2017-0013/full/html>.

A. *Risk from the Growing Rate of FinTech Development*

The first layer of cyber risk stems from the high rate and typology of technological development and adoption of digital systems in finance. The growing transition to cloud infrastructure creates more concentrated data nodes, with less software diversity, requiring higher security measures.[19] Endogenous threats to such nodes stem from compromises of internal firm or client information and unauthorised access to systems by or via users or employees. Exogenous threats involve breaches from interfacing with other third-party systems or using fraudulently acquired privileged account credentials to access data and perform transactions. Both threats form several concentric layers of security risk by depending on the security of third-party software in the likes of (i) colocation centres holding primary server data or (ii) employee mobile and other IoT devices. For example, in 2016 criminals stole $81 million from the central bank of Bangladesh, by infecting a Swift server with malware.[20] With more interconnected and digitised technology, cyber security is only as strong as the weakest link in the network.

New FinTech, like distributed ledger technologies, blockchain, and stablecoins, comes with their own set of risks. While their novel methods of centralisation (or decentralisation) provide unique value to their users, they still tend to be based on traditional or cloud-based infrastructure. Depending on the level of centralisation and 'chain'-related status, updating the infrastructure of the technology can be difficult. With no clear contingency mechanism, a security breach can instantly disrupt the network. One of the ironies is that much of the appeal of cryptocurrencies for some investors is their decentralised nature, and yet the difficulties around self-custody of one's private key almost invariably mean investors trusting the custody of their cryptocurrency to exchanges which have often proven to be the weakest link in the system and the most frequent target of successful hacks.

B. *Risk from Lagging and Divergent International FinTech Governance*

The second layer of risk stems from lag and divergence in cyber governance in different countries. While cyberspace is a high-speed, frictionless global network, its regulation is fragmented, with at best significant gaps and at worst normative clashes between various actors. At national levels, particularly in less mature regulatory environments, severe discrepancies leave smaller private and public entities

---

[19] Centre for Risk Studies, Cyber Risk Outlook 2019 (Report, University of Cambridge Judge Business School, May 2019) <www.jbs.cam.ac.uk/faculty-research/centres/risk/publications/technology-and-space/cyber-risk-outlook/cyber-risk-outlook-2019>.

[20] Emanuel Kopp, Lincoln Kaffenberger and Christopher Wilson, 'Cyber Risk, Market Failures, and Financial Stability' (International Monetary Fund Working Paper WP/17/185, 2017) 4 <www.imf.org/en/Publications/WP/Issues/2017/08/07/Cyber-Risk-Market-Failures-and-Financial-Stability-45104>.

vulnerable, opening the wider system to cascading effects from breached entities. Attempts to lessen such sectoral discrepancies are nascent.

The United States, for example, has embraced public–private partnerships, with the *Cybersecurity Information Sharing Act of 2015* inviting private entities and certain government agencies to share information on threats with federal agencies. The National Institute of Standards and Technology and the Financial Industry Regulatory Authority collect, identify, assess, and respond to risks between public and private entities, exchanging best practices. However, these are largely soft measures with varying membership across sectors and size. Hard measures generating systemic protection are also increasing. For example, New York has implemented comprehensive cybersecurity rules requiring financial service firms to appoint chief information security officers, conduct periodic risk assessments, and protect sensitive data,[21] while California, for example, avoids prescriptive requirements in favour of risk-based security centred on consumer data protection.[22]

Likewise, the EU Network and Information Security Directive adopted in 2016 sets a minimum level of harmonisation among Member States, setting a single point of contact and creating computer security incident response teams (CSIRTs).[23] Yet, Czechia has two national CSIRTs, Estonia has one, and Spain has one each for the public and private sectors.[24] In the case that an incident is recorded, cooperation among law enforcement is difficult, given the number of jurisdictions involved and the inefficiencies persisting in cross-border collaboration.[25] These differences are capable of placing additional burdens on attempts at cooperation, thereby facilitating hackers' business and extending cyber incident contagion.[26]

C. *Risk from Conflating National Security and Financial Stability*

The third layer of risk is tied to the convergence of national security and financial stability in the cyber domain. Where cybersecurity has conventionally been understood

---

[21] NYCRR tit 23 § 500.00 (2017).

[22] US, AB 375, *California Consumer Privacy Act*, 2017–2018, Reg Sess, Cal, 2018 (enacted).

[23] *Directive (EU) 2016/1148 of the European Parliament and of the Council of 6 July 2016 Concerning Measures for a High Common Level of Security of Network and Information Systems across the Union* [2016] OJ L 194/1.

[24] European Union Agency for Cybersecurity, 2021 Report on CSIRT-LE Cooperation: A Study of the Roles and Synergies among Sixteen Selected EU/EEA Member States (Report, March 2022) <www .enisa.europa.eu/publications/2021-report-on-csirt-law-enforcement-cooperation>.

[25] See Sabrina Galli, 'NYDFS Cybersecurity Regulations: A Blueprint for Uniform State Statute' (2018) 22(1) *North Carolina Banking Institute Journal* 235; John Ogle, 'Identities Lost: Enacting Federal Law Mandating Disclosure and Notice after a Data Security Breach' (2019) 72(1) *Arkansas Law Review* 221.

[26] See Loretta J Mester, 'Perspectives on Cybersecurity, the Financial System, and the Federal Reserve' (Speech on 2019 Ohio Bankers Day, Ohio Division of Financial Institutions, 4 April 2019) <www .clevelandfed.org/newsroom-and-events/speeches/sp-20190404-perspectives-on-cybersecurity-the-financial-system-and-the-federal-reserve>.

as a state responsibility, aimed at protecting internal critical infrastructure and cyberspace from national security incidents, increasingly interconnected data and transaction flows necessitate broadening the mandate. However, the defence origins of cybersecurity can lead to vastly varying approaches to transnational cybersecurity cooperation, which may hamper the intelligence pooling necessary to effectively prevent cyber incidents. Recent challenges for CSIRTs often display this.

Hundreds of CSIRTs across the world perform similar primary functions in both the public and private sectors. They (i) coordinate prevention efforts against cyberthreats, (ii) disseminate information regarding cybersecurity practices and incidents, (iii) remediate damage by securing breached data, and (iv) recover public and private systems after a cyber-attack on national infrastructure.[27] To disseminate and develop intelligence and best practices among themselves, various informal cybersecurity networks were established connecting CSIRTs to one another, aiming to foster collective cybersecurity.[28] Such 'walled-gardens' remain the main vehicles of best practice, toolsets, and communication exchange between CSIRTs, mitigating the asymmetry of capacity between various teams.[29]

As CSIRT functions evolve to meet the demands of their respective governments, their duties can expand to include law enforcement or intelligence activity. This can alter their ability to reveal vulnerabilities or raise the suspicion of network members to the use of received information for political purposes. Through no fault of their own, CSIRTs risk being isolated from the 'web of trust', cutting them off from access to the latest vulnerabilities and leaving them in something of an information vacuum.[30] CSIRT groupings can create significantly more cyber-resilience than individual units.[31] As these networks are comprised of both public and private

---

[27] Christopher S Yoo, 'Cyber Espionage or Cyberwar? International Law, Domestic Law, and Self-Protective Measures' in Jens David Ohlin, Kevin Govern, and Clair Finkelstein (eds), *Cyber War: Law and Ethics for Virtual Conflicts* (Oxford University Press, 1st ed, 2015) 175–94.

[28] The largest network, FIRST (Forum of Incident Response and Security Teams) was established in 1990. Membership has grown from a handful of CSIRTs in North America in the year of formation, to 661 from 102 countries by December 2022: 'First Members around the World', *FIRST* (Web Page, December 2022) <www.first.org/members/map>.

[29] Isabel Skierka et al, 'CSIRT Basics for Policy-Makers: The History, Types, and Culture of Computer Security Incident Response Teams' (Working Paper, New America and the Global Public Policy Institute, 2015) 8 <www.gppi.net/publications/global-internet-politics/article/csirtbasics-for-policy-makers>.

[30] Jaco Robertson, Marthie Lessing, and Simon Nare, 'Preparedness and Response to Cyber Threats Require a CSIRT' (International Federation for Information Processing TC9 Workshop on ICT Uses in Warfare and the Safeguarding of Peace, 2008); see also Robert Morgus et al, 'National CSIRTS and Their Role in Computer Security Incident Response' (Report, New America and the Global Public Policy Institute, November 2015) 22–8 <www.newamerica.org/cybersecurity-initiative/policy-papers/national-csirts-and-their-role-in-computer-security-incident-response>, for the recommendation to disassociate national CSIRTs from law enforcement and intelligence agencies.

[31] Joseph S Nye, 'The Regime Complex for Managing Global Cyber Activities' (Global Commission on Internet Governance Paper Series No. 1, Centre for International Governance Innovation, May 2014) <www.cigionline.org/sites/default/files/gcig_paper_no1.pdf>.

sector teams, limiting the access of one team to information can disable cybersecurity capacity, increasing financial destabilisation risk.

Similar misalignments are present at higher policy levels. For instance, the US strategy labels certain private sector firms as a subset of critical infrastructure due to their potentially catastrophic national effects on economic security, and US cybersecurity policy has pivoted from defence to deterrence. The Financial Systematic Analysis and Resilience Center, established in 2016 by the heads of eight large US financial service providers, launched a pilot project together with the US government to share threat data on nation-state actors that may pose threats to US national security.[32] The shift towards increasing the role played by major financial players in US intelligence challenges other nations in implementing their own approaches.[33] States must now carefully consider the extent to which US financial service providers with branches in their jurisdictions may collect and transfer information to the US government, which may deter some from information sharing. As other states adopt similar approaches, the risks of fragmentation increase. A final challenge arises from adversarial regimes intentionally and surreptitiously utilising cyberspace against their rivals, which precludes cooperation in cyber with such regimes for the purpose of financial stability. Mitigating this effect to some extent is that such states and regions tend to have separate, mutually independent, FinTech networks.

D. *Risk from Cyber-Monoculture*

One additional cyber risk comes from the lack of cyberdiversity, that is: where most large institutions use the same IT (software, infrastructure, cloud computing), cyber risks increase since cyberattacks against one institution may also succeed against another institution running similar IT systems. Hence, not only the use of tech but also the uniformity of tech applications (which are inherent in the tech economy) create new risks.

IV. ADDRESSING THE SYSTEMIC RISKS OF CYBERSECURITY

Cybersecurity is generally considered mature when concerned with traditional critical infrastructure,[34] but the growth of data and money flows enabled by FinTech may create a dangerous interdependence that tends to avert stakeholder attention from cyber-resilience. To address the aforementioned risks, we suggest expanding the

---

[32]   Chris Bing, 'Inside "Project Indigo": The Quiet Info-Sharing Program between Banks and U.S. Cyber Command', CyberScoop (Web Page, 21 May 2018) <www.cyberscoop.com/project-indigo-fs-isac-cyber-command-information-sharing-dhs>.

[33]   Gil Baram et al, 'Strategic Trends in the Global Cyber Conflict' (2018) 2(3) *Cyber Security: A Peer-Reviewed Journal* 238.

[34]   Basel Committee on Banking Supervision, Cyber-Resilience: Range of Practices (Report, Bank for International Settlements, December 2018) 5, 21 <www.bis.org/bcbs/publ/d454.htm>.

breadth of cyber incident scenarios internationally, involving a variety of FinTechs to not only assess system weaknesses and costs but also clarify liability assignment, which may be instrumental to reduce uncertainty in case of a cyber-caused crisis and aid in promoting a common legal framework. Such tests may also highlight the problems associated with moral hazard and TBTF and TCTF.

Considering national security concerns, we also suggest a comprehensive regulatory effort founded on already established grassroots operational initiatives with experience in pooling preventative, reactive, and proactive cybersecurity efforts. Careful examination should identify entities vulnerable to cyber breaches and capable of impacting financial stability, and relevant intelligence should be shared with other stakeholders at an international level. Policy differences are capable of inhibiting trust between stakeholders, so an apolitical mechanism may be appropriate. The International Committee of the Red Cross offers a model for a confidential and impartial coordinator entity working with independent national sub-structures, capable of tracking threats of contagion internationally.

At the domestic level, there is a clear need for a multi-tiered approach, with coordination efforts at the national level (for national security issues), at the sectoral level (for instance the financial sector, for financial stability issues), and at the industry level, internally and externally, in the context of the so-called 'three lines of defense' (management control, risk and compliance controls, and independent assurance) at both individual institutions and across the financial industry.

Effective cybersecurity is presently one of the largest challenges facing financial institutions, financial systems, and major corporates, more generally, and a major potential source of systemic risk in financial systems. Massive efforts are underway to address it, and more needs to be done.

V. DATA RISKS

In addition to cybersecurity, the increasingly central role of data in the financial sector highlights the second major area of concern: data protection. As highlighted in Chapter 10, different policies are being developed in different economies, partially because of fundamentally different societal approaches, with the United States, China, and EU being the leading examples of legal approaches to use, ownership, and protection of data. Most notably, the EU's General Data Protection Regulation (GDPR) is the most ambitious, harmonised legal approach to date reflecting concerns for an individual's privacy (and in turn establishing a user's rights vis-à-vis the data comptroller).[35] The United States has so far generally taken a business-friendly approach based on limited regulation and full transferability,

---

[35] See, for a short description of the GDPR and its impact on data-driven finance, Dirk A Zetzsche et al, 'The Evolution and Future of Data-Driven Finance in the EU' (2020) 57(2) *Common Market Law Review* 331.

with data governance issues only addressed through federal agencies such as the Federal Trade Commission.[36] This characterisation and approach, however, are now changing, with the enactment of new legislation in California not dissimilar in many ways to the GDPR and with both political parties and most major technology companies now agreeing on the need for new federal legislation in the area. China largely followed a US style laissez-faire approach to data markets until 2020, albeit with a very high level of comfort in state collection and use of data. Since 2020, China has increasingly been developing a framework to maximise the value of aggregate data as a state resource while reducing the concentration and dominance that had emerged from its earlier approach. These variations of approach highlight the major questions about the role of data in digitised and datafied societies and economies: who owns and controls data, and what does ownership and control entail?

In looking at related issues, it is important to distinguish between data security or protection risks, with data privacy risks (which are about the collection and use of personal data, particularly in jurisdictions with extensive privacy protections such as GDPR).

As dissimilitude in national legal approaches and capacities tend to heighten data security and privacy TechRisks,[37] we identify three data security and privacy risks in particular: (1) data manipulation uncertainty risk, (2) FinTech systemic integration risk, and (3) RegTech monitoring and intervention capacity risk.

A. *Data Manipulation Uncertainty Risk*

The compound effects of increasingly concentrated data nodes with more linkages and levels of analysis and subsequent use are as yet unclear. Legal frameworks are generally not constructed to take into account macroprudential data risks. The principle of precaution for data and privacy is thus still nascent. Impact assessment tests required by data controllers under the EU's GDPR, for example, remain 'abstract or imprecise'.[38] Regulators lack a clear understanding of harm caused by bad faith or negligent data transfers across jurisdictions.

To avoid misconstruing data risks by setting narrow goal-based rules, a regulatory shift is taking place towards increasing the accountability of data manipulators by scrutinising the technical construction of algorithms and the auditability of their

---

[36] See, for instance, on Facebook's Cambridge Analytica scandal, Federal Trade Commission, 'FTC Sues Cambridge Analytica, Settles with Former CEO and App Developer: FTC Alleges They Deceived Facebook Users about Data Collection' (Press Release, 24 July 2019) <www.ftc.gov/news-events/press-releases/2019/07/ftc-sues-cambridge-analytica-settles-former-ceo-app-developer>.

[37] World Bank, Trading for Development in the Age of Global Value Chains (World Development Report, 2020) 245 <www.worldbank.org/en/publication/wdr2020>.

[38] Amir Shayan Ahmadian et al, 'Supporting Privacy Impact Assessment by Model-Based Privacy Analysis' (Proceedings of the 33rd Annual ACM Symposium on Applied Computing, April 2018) 1467.

data analytics.[39] While helpful in retrospective investigations, these factors do not work well in mitigating or preventing loss.

B. *FinTech Systemic Integration Risk*

In 2018, Agustin Carstens highlighted the risks associated with FinTech expansion into financial intermediation or 'online money market funds'.[40] The size of certain FinTechs may lead to credit and liquidity, and cascading investor run, risks. The use of proprietary or second-hand non-traditional banking data to evaluate credit risk may import different levels of risk depending on the size of the data samples available, thereby precluding one-size fits all regulatory solutions. China, for instance, established *sui generis* norms for BigTech companies, which required reserves on custodial accounts and for payments to be channelled through an authorised clearing house.

The compound network effects enjoyed by firms with access to large data pools allow for pattern recognition unattainable by new entrants, thereby dampening competition.[41] Even if policy attempts to remedy such imbalances by restricting data collection and retention, the incumbent's existing data provide a rich resource capable of being analysed in a myriad of ways, which can challenge regulators.

C. *RegTech Monitoring and Intervention Capacity Risk*

If data risks are shared between the public and private sectors, regulators will require sufficient legal and technical capacity to effectively assess the data-driven economy. In this regard, three data attributes create particular challenges: (1) the strain placed on resources by the vastly varying range of data that need to be monitored for a holistic investigation, (2) the vast variety of data structures running through proprietary systems that may need to be transposed into a form that meets regulatory standards, and (3) data quality assessment that requires understanding and comparing to upstream and vertical data origins and points, thereby multiplying the investigative burden. Data investigation difficulties are also particularly strained

---

[39] Paulette Lacroix, 'Big Data Privacy and Ethical Challenges' in Mowafa Househ, Andre W Kushniruk, and Elizabeth M Borycki (eds), *Big Data, Big Challenges: A Healthcare Perspective: Background, Issues, Solutions and Research Directions* (Springer, 2019).

[40] Agustín Carstens, 'Big Tech in Finance and New Challenges for Public Policy' (Keynote Address, FT Banking Summit, 4 December 2018) <www.bis.org/speeches/sp181205.htm>. See also Giorgio Barba Navaretti, Giacomo Calzolari, and Alberto Franco Pozzolo, 'FinTech and Banks. Friends or Foes?', European Economy (Web Page, 23 December 2017) <https://european-economy.eu/2017-2/fintech-and-banks-friends-or-foes>.

[41] Financial Stability Board, FinTech and Market Structure in Financial Services: Market Developments and Potential Financial Stability Implications (Report, 14 February 2019) 18 <www.fsb.org/2019/02/fintech-and-market-structure-in-financial-services-market-developments-and-potential-financial-stability-implications>.

by cross-jurisdictional coordination burdens, like heterogenous methodological approaches and investigative mandates and capacities.

Globally, standardisation initiatives, such as legal entity identifiers, have great potential to assist with data alignment, but they are slow and offer limited macroprudential entry points. Furthermore, data access and sharing is scarce and even contentious. For example, the US CLOUD Act (*Clarifying Lawful Overseas Use of Data Act*) obliges cloud providers like Google and Amazon to submit data to law enforcement under warrant or subpoena, even if the data are in another country. EU authorities report that the Act clashes with the EU's GDPR, highlighting an 'urgent' need for updates to Mutual Legal Assistance Treaties encompassing principles of proportionality and data minimisation. For companies to comply with both, they may need to fully segment their network, relegating vulnerabilities to divested branches. If data access remains an uneven playing field, the asymmetry of information will limit preventative and reactive risk management.

D. *Addressing Data Security and Privacy Risks*

Data security and privacy risks differ from cybersecurity by relating to the collection as well as the utilisation and veracity of collected data, instead of its protection. Consequently, regulators should consistently canvas the public sector for weaknesses in its integrity, risks of re-identification, etc. This demands sufficient resources and mandates to investigate the complex data streams. Once investigated, legal risk management frameworks can be created and updated. To effectively follow data trails, regulation should be harmonised internationally.

Similar to cyberactivity, the most effective way to advance more effective data assessments is through networks of data specialists exchanging best practices.[42] We posit supporting already existing initiatives and reinforcing public–private partnerships to better understand technical risks and events capable of drawing opprobrium from stakeholders, especially firms with potential impacts on cross-jurisdictional institutional trust.

VI. THE NEW RISK PARADIGM: IT AND MODEL RISK AS DRIVERS OF SYSTEMIC RISK

To date there appears to be little evidence of digital financial products and investments generating systemic risk. Even the collapse of the so-called crypto exchange, FTX, didn't generate systemic effects across the financial system.

Rather, the clear risk of digitisation – a process that in many cases covers entire businesses – is that of security, namely cybersecurity and data protection. Cyber

---

[42] Konstantina Vemou and Maria Karyda, 'Evaluating Privacy Impact Assessment Methods: Guidelines and Best Practice' (2019) 28(1) *Information and Computer Security* 35.

risks, data risks, technological risks, and financial risks accumulate. This new type of risk, tech risk, now comprises another major form of risk, alongside the other traditional categories of financial risks. Digitisation/datafication, cybersecurity and TBTF/TCTF considerations together create a world where the financial system is more vulnerable than before. Where tech risks are new drivers of instability, regulators are well advised to focus on these new forms of risk both in their own right and in terms of their connections to other forms of risk.

In a sense, many of the characteristics of the international financial system and its participants can be transposed to the international cyber networks and their participants – in particular, TechFins. Both concern large, concentrated, relatively frictionless movements, necessitating increased transparency and control. Both are undergoing discussions regarding the merits of international centralisation, or regionalisation – except instead of currency, it is data. Both are now scrutinised for their potential volatility, risk susceptibility, and contagion effects. Both have demanded structural attention. It is therefore unsurprising that TechFins require prudential regulation and supervision.

To conclude, we present some basic principles of how cybersecurity and tech risks can be regulated and monitored, and outline the deficiencies of existing/traditional approaches.

In terms of importance, cybersecurity and tech risk, as categories of operational risk, now complement (traditional) financial risks. Tech risk functions as a new driver of potential instability, and regulators should focus on this new risk category.

How might regulators best respond to this new reality? The deficiencies in the regulatory system with regard to global technology risks are similar to those that we experienced with regard to other new forms of systemic risk prior to the GFC. Those deficiencies include loopholes in regulation, lack of coordination among regulators, information asymmetry, lack of expertise on side of financial intermediaries and regulators, and lack of awareness or investment on the side of intermediaries.

We encourage a new risk agenda that responds to global technology risks proactively. Such an agenda must include, from a regulatory perspective, seven steps.[43]

First, regulators must *prioritise tech risks*, and this prioritisation must take place both internally and externally. The result of this prioritisation is that tech risks should be treated as equal to financial risks. This is particularly important in the context of monitoring these new sorts of risk and collecting non-traditional forms of information. This could be done by appointing a Chief Technology Risk Officer (CTRO) for the supervisory authority in order to emphasise the significance of these sorts of risks. At the same time, financial intermediaries should be required to appoint Chief Technology Risk Officers or equivalent senior management officers responsible for

---

[43] We have advanced this agenda before in Douglas W Arner, Ross P Buckley, and Dirk A Zetzsche, 'FinTech, RegTech and Systemic Risk: The Rise of Global Technology Risk' in Douglas W Arner et al (eds), *Systemic Risk in the Financial Sector: Ten Years after the Great Crash* (CIGI Press, 2019) 69.

cyber, technology, and data risks, as a main contact point, with board monitoring, perhaps at the least in the firm's risk committee. Further, the CTRO's report on cyber risk should be a core agenda item at all meetings of the Board and of senior management.

Second, regulators need to *strengthen in-house tech expertise* to understand the sources of these new exposures in the ecosystems that they monitor and supervise, and to be able to discuss tech matters with intermediaries. We encourage, in particular, tech councils and tech expert groups at global policy bodies such as the FSB, IOSCO, and others.

Third, regulators must continue to *enhance reporting requirements* with regard to details of the intermediaries' tech risk management strategies and the budget invested in and human resources devoted to cybersecurity. These reports should include tech details and be read by the supervisor's tech department.

Fourth, *regulators must prioritise* these sorts of risks in the context of both on-site and off-site supervision to understand whether intermediaries have understood those risks and how they address them, and when they visit, they need to speak to tech experts as well as upper management or the legal department. Of course, on the authorities' side, technology and regulatory experts should be present as well.

Fifth, regulators must strive to *depoliticise* cybersecurity where it is related to financial stability, to foster the development of intergovernmental or sectoral networks capable of preventing and defending against cyber incidents, especially considering the growing financial interconnectedness. An isolated cybersecurity island connected to the datafied financial network poses increasing risks of contagion.

Sixth, regulators should *use the new technologies themselves*, since only users fully understand the issues with an application. This can be part of a major RegTech strategy, which – in many instances – is overdue anyway, in order to respond to the enormous data streams regulators receive in response to GFC-related additional reporting requirements. Regulators may suffer from technology failures, but in doing so, they will learn to handle large tech projects – and know what they have to ask for from the intermediaries.

Seventh, regulators should continually seek to *harmonise* normative cyber and data policies to avoid friction and uncertainty, and not allow rules with potential impacts on financial stability to entrench themselves in the long run. This may prevent races to the bottom, which can intensify destabilising behaviour.

The world has become riskier as tech risk has become a prime driver of risk levels. The new tech risk will translate into financial risk sooner or later. A regulatory system that waits until financial risks have materialised as long-term impacts of tech risk has failed in its core function. Regulators need to face rather than fear the unknown and develop a degree of tech expertise matched only by the large – but as yet unregulated – data-driven firms. This is a very demanding challenge indeed for all regulators, but not one they can avoid.

18

The New SIFIs

FinTech, TechFin, Scale, and Connectivity

SUMMARY

In addition to cybersecurity, the digitisation and datafication of finance at the centre of FinTech raise a range of data-related risks, in particular to data security and privacy (the focus of Chapter 17) and from concentration and the emergence of new Systemically Important Financial Institutions (SIFIs) in the form of digital finance platforms, TechFins and BigTechs. These new entrants bring with them a range of regulatory challenges we analyse here.

I. INTRODUCTION

Beyond the cybersecurity and data protection concerns addressed in Chapter 17, the growth of new financial participants such as FinTechs, TechFins, and BigTechs raises potential concerns.[1]

At this point in time, the principal risks do not tend to arise from FinTechs as such. FinTechs are typically brought into existence to address pain points and problems in financial services – while trying to become big, they tend to start small.[2] Most FinTechs do not seek to disrupt the existing intermediaries; rather they want to collaborate with the intermediaries and seek them as clients. It is here that much true FinTech innovation takes place, and at a rapid pace. As such, balanced proportional approaches to regulation are most appropriate, as we have suggested in Chapter 3.

---

[1] See Jon Frost et al, 'BigTech and the Changing Structure of Financial Intermediation' (BIS Papers No. 779, Monetary and Economic Department, Bank for International Settlements, April 2019) <www.bis.org/publ/work779.htm>.

[2] Daniel Drummer et al, *Fintech: Challenges and Opportunities* (Report, McKinsey & Company, May 2016) <www.mckinsey.com/industries/financial-services/our-insights/fintech-challenges-and-opportunities>.

However, the involvement of large data firms (TechFins and BigTechs) in financial matters is a reason for concern, particularly from the standpoint of data protection and use.[3]

II. TECHFIN

In contrast to FinTechs, TechFins – BigTech firms entering into finance – are often very significant firms outside of the financial services sector prior to stepping into it. Due to their scale, TechFins are connected to many institutions from the moment they enter the financial services market by, for example, functioning as a conduit to licensed institutions. Moreover, because of their data power, TechFins exercise influence over connected financial institutions from their moment of entry, and may often quickly control whole market segments when they finally begin to provide regulated financial services.

The governance and disclosure frameworks for financial services are not designed to accommodate TechFins: Financial intermediaries should be experts in processing financial information to channel cash flows to their most efficient use, in terms of expected risk-return ratios. This paradigm is challenged by TechFins. If TechFins have better data than traditional financial institutions, TechFins may provide the financial intermediary function more effectively. However, TechFins, at least today, operate for the most part in an unregulated environment. Until rather late in their journey into financial services, when they apply for a financial services license, TechFins will not be subject to customer and investor protection rules, nor to measures that ensure the functioning of financial markets and prevent the build-up of systemic risk.[4]

Moreover, from the perspective of incumbent licensed financial intermediaries, TechFins may provide unbalanced, and arguably unfair, competition. The fixed costs of an initial license and the ongoing costs of supervision and related reviews by advisors, and so forth, will mean licensed intermediaries bear higher costs than unlicensed ones. In the long run, licensed intermediaries are doomed to lose these contests, given their higher cost base and limited flexibility to respond to competitive challenges. Such an uneven playing field clearly raises risks of regulatory arbitrage as well as unfair competition.

Risks arise from the potential for very rapid scaling in the TechFin context, something we have previously highlighted in the context of the speed with which a firm

---

[3] Current regulatory attention focuses on the systemic risk dimension of technology firms. The BIS/ BCBS has entered into a global consultation, in particular, on the role of 'BigTech'. See Basel Committee on Banking Supervision, *Sound Practices: Implications of FinTech Developments for Banks and Bank Supervisors* (Report, February 2018) 15 <www.bis.org/bcbs/publ/d431.htm>.

[4] Cf Dirk Zetzsche, 'Investment Law as Financial Law: From Fund Governance over Market Governance to Stakeholder Governance?' in Hanne Søndergaard Birkmose, Mette Neville and Karsten Engsig Sørensen (eds), *The European Financial Market in Transition* (Kluwer Law International, 2012), 339–43.

or product can now move from 'too small to care' to 'too big to fail' (TBTF) – a core feature of the FinTech era which has emerged over the past decade.[5] For instance, in its first 10 months of operation, Yu'e Bao,[6] Ant Financial's wealth management platform, became the fourth largest money market fund in the world and encountered a swift, restrictive response from Chinese regulators.[7] In April 2017, after China's regulators had lifted the shackles, and only four years after its creation, Yu'e Bao became the largest money market fund globally. Alibaba's decision to separate Ant into a separate licensed financial services holding company – albeit under its continued control – by renaming its subsidiary Alipay in October 2014 was the direct result of regulators' fears over possible systemic risk arising from both Alipay and Yu'e Bao. In a similar way, mobile money platforms such as M-Pesa have assumed systemic importance in some African countries,[8] as well as MercadoLibre (with payments and financial subsidiaries) and Russian financial platform provider Tinkoff in their respective home markets.

While arguably bringing important consumer benefits, the emergence of TechFins highlights the emergence of large new firms which must be carefully considered from the standpoint of potential risks arising from their size, interconnectivity, and roles in providing systemically important infrastructure. Often, control of important market segments in financial services being concentrated in the hands of the few has led to major financial crises.[9] Examples include the early-2000s accounting frauds[10] and the role of the credit rating agencies in the 2008 crisis as well as the roles of SIFIs in many crises.[11] Accounting firms and rating agencies are mere data providers linked to the system (much like early-stage TechFins), while

[5] Douglas W Arner, Janos Baberis, and Ross P Buckley, 'The Evolution of FinTech: A New Post-Crisis Paradigm' (2016) 47(4) *Georgetown Journal of International Law* 1271.

[6] Jamil Anderlini, 'Explosive Growth Pushes Alibaba Online Fund up Global Rankings', *Financial Times* (online, 10 March 2014) <www.ft.com/content/748a0cd8-a843-11e3-8ce1-00144feab7de>.

[7] Zhou Weihuan, Douglas W Arner and Ross P Buckley, 'Regulation of Digital Financial Services in China: Last Mover Advantage' (2015) 8(1) *Tsinghua China Law Review* 25.

[8] See, for example, Kiarie Njoroge, 'Report: This Is What Would Happen to Kenya's Economy if M-Pesa Was to Collapse', Nairobi News (online, 30 November 2016) <http://nairobinews.nation.co.ke/news/treasury-report-reveals-fears-m-pesas-critical-role-economy>; Frank Jacob, 'The Role of M-Pesa in Kenya's Economic and Political Development' in Mickie Mwanzia Koster, Michael Mwenda Kithinji and Jerono P Rotich (eds), *Kenya after 50: Reconfiguring Education, Gender, and Policy* (Palgrave MacMillan, 2016) 89.

[9] Ross P Buckley and Douglas W Arner, *From Crisis to Crisis: The Global Financial System and Regulatory Failure* (Wolters Kluwer, 2011).

[10] See, for example, Sean Farrell, 'The World's Biggest Accounting Scandals', *The Guardian* (online, 22 July 2015) <www.theguardian.com/business/2015/jul/21/the-worlds-biggest-accounting-scandals-toshiba-enron-olympus>; C William Thomas, 'The Rise and Fall of Enron' (2002) 193(4) *Journal of Accountancy* 41.

[11] See Financial System Inquiry Committee, Parliament of Australia, Financial System Inquiry (Final Report, November 2014) <https://treasury.gov.au/publication/c2014-fsi-final-report>, discussing 'too-big-to-fail' (at 99) and 'moral hazard' (at 38).

SIFIs are typically very large (like TechFins that offer regulated services).[12] All three, unlike the TechFins, are at last strictly regulated today.[13]

Yet TechFins are by no means risk free. Typically, all the risks created by TechFins are unknown as the information flow to financial regulators is not mandatory for as long as TechFins are beyond the scope of monitoring or supervision. We will only learn of the outcomes when the service is not performed properly, with often surprising results. This will be particularly so as artificial intelligence and machine learning (AI/ML) applications to large and novel datasets become more prevalent in financial services, because the underlying algorithms are very complex, almost opaque, and the behaviour of the self-learning algorithms will become impossible to predict. Further, we lack experience with AI/ML-based pricing models over a full business cycle.

If financial law does not apply, potential systemic risk may build up unobserved, unmitigated, and uncontrolled, and, in the longer term, the next global financial crisis may well come from weaknesses in TechFins rather than in authorised financial institutions. Such concerns led to the decision in China to classify Ant Financial as a SIFI in late 2018, a move we strongly support.

Established thresholds for the imposition of financial regulation, such as the solicitation of customers, deposit-taking, pooling of assets, or discretion over client assets, often fail to bring TechFins within the regulatory perimeter. Regulators are unable to enforce customer protection measures to monitor and mitigate systemic risk. Protected factors are often put at risk by TechFins.

As financial regulation plays an important role in furthering market efficiency and customer protection, TechFins should be regulated when offering financial services. An imbalance of competition will arise if TechFins are not regulated in the 'too large to ignore' phase of their development cycle and do not bear the same regulatory costs as the licensed financial services providers.

In the world of TechFins, most customers provide their data for free in exchange for a free service. Therefore, the 'follow the money' traditional financial legal approach is likely to fail. The new regulatory approach should be 'follow the data', not as a mere policy choice but as a necessity. In a world where data are the new currency and where legislation regulates intermediaries managing financial assets (e.g., banks and asset managers), there is an urgent need to regulate data intermediaries in a similar way.

Regulators should consider regulating financial data collection and analytics when such activities exceed certain thresholds. A threshold set as a percentage of

[12] Mustafa Yuksel, 'Identifying Global Systemically Important Financial Institutions' (Bulletin of December Quarter 2014, Reserve Bank of Australia, December 2014) <www.rba.gov.au/publications/bulletin/2014/dec/pdf/bu-1214-8.pdf>.

[13] See, for example, Siegfried Utzig, 'The Financial Crisis and the Regulation of Credit Rating Agencies: A European Banking Perspective' (Asian Development Bank Institute Working Paper No. 188, January 2010).

the overall population or amount of datapoints in the reference market could represent the threshold between 'too small to care' and 'too large to ignore'. Above this threshold, TechFin regulation should focus on information collecting and ensuring regulatory access to data-based business models. This will ensure sound analytical methods and adherence to protected factors relevant to that reference market. If the risk analysis arising from the regulatory enquiry reveals systemic risk, relevant preventative measures must be applied. We return to some of these issues in Chapter 19 regarding the challenges of concentration.

We consider BigTechs in more detail in the following sections.

III. BIGTECH

According to the Basel Committee on Banking Supervision,

> Bigtech refers to large globally active technology firms with a relative advantage in digital technology. Bigtech firms usually provide web services (search engines, social networks, e-commerce, etc) to end users over the internet and/or IT platforms or they maintain infrastructure (data storage and processing capabilities) on which other companies can provide products or service.[14]

These BigTechs can be involved in financial markets in two ways. First, they can function as third-party providers to financial intermediaries. Use cases include the cloud services provided by Amazon and others, or data feeds to banks and asset managers which are used to inform risk models and calculations. Second, BigTech firms can serve as conduits linking the financial service providers with the customers that the BigTech typically already has, and over time potentially beginning to provide the financial service itself directly to customers – thus functioning as TechFins (Figure 18.1).[15]

Both BigTech business models – be it third-party IT services (Big Data) or TechFin-like provision of financial services – have the potential to create systemic risk, albeit in different ways.

BigTechs providing third-party IT services to the financial services industry import the risks examined in Chapter 17 that arise from a cyber monoculture.

BigTechs functioning as TechFins typically benefit from: (a) regulatory gaps and/or disparities in treatment with traditional financial institutions, (b) economies of scope and scale, and (c) network effects (i.e., a tendency towards concentration in both data and finance). This combination suggests TechFins may in time increase TBTF risks, in addition to raising concerns about competition and data protection.

---

[14] Basel Committee on Banking Supervision (n 3).
[15] Dirk A Zetzsche et al, 'From FinTech to TechFin: The Regulatory Challenges of Data-Driven Finance' (2018) 14(2) *New York University Journal of Law and Business* 393.

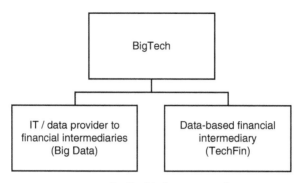

FIGURE 18.1 BigTech's function in finance

As to 'too connected to fail' (TCTF), in the world of digitised finance all is connected via the data feed, and such connectivity creates systemic risk. In particular, traditional bank-owned and bank-run infrastructure is replaced by new systemically important infrastructure that is owned by someone else who is usually not a financial intermediary in the traditional sense, and not regulated as such, and thus not subject to the measures we associate with systemic risk (bail-in/bail-out, segregation of critical infrastructure, etc.). Examples include market concentration in data feeds and in cloud services as non-financial firms provide data and hosting services for financial firms and regulators.

BigTech's involvement in finance tends to link size and connectivity – a combination that creates sizable potential systemic risks. The lack of transparency and the potential to build up (further) size in financial services very rapidly complete a story that suggests strongly that regulatory action with regard to BigTechs needs to be a high priority.

IV. NEW FORMS OF FINANCIAL INFRASTRUCTURE

In addition to new risks from the digital environment (particularly relating to cybersecurity and data protection and privacy) and from new financial institutions (particularly scale and network effects), new risks also arise from the evolution of new forms of digital financial infrastructure. BigTech has played a major role in this development. In China, for example, BigTechs in the form of AliPay and WeChatPay have revolutionised payments. The activities of these firms have expanded into credit provision, insurance, and investment services, creating complex interconnected webs across several sectors. The situation is similar in an increasing range of other nations.

In regions where incumbent bank-based payments remain dominant, like the United States or Europe, new payment services are still underpinned by traditional bank infrastructure. However, the growth in FinTechs foreshadows a convergence of traditional banking and this new infrastructure. The rate and scope of such change, as exemplified by China, can cause tectonic shifts in a financial system's structure.

Concerns about financial infrastructure are by no means new, with financial regulation focusing on payment systems since the failure of Bankhaus Herstatt in 1974 and on securities clearing and settlement systems particularly since the failure of the Hong Kong stock and futures exchanges in 1987. Both issues were addressed by the BIS Committee on Payment and Settlement Systems and the International Organisation of Securities Commissions (IOSCO). Since 2008, concerns about and focus on 'financial market infrastructures' (FMIs) have increased dramatically, with leadership taken by the FSB and the joint BIS-IOSCO Committee on Payment and Market Infrastructures. Since 2008, there has been an ongoing debate about risks in central clearing houses and whether the benefits in terms of reducing counterparty risk are exceeded by new risks of concentration and systemic reliance. Clearly, cybersecurity issues relate directly to CCPs and similar infrastructures. There are also TBTF/TCTF concerns, particularly as new entrants using new technologies such as blockchain or stablecoins try to disrupt existing markets and participants.

However, beyond these, we have also seen the emergence of new forms of digital financial infrastructure, particularly in the context of cloud services. Cloud services and cloud service providers are playing an increasing role in the financial sector. This is particularly the case with new FinTechs which are often cloud natives, with often their entire business being cloud based. At the same time, traditional financial institutions are increasingly using cloud services to provide backup to existing systems and to build new systems, often to replace existing outdated core systems (often based on old mainframes running seriously out-of-date software).

In the case of IT/data provision to financial intermediaries, the intermediaries are exposed to operational, particularly cyber, risks from those third-party service providers. For instance, when Amazon's cloud computing data centre in Hong Kong failed, the website of the US SEC, plus many consumer-oriented services, such as Netflix, went down.[16]

Financial supervision typically does not apply to the Big Data providers. IT/data providers usually fall outside the scope of financial regulation. Therefore, financial regulators lack information regarding such firms and their potential roles in interconnectivity across the financial sector as well as appropriate tools of supervision or regulation with which to regulate them.

Financial law usually responds to risks created by non-supervised firms by imposing strict outsourcing requirements on financial firms. In particular, the financial firm needs to ensure systemic stability at all times, regardless of the outsourcing of information technology. But difficulties may arise for a bank (even a JP Morgan or Goldman Sachs) in ensuring that a major tech company (e.g., Amazon, Apple,

---

[16] Elaine Ou, 'Can't Stream Netflix? The Cloud May Be to Blame', Bloomberg (online, 3 March 2017) <www.bloomberg.com/view/articles/2017-03-02/can-t-stream-netflix-the-cloud-may-be-to-blame>.

Google, or Microsoft) provides appropriate service when the tech company is many times the size of the bank and has more market power.

Such issues in the context of cloud services are leading to increasing discussion of whether such tech firms should be regarded as systemically important infrastructure providers and regulated accordingly, in the same way that certain payment systems or securities and derivatives central counterparties (CCPs) are. Related discussions are also taking place about whether or not cloud services are in fact a form of utility and need to be separated from other tech businesses.

The alternative to control over the service provider is diversification. For instance, financial law could require that any financial firm must have mirror cloud servers at three different providers, and that these providers be unrelated to each other. While mandatory diversification ensures some additional security and also has some positive effects on market structure in the provider market, it comes with increased costs and other problems (which we discuss further in Chapter 19 in the context of digital financial platforms).

The other problem is cybersecurity. The more providers hold the intermediaries' financial data, the greater the risk of internal data corruption (stealing, manipulation, or abuse) or an external cyber-attack. Second, mandatory diversification of data streams and server space takes away some of the benefits of datafication. It slows down IT processes and creates risk of confusion: if data are stored on a blockchain with many different cloud providers, the storing of data on the blockchain itself costs time and resources. If a brokerage system runs on three different data streams simultaneously, and one of the streams shows different data from the other two, which of the three datasets is correct, and on which should the broker base a billion US$ transaction? These risks are exacerbated by the fact that the market for cloud storage and related analytics as well as data provision for financial markets is highly concentrated.[17] Financial intermediaries may have little choice as to providers, while cyber attackers are given easy targets.

V. NEW SIFIS: THE THREE REGULATORY PERSPECTIVES

The resulting concentration and dominance now also risks the very innovation promoted by regulators to encourage FinTech. Regulators around the world now seek to balance the benefits of these dominant platforms against concerns about abuses of data and market position.[18] How regulators might best strike a balance between innovation and competition is the subject matter of this section.

---

[17] See Dirk A Zetzsche et al, 'The Evolution and Future of Data-Driven Finance in the EU' (2020) 57(2) *Common Market Law Review* 331. See Douglas W Arner, Ross P Buckley and Dirk A Zetzsche, 'FinTech, RegTech and Systemic Risk: The Rise of Global Technology Risk' in Douglas W Arner et al (eds), *Systemic Risk in the Financial Sector: Ten Years after the Great Crash* (CIGI Press, 2019) 69.

[18] See Shoshana Zuboff, *The Age of Surveillance Capitalism: The Fight for a Human Future at the New Frontier of Power* (PublicAffairs, 2019) 8.

A. *Competition*

The purpose of antitrust and competition laws is to protect consumers and small businesses from abusive business practices arising from the concentration of market power in the hands of dominant firms.[19] These laws help to maintain a competitive market environment by limiting predatory practices such as market allocation, bid-rigging, price-fixing, and others. As such, antitrust and competition laws apply to various economic activities that can intentionally or unintentionally stifle competition.

At the international level, bodies such as the Organisation for Economic Cooperation and Development, the International Competition Network, and the UN Conference on Trade and Development develop voluntary recommendations, best practices, and policy guidelines aimed at harmonising competition laws across different jurisdictions. In addition to multilateral cooperation, regulators from different jurisdictions can adopt bilateral Memoranda of Understanding or collaboration agreements to harmonise the enforcement of competition laws.[20]

At the national and regional level, regulators have broad discretion in their approaches to competition policy and its goals. For example, the United States and the European Union (EU) often pursue different goals with their competition policies. In the United States, antitrust law is primarily focused on the protection of consumer welfare;[21] whereas, in the EU, competition law is aimed at both protecting consumers and facilitating market integration.[22] The difference in competition policy goals translates into different regulatory requirements: the EU has a much lower threshold for qualifying economic activities as anti-competitive than the United States does.

Competition laws are becoming increasingly relevant for platform finance, which is challenging dominant paradigms around competition, innovation, inequality, and other aspects of balanced sustainable development. In particular, BigTechs tend to have massive advantages in data collection and digital infrastructure control. These advantages can lead to conflicts of interest and allow platforms to undermine market competition. For example, digital finance platforms can maintain digital monopolies by acquiring smaller competitors, thus solidifying their market position,[23] or by

---

[19] Joshua D Wright and Douglas H Ginsburg, 'The Goals of Antitrust: Welfare Trumps Choice' (2013) 81(5) *Fordham Law Review* 2405, 2406.

[20] See, for example, Directorate for Financial and Enterprise Affairs Competition Committee, Inventory of Provisions in Inter-Agency Co-Operation Agreements (MoUs) (Report, OECD, 2016) 3 <www.oecd.org/officialdocuments/publicdisplaydocumentpdf/?cote=DAF/COMP/WP3(2016)1/REV2&docLanguage=En>.

[21] 'The Antitrust Laws', *Federal Trade Commission* (Web Page) <www.ftc.gov/tips-advice/competition-guidance/guide-antitrust-laws/antitrust-laws>.

[22] See Shanker Singham, 'Approach of the European Commission to Competition in the High Technology Sector' (European Policy Information Center, 2018) 4 <https://ec.europa.eu/competition/information/digitisation_2018/contributions/epicenter.pdf>.

[23] See, for example, Mark Glick, Catherine Ruetschlin, and Darren Bush, 'Big Tech's Buying Spree and the Failed Ideology of Competition Law' (2021) 72(2) *Hastings Law Journal* 465 (analysing the acquisition of Instagram and WhatsApp by Meta).

raising barriers to market entry by using their data and dominant platforms to force specialist applications to forgo part of their revenue in return for being connected to the platform.

These risks are attracting the attention of regulators in developed and developing countries. Meta, for example, has faced antitrust scrutiny and investigations in India, Turkey, Argentina, the United Kingdom, and the EU for changes to its privacy policy and terms of service, which would allow it to collect data without permission from its WhatsApp users to enhance activities on its Facebook platform. In turn, the EU adopted the *Digital Markets Act* and the *Digital Services Act*, designed to foster competitiveness among digital service providers and to enhance the protection of digital consumer rights by identifying 'gatekeepers' and imposing new obligations on digital service providers. US regulators have found that the market power of major tech companies can undermine competition, warranting antitrust reforms approved by the House in September 2022,[24] while Google has been sued for maintaining a monopoly in internet search and search advertising markets.[25]

In a similar vein, China in 2021 enacted a series of revisions to its Antitrust Law aimed at the protection of fair competition, a reduction in operator compliance costs, and the improvements of competition supervision in the internet sector.[26] The regulations restrict subsidies, discounts, and other business practices that can affect competition. India has prohibited e-commerce platforms from selling products from affiliated companies to avoid potential conflicts of interest and concentration of market power. These developments suggest that regulators around the world will continue to re-examine their existing competition laws to address the risks arising from digital finance platforms.

Competition laws can limit the negative impacts of digital finance platforms where the resulting concentration of market power undermines the resilience of existing business models and prevents the development of emerging local enterprises.

---

[24] Subcommittee on Antitrust, Commercial and Administrative Law of the Committee on the Judiciary (US), Investigation of Competition in Digital Markets: Majority Staff Report and Recommendations (Report, 2020); see also 'White House Still Committed to Tech Antitrust Bill', *Reuters* (online, 18 November 2022) <www.reuters.com/world/us/white-house-still-committed-tech-antitrust-bill-2022-11-17>.

[25] See Department of Justice, 'Justice Department Sues Monopolist Google for Violating Antitrust Laws' (Media Release, 20 October 2020) <www.justice.gov/opa/pr/justice-department-sues-monopolist-google-violating-antitrust-laws>; see also 'Google Asks Court to Toss Out Federal Antitrust Lawsuit', *Reuters* (online, 14 December 2022) <www.reuters.com/legal/google-asks-court-toss-out-federal-antitrust-lawsuit-2022-12-13>.

[26] See Leo Xin, 'China Drafts New Antitrust Guideline for Internet Companies', Pinsent Masons (19 November 2020) <www.pinsentmasons.com/out-law/news/china-drafts-new-antitrust-guideline-for-internet-companies>; Anti-Monopoly Bureau of State Administration for Market Regulation (CN), 'Invitation for Submission on the "Guidelines for Anti-Monopoly in the Field of Platform Economy (Draft for Comment)"' (11 November 2020) <www.samr.gov.cn/hd/zjdc/202011/t20201109_323234.html>; see also 'China: China Issues Anti-Monopoly Guidelines for the Internet Platform Economy', *Baker McKenzie* (Web Page, 11 February 2021) <https://insightplus.bakermckenzie.com/bm/antitrust-competition_1/china-china-issues-anti-monopoly-guidelines-for-the-internet-platform-economy>.

B. *Financial Regulation*

Based on the assumption that a well-functioning financial market is a public good, financial regulation aims to address issues of financial stability, market efficiency, financial integrity, consumer and investor protection, and fairness. Regulation generally arises in response to societal harms that policymakers and the public do not want to see repeated – namely financial crises, bank failures, fraud and money laundering, and abuse of consumers. Regulators are the representatives of society who are 'paid to worry' and mitigate these risks. In this sub-section, we focus on microprudential risks, viz., those that materialise on the individual firm's level.

Financial regulation generally requires companies to obtain special licenses from relevant regulators to provide financial services. For example, companies that wish to provide banking services need to obtain a banking license and comply with a range of related regulatory standards. Most jurisdictions apply existing regulatory standards to govern the financial activities of digital finance platforms.[27] Hence, if such platforms want to engage in regulated activities that require a license, they typically can do so by applying for a general (i.e., non-tech-specific) financial license.

Two problems arise with this approach for these platforms. First, such firms often structure their activities so as to not need banking or other licenses. To limit their regulatory compliance costs, these firms typically seek to control the customer interface and offer their customers white-labelled financial services and products from existing financial institutions. This typically removes the need for the platform to have its own licence. This means platforms can potentially affect financial markets while remaining beyond regulatory supervision. Second, it is often quite unclear whether the financial activities of digital finance platforms fall within the scope of relevant licensing or other financial regulations. For example, money balances in wallets, peer-to-peer lending, and some blockchain-based financial products might not fit within traditional definitions of deposits, lending, and securities trading and brokerage. How, when, and where these new digital products fall under existing rules is often far from clear in many jurisdictions.

As a result of these two features of platforms, the prevention of regulatory arbitrage through entirely new regulation, or functional approaches to existing regulation, has emerged in many jurisdictions.

To improve the licensing process and enhance competition, some regulators have amended their regulatory frameworks to govern the activities of digital finance platforms. For example, the US Office of the Comptroller of the Currency approved special national bank charters for FinTech companies (including digital

---

[27] Juan Carlos Crisanto, Johannes Ehrentraud, and Marcos Fabian, 'Big Techs in Finance: Regulatory Approaches and Policy Options' (Financial Stability Institute Brief No. 12, March 2021) 5 <www.bis.org/fsi/fsibriefs12.pdf>.

finance platforms).[28] The charters are subject to similar regulatory frameworks to those that apply to banks but with some relaxations such as exemptions from deposit requirements and state money-transmitter laws. Similar developments can be found in other jurisdictions, such as Australia, the United Kingdom, and the EU, where regulators allow FinTech companies to provide limited financial services, in some cases with limited or conditional licences. In a similar vein, China adopted a unified regulatory regime for all firms engaging in financial services-related business without distinctions from a technological platform standpoint or otherwise.[29]

Besides licensing, other financial regulatory requirements may be applicable to digital finance platforms, such as know your customer and anti-money laundering obligations and securities regulations. These regulations are likewise designed to secure the stability of the financial sector, deter criminal activities, and protect consumers.[30]

C. *Innovation*

From an innovation perspective, a certain degree of platformisation is desirable, as it promotes and facilitates new services. Yet, this pro-innovative effect may be quickly muted once it is the platform which determines what may be linked to it, because the platform will prefer businesses that do not compete with services and products the platform wishes to offer itself.

Furthermore, the perspective of the platform provider may change over time: if the data stream flowing through the platform indicates a given service or product is proving particularly popular, the platform provider will often seek to internalise that service, either by acquiring its provider or by adding its own, competitive service via the platform, at potentially preferable terms and typically with better technical access options, given the new service or product will be integrated with existing offerings developed and hosted by the platform provider. Similar strategies are seen by providers of traditional website and platform services for e-commerce and search. Platforms thus may work to promote or severely retard competition and innovation.

VI. ADDRESSING NEW SIFIS

At the core of our concern is the TechFins' conduit function in their early stage when they stand between the financial intermediary and their customers. One

---

[28] See Office of the Comptroller of the Currency, 'Policy Statement on Financial Technology Companies' Eligibility to Apply for National Bank Charters' (Policy Statement, 31 July 2018) <www.occ.gov/news-issuances/news-releases/2018/pub-other-occ-policy-statement-fintech.pdf?utm_campaign=ABA-Newsbyteso80118&utm_medium=email&utm_source=Eloqua>.

[29] See Zhong Xu and Ruihui Xu, 'Regulating Fintech for Sustainable Development in the People's Republic of China' (Asian Development Bank Institute Working Paper No. 1023, October 2019) 14–15.

[30] Dirk Zetzsche, Douglas W Arner and Ross P Buckley, 'Digital ID and AML/CDD/KYC Utilities for Financial Inclusion, Integrity, and Competition' (2018) 47 *CAPCO Institute Journal of Financial Transformation* 133.

could respond that the early-stage TechFin function is merely one of data delivery; and data delivery is not a special activity warranting regulation. Yet data provision in a highly concentrated market has prompted regulators to require financial institutions to diversify their data sources, and in our view, rightly so. The difference with TechFins is that while data delivery is a back-end function, TechFins also provide a front-end function of connecting the customers and the actual provider of the white-labelled financial services. TechFins' conduit function cannot be addressed by diversification requirements since the financial institution cannot change the 'service provider' as readily as it can change a back-end relationship – terminating the cooperation with the TechFin would cost the financial institution the link to its most precious asset: its customers.

For that reason, we propose regulating data gathering and analytics by virtue of a moderate regulatory intervention, along the business evolution from (1) too small to care to (2) too large to ignore and then to (3) too big to fail.

As TechFins often do not seek access to client funds directly, many established financial regulatory thresholds based on balance sheet size, exposures, or assets under management will fail to be triggered. In order to set appropriate thresholds, regulators must develop new criteria. These could include an overall number of data points, or holding data on a significant share of a population in the reference market, or other measures that reflect a very substantial dataset.

If financial data gathering and analytics becomes a regulated activity, systemic risk measures will apply as soon as TechFins become essential to financial stability, and this will be determined by the TBTF or TCTF tests. If the TechFin is the main client channel for one important bank or for many banks which together are of systemic importance, the importance of the TechFin becomes like that of a new CEO or a new business model rather than merely that of infrastructure. To the same extent that a new bank CEO and other key staff would be subject to regulatory scrutiny, we would ask the TechFin to meet the 'fit and proper' requirement, and ask for adequate resources to maintain that function on the side of the TechFin. This is where a systemic risk perspective indicates a case for regulation of TechFins.

Once regulators come to the conclusion that the TechFin is of systemic importance – for instance, once TechFin data are essential for a systemically significant financial institution, or the TechFin provides the main client access for several financial institutions which together are of systemic significance – we recommend measures to control and limit systemic risk. In the first case, this could require the significant financial institution to diversify its data sources. In the second case, we recommend (a) structural requirements for TechFins (such as capital levels, segregation of activities, data storage and reliability standards), (b) empowering regulators to shut down the activity (while preserving customer data), or (c) appointing a commissioner to run the quarantined TechFin part of the business in the public interest. As part of the resolution scheme, regulators must ask the service provider how to ensure access to essential facilities in times of a crisis. In the case of data-driven business models such as those of a TechFin, the resolution plan must lay out how continued access to data is ensured even if the financial business is bankrupt. For instance, we would ask data-intensive financial firms to provide for licensing contracts with their data-driven mother subsidiaries that ensure business continuity (i.e., further data feeds) even if the financial firm itself is bankrupt for a certain period of time. Without the data the whole firm will be threatened, and rarely will the TechFin arm of a BigData firm have full ownership of the data it is supplying.

Systemic risk intervention could go even one step further. Since running a crucial data provider in the public interest is not a long-term solution, mandating an open data policy under certain circumstances, as a particular systemic risk measure for data-driven financial services, may reduce the need for additional regulatory intervention long term. Note that, in contrast to open banking proponents, we do not argue for open data policies in all cases, but only as a specific crisis measure imposed on very large data-driven financial services firms.

The emergence of concentration and dominance in digital finance poses real challenges for regulation and is the subject of our final substantive chapter, Chapter 19.

19

The Challenge of Scale

Addressing Concentration and Dominance in Digital Finance

SUMMARY

The economies of scope and scale of finance combined with the network effects of data and technology create benefits and pose risks to competition within financial markets. The same FinTech economies that reduce costs and increase efficiencies often contribute to decreasing competition in FinTech market segments. This market concentration is at odds with key objectives of financial regulation, including market efficiency, investor/client protection, and systemic risk prevention, and may require regulators to intervene.

I. INTRODUCTION

Very large FinTech and technology firms (hereafter 'BigTechs') have developed from the combination of technological evolution (see Chapter 2), conducive regulatory approaches (Chapter 3), and the pro-concentration effects that characterise data and financial industries (Chapter 6). These BigTech firms, and the financial ecosystems built on their platforms, provide financial and other services to users throughout their lives. The pro-concentration effects stemming from digital finance platforms and financial ecosystems often turn FinTech market segments into winner-takes-all races, resulting in technology-induced centralisation in the platform provider and ironically reversing FinTech's tendency towards disintermediation and decentralisation.

The emergence of scale, concentration, and dominance in digital finance platforms poses significant challenges to policymakers and regulators from both conceptual and execution standpoints. The sprawling cross-border nature of these business models impacts a multitude of distinct yet related sectors, such as telecommunications, finance, and data protection, and requires authorities to consider the question of how to regulate along several axes and dimensions. This is particularly so as digital finance platforms can be global in scope and have widely differing local impacts.

Regulators can deploy a range of approaches to govern finance platforms and financial ecosystems. Given a certain degree of platformisation is desirable to achieve the advantages of FinTech explored in Chapter 6, regulatory approaches can be seen on a spectrum from permissive to restrictive, with laissez-faire at one end and prohibition at the other. In between lie a range of techniques: active encouragement such as industrial policy, infrastructure development or innovation hubs; test-and-learn approaches, such as piloting or sandboxes; self-regulation; minimal registration or licensing; disclosure; co-regulation; internal governance requirements; external monitoring via penalties and enforcement; graduated proportional regulation; public utility regulation; and structural reform, such as unbundling or nationalisation. We consider each next.

II. PERMISSIVE AND FACILITATIVE APPROACHES

The first possible approach to digital finance platforms is simply not to regulate them. By doing nothing, the result may be either rigorous or laissez-faire depending upon whether current financial regulation applies to the operations of a particular platform.[1] Doing nothing may involve requiring new entrants to comply with the existing financial regulation, often with highly restrictive results and adverse effects on financial innovation, or it may leave new entrants unregulated.

Alternately, a do-nothing approach could simultaneously accelerate financial innovation *and* exacerbate data-driven market dynamics. We have described China's experience with permissiveness before 2015 in Chapter 2. Most notably, during its unregulated period, Alibaba laid the foundation for the world's largest financial ecosystem (measured by number of clients). While the soundness of the Chinese financial system, or the dire need for competition within it, prior to the FinTech boom may explain the benefits of doing nothing in this particular case, and while non-legal means eventually allowed political control over the emerging providers of financial ecosystems, the Chinese example clearly demonstrates the systemic risks that can arise from uninhibited growth of certain market participants (and which were the reason for the far more cautious regulatory approach since 2015).

In the context of digital finance platforms, however, a laissez-faire approach would be likely to further the growth of existing platforms, quite probably by the undesirable practices laid out above. Although this is the approach most countries have taken so far, it will likely result in undesirable winner-take-all outcomes. Going forward, policymakers and regulators need to provide supporting frameworks to maximise the benefits of data aggregation and use in finance, including by platformisation, while at the same time, monitoring the market and building proportional regulatory approaches to minimise emerging risks, particularly from scale and dominance.

---

[1]   Dirk A Zetzsche et al, 'Digital Finance Platforms: Toward a New Regulatory Paradigm' (2020) 23(1) *University of Pennsylvania Journal of Business Law* 273.

Beyond simply a permissive approach, governments around the world are increasingly considering ways in which to directly support innovation, typically through early-stage research and development investment.[2] In addition, in recognising the importance of data to future innovation, development, and competitiveness, regulators and policymakers are considering how to support the role of data in sustainable development.[3] The most advanced of these relate to 'open banking', 'open finance', and 'open data', with the European Union (EU), United Kingdom, and, particularly, Australia having the most developed approaches so far.[4] Others – such as China – are considering how to maximise the benefits of data for future innovation and development by, for instance, recognising data as a public good or commons which can then be used across society.[5] Similar discussions are taking place in the technological context, particularly in discussions of the potential role of decentralisation and blockchain.[6] In the specific context of FinTech innovation, the test-and-learn approaches discussed in Chapter 3 – including piloting, regulatory sandboxes, and special charters and licences – while far from being a panacea, certainly enhance the critical flow of information between innovative firms and their regulators. Some may argue that in the face of BigTechs or digital finance platforms, these tools may prove of little value since they are designed to promote testing of new technologies and business models rather than to regulate global players. However, the countervailing argument is that such initiatives promote the creation of new financial services by smaller players which may have disproportionately large impacts in shaping digital financial services, especially in developing countries. Moreover, digital finance platforms will most likely continue to innovate and provide new offerings that will ideally be tested within sandboxes to minimise potential negative impacts.

---

[2] Organisation for Economic Co-operation and Development, *OECD Science, Technology and Innovation Outlook 2021: Times of Crisis and Opportunity* (OECD, 2021).

[3] The United Nations Secretary-General's Task Force on Digital Financing of the Sustainable Development Goals, *People's Money: Harnessing Digitalization to Finance a Sustainable Future* (Report, August 2020) <https://unsdg.un.org/resources/peoples-money-harnessing-digitalization-finance-sustainable-future>.

[4] Douglas W Arner, Ross P Buckley, and Dirk A Zetzsche, 'Open Banking, Open Data and Open Finance: Lessons from the European Union' in Linda Jeng (ed), *Open Banking* (Oxford University Press, 2022) 147, ch 8.

[5] See, for example, National Infrastructure Commission (UK), *Data For The Public Good* (Report) 8 <https://nic.org.uk/app/uploads/Data-for-the-Public-Good-NIC-Report.pdf>. See also World Economic Forum, 'World Economic Forum Launches Initiative to Enable Equitable and Trusted Use of Data for Global Common Good' (News Release, 8 December 2020) <www.weforum.org/press/2020/12/world-economic-forum-launches-initiative-to-enable-equitable-and-trusted-use-of-data-for-global-common-good>.

[6] United Nations Development Programme, The Future Is Decentralised: Block Chains, Distributed Ledgers, and the Future of Sustainable Development (Report, 2018) 7 <www.undp.org/publications/future-decentralised>.

III. FOUNDATIONAL REGULATION: DATA APPROACHES

A second regulatory approach focuses on enhancing competition to ensure that competitive market forces play a beneficial role rather than contribute to an already concentrated financial sector. Pro-competition measures have been considered in regard to IT and software,[7] critical financial market infrastructure (FMI) such as payment, clearing, and settlement systems, and in 'open banking' initiatives.[8] This section reviews some of the pro-competition strategies from which regulators can choose in their pursuit of digital finance platform governance.

Regulation should aim at securing objective, transparent, and fair, rather than profit-based, conditions of access. Open interfaces, open-source code of the technology core, fair and non-discriminatory access requirements, and a transparent fee structure enable third-party developers to write proprietary applications for platform clients.[9] Principle 18 of the IOSCO principles on access to the services of critical infrastructure providers is relevant here:

> An FMI's participation requirements should be justified in terms of the safety and efficiency of the FMI and the markets it serves, be tailored to and commensurate with the FMI's specific risks, and be publicly disclosed. Subject to maintaining acceptable risk control standards, an FMI should endeavour to set requirements that have the least-restrictive impact on access that circumstances permit.[10]

One feature that would enable competition while retaining the benefits of digital finance platforms is an open data requirement for dominant firms that would allow innovative competitors to offer services that make use of existing data pools rather than having to build their own new ones at great expense.

Regulators should require digital finance platforms and other incumbents to grant new entrants access to client account data as this will reduce client switching costs because the newcomer can ensure a smooth tech migration. While standardisation of client data is a crucial precondition for smooth migration, doubts remain about whether such initiatives do, in fact, benefit small, innovative, new entrants.[11] For example, some evidence from the EU's open banking initiative suggests that access to client data appears to facilitate the market access of large technology

---

[7] See, for example, Luca Rubini (ed), *Microsoft on Trial: Legal and Economic Analysis of a Transatlantic Antitrust Case* (Edward Elgar Pub, 2010) 39–43.

[8] See Markos Zachariadis and Pinar Ozcan, 'The API Economy and Digital Transformation in Financial Services: The Case of Open Banking' (Working Paper No. 2016-001, SWIFT Institute, 15 June 2017) 10–12.

[9] See United States v Microsoft Corp, 231 F Supp 2d 144, 191 (D DC, 2002).

[10] Committee on Payment and Settlement Systems (Bank for International Settlements) and Technical Committee of the International Organization of Securities Commissions, *Principles for Financial Market Infrastructures* (Report, April 2012) 101 <www.bis.org/cpmi/publ/d101a.pdf>.

[11] See Dirk A Zetzsche et al, 'The Evolution and Future of Data-Driven Finance in the EU' (2020) 57(2) *Common Market Law Review* 331, 342–6.

companies that have the resources to (1) attract a sufficient number of new clients, (2) develop large-scale data transfer interfaces, and (3) master the complex EU regulation in this field.

Thus, we propose requiring open client data from firms with a strong, potentially dominant position, regardless of their sector of origin. In an effort to reduce further concentration of financial service providers, an open data requirement, paired with a data governance requirement that requires data administration on a standardised basis, could attach once a provider exceeds a certain set share of a given financial market. This would allow easier entry for smaller competitors.

Regulators should also ask potential users of digital finance platforms to diversify their own risks deriving from their dependency on a certain platform. For example, a regulation could require that any *financial* firm must employ at least two or more unrelated providers or systems. While mandatory diversification has some positive effects on market structure, it also brings increased costs, imposes redundancy, adds further cybersecurity risks (given that multiple systems have access to the consumer data), and reduces benefits of datafication (because of slowed IT processes). Most importantly, mandated diversification could reduce platform-specific benefits for users by moving away from one look and feel and one quality and level of service, as well as the accumulation and best use of a client's liquidity for ensuring lower costs on the back end. Mandatory diversification, if imposed, might work only on the back end. Further, mandatory diversification may well not work in developing economies that lack a sufficient number of service providers for diversification. An alternative to this mandatory diversification suggestion, which would achieve the same end, would be to limit a platform's maximum share of clients in a given market.

In markets where there are more than one significant digital finance platform or other platform services, users under this proposal might be required to switch providers every few years. Rotation would likely be costly: all weblinks, data interfaces, and, in some cases, brokerage connections would need readjustment after each change, giving the institution's clients ever more reasons to contract directly with the platform provider. Providers will also find it difficult to negotiate fee reductions based on revenues earned if the law mandates regular displacements of the very revenue for which the discount provides an incentive to stay. Further, if the technology of *their* consumers is linked – either technically or economically – to the platform, an institution's users will have even more reasons to contract directly with the platform, thereby exacerbating, rather than slowing, market concentration.

Finally, merger control is the standard competition approach to overly concentrated markets. Though antitrust law's main rationale is market efficiency, our analysis of digital finance platforms suggests that merger control can also be justified from a financial regulation perspective: mergers of very large platforms could be prohibited not only because of competition concerns but also for client protection, innovation, and, especially, financial stability concerns.

IV. DESIGNATION AS A REGULATED INDUSTRY

Regulators have at their disposal moderate regulatory interventions such as various types of command-and-control, self-regulatory, and co-regulatory approaches. The most effective approach will depend on the platform's stage of evolution. As a general matter, the greater the scale and/or significance of a digital finance platform, the stronger the case for an intervention.[12]

A. *Command-and-Control Regulation*

A standard response of regulators to increasing concentration within a given industry is adding an additional layer of regulation upon the firms, particularly through requiring licensing for regulated activities. In doing so, they enhance control over the sector and obtain better data for regulatory decisions. The difficulty in submitting digital finance platforms to regulation is finding a common denominator of activities that accurately describes the range of activities of a platform.

Given that the core of platform activity is data collection and processing, regulators could define 'financial data gathering and analytics' as a regulated activity and exempt participants that do not meet certain size or scope requirements. The result of such regulation could be a differentiated regime with tiered rules for large platforms, similar to the rules applicable to SIFIs, moderate reporting requirements for mid-size platforms, and a mere registration requirement for small ones.[13] Such a regime would probably have to state expressly that it does not apply to regulated banks and financial institutions, or otherwise it would so apply given the extent of data gathering and analysis in a modern bank and the undesirability of regulatory overlaps.

A different regulatory approach could focus on the underlying code, that is, its technical functionality. Supervisory agencies could seek to understand the technology and require additional code aimed at meaningfully balancing private incentives with public interests. For example, regulators can choose to monitor credit risk assessment software for hidden gender, race, or other biases and require companies to amend the underlying code if such biases are detected. Such a code-focused approach would ask much from regulators trained in financial and legal matters but will almost certainly become necessary in time.

---

[12] See Committee on Payment and Settlement Systems (n 10) 10–12, discussing applicability and proportionality of the FMI principles.

[13] See, for example, Basel Committee on Banking Supervision, 'Scope and Definitions: Global Systemically Important Banks' (SCO40, Bank for International Settlements, 9 November 2021) <www.bis.org/basel_framework/chapter/SCO/40.htm?inforce=20211109&published=20211109>.

B. Self-Regulation

Self-regulation is a critical means of drawing upon the knowledge of participants when regulators reach the limits of their own expertise. Thus, FMI providers typically establish a common set of rules and procedures for all participants, including a technical infrastructure and a specialised, customised risk-management framework.[14] While these rules and procedures often take a contractual form, a self-regulatory approach can formalise the adoption and amendment of these rules and establish a minimum publication and notice period. Regulators can then use these frameworks to enhance control over platforms.

The downside of self-regulation is the dependency of the self-regulated constituency on adopting rules.[15] Where private and public interests collide, we should expect few serious efforts at self-regulation. In particular, although we may well see basic investor protections, the provider and its participants will have little interest in slowing growth by curtailing the network effects from which they benefit, and so will do little to combat antitrust concerns and size-based systemic risk. Self-regulatory organisations thus regularly face the tension between remaining light touch and interest friendly or turning into more of a public oversight body focused on technicalities *in addition to* mandatory regulation, like the Financial Industry Regulatory Authority.[16]

C. Co-regulation

Regulators could also pursue a co-regulation strategy. Co-regulation has been defined as a:

> mechanism whereby [a] legislative act entrusts the attainment of the objectives defined by the legislative authority to parties which are recognized in the field (such as economic operators, the social partners, non-governmental organizations, or associations).[17]

Co-regulation has been discussed as potentially effective for non-financial platform industries, as its inclusion of a broad pool of innovators 'in the articulation, execution and evolution of policy, law, norms development, oversight and regulation',[18]

---

[14] See Committee on Payment and Settlement Systems (n 10) 7.

[15] Jan Sammeck, *A New Institutional Economics Perspective on Industry Self-Regulation* (Gabler Verlag, 2012) 60.

[16] See William A Birdthistle and M Todd Henderson, 'Becoming a Fifth Branch' (2013) 99 *Cornell Law Review* 1, 12–15 (analysing the evolution of FINRA from a self-regulatory organisation to a quasi-governmental organisation).

[17] See Michèle Finck, 'Digital Regulation: Designing a Supranational Legal Framework for the Platform Economy' (Law, Society and Economy Working Papers 15/2017, London School of Economics and Political Science, 2017) 15–16 <https://eprints.lse.ac.uk/87568/1/Finck_Digital%20Co-Regulation_Author.pdf> (defining co-regulation).

[18] See Raymond H Brescia, 'Regulating the Sharing Economy: New and Old Insights into an Oversight Regime for the Peer-to-Peer Economy' (2016) 95(1) *Nebraska Law Review* 87, 134.

may well elicit more balanced views. An example is when some local authorities and Airbnb agreed on the collection of a tourist tax.

For digital finance platforms, regulators could seek to enter into co-regulation agreements with operators that reflect public concerns such as systemic risk, customer protection, market integrity, and national security. As with any other regulatory tool, however, co-regulation has its limits which arise particularly when the public interest collides with the provider's profit-seeking behaviour. Thus, although co-regulation could be a way to implement moderate investor protection and national security measures, it may be less effective than some of the other strategies suggested in combating the competition and financial stability concerns we outline.

V. PUBLIC UTILITY REGULATION

In line with the broader scholarship on platform industries,[19] digital finance platforms could be regulated as public utilities. Regulation characteristics of public utilities include, for instance, rate regulation, minimum service level and quality assurance prescriptions, and a defined or capped rate of return on investments. This list demonstrates that traditional public utility regulation fits best for highly standardised services such as energy and water supply. Regulators seeking to set the aforementioned limits in a highly innovative, rapidly growing environment such as digital financial services will face potentially insurmountable challenges.

A less intrusive form of public utility status is the designation of certain systems as Financial Market Utilities (FMUs) which require advanced risk-management methods, intensified supervision, and advance notice of rule changes.[20] The FMU rules were drafted for clearing organisations and central counterparties and would need amendments to reflect, among other things, the data and liquidity dimension of digital finance platforms. This is the approach being taken in China in the context of Ant and other digital finance platforms: designating them as SIFIs and subjecting them to higher regulatory and supervisory attention.[21]

As a form of indirect regulation, supervisory authorities could become significant shareholders or operators of a digital finance platform. One example is the real-time gross settlement payment system in which the technology core is developed with the involvement of central banks that, in some cases, also engage in operations.[22] Similar

---

[19] See K Sabeel Rahman, 'The New Utilities: Private Power, Social Infrastructure, and the Revival of the Public Utility Concept' (2018) 39(5) *Cardozo Law Review* 1621, 1634–5.

[20] See 'Designated Financial Market Utilities: Title VIII of the Dodd-Frank Act', *Federal Reserve* (Web Page, 29 January 2015) <www.federalreserve.gov/paymentsystems/title-viii-dfa.htm>.

[21] See, for example, Xinmei Shen, 'China Amends Anti-Monopoly Law for the First Time amid Tech Crackdown, Increasing Penalties and Regulatory Control', South China Morning Post (online, 27 October 2021) <www.scmp.com/tech/policy/article/3153881/china-amends-anti-monopoly-law-first-time-amid-tech-crackdown>.

[22] See, for example, Morten Bech, Yuuki Shimizu, and Paul Wong, The Quest for Speed in Payments (Bank for International Settlements Quarterly Review, March 2017) <www.bis.org/publ/qtrpdf/r_qt1703g.htm>.

approaches are now being seen in an increasing number of jurisdictions at the retail level with 'fast payment systems'.[23] Putting aside the obvious capacity constraints of many competent authorities, having a stake in a digital finance platform brings potential informational advantages for a central bank or other regulatory agency.

On the downside, authority stakes in a platform create a potentially undesirable outcome. The platform in which a central bank or other authority might take a stake is likely to be, or become, a monopolist that will plausibly leave little room for additional market-led innovation. Government investment makes the most sense in markets where competition is unlikely to develop in the first place, such as where existing financial institutions are insufficiently funded, tech expertise is scarce, or competition is undesirable because all financial institutions must meet the same standard to reduce *their customers'* transaction costs (such as in payment systems). For these reasons, central banks often develop and operate core infrastructure for financial services through public–private partnerships. FinTech is no exception: for instance, in India the National Payments Corporation of India plays a core role in the development of the payment infrastructure as we discussed in Chapter 16. In line with this strategy, the PBOC has required Ant Group (formerly known as Ant Financial) to outsource its core credit scoring data business into a public–private partnership in which state-owned enterprises have the majority ownership.[24]

VI. UNBUNDLING

A more interventionist approach would mandate unbundling. Unbundling is well established as a competition measure, yet financial law also frequently imposes it.[25] Indeed, some contend that a 'core principle' of banking law is the 'separation of banking and commerce'.[26] At least in the United States, firms that own or control a US bank are prohibited from engaging in business activities other than banking or managing banks.

Another regulatory strategy would be to mandate separate service pricing and require an option for consumers to source distinct and separate services from different digital finance platforms. Unbundling seeks to separate fees for different services previously sold as a package and prohibit hidden bundling rebates ('tying'). Unbundling aims at two different goals.[27] First, it establishes the price of a single

---

[23] Anton N Didenko and Ross P Buckley, 'The Evolution of Currency: Cash to Cryptos to Sovereign Digital Currencies' (2019) 42(4) *Fordham International Law Journal* 1041.

[24] Julia Zhu and Xie Yu, 'Exclusive: China's Central Bank Accepts Ant's Application for Financial Holding Company', *Reuters* (online, 18 June 2022) <www.reuters.com/business/finance/exclusive-chinas-central-bank-accepts-ants-application-financial-holding-company-2022-06-17>.

[25] Dan Awrey, 'Unbundling Banking, Money, and Payments' (2022) 110(4) *Georgetown Law Journal* 715.

[26] See Saule T Omarova, 'The Merchants of Wall Street: Banking, Commerce, and Commodities' (2013) 98(1) *Minnesota Law Review* 265, 268, 274–5.

[27] Awrey (n 25).

service, allowing new entrants to review whether they can compete by offering a better single service, if they cannot compete with the whole platform. Second, unbundling prohibits the cross-subsidisation of some services from the proceeds of other services for which there may be less competition.

Unbundling as a regulatory requirement, however, must be handled with care. Unbundling reduces some efficiencies that stem from bundled consumer contacts and the better data inherent in handling services simultaneously.[28] After all, unbundling involves ripping the integrated platform apart when, oftentimes, its integration is one of its main benefits. Regulators imposing unbundling requirements face the further difficulty of determining which part of a service may be untied at what point in time without impeding innovation based upon disintermediation. Finally, there is a stronger alternative to unbundling which is to prohibit the offering of certain services along with others.

Applying these concepts to digital finance platforms, regulators may wish to adopt unbundling rules that limit the financial or other services that digital finance platforms can provide. For example, digital finance platforms that provide IT infrastructure services to financial institutions may be prohibited from branching out into financial services themselves to avoid conflicts of interest or market concentration. This would prevent major cloud service providers, such as Amazon, from also providing financial services.

A softer form of unbundling and separation would require segregation. For instance, regulations may prohibit an investment advisor from booking mutual fund assets in its own accounts and require the advisor to hold such assets in an account earmarked for the investors. This softer form would merely manage conflicts: two functions could be provided by one entity, but an information barrier would have to be erected and conflicts monitored and managed.

Along these lines, regulation could require the unbundling and separation of functions not only legally – as the law currently does by requiring separate legal entities to perform these tasks – but also technically. A technical unbundling requirement would prohibit a platform from simultaneously providing fund manager, custodian, and investor functions, or offering insurance and banking functions, or using data and liquidity access to secure control over the whole fund value chain.

VII. PROHIBITION

Given that digital finance platforms can provide crucial infrastructure for financial markets and benefits for sustainable development, prohibition is unlikely to be an

---

[28] There is a wide body of antitrust literature discussing tying practices and unbundling requirements. See Keith N Hylton and Michael Salinger, 'Tying Law and Policy: A Decision-Theoretic Approach' (2001) 69(2) *Antitrust Law Journal* 469, 470; Nicholas Economides and Ioannis Lianos, 'The Elusive Antitrust Standard on Bundling in Europe and in the United States in the Aftermath of the Microsoft Cases' (2009) 76(2) *Antitrust Law Journal* 483.

appropriate option in most cases. With that said, some jurisdictions have sought to prevent or limit the entry of foreign digital finance platforms. Nonetheless, while various regulatory approaches may be valid, generally, prohibition will not be in the interests of viable long-term financial market development.

VIII. REGULATING DIGITAL FINANCE PLATFORMS

Digital financial ecosystems bring many advantages. Yet, the rapid emergence of concentration and dominance in digital finance that arises from platformisation has taken many by surprise. Financial regulators must be concerned about, and authorised to intervene in, the structure of FinTech markets with a view to ensuring the delivery of all regulatory objectives – protecting clients and customers, limiting systemic risks, and ensuring market efficiency and innovation in financial markets.

As we have laid out in this chapter, the dominant position of platforms stems from their control over both data and liquidity. In this regard, digital finance platforms differ from the TechFins analysed in Chapter 16 which are characterised, primarily, by access to and analysis of massive amounts of diverse data. Based on this analysis, we suggest three measures to regulate digital finance platforms.

A. *Defining Financial Data Gathering and Analytics as Regulated Activity*

While avoidance of full financial supervision by not activating the triggers for financial regulation has been important to TechFins, avoidance of financial supervision is less important for digital finance platforms, given licensed intermediaries are at the core of many such platforms. Nonetheless, regulation and supervision only cover a small part of the activities of most digital financial platforms as they do not extend to one of the core elements of their market power which is the accumulation and analysis of data.

Hence, as an initial measure, to reflect the importance of the data dimension and following the same logic we applied to TechFins in Chapter 16, we propose regulating data gathering and analytics by virtue of a moderate regulatory intervention, which will be triggered at some predefined point along the business evolution from (1) too small to care, to (2) too large to ignore, and then to (3) too big to fail (TBTF). To adequately assess market size and efficiency, regulators are encouraged to develop expertise in defining sub-segments of data gathering and analytics, for instance, on data of importance for lending, asset management, custody, risk management, and so forth. By this measure, almost certainly, the large digital finance platforms will qualify as TBTF in *some* segments given the extent of their access to both client data and (in many cases) liquidity, and thus attract appropriate regulation (as has been imposed on Ant Financial in China). Smaller platforms, of course, will need to report their data position to regulators so that the latter can ascertain when similar regulation should be applied to them.

B. *Proportionate Regulation*

When both the financial intermediation activity (regulated by traditional means) *and* the data processing fall within the scope of financial regulation, regulators will have the right to control the core factors of digital financial platform market dominance and will be able to respond accordingly through setting proportionate requirements.

Such requirements may well include, *for all such platforms*, business continuity requirements including back-up systems, restructuring arrangements, and designated tech and financial staff to serve as experts in the context of a crisis and as key access points for regulators. Further, it may well prove desirable, as we proposed above, to require the unbundling of business functions such as payments, brokerage, custody, asset managements, and lending into separate legal entities with separate data and technical infrastructure. This unbundling may well provide transparency for each service segment and facilitate restructuring when necessary as each of these separate activities have different types of risks and require different methods to restructure.

For platforms identified as TBTF, that is, SIFI platforms, we propose a systemic risk surcharge that reflects the platforms' control over both data and liquidity. If the platform can be classified as a SIFI on both the data and liquidity dimensions, additional surcharges may be justified to provide a security cushion for economic shocks and technical malfunctions.

C. *From Open Data to Nationalisation*

However, neither business continuity arrangements nor capital provisioning will stop the scale economies and networks effects from driving further rapid growth in the platform once a certain threshold is passed in each market segment. We thus propose a four-step approach based on the growth dynamic in each given segment.

As a first step, we propose that regulators seek to facilitate and mandate effective open data approaches by requiring disclosure of *raw* data in a granular, structured manner following ISO norms to a data repository under public supervision, for public access by all competing providers.

As a second step, if the market share in the respective markets exceeds a further threshold, we propose that regulators partially nationalise the data pools by turning the data pool entity into a public–private joint venture. The data in the pool then become a public utility rather than a private property, with the platform provider requested to pay licensing fees to use the data (which may be partly offset by dividends it receives from the data pool entity). This step will limit refinancing opportunities based on data economics as the property rights in the data change hands. In addition, traditional antitrust measures like merger control will apply from this stage onwards.

As a third step, we propose the possible forced sale of certain business activities to stop a monopoly from developing.

We acknowledge that these three steps are increasingly severe in their impact on the platform owners' property rights, yet they may well be necessary to avoid the fourth and most severe regulatory intervention, nationalisation of the platform. We stress (again) that public (co-)ownership in critical FMI is quite common – for instance, large-scale payment systems are often operated and at least partially owned by central banks, to ensure access and operational resilience. The direct access to the central bank ensures support of the critical FMI in times of liquidity or economic crises. One example we discussed comprehensively in Chapters 12 and 13 is the digital financial infrastructure of India. Nationalisation is a drastic but overall not outlandish measure for systemically important critical financial infrastructure.

Whether and when a platform qualifies as critical financial infrastructure will depend upon its dominance in the respective market segments. We propose that financial regulation be empowered to take each of the four steps laid out above, as needed in their market, to ensure competition, operational resilience, and openness to innovation in critical FMI.

PART V

Conclusion

20

Building Better Financial Systems

SUMMARY

We considered in Part I the evolution of FinTech. Part II discussed approaches to the range of new technologies at the heart of FinTech and the use of facilitation mechanisms to support the development of balanced risk-based proportional regulatory approaches. Part III discussed the central role of infrastructure in the context of digital financial transformation and how it can and should be built. Part IV focused on the risks associated with FinTech, ranging from market concentration to monopolisation, and from technological operating risks to financial systemic risks.

This chapter concludes. It does so in six sections. In Section I, we revisit the major drivers of FinTech: finance, technology, and regulation. In Section II, we examine how each of these drivers brings its own challenges, which one or two of the other domains have the potential to mitigate. In Section III, we show how the global discussion on how to regulate FinTech is indicative of a broader regulatory trend to expect more from the financial system than the mere efficient distribution of capital; and we argue how financial regulation which promotes resilience, financial inclusion, and expansion of financial resources is well equipped to further the overarching objective of sustainable development. In Section IV, we analyse further how FinTech (and FinTech-oriented financial regulation) may be used to advance sustainable development. In Section V, we analyse the constituent building blocks of a comprehensive FinTech strategy. Section VI concludes.

I. FINTECH: THE NEW NORMAL

We have identified finance, technology, and regulation as the main drivers of the developments covered by the term FinTech. The negative side of finance, expressed in major crises associated with large incumbent financial institutions, prompted the need for new solutions. These solutions have been found, on the one hand, in tightening existing financial legislation and enhancing reporting requirements, and on the other hand, in financial entrepreneurs whose business models rest on

technological innovation, using elements of a range of new technologies including artificial intelligence, distributed ledgers, blockchain and smart contracts, cloud
computing and/or data gathering and data analytics.

Early outstanding examples of what FinTech could achieve opened the eyes
of decision-makers worldwide: Kenya's M-Pesa, China's Ant, and India's Aadhaar
regime were exemplars that showed how technology and finance *could* make a difference in terms of financial inclusion and speed and service levels, thereby furthering digital transformation for billions of people worldwide and helping in myriad
ways to lift them from poverty.

Financial regulators welcomed the new entrants in financial services markets
as they promised an entirely new service level paired with, at least initially, lesser
systemic risk in the financial system compared to incumbents. Yet they provided
two challenges. First, regulators knew very little indeed about the new technologies
and related risks associated with small FinTech firms. Second, FinTech entrepreneurs knew very little indeed (and sometimes had very little respect for) financial
regulation.

To enhance mutual learning and accommodate the new entrants' demands for
guidance in the regulatory thicket, some regulators turned to new regulatory tools
such as regulatory sandboxes and piloting regimes which de facto discriminated
between traditional business (subjecting those entities to the full force of the post-
GFC regulations) and FinTech start-ups (which were subject to more lenient standards and given assistance to meet regulatory requirements). Other jurisdictions,
following a more cautious approach, turned to innovation hubs as informal coach-
ing and learning zones for both FinTech entrepreneurs and regulators.

Fairly swiftly the incumbents – both technology and financial firms – fought back
and sought to establish large financial platforms, mimicking the model of Ant in
China, in attempts to create a reach to retail clients, a grip on information flows,
and a market dominance never seen before in finance. FinTech start-ups, originally
seen as a cure for the ills of incumbent financial systems, were soon marginalised
and turned from disruptors to collaborators, providing ancillary services to banks
and the digital financial platforms that seek to combine significant shares of the
financial data and liquidity of the world.

The pandemic, by increasing the need for datafication to underpin digital
finance, contributed to the development of large datafied solutions for the financial
system and society at large. Furthermore, as explored in Chapter 6, the various crises
of the early 2020s confirmed that digital transformation is key to ensuring consistent functioning of the private and public sectors. The private sector in developed
countries – save for industries including travel, health and energy – was mostly able
to accommodate the needs of individuals with its current state of digitisation: mobile
payments, e-commerce, and delivery apps allowed for online payments and essential shopping. The story was far more mixed in the public sector in most countries.
Distribution of emergency relief funds in many countries would have benefitted

greatly from the further use of FinTech. As argued in Part III, timely provisioning of public funds for the most disadvantaged is essential. The effective distribution of such funds requires digital finance infrastructure and governmental experience with large-scale digital financial transactions.

The Crypto Winter of 2022–2023 diminished the hope of some FinTech enthusiasts with falls in the price of BitCoin, the insolvencies of major crypto intermediaries and projects, and a crisis in decentralised finance business models. While the Crypto Winter extended to the failure of a series of technology-oriented banks, most significantly Silicon Valley Bank, exacerbated in terms of speed via digital communications and linkages, nonetheless, today the promise of FinTech remains, but mostly in large incumbents that can provide financial stability and technological sophistication, and have the capacity to adapt to ever faster changing circumstances.

FinTech has indeed made the journey from the outer reaches of the financial system to both Main Street and Wall Street, although in a rather different way than was hoped for by FinTech entrepreneurs a decade ago. FinTech is everywhere in finance today. In all its myriad of manifestations, FinTech today is the 'new normal'. Just as engaging in e-commerce a decade ago is now shopping (online – but still shopping), so will so much of FinTech today simply be routine banking in a decade's time.

II. FINANCE, LAW, AND TECHNOLOGY AS AN INTERACTIVE SYSTEM

FinTech brings with it all the reasons finance is the most regulated sector of any modern economy. Fear and fraud, the siblings that have long accompanied finance, are abundantly present in FinTech: fraudulent ICOs during the ICO bubble, technical malfunctions resulting in system shutdowns and trading halts in new and old asset classes, large-scale overnight bankruptcies of former FinTech heroes, fee schemes better hidden than ever as the currency is data rather than money, and data abuses.

Each of these phenomena, all too familiar as the common market failures from the 'old finance', provide good reasons for a prudent balanced approach to FinTech so that it is open to innovation but has a sentry at the gates.

Where financial issues (such as information asymmetry, agency, and transaction costs and fragmented liquidity) are addressed by technology (such as AI, advanced data analysis, or technology-enabled disintermediation), law and regulation follow to address the risks created by the technology.

Where technology provides new financial models (such as bundling retail liquidity in crowdfunding or AI-based allocation of SME credit), financial entrepreneurs will enter the market to distinguish the better investment opportunities from the others and law and regulation will seek to protect retail investors from overly optimistic promises.

Finally, where law and regulation impose extensive and burdensome reporting requirements, technology will be used to make affordable financial services viable – a phenomenon discussed in Chapter 4 as RegTech.

FinTech, in short, is a field where finance, technology, and regulation interact and where changes in one trigger adjustments and amendments in the other two. In today's FinTech markets, none of its three dimensions can operate without a keen eye on developments in the other two.

III. TOWARDS BETTER FINANCIAL SYSTEMS: BROADENING REGULATORY OBJECTIVES

FinTech and digital finance have paved the way for a broader understanding of financial regulation that takes into account the full panoply of contemporary regulatory objectives that were previously understood to be beyond the mission of financial regulation.

FinTech has forced regulators and regulation to grapple with technology, a field previously outside their domain, so they have built capacity and become accustomed to making foreign fields their own. FinTech can be seen as one factor underpinning the new trend of rapidly widening objectives of financial regulation, from market integrity (through AML/CTF rules) to financial inclusion, and from sustainable development to a weapon of financial warfare. All of these changes put entirely new demands on a financial system and its regulators.

Every widening of regulatory objectives brings its own challenges. Yet this train has left the station, and there are very few indicators that the trend to demand ever more from the financial system will soon be reversed in our contemporary world characterised, as it is, by an endless chain of crises.

All of these demands on regulation were unlikely to succeed without the decade of FinTech we now have behind us. Datafication was a necessary precondition for turning a problem child into an effective tool to tackle the great challenges mankind now faces. This is because the core of problem solving now involves data gathering and analytics, a capacity developed in the FinTech age.

To take further the idea of finance as one of humankind's more effective tools for problem solving across broad areas, four elements must remain at the core of regulatory attention: resilience, financial inclusion, expansion of financial resources, and generalised sustainable development.

A. *Resilience*

Before 2020, digital finance had emerged as a clear way to improve financial inclusion and sustainable development. The pandemic highlighted the need for accelerating the development of digital finance and digital financial infrastructure, particularly in developing countries, to provide secure and timely channels through which resources can be sent to those in need. Despite the rapid pace of digitalisation across the world, when the pandemic of 2020–2022 hit, most countries were underequipped in this regard. Existing digital financial infrastructure needed, and still needs, improvement by cooperation between governments, international organisations, financial institutions, and tech companies. Digital transformation is key to ensuring consistent functioning of the private and public sectors in the context of future sustainability and other crises.

Looking forward, crises will likely be common, and thus financial regulation needs to embrace its new role as a crisis mitigant and management tool. In particular, the financial system needs to be ready to respond to three types of external impacts: fragmentation, ad-hoc disasters, and the longer-term challenge of transforming the world's economies in the context of climate change.

With the re-emergence of major conflicts and tension between superpowers, we expect the future global financial system may well fragment to reflect the various blocs' struggle for political, military, and economic superiority. The fragmentation of the global financial system into a new multipolar dynamic is the most likely result of the current struggle between the superpowers, with the US dollar losing some of its centrality and the global economy suffering as a consequence. We may well see new CBDCs, as discussed in Chapter 15, in particular the eCNY, gradually becoming more widely used as China and Russia supply crucial commodities and financing to emerging and developing economies.

At the same time, the impact of climate change appears to be striking with increasingly tremendous force. Mankind is facing increasing numbers and severity of disasters like droughts, storms, and floods more frequently than ever before. These climate challenges range from inadequate water supplies in many countries to the so-called 'once in a hundred year' floods occurring in successive years in Australia and 'once in a thousand year' events occurring in an increasing range of locales. All countries now face multiple challenges, ranging from the need to improve the energy efficiency of the housing stock through to impacts upon the financial system, with the insurance sector, in particular, severely challenged. Going forward, climate change and other natural and manmade disasters seem set to pose increasing financial stability, economic and social risks.

But the regulatory challenges do not stop at impact mitigation. As we lay out in detail below, the financial system is also expected to finance, and thus further, a transition to a more sustainable economy. Given the financial system must function well despite these additional missions and under challenging circumstances, the promotion of resilience, in all its dimensions, becomes a core regulatory objective.

B. *Financial Inclusion*

The second element is financial inclusion, particularly through enhanced access to payments and savings capacities, which allow people to conduct their lives far more efficiently, and to think and plan longer term. Financial inclusion will support resilience in the face of future crises, particularly when combined with a continued focus on financial stability and other traditional financial regulatory objectives.

Approaches focusing on digital financial infrastructure as laid out in Part III are particularly important in this respect.

C. *Expansion of Financial Resources*

The third element is the expansion of resources in the financial system. More people saving and investing provides more financial resources which can be used to mitigate likely future crises and support sustainable development. FinTech in many countries has initially supported only payments and basic lending. Once these basic aspects of financial inclusion have been achieved, regulators must move on and expand the use of digital finance in areas including wholesale lending, asset management, and insurance, and promote the use of technology to further market efficiency and the effective distribution of scarce capital across the economy.

D. *Towards Sustainable Development*

The fourth element is the use of finance to support sustainable development. Beyond disaster response, this includes in particular the financing of transition technologies and less-resource-intense business models. Examples include support payments for disaster- and crisis-impacted people and businesses, and ESG and green investment strategies and green investing quotas. In this respect, new regulatory requirements can provide tools to further the analysis of the impact of sustainable investments and policies. We discuss how FinTech regulation can support sustainable development in the following sections.

IV. SUSTAINABILITY, FINANCE, AND REGULATION: A NEW PARADIGM

As a starting point, we posit that sustainable development has become a core and independent central bank and financial regulatory objective, joining the traditional objectives of monetary stability, financial stability, consumer/client protection, market efficiency, and market integrity.

We support this statement in three steps. First, we argue that sustainable development is a shared goal of regulators worldwide. Second, we briefly describe the tools of sustainable finance regulation. Third, we explore the role macroeconomic regulators, in particular central banks, play in furthering sustainable development, as sustainability risks can be long-term systemic risks.

A. *Sustainable Development as Global Regulatory Goal*

Sustainable development is one of the most important shared objectives globally. The focus today increasingly centres on the UN's Sustainable Development Goals

(SDGs), which outline a set of universally agreed goals including the eradication of poverty, elimination of hunger, access to healthcare, and economic growth, among others. All UN Member States have committed to achieving the SDGs by 2030. While progress is being made – building on the earlier Millennium Development Goals – there is a long way to go indeed to address a range of risks, particularly around climate change, biodiversity loss, and inequality.

B. *Towards Appropriate Sustainable Financial Regulatory Policy*

Financial regulators across the globe are considering how they can support sustainable development while still attending to the traditional core objectives of financial regulation discussed above. Regulators and scholars are exploring how financial systems can best assist in managing environmental and social change, and mitigate environmental impacts, under the rubric of sustainable finance regulation. Foundational elements of a market-based, sustainability-oriented financial regulation include:[1] (1) a double materiality regulatory objective, focusing on both sustainability risks and the impact of economic activities on sustainability factors, (2) a classification system ('Taxonomy') identifying desirable and undesirable conduct, (3) disclosure rules on ESG factors, and (4) fiduciary duties of financial intermediaries that consider both financial and sustainability preferences when making investment and lending decisions. The former may be supplemented by financial incentives (through credit guarantees or risk-sharing with public institutions) and by required capital provisioning for sustainability risks that can be clearly identified and measured.

All these new tools require data and technology to operate, which Green FinTech may provide well. We will discuss how we might get there in the next section. But before we turn to this subject matter, we consider the role of central banks in reigning in sustainability risks.

C. *Central Banks' Role in Limiting Systemic Sustainability Risk*

Central banks are today most often both macro-prudential and micro-prudential banking regulators, and thus the primary focal points in discussions of financial regulation and governance, including sustainable finance.

From the 1970s until 2008, the consensus focus for central banks was monetary policy. Independent central banks focused on price stability were viewed as the

---

[1]   See Douglas W Arner, Ross P Buckley and Dirk A Zetzsche, 'FinTech and the Four Horsemen of the Apocalypse: Building Financial Ecosystems for Resilience, Innovation and Sustainable Development' (2022) 39(1) *Banking and Finance Law Review* 5; Alliance for Financial Inclusion, *Roadmap for Inclusive Green Finance Implementation: Building Blocks to Implement IGF Initiatives and Policies* (Special Report, November 2022) <www.afi-global.org/wp-content/uploads/2022/11/Roadmap-for-Inclusive-Green-Finance-Implementation_isbn.pdf>; Dirk A Zetzsche and Linn Anker-Sørensen, 'Regulating Sustainable Finance in the Dark' (2022) 23(1) *European Business Organization Law Review* 47.

optimum structural design to lower the rate of inflation. At this time, central bank independence became statutorily reinforced around the world. While central banks often received financial stability mandates during this period, financial stability beyond monetary stability was in practice largely de-emphasised as a role for central banks. Furthermore, systemic risks were typically understood as being beyond the concern and risk management requirements of financial institutions.

The 2008 Crisis shattered this consensus by exposing the need for central banks to return to a more traditional and broader macro-prudential stability role as well as retaining a micro-prudential regulatory role. Central banks took on pivotal responsibilities to maintain the functioning of the financial system and to mitigate the spread of systemic risks from systemically important financial institutions, other financial institutions, and markets. Macro-prudential supervision and systemic risk were brought to the fore of institutional design, regulation, and financial stability management in the years after 2008.

In the last decade, sustainability risks have been increasingly identified as long-term systemic risks best mitigated by regulatory action. Given this perspective on sustainability risk as being systemic is relatively new, questions arise as to whether financial regulators and central banks in their current form are appropriate fora for sustainability discussions and whether they have the necessary mandates and tools. We suggest these roles are entirely appropriate for central banks, given their economic, monetary, and financial stability mandates. The further question then arises: how to do this? Our answer is by making financial regulators and central banks with their broadened mandates a core part of a comprehensive FinTech strategy.

V. BUILDING BLOCKS OF COMPREHENSIVE FINTECH STRATEGIES

We have explained how the objectives of financial regulation have been widened in response to humanity's ongoing challenges and crises. We next analyse what type of strategies regulators need to adopt to make the financial system fit for the future. We do this on the premise that, going forward, finance will be important for stability, resilience, crisis response, and inclusion, and also for supporting the economic and social transformation needed for sustainable development. If sustainable development is an overarching policy objective, as it is now commonly perceived, it must also be a priority in regulating FinTech. For that purpose, we synthesise the core lessons of the past decades to suggest a strategy for achieving these objectives – the core of which focuses upon building digital infrastructure and developing new regulatory approaches.

A. *Digital Infrastructure*

As highlighted in Part III, digital financial infrastructure is key to achieving all the objectives of finance, from financial inclusion to resilience, financial stability, sustainability, and beyond. Our experience of crises has reinforced the fundamental role of digital infrastructure: various crises have confirmed the need for digital financial infrastructure for crisis management, economic recovery, and sustainable development. The most fundamental aspects of this digital infrastructure are mobile payments and the required foundational layer of digital identity. Central to the impact of digital payments is interoperability, which governments are increasingly mandating to maximise social and economic benefits and innovation. In addition to supporting transfers, payments, and e-government initiatives, this infrastructure framework reduces transaction costs and facilitates a wide range of commercial activities, new businesses, and opportunities.

B. *New Financial Regulatory Approaches*

Digital infrastructure needs to be supported by appropriate regulatory frameworks. How can law and regulation support the creation of resilient, inclusive, and sustainable digital finance? Our answer to this question has seven elements: (i) a broader analytical framework, (ii) expanded expertise, (iii) promotion of innovation, (iv) use of RegTech and SupTech, (v) a beta approach to regulation, (vi) cross-border harmonisation, and (vii) an awareness of the broader ecosystem.

1. Broader Analytical Framework

To address the risks from innovation, an appropriate analytical framework needs to address: (1) new sources of traditional risk, (2) new forms of risk, and (3) new markets and systems. In applying this framework, it will be helpful to closely consider several key areas of concern which have arisen during the process of digital financial transformation, including cybersecurity, data security, and data privacy, and the emergence of new systemically important data-driven financial institutions including new forms of financial market infrastructure such as platforms.

2. Expanding Expertise

Regulators today need an even deeper understanding of the link between finance and the real economy. This requires a markedly expanded skill set. Regulators need insights from across the formal and natural sciences, and the social sciences, to monitor and reassess risk exposures and assess the impacts on sustainability and recovery of each regulation. Financial regulators need to hire more staff with scientific, analytical, and interdisciplinary skills. This includes expertise in the interactions with the subject of systems science – for instance, how climate change is likely to affect storm, flood, and fire risks and the attendant impacts on insurers and crucial financial intermediaries including large banks and pensions funds.

This broader skill set will also need to be mirrored in these major regulated financial entities. The landscape of financial services is growing ever more complex, requiring both more sophisticated and innovative approaches from providers and their employees.

3. Promotion of Innovation: Balanced Proportional Risk-based Regulation

Regulators should take three steps to make their financial system fit for purpose. First, regulators should *identify and modernise unsuitable regulation* based on a regulatory impact assessment that determines whether legacy rules remain useful. Second, regulators should implement *risk-based graduated proportional regulation*. Third, regulators should implement effective regulatory facilitation arrangements that promote innovation as we have laid out further in Chapters 3 and 11.

4. Regulatory and Supervisory Technology

The task of regulators will be greatly assisted by higher levels of datafication. The effective regulation of finance is going to require ever greater use of technology by regulators: RegTech. Regulators should upgrade supervisory data systems and regulatory technologies (SupTech and RegTech) and work to support the development of core digital infrastructure. The targeted implementation of SupTech and RegTech tools will enable appropriate proportional regulation of innovative financial products and services, including sustainable ones which will benefit financial inclusion and address attendant risks.

5. A Beta Approach to Regulation

Regulators and regulated entities will likely need to begin to adopt the 'beta approach' common in software development. Regulation will never be perfect, and using finance to mitigate the impact of external shocks will require constantly adjusting the rules and standards. Financial regulation, of necessity in some aspects, will be characterised by a process of trial and error – of learning from experience and adjusting on the run – which will be anathema to many traditional regulators. This will require a mix of hard and soft law and binding and indicative types of regulation.

6. Cross-Border Harmonisation and Market Access

Both the effectiveness of financial regulation and sustainable development can be further advanced by regional regulatory approaches to support necessary scale. Policymakers and regulators in many countries will need to promote regionally harmonised regulatory frameworks. The more consistent regulatory approaches are across a region, the more attractive each national market will be to innovative financial service providers. In turn, more providers in a region will allow customers to choose from a wider range of services and benefit from more competitive prices, while also increasing the likelihood of firms developing innovative solutions to a wide range of issues.

7. Awareness of the Broader Ecosystem

A much-widened regulatory mandate requires regulators to take into account the wider societal ecosystem in which FinTech operates to maximise resilience, inclusion, innovation, and sustainable development. From the standpoint of digital finance, the wider ecosystem focuses on education, skills and funding and the development of expertise through related professional and other associations. This wider focus supports the effectiveness of regulatory facilitation arrangements such as innovation hubs. Of particular importance in many countries is a far greater focus on education in the STEM disciplines (i.e., science, technology, engineering, and mathematics) and on social science research into the impacts of technology on humanity.

The targeted implementation of these new regulatory approaches will encourage and facilitate the development of innovative financial products and services while addressing attendant risks. These measures form an overall strategy to support FinTech, financial inclusion, innovation, and sustainable development. These goals can be further advanced by the requisite focus on building digital financial infrastructure and on regional regulatory approaches to support necessary scale.

VI. CONCLUSION

Global finance in the next decade will be driven by three central themes: increasingly rapid advances in technology, the need for sustainable development, and a continual tension between economic, financial, and technological globalisation and fragmentation. These themes will create new opportunities, risks, and challenges for finance and financial governance, and we have laid out many of the factors that will impact the outcome in this book.

In this environment, policymakers and regulators need to focus on three elements. The first is the expansion of financial inclusion, particularly through enhanced access to payments and savings capacities, which allow people to conduct their lives far more efficiently and to think and plan longer term. Approaches focusing on digital financial infrastructure are particularly important in these respects. The second is improving the allocation of existing financial resources to support sustainable development. In this respect, new regulatory requirements can support financial stability, resilience, and response to the many challenges and crises societies will have to face. The third is the expansion of resources in the financial system: more people saving and investing provides more financial resources which can be used in supporting change and crisis response.

The additional functions the financial system needs to deliver, from crisis response to promoting innovation and sustainable development, require higher levels of digitalisation and datafication. The broadening of financial systems' missions cannot succeed without datafication, and datafication requires digitalisation and resilient digital infrastructure.

As we have argued in Part III, if the financial system is to be utilised for crisis management and promoting resilience of the economy, it must itself be resilient, sustainable, and inclusive – and this requires it to be more digital. Digital channels will often be the optimal, and in crises may be the only, way of providing public services such as education, healthcare, immigration, taxation, and customs. Furthermore, for steering the overall economy in a sustainable direction, any approach not built upon digitalisation and datafication is likely to fail. What cannot be measured cannot be adequately regulated or supervised. The sheer mass of datapoints needed for rendering broader regulatory objectives feasible will further prompt digitalisation of large parts of finance, which will lead to advanced measurement and modelling in line with the RegTech cycle we identified in Part I.

To ensure the financial system *can* contribute to this full range of roles and objectives, digitalisation needs to be paired with fit-for-purpose financial regulation. This will require (1) a broader analytical framework, (2) an expansion of regulatory skill sets, (3) promotion of innovation, (4) expanded use of RegTech and SupTech, (5) acknowledging the necessity of learning from trial and error and of adjusting regulations on the run, (6) ensuring at least regional, harmonisation of regulatory frameworks, and (7) awareness of the broader societal ecosystem in which FinTech functions.

If rightly designed and regulated, digital finance is one of the world's best hopes for ameliorating the impacts of the series of crises likely to characterise our future and supporting the realisation of inclusive sustainable development.

Index